Principles of Information Security

Principles of Information Security

Editor:

Prof. Dr. Zoran Gacovski, Ph.D.

ArclerPress

www.arclerpress.com

Principles of Information Security

Editor: Prof. Dr. Zoran Gacovski, Ph.D.

708 3rd Avenue, 6th Floor
New York
NY 10017
United States of America
www.arclerpress.com

ISBN: 978-1-68094-462-4

Library of Congress Control Number: 2016951156

About the Editor

Prof. Dr. Zoran Gacovski, Ph.D.

Dr. Zoran Gacovski has earned his PhD degree at Faculty of Electrical engineering, Skopje. His research interests include Intelligent systems and Software engineering, fuzzy systems, graphical models (Petri, Neural and Bayesian networks), and IT security. He has published over 50 journal and conference papers, and he has been reviewer of renowned Journals. In his career he was awarded by Fulbright postdoctoral fellowship (2002) for research stay at Rutgers University, USA. He has also earned best-paper award at the Baltic Olympiad for Automation control (2002), US NSF grant for conducting a specific research in the field of human-computer interaction at Rutgers University, USA (2003), and DAAD grant for research stay at University of Bremen, Germany (2008). Currently, he is a professor in Computer Engineering at European University, Skopje, Macedonia.

Contents

Section II: Intrusion Detection and Prevention

Section III: Cloud Security Methods

Section IV: Cryptographic Methods

List of Contributors

Ren Fujii
Graduate School of Life and Environmental Sciences, Kyoto Prefectural University, Kyoto, Japan

Yasunari Yoshitomi
Graduate School of Life and Environmental Sciences, Kyoto Prefectural University, Kyoto, Japan

Taro Asada
Graduate School of Life and Environmental Sciences, Kyoto Prefectural University, Kyoto, Japan

Masayoshi Tabuse
Graduate School of Life and Environmental Sciences, Kyoto Prefectural University, Kyoto, Japan

Yoshitomo Matsubara
Graduate School of Applied Informatics, University of Hyogo, Kobe, Japan

Toshiharu Samura
Department of Electrical and Computer Engineering, National Institute of Technology, Akashi College, Akashi, Japan

Haruhiko Nishimura
Graduate School of Applied Informatics, University of Hyogo, Kobe, Japan

Hu Xiong
Key Laboratory of Network and Software Security Assurance of the Ministry of Education, Institute of Software, School of Electronics Engineering and Computer Science, Peking University P. R. China

Zhi Guan
Key Laboratory of Network and Software Security Assurance of the Ministry of Education, Institute of Software, School of Electronics Engineering and Computer Science, Peking University P. R. China

Jianbin Hu
Key Laboratory of Network and Software Security Assurance of the Ministry of Education, Institute of Software, School of Electronics Engineering and Computer Science, Peking University P. R. China

Zhong Chen
Key Laboratory of Network and Software Security Assurance of the Ministry of Education, Institute of Software, School of Electronics Engineering and Computer Science, Peking University P. R. China

Jaydip Sen
Innovation Lab, Tata Consultancy Services Ltd. India

Md. Al Mehedi Hasan
Department of Computer Science & Engineering, University of Rajshahi, Rajshahi, Bangladesh

Mohammed Nasser
Department of Computer Science & Engineering, University of Rajshahi, Rajshahi, Bangladesh

Shamim Ahmad
Department of Computer Science & Engineering, University of Rajshahi, Rajshahi, Bangladesh

Khademul Islam Molla
Department of Computer Science & Engineering, University of Rajshahi, Rajshahi, Bangladesh

Hossain Shahriar
Kennesaw State University, Marietta, Georgia, USA

Tulin Klintic
Kennesaw State University, Marietta, Georgia, USA

Victor Clincy
Kennesaw State University, Marietta, Georgia, USA

Eman Alharbi
Information Technology Department, King Abdul-Aziz University, Jeddah, KSA

Noha Alsulami
Information Technology Department, King Abdul-Aziz University, Jeddah, KSA

Omar Batarfi
Information Technology Department, King Abdul-Aziz University, Jeddah, KSA

Indraneel Mukhopadhyay
Department of Information Technology, Institute of Engineering & Management, Kolkata, India

Mohuya Chakraborty
Department of Information Technology, Institute of Engineering & Management, Kolkata, India

Andrew Blyth
Information Security Research Group, University of South Wales, Pontypridd, UK

Arif Sari
Department of Management Information Systems, European University of Lefke, Lefke, Cyprus

Sai Kiran Mukkavilli
Department of Electrical & Computer Engineering, Tennessee State University, Nashville, TN, USA

Sachin Shetty
Department of Electrical & Computer Engineering, Tennessee State University, Nashville, TN, USA

Liang Hong
Department of Electrical & Computer Engineering, Tennessee State University, Nashville, TN, USA

Samuel Paul Kaluvuri
Eindhoven University of Technology, Eindhoven, Netherlands

Alexandru Ionut Egner
Eindhoven University of Technology, Eindhoven, Netherlands

Jerry den Hartog
Eindhoven University of Technology, Eindhoven, Netherlands

Nicola Zannone
Eindhoven University of Technology, Eindhoven, Netherlands

Amir Mohamed Talib
College of Computer and Information Sciences, Al-Imam Muhammad Ibn Saud Islamic University, Riyadh, KSA

Abdallah Handoura
Ecole Nationale Supérieure des Télécommunications de Bretagne France

Omer K. Jasim
Computer Science, Al-Ma'arif College University, Anbar, Iraq

Safia Abbas
Faculty of Computer and Information Sciences, Ain Shams University, Cairo, Egypt

El-Sayed M. Horbaty
Faculty of Computer and Information Sciences, Ain Shams University, Cairo, Egypt

Abdel-Badeeh M. Salem
Faculty of Computer and Information Sciences, Ain Shams University, Cairo, Egypt

Saleh Al-Omar
Department of Engineering, Al-Ahliyya Amman University, Amman, Jordan

Moad Mowafi
Department of Network Engineering and Security, Jordan University of Science and Technology, Irbid, Jordan

Lo'ai Tawalbeh
Department of Computer Engineering, Jordan University of Science and Technology, Irbid, Jordan

Walid Aljoby
Department of Network Engineering and Security, Jordan University of Science and Technology, Irbid, Jordan

Mohammad Al-Rousan
Department of Network Engineering and Security, Jordan University of Science and Technology, Irbid, Jordan

Adel Hammad Abusitta
College of Engeenering & IT, Al Ain University of Science and Technology, Al Ain, UAE

Preface

The need for computer and network security dates since the '80-s of the last century. The first computer networks were local and in an academic setting, so there was large confidence among users associated with them (there were almost no security problems). With the sudden development of the information technology and the today's Internet, the first abuses occurred along with the need to protect private and corporate data. Today, information safety is crucial and it is most evident especially in the e-commerce and e-business. The information is a vital corporate's property and it has enormous value. The information security, primarily comprising computer and the network security, is mainly concerned with the data protection (privacy), data integrity and data availability. This edition covers main security concepts, such as authentication methods, intrusion detection and prevention, cloud security protocols, and cryptography.

Section 1 focuses on user authentication, describing a discrete wavelet transforming of a digital moving image, personal identification by keystroke dynamics, anonymous authentication protocols for vehicular ad hoc networks, and privacy-preserving authentication protocols for wireless mesh networks.

Section 2 focuses on intrusion detection and prevention, describing feature selection for intrusion detection by random forest, mobile phishing attacks and mitigation techniques, enhanced dragonfly key exchange protocol, intrusion detection & prevention system based on artificial neural network, and detection of sophisticated network threats via novel micro-proxy architecture.

Section 3 describes cloud security, including anomaly detection systems in cloud networks, quantifying the impact of security threats to cloud data centers, extensible authorization service for cloud environments, and confidentiality and fine-grained data access control of cloud data storage.

Finally, Section 4 discusses about cryptographic methods, describing telecom services using quantum cryptographic mechanisms, evolution of a symmetric quantum cryptographic algorithm, generators of pseudorandom sequences based on shift register, information assurance based on cryptographic checksum, and visual cryptography based digital image copyright protection.

Editor
Prof. Dr. Zoran Gacovski, Ph.D.

INTRODUCTION

Information security is the process of protecting the availability, privacy, and integrity of data. While the term often describes measures and methods of increasing computer security, it also refers to the protection of any type of important data, such as personal diaries or the classified plot details of an upcoming book. No security system is foolproof, but taking basic and practical steps to protect data is critical for good information security.

Password Protection

Using passwords is one of the most basic methods of improving information security. This measure reduces the number of people who have easy access to the information, since only those with approved codes can reach it. Unfortunately, passwords are not foolproof, and hacking programs can run through millions of possible codes in just seconds. Passwords can also be breached through carelessness, such as by leaving a public computer logged into an account or using a too simple code, like "password" or "1234."

To make access as secure as possible, users should create passwords that use a mix of upper and lowercase letters, numbers, and symbols, and avoid easily guessed combinations such as birthdays or family names. People should not write down passwords on papers left near the computer, and should use different passwords for each account. For better security, a computer user may want to consider switching to a new password every few months.

Antivirus and Malware Protection

One way that hackers gain access to secure information is through malware, which includes computer viruses, spyware, worms, and other programs. These pieces of code are installed on computers to steal information, limit usability, record user actions, or destroy data. Using strong antivirus software is one of the best ways of improving information security. Antivirus programs scan the system to check for any known malicious software, and most will warn the user if he or she is on a webpage that contains a potential virus. Most programs will also perform a scan of the entire system on command, identifying and destroying any harmful objects.

Most operating systems include a basic antivirus program that will help protect the computer to some degree. The most secure programs are typically those available for a monthly subscription or one-time fee, and which can be downloaded online or purchased in a store. Antivirus software can also be downloaded for free online, although these programs may offer fewer features and less protection than paid versions.

Even the best antivirus programs usually need to be updated regularly to keep up with the new malware, and most software will alert the user when a new update is available for downloading. Users must be aware of the name and contact method of each anti-virus program they own, however, as some viruses will pose as security programs in order to get an unsuspecting user to download and install more malware. Running a full computer scan on a weekly basis is a good way to weed out potentially malicious programs.

Firewalls

A firewall helps maintain computer information security by preventing unauthorized access to a network. There are several ways to do this, including by limiting the types of data allowed in and out of the network, re-routing network information through a proxy server to hide the real address of the computer, or by monitoring the characteristics of the data to determine if it's trustworthy. In essence, firewalls filter the information that passes through them, only allowing authorized content in. Specific websites, protocols (like File Transfer Protocol or FTP), and even words can be blocked from coming in, as can outside access to computers within the firewall.

Most computer operating systems include a pre-installed firewall program, but independent programs can also be purchased for additional security options. Together with an antivirus package, firewalls significantly increase information security by reducing the chance that a hacker will gain access to private data. Without a firewall, secure data is more vulnerable to attack.

Codes and Cyphers

Encoding data is one of the oldest ways of securing written information. Governments and military organizations often use encryption systems to ensure that secret messages will be unreadable if they are intercepted by the wrong person. Encryption methods can include simple substitution codes, like switching each letter for a corresponding number, or more complex systems that require complicated algorithms for decryption. As long as the code method is kept secret, encryption can be a good basic method of information security.

On computers systems, there are a number of ways to encrypt data to make it more secure. With a symmetric key system, only the sender and the receiver have the code that allows the data to be read. Public or asymmetric key encryption involves using two keys — one that is publicly available so that anyone can encrypt data with it, and one that is private, so only the person with that key can read the data that has been encoded. Secure socket layers use digital certificates, which confirm that the connected computers are who they say they are, and both symmetric and asymmetric keys to encrypt the information being passed between computers.

Legal Liability

Businesses and industries can also maintain information security by using privacy laws. Workers at a company that handles secure data may be required to sign non-disclosure agreements (NDAs), which forbid them from revealing or discussing any classified topics. If an employee attempts to give or sell secrets to a competitor or other unapproved source, the company can use the NDA as grounds for legal proceedings. The use of liability laws can help companies preserve their trademarks, internal processes, and research with some degree of reliability.

Training and Common Sense

One of the greatest dangers to computer data security is human error or ignorance. Those responsible for using or running a computer network must be carefully trained in order to avoid accidentally opening the system to hackers. In the workplace, creating a training program that includes information on existing security measures as well as permitted and prohibited computer usage can reduce breaches in internal security. Family members on a home network should be taught about running virus scans, identifying potential Internet threats, and protecting personal information online.

In business and personal behavior, the importance of maintaining information security through caution and common sense cannot be understated. A person who gives out personal information, such as a home address or telephone number, without considering the consequences may quickly find himself the victim of scams, spam, and identity theft. Likewise, a business that doesn't establish a strong chain of command for keeping data secure, or provides inadequate security training for workers, creates an unstable security system. By taking the time to ensure that data is handed out carefully and to reputable sources, the risk of a security breach can be significantly reduced.

Information Security Analyst

An information security analyst is an important team member in an Information Technology department. People in this position help organizations take measures to protect sensitive and mission-critical data. The analyst will help develop, implement, and ensure compliance of policies to protect an organization's data from being inappropriately accessed or used.

Excellent technical skills are critical so that the information security analyst can discern and take measures to prevent data security attacks. These attacks may come from inside or outside the organization. The analyst may be included in planning for other threats to the organization's data, such as threats caused by severe weather, maintaining power to servers in case of a local outage, and planning for continuing operations at alternate sites in case the main operations site needs to be shut down.

Some common duties of a person in this position are to create plans to prevent malicious or inadvertent use of data, create plans for emergency use, train users on security measures, and monitor access to data. Along with these duties, the information analyst may also be tasked with reviewing information on viruses and ensuring virus protection is in place. They may be asked to assess risks of data exposure as well as validate that security systems are in place and working as designed. The analyst may serve as experts on application development project teams to ensure the application complies with the organization's information security standards.

An information security analyst job description may include a need for expert knowledge in the systems technology used by the hiring organization. Some organizations may require a certain number of years of experience. Additional requirements that an organization may find desirable are a four-year degree in a technical field, network and system administration experience, and programming experience.

There are other skills helpful for information security analysts. Developing an ability to communicate with audiences of differing technical skills is valuable. When communicating security concerns to non-technical staff, the analyst must be able to make technical concepts understandable by a general audience. A good understanding of the organization's business will help the analyst perform more effectively, as it is useful to understand which information is most critical to the organization's mission and more likely to need protection.

Those who are interested in an information security analyst job must be willing to keep up on technology developments that affect the field of information security. Similarly, the analyst will need to keep abreast of trends in attacks such as viruses and hacker attacks. Moreover, information security legal requirements may change, and so the analyst must also stay abreast of regulatory requirements.

The Seven Basic Principles of IT Security

Security is a constant worry when it comes to information technology. Data theft, hacking, malware and a host of other threats are enough to keep any IT professional up at night. In this article, we'll look at the basic principles and best practices that IT professionals use to keep their systems safe.

The Goal of Information Security

Information security follows three overarching principles:

- Confidentiality: This means that information is only being seen or used by people who are authorized to access it.
- Integrity: This means that any changes to the information by an unauthorized user are impossible (or at least detected), and changes by authorized users are tracked.
- Availability: This means that the information is accessible when authorized users need it.

So, armed with these higher-level principles, IT security specialists have come up with best practices to help organizations ensure that their information stays safe.

IT Security Best Practices

There are many best practices in IT security that are specific to certain industries or businesses, but some apply broadly.

Balance Protection with Utility

Computers in an office could be completely protected if all the modems were torn out and everyone was kicked out of the room - but then they wouldn't be of use to anyone. This is why one of the biggest challenges in IT security is finding a balance between resource availability and the confidentiality and integrity of the resources.

Rather than trying to protect against all kinds of threats, most IT departments focus on insulating the most vital systems first and then finding acceptable ways to protect the rest without making them useless. Some of the lower-priority systems may be candidates for automated analysis, so that the most important systems remain the focus.

Split up the Users and Resources

For an information security system to work, it must know who is allowed to see and do particular things. Someone in accounting, for example, doesn't need to see all the names in a client database, but he might need to see the figures coming out of sales. This means that a system administrator needs to assign access by a person's job type, and may need to further refine those limits according to organizational separations. This will ensure that the chief financial officer will ideally be able to access more data and resources than a junior accountant.

That said, rank doesn't mean full access. A company's CEO may need to see more data than other individuals, but he doesn't automatically need full access to the system. This brings us to the next point.

Assign Minimum Privileges

An individual should be assigned the minimum privileges needed to carry out his or her responsibilities. If a person's responsibilities change, so will the privileges. Assigning minimum privileges reduces the chances that Joe from design will walk out the door with all the marketing data.

Use Independent Defenses

This is a military principle as much as an IT security one. Using one really good defense, such as authentication protocols, is only good until someone breaches it. When several independent defenses are employed, an attacker must use several different strategies to get through them. Introducing this type of complexity doesn't provide 100 percent protection against attacks, but it does reduce the chances of a successful attack.

Plan for Failure

Planning for failure will help minimize its actual consequences should it occur. Having backup systems in place beforehand allows the IT department to constantly monitor security measures and react quickly to a breach. If the breach is not serious, the business or organization can keep operating on backup while the problem is addressed. IT security is as much about limiting the damage from breaches as it is about preventing them.

Record, Record, Record

Ideally, a security system will never be breached, but when a security breach does take place, the event should be recorded. In fact, IT staff often record as much as they can, even when a breach isn't happening. Sometimes the causes of breaches aren't apparent after the fact, so it's important to have data to track backwards. Data from breaches will eventually help to improve the system and prevent future attacks - even if it doesn't initially make sense.

Run Frequent Tests

Hackers are constantly improving their craft, which means information security must evolve to keep up. IT professionals run tests, conduct risk assessments, reread the disaster recovery plan, check the business continuity plan in case of attack, and then do it all over again.

The Takeaway

IT security is a challenging job that requires attention to detail at the same time as it demands a higher-level awareness. However, like many tasks that seem complex at first glance, IT security can be broken down in to basic steps that can simplify the process. That's not to say it makes things easy, but it does keep IT professionals on their toes.

In Information Security, What Is the Attack Surface?

An attack surface in information security is any area where an unauthenticated user can run or input code into the system. This is split into three areas: network, software and human attack surface. While surfaces are technically only a measure of how unauthenticated users can access the system, another attack can come from a trusted employee. There are ways of reducing an attack, such as making fewer functions to which users can add code, having less code in general, and splitting up these functions so only trusted users can access them. Reducing attack surfaces does not reduce the damage an attack can inflict, only the odds that an attack will occur.

When dealing with programs, networks and websites, there is always going to be an attack surface. Some surfaces can be reduced or eliminated, but some are vital to the success of a program. For example, an input form that lets users write messages is considered a security threat. At the same time, if there is a program or website that needs to gather information from users, and the user needs to type the information manually, an input field is the only way to make this possible.

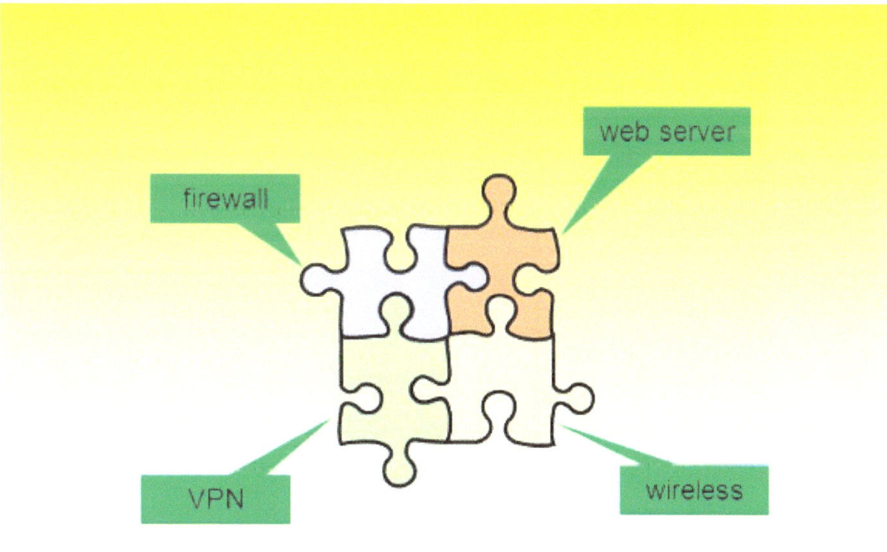

Attack surfaces are measured in three categories. Network attack surfaces are in the network and are primarily caused by open ports or sockets, or by having tunnels boring into the network. Tunnels are sometimes hard to find, because they may appear to be regular traffic on the network. A software attack surface is any area or function in a program that a user can use, regardless of position or authentication.

The human attack surface is different from the other two, because network and software surfaces are based on unauthenticated users. The human surface involves disgruntled or unscrupulous employees stealing or destroying data. If an employee leaves the company and a new employee has to gain access to data, this also is considered a security threat, because it's not yet clear how much trust can be placed in the new employee.

Reducing an attack surface differs, depending on what area is being reduced. With network surfaces, all ports and sockets should be closed to all users other than trusted sources. In software surfaces, the amount of overall code should be limited to its minimum, and the amount of functions available to unauthenticated users should be confined to just a few areas. Human surface reducing can be difficult, and this can only be done effectively by giving new employees the minimum amount of freedom to perform functions until he or she is trusted with the data.

SECTION I: USER AUTHENTICATION METHODS

CHAPTER 1

AUTHENTICATION METHOD USING A DISCRETE WAVELET TRANSFORM FOR A DIGITAL MOVING IMAGE

Ren Fujii, Yasunari Yoshitomi, Taro Asada, Masayoshi Tabuse

Keywords: Authentication, Moving Image, Copyright Protection, Tolerance to Compression, Wavelet Transforms

INTRODUCTION

Recent progress in digital media technology and distribution systems, such as the Internet and cellular phones, has enabled consumers to easily access, copy, and modify digital content, which includes electric documents, images, audio, and video. Therefore, techniques to protect the copyrights for digital data and to prevent unauthorized duplication or tampering are urgently needed.

Digital watermarking (DW) is a promising method for copyright protection of digital data. Several studies have developed a method in which 1) the DW can be sufficiently extracted from the watermarked digital data, even after compression, and 2) the quality of the digital data remains high after the DW is embedded [1] -[8] . However, a tradeoff generally exists between these two properties. Two important properties of the DW for digital data are imperceptibility of DW-introduced distortion, and robustness to signal processing methods, such as compressions and vicious attacks. However, the data rate and complexity of the DW have attracted attention when discussing the DW performance.

For overcoming the issue of performance, we previously developed authentication methods for digital audio [9] and a static image [10] without inserting a DW into them by using a discrete wavelet transform (DWT). In contrast to the DW, no additional information is inserted into the original digital data by the previous method [10] , and the digital data are authenticated by features extracted by the DWT and characteristic coding [10] . In the present study, we developed an authentication method for a digital moving image to protect the copy rights by using the previously proposed method [10] for a static image and our newly proposed method for selecting several frames in the moving image. No additional information is inserted into the original moving image by the proposed method or into the original static image by the previously proposed method [10] . The digital moving image is authenticated by features extracted by the DWT and characteristic coding of the proposed method. This paper presents the method and also an analysis of its performance, including the tolerance of authentication to both compressions and vicious attacks.

WAVELET TRANSFORM

In the present study, we use the authentication method for a static image [10] to authenticate a moving image. First, we briefly describe the procedure of the DWT used in the authentication for a static image.

The original image $F(u,v)$, which is used as the level-0 wavelet decomposition coefficient sequence $s^{(0)}_{u,v}$, is decomposed into the multi-resolution representation (MRR) and the coarsest approximation by repeatedly applying the DWT. The wavelet decomposition coefficient matrix $s^{(j)}_{u,v}$ at level j is decomposed into four wavelet decomposition coefficient matrices at the level $j+1$ by using (1), (2), (3), and (4).

$$s^{(j+1)}_{u,v} = \sum_{l} \sum_{k} \overline{p_{k-2u}}\, \overline{p_{l-2v}}\, s^{(j)}_{k,l} \tag{1}$$

Citation: Fujii, R. , Yoshitomi, Y. , Asada, T. and Tabuse, M. (2016) Authentication Method Using a Discrete Wavelet Transform for a Digital Moving Image. Journal of Information Security, 7, 1-13. doi: 10.4236/jis.2016.71001.

$$w_{u,v}^{(j+1,h)} = \sum_{l} \sum_{k} \overline{p_{k-2u}}\,\overline{q_{l-2v}}\, s_{k,l}^{(j)} \quad (2)$$

$$w_{u,v}^{(j+1,v)} = \sum_{l} \sum_{k} \overline{q_{k-2u}}\,\overline{p_{l-2v}}\, s_{k,l}^{(j)} \quad (3)$$

$$w_{u,v}^{(j+1,d)} = \sum_{l} \sum_{k} \overline{q_{k-2u}}\,\overline{q_{l-2v}}\, s_{k,l}^{(j)}, \quad (4)$$

where u and v denote the horizontal and vertical directions, respectively, and p_k and q_k denote the scaling and wavelet sequences, respectively. In addition, $w_{u,v}^{(j+1,h)}$ denotes the development coefficient obtained by operating the scaling function in the direction of the horizontal axis and the wavelet in the vertical axis; $w_{u,v}^{(j+1,v)}$ denotes the development coefficient obtained by operating the wavelet in the direction of the horizontal axis and the scaling function in the vertical axis, and; $w_{u,v}^{(j+1,d)}$ denotes the development coefficient obtained by operating the wavelet in the direction of both the horizontal and vertical axes. The development coefficients at level J are obtained by repeatedly using (1), (2), (3), and (4) from $j=0$ to $j=J-1$. In this method, the image must be a square composed of $2^L \times 2^L$ $(J \le L)$ pixels. For example, the image is decomposed by the DWT to level 3, as shown in Figure 1, where the original image $s_{u,v}^{(0)}$ is decomposed into $s_{u,v}^{(1)}$ expressed by 1LL, $w_{u,v}^{(1,v)}$ is expressed by 1HL, $w_{u,v}^{(1,h)}$ is expressed by 1LH, and $w_{u,v}^{(1,d)}$ is expressed by 1HH. Here, H and L denote the high- and low-frequency components, respectively.

AUTHENTICATION ALGORITHM FOR STATIC IMAGE

It is known that the histogram of wavelet coefficients of each domain at MRR parts has a distribution in which the center is almost 0 when the DWT is performed on a natural image (Figure 2) [4] . Exploiting this phenomenon, we developed an authentication method for a static image [10] .

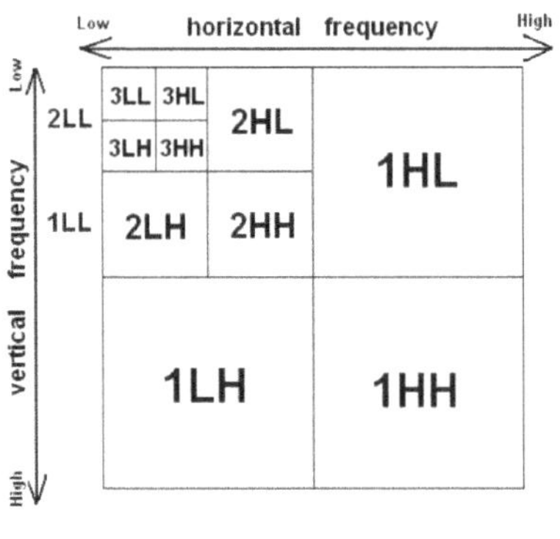

Figure 1: Mallat division [8].

Coding

For coding the image, we obtain the histogram of wavelet coefficients V at the selected level of an MRR sequence (Figure 3). As with the DW techniques for images [10] and digital audio [9] , we set the following coding parameters.

The values of Th(minus) and Th(plus) in Figure 3 are chosen such that the non-positive wavelet coefficients (S_m in total frequency) are equally divided into two groups by Th(minus), and the positive wavelet coefficients (S_p in total frequency) are equally divided into two groups by Th(plus). Next, the values of $T1$, $T2$, $T3$, and $T4$, which are the parameters for controlling the authentication precision, are chosen to satisfy the following conditions:

1) $T1 < Th(\text{minus}) < T2 < 0 < T3 < Th(\text{plus}) < T4$.

2) The value of S_{T1}, which is the number of wavelet coefficients in $(T1, Th(\text{minus}))$, is equal to S_{T2}, which is the number of wavelet coefficients in $[Th(\text{minus}), T2)$, i.e., $S_{T1} = S_{T2}$.

3) The value of S_{T3}, the number of wavelet coefficients in $(T3, Th(\text{plus})]$, is equal to S_{T4}, the number of wavelet coefficients in $(Th(\text{plus}), T4)$, i.e., $S_{T3} = S_{T4}$.

4) $S_{T1}/S_m = S_{T3}/S_p$.

In the present study, the values of both S_{T1}/S_m and S_{T3}/S_p are set to 0.25, which was determined experimentally.

To prepare the coding for authentication, the procedure separates the wavelet coefficients V of an MRR sequence into five sets (hereinafter referred to as A, B, C, D, and E), as shown in Figure 4, by using the following criteria:

- $A = \{V \mid V \in V^{SC}, V \le T1\}$,
- $B = \{V \mid V \in V^{SC}, T1 < V < T2\}$,
- $C = \{V \mid V \in V^{SC}, T2 \le V \le T3\}$,
- $D = \{V \mid V \in V^{SC}, T3 < V < T4\}$,
- $E = \{V \mid V \in V^{SC}, T4 \le V\}$,

where V^{sc} is the set of wavelet coefficients in the original image file.

The wavelet coefficients of an MRR sequence are coded according to the following rules, in which V_i denotes

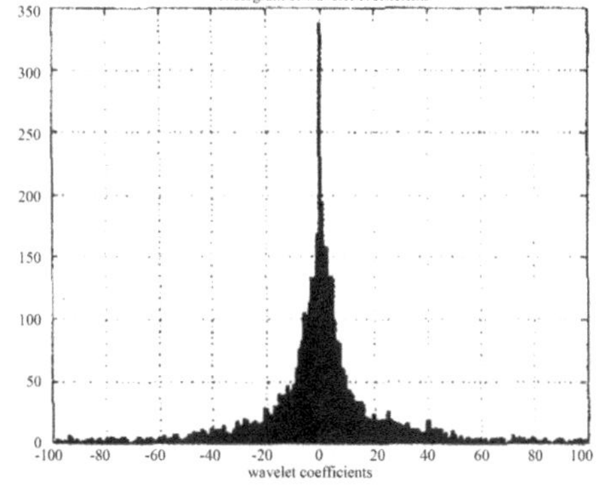

Figure 2: Histogram of the wavelet coefficients [4] .

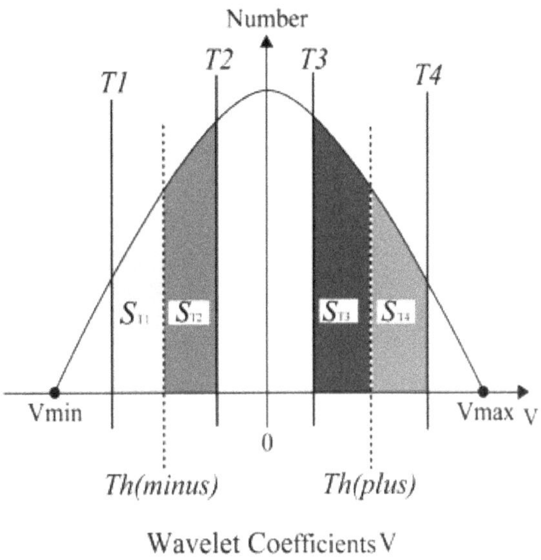

Figure 3: Schematic diagram of the histogram of MRR wavelet coefficients [9] .

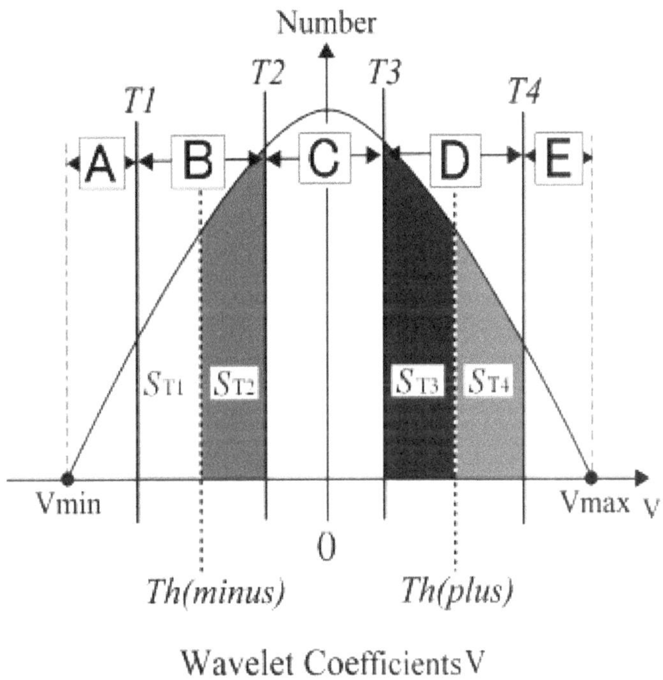

Figure 4: Five sets (A, B, C, D, and E) of the histogram of wavelet coefficients V of an MRR sequence for the assignment of a bit [9] .

one of the wavelet coefficients:

When $V_i \in C$, flag f_i is set to 1, and bit b_i is set to 0.

When $V_i \in (A \cup E)$, flag f_i is set to 1, and bit b_i is set to 1.

When $V_i \in (B \cup D)$, flag f_i is set to 0, and bit b_i is set to 0.5.

For authentication of the digital image, we use a code C (hereinafter referred to as an original code), which is the sequence of b_i defined above. For coding and authentication, we assign a sequence number and a flag for each wavelet coefficient. The flag $f_i = 1$ for V_i means that V_i is assigned a bit ($b_i = 0$ or 1) for the coding. The flag $f_i = 0$ for V_i means that V_i is not assigned a bit of 0 or 1: b_i is externally set to 0.5 as an arbitrary constant, and the value of b_i does not influence the performance of the proposed method described in Section 3.2. The coding with the exclusion of all V_i belonging to sets B and D, where the magnitudes of V_i are intermediate, is a novel feature of our previously reported studies [9] [10] .

Authentication

We authenticate not only an original digital image file but also a signal-processed version. Compression, which is one example of signal processing, is often applied to a digital image for the purposes of distribution via the Internet or for saving on a computer. Through the same coding procedure described in Section 3.1, we applied the DWT to a digital image and obtained a histogram of wavelet coefficients V' at the same level of the DWT as that coded for the original image file, as described in Section 3.1. Then, we set the authentication parameters as follows. The values of $Th'(\text{minus})$ and $Th'(\text{plus})$ (Figure 5) are chosen such that the non-positive wavelet coefficients (S'_m in total frequency) are equally divided into two groups by $Th'(\text{minus})$, and the positive wavelet coefficients (S'_P in total frequency) are equally divided into two groups by $Th'(\text{plus})$. Next, the values of $T1'$, $T2'$, $T3'$, and $T4'$, the parameters for controlling the authentication precision, are chosen to satisfy the following conditions:

1) $T1' < Th'(\text{minus}) < T2' < 0 < T3' < Th'(\text{plus}) < T4'$.

2) The value of S'_{T1}, the number of wavelet coefficients in $(T1', Th'(\text{minus}))$, is equal to S'_{T2}, the number of wavelet coefficients in $[Th'(\text{minus}), T2')$, i.e., $S'_{T1} = S'_{T2}$.

3) The value of S'_{T3}, the number of wavelet coefficients in $(T3', Th'(\text{plus})]$, is equal to S'_{T4}, the number of wavelet coefficients in $(Th'(\text{plus}), T4')$, i.e., $S'_{T3} = S'_{T4}$.

4) $S'_{T1}/S'_m = S'_{T3}/S'_P$.

In the present study, the values of both S'_{T1}/S'_m and S'_{T3}/S'_P are set to 0.25, which is the same setting used for coding of the original image file, as described in Section 3.1.

In preparation of the coding for authentication, the procedure separates the wavelet coefficients V' of an MRR sequence into three sets (hereinafter referred to as F, G, and H), shown in Figure 5, by using the following criteria:

- $F = \{V' \mid V' \in V'^{AC}, V' < Th'(\text{minus})\}$,
- $G = \{V' \mid V' \in V'^{AC}, Th'(\text{minus}) \le V' \le Th'(\text{plus})\}$,
- $H = \{V' \mid V' \in V'^{AC}, Th'(\text{plus}) < V'\}$,

where V'^{AC} is the set of wavelet coefficients of the target image file for making the code for authentication.

The wavelet coefficients of an MRR sequence are coded according to the following rules, in which V'_i denotes one of the wavelet coefficients:

When $f_i = 1$ and $V'_i \in G$, bit b'_i is set to 0.

When $f_i = 1$ and $V'_i \in (F \cup H)$, bit b'_i is set to be 1.

When $f_i = 0$, bit b'_i is set to 0.5.

When $f_i = 0$, b'_i is externally set to 0.5 as an arbitrary constant, and the value of b_i does not influence the performance of the proposed method described below.

For authentication of the digital image, we use the code C' (hereinafter referred to as an authentication code), which is the sequence of b'_i defined above. The authentication ratio AR (%) is defined by the following:

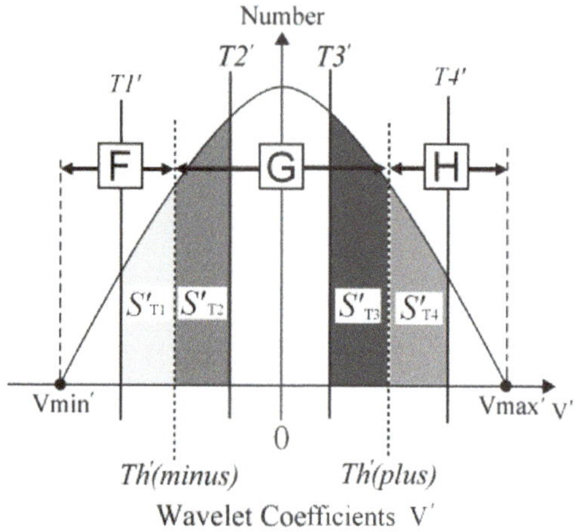

Figure 5: Three sets (F, G, and H), indicated on the histogram, of MRR wavelet coefficients used for authentication [9].

$$AR = \frac{100\sum_{i=1}^{N} f_i\left(1 - \left|b_i - b'_i\right|\right)}{\sum_{i=1}^{N} f_i}, \quad (5)$$

where N is the number of wavelet coefficients assigned flags in the coding for the original image file, described in Section 3.1. According to (5), the values of neither b_i nor b'_i influence the value of AR in the case that $f_i = 0$, which means the corresponding V_i is not assigned a bit of 0 or 1 in the coding for the original image file.

To use the proposed method, we need to store flags f_i and the original code C of each image file having a copyright we want to protect. In calculating (5) for the authentication of an original image file, we do not use an original image file; instead, we use the flags f_i and the original code C of the original image file.

AUTHENTICATION ALGORITHM FOR MOVING IMAGE

Coding

We obtain 10 pieces of coding per moving image, which is assumed to have 13 or more frames, in a database as follows.

Step 1: Calculate frame No. k_B, which is the smallest integer not less than $0.1 \times N_{total}$, and calculate frame No. k_E, which is the largest integer not greater than $0.9 \times N_{total}$. Here, N_{total} is the total number of frames of the moving image. Then, go to Step 2.

Step 2: Output the images of frame Nos. k_B and $k_B + 1$ as BMP files. Calculate the total sum $S[1]$ of the squares with a gray level difference at each pixel between frame Nos. k_B and $k_B + 1$. Store the gray levels of frame No. $k_B + 1$ in an array, A_1. Give the initial condition as $C[1] := k_B + 1$, $count := 1$, $k := k_B + 2$. Then, go to Step 3.

Step 3: If $k = k_E + 2$, go to Step 8. Otherwise, go to Step 4.

Step 4: Overwrite the image of frame No. k on that of $k_B - 2$ as the BMP file. Store the gray levels of frame No. k in array B. Calculate the total sum T of the squares with a gray level difference at each pixel between frame Nos. $k-1$ and k. Update the value of k as $k := k+1$. Then, go to Step 5.

Step 5: If $count < 10$, update the value of $count$ as $count := count + 1$ and go to Step 6. Otherwise, go to Step 7.

Step 6: Overwrite the array as $A_{count} := B$. Set the values as $S[count] := T$, $C[count] := k-1$. Then, go to Step 4.

Step 7: Calculate $l = \arg\max_{i=1,2,\cdots,10} S[i]$. If $S[l] > T$, overwrite the array as $A_l := B$ and set the values as

$S[l] := T$, $C[l] := k-1$. If $k = k_E + 1$, go to Step 8. Otherwise, go to Step 4.

Step 8: Output the arrays $A_i\,(i = 1,2,\cdots,10)$ as BMP files. Obtain the codes and flags used for selective coding by using the method described in Section 3.1. Output the codes, the flags, $C[i]\,(i = 1,2,\cdots,10)$, and $S[i]\,(i = 1,2,\cdots,10)$. Then finish.

According to our experience, sometimes several consecutive frames including the first or the last frame of a moving image have black for almost all pixels or white for almost all pixels. If such a frame is selected for coding despite that it is neither a representative nor a unique frame for the moving image, the code of the frame might be very detrimental to the authentication of the moving image. Therefore, in Step 1, as the objects for coding, we exclude the first and last 10% of the frames.

Authentication

The selection of frames is performed for test moving images with the same method described in Section 4.1. Assuming that the codes and the flags for selective coding for selected frames of moving images in a database were obtained by using the methods described in Section 4.1, the authentication ratios of each selected frame of a test moving image to each selected frame of the moving image in the database are calculated with the method described in Section 3.2. The authentication ratio of a test moving image to a moving image in a database is defined as the highest among all values of authentication ratios of selected frames of the test moving image to selected frames of the moving image in the database. Then, the moving image having the highest authentication ratio among all moving images in the database is found.

EXPERIMENT

In this section, we describe computer experiments and the results for evaluating the performance of the proposed method.

Method

The experiment was performed in the following computational environment: the personal computer was a DELL OPTIPLEX3020 (CPU: Intel(R) Core(TM) i5-4570 3.20 GHz, memory: 4.0 GB); the OS was Microsoft Windows 7 Professional; the development language was Microsoft Visual C++6.0.

The process of the experiment was as follows. Obtain 100 sets of codes consisting of ten codes for the Y components, which are obtained by the conversion from RGB components into YCrCb components per moving image from the original 100 MPEG-1 files of MUSCLE-VCD-2007 [11]. Use these sets for the authentication among themselves. Convert three target files, which are selected according to the recording time of the shortest (No. 31: 17 s), the closest to the average recording time (No. 49: 34 min 56 s), and the longest (No. 47: 1 hour 55 min 46 s) among the moving images in the database into MPEG-2 and MPEG-4, followed by the authentication to the converted files. Investigate the tolerance of the authentication ratios to the frame rate of three target files after converting their file format from MPEG-1 with the frame rate of 25 fps to MPEG-4 with the frame rate of 5 to 60 fps. Investigate the tolerance of the authentication ratios to the compression of three selected files by using libjpeg [12] to change the values of the quality of the images obtained from the selected frames and by using FFmpeg [13] to generate moving images with the images modified by libjpeg, Investigate the authentication ratios to the frames whose frame distance from a selected frame of a target file is within 5.

We used FFmpeg to output a BMP file having 24 bits as the gray level and 256 × 256 pixels from the moving image. For the DWT, we use Daubechies wavelets. The 4LH components obtained from the DWT up to Level 4 were chosen for coding and authentication, based on the analysis in the preliminary experiments. Figure 6 shows ten image examples consisting of one frame per moving image.

Several consecutive frames having black for almost all pixels or white for almost all pixels are sometimes inserted in a moving image because they can be useful for scene transitions. If such a frame is selected for coding despite that it is neither a representative nor a unique frame for the moving image, the code of the frame might be very harmful for authentication of the moving image. Therefore, in addition to the exclusion of frames as the objects of coding described in Step 1 in Section 4.1, we used only the frames having an average gray level of α

Figure 6: Ten image examples consisting of one frame per moving image of the specified number.

to 250 for the Y component, which has a gray level range of 0 to 255. The value of α was decided to be 11.1 by trial and error. However, when we did not obtain ten frames with α set to 11.1, we changed the value of α to 5 and were able to obtain ten frames for coding.

Results and Discussion

Authentication for MPEG-1 Files

The purpose of authentication is to protect the copyrights on moving image data. In the ten moving images listed in Table 1, when the moving image file targeted for authentication was different from that used for making the code of the original moving image file, the average authentication ratio was 60.2% (more precisely, in the range 40.9% to 81.1%), which was much smaller than the authentications ratios when authenticating the same moving image file as the original moving image file (100% in all cases in this experiment; see Table 1). An authentication ratio of 50% corresponds to the value in the case that randomly generated bits are used for b_i and/or b_i' in (5). Accordingly, the proposed method distinguished the original moving image file from each of the other nine shown in Table 1. When all moving images in thc databasc [11] were authenticated by using all moving images in the database [11] , the average authentication ratios between each pair of different moving images was 66.0% (more precisely, in the range 34.1% to 94.1%), which was fairly smaller than the authentications ratios when authenticating the same moving image file as the original moving image file (100% in all cases in this experiment) [14] . In other words, we could identify all moving image files in the database [11] by using all moving image files in the database [11] . When authenticating the No. 59 moving image file with the codes of the No. 73 moving image file as the original moving image file, the authentication ratio was 94.1%. The high authentication ratio was caused by the pair of similar frames shown in Figure 7 [14] .

Robustness to Conversion into MPEG-2 or MPEG-4

When the three moving images of Nos. 31, 47, and 49, converted from MPEG-1 to MPEG-2 or MPEG-4, were authenticated by using 100 moving images (MPEG-1) in the database [11] , the authentication ratios was between each pair of different moving images (in the range 43.9% to 79.5%), and were much smaller than the authentications ratios when authenticating the same moving image file as the original moving image file (100% in all cases in this experiment). Therefore, we could conclude that the proposed method has excellent robustness to conversion to MPEG-2 or MPEG-4. Table 2 shows several authentication ratios from this experiment.

Robustness to Frame Rate

Table 3 shows the robustness of the proposed method according to the frame rate. In the cases of Nos. 31 and 47 moving image files, the authentication ratios were kept at 100% for 5 to 60 fps of the file authenticated when authenticating the moving image file with 5 to 60 fps by using the original moving image file with 25 fps. Moreover, in the case of the No. 49 moving image file, the authentication ratios were kept to 100% only for 20 and 25 fps of the file authenticated when authenticating in the same manner (Table 3). The frame rate of the moving image file could be changed to avoid the copyright protection by the proposed method; it was effectively more beneficial to use the higher authentication ratio between the authentication ratio obtained by using the raw frame rate of the authenticated file and that obtained by converting the frame rate of the authenticated file into the same value as that in the database (Tables 3-5).

Table 1: Authentication ratios in 100 combinations of original moving images expressed by file No. for columns and by authentication targets expressed by file No. for rows]

File No.	3	24	25	31	61	69	70	81	94	100
3	100	61.4	56.8	62.9	55.2	55.8	60.6	47.7	63.6	72.0
24	64.4	100	54.5	60.6	50.0	48.5	62.9	51.5	68.2	65.9
25	61.4	56.1	100	57.6	50.0	50.0	70.5	44.7	61.4	63.6
31	62.1	61.4	56.1	100	55.9	50.8	62.9	40.9	70.5	71.2
61	59.1	56.1	50.8	58.3	100	77.5	76.5	56.8	62.9	53.0
69	57.6	51.5	59.1	51.5	78.5	100	75.8	81.1	56.8	49.2
70	66.7	58.3	68.2	65.9	69.8	72.5	100	50.0	70.5	69.7
81	51.5	56.8	51.5	44.7	57.5	81.1	50.0	100	50.0	41.7
94	65.9	68.9	65.2	73.5	60.2	50.7	67.4	46.2	100	72.0
100	72.0	67.4	61.4	68.9	55.2	47.1	72.0	40.9	67.4	100
										(%)

Table 2: Authentication ratios of target files with MPEG-2 or MPEG-4 formats

Original file No. (format)	Target file No. & format					
	31		47		49	
	MPEG-2	MPEG-4	MPEG-2	MPEG-4	MPEG-2	MPEG-4
31 (MPEG-1)	100	100	58.3	59.8	65.9	56.8
47 (MPEG-1)	63.6	65.2	100	100	63.6	59.8
49 (MPEG-1)	62.9	63.6	59.1	59.8	100	100
						(%)

Table 3: Tolerance of authentication ratio to frame rate of target file having a MPEG-4 format

Original file No. (fps)	Fps of target file No. 31							
	60	50	30	25	20	15	10	5
31 (25)	100	100	100	100	100	100	100	100
47 (25)	65.9	65.9	65.9	63.6	65.9	65.9	65.2	63.6
49 (25)	55.3	55.3	56.1	53.0	54.5	54.5	53.8	53.8

Original file No. (fps)	Fps of target file No. 47							
	60	50	30	25	20	15	10	5
31 (25)	59.1	59.1	59.1	59.1	59.1	59.1	59.1	59.1
47 (25)	100	100	100	100	100	100	100	100
49 (25)	59.1	60.6	60.6	60.6	59.8	59.8	59.8	60.6

Original file No. (fps)	Fps of target file No. 49							
	60	50	30	25	20	15	10	5
31 (25)	56.8	54.5	55.3	53.8	53.0	53.0	62.9	54.5
47 (25)	52.3	47.0	47.7	56.1	60.6	47.7	59.8	52.3
49 (25)	75.8	79.5	72.7	100	100	98.5	69.7	98.5
								(%)

Figure 7: Images of a pair of similar frames; left figure: selected from No. 73 moving image, right figure: selected from No. 59 moving image [14] .

Robustness to Compression Rate

Figure 8 illustrates the flow for generating new MPEG-1 files from an original MPEG-1 file through JPEG files with several compression rates. When the moving image file targeted for authentication was different from that used for making the code of the original moving image file, the average authentication ratio was 68.9% (more precisely, in the range 62.9% to 75.0%), which was fairly smaller than the authentications ratios when authenticating the same moving image file as the original moving image file (100% in almost all cases with the JPEG quality of 0 to 100 in this experiment; see Table 6). The image obtained with very low JPEG quality had a very poor appearance (see the left figure in Figure 9). Therefore, we could conclude that the proposed method has excellent robustness to the compression rate when keeping a good image appearance.

Robustness to Frame Exclusion

Table 7 shows authentication ratios for frames near each selected frame. When authenticating the frame near the selected one in the same moving image file by using the code of the selected frame of the original moving image file, the authentication ratio was100% in most cases (Table 7). However, in some cases, the attack of frame extraction effectively avoided the copyright protection by using the proposed method (see the three cases of frames from the bottom of the No. 49 moving image file in Table 7). The three frames in the No. 49 moving image file were within continual frames under the conditions of both rapid rotation and fairly dark appearance. Therefore, the robustness of the proposed method to frame extraction for authentication might be effectively improved by selecting frames that do not have a dark appearance, which could be judged by using the information of its gray levels.

Table 4: Authentication ratios after the frame rate of target file No. 49 is changed twice to 25 (original file; MPEG-1) → [5 to 60] (MPEG-4) → 25 (MPEG-4) fps

Original file No. (fps)	Fps of target file No. 49 before changed to 25							
	60	50	30	25	20	15	10	5
31 (25)	51.5	59.1	55.3	53	51.5	59.1	56.1	56.1
47 (25)	46.2	53.8	50.0	56.8	53.8	52.3	59.1	63.6
49 (25)	73.5	100	69.7	100	81.1	79.5	76.5	78.8
								(%)

Table 5: Highest authentication ratios of those in Table 3 and Table 4

Original file No. (fps)	Fps of target file No. 49 before changed to 25							
	60	50	30	25	20	15	10	5
31 (25)	56.8	59.1	55.3	53.8	53.0	59.1	62.9	56.1
47 (25)	52.3	53.8	50.0	56.8	60.6	52.3	59.8	63.6
49 (25)	73.8	100	72.7	100	100	98.5	76.5	98.5
								(%)

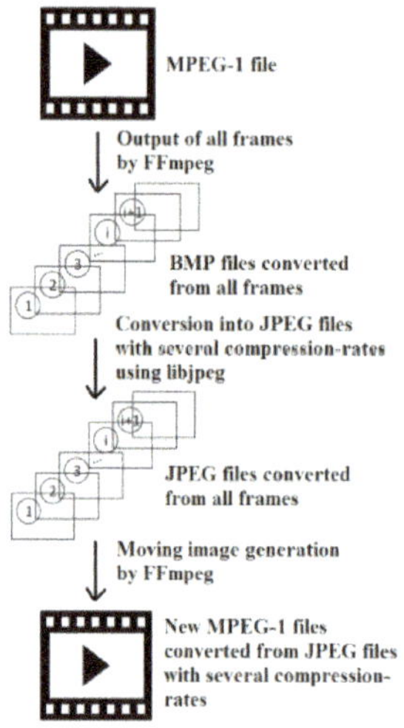

Figure 8: Flow for generating new MPEG-1 files from an original MPEG-1 file through JPEG files, corresponding to all frames of an original MPEG-1 file. The JPEG files have several compression rates.

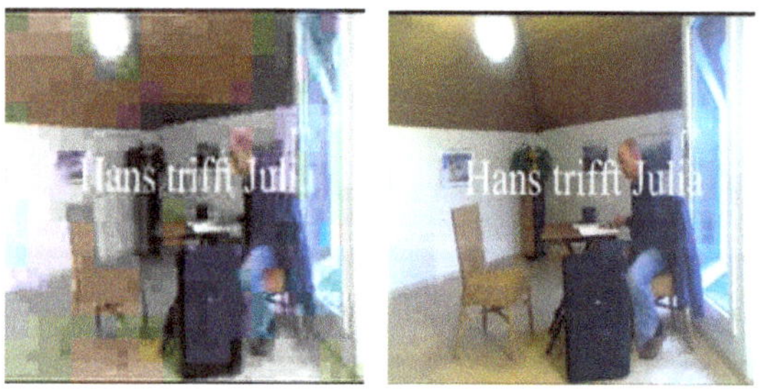

Figure 9: Example of compressed image of moving image No. 31; left figure: quality 5, right figure: quality 100.

Table 6: Tolerance of authentication ratios to compression of target file

Original file No.	Quality value of JPG compression for each frame of target file No. 31						
	0	5	10	15	50	75	100
31	96.2	98.5	100	100	100	100	100
94	70.5	73.5	72.7	74.2	73.5	74.2	75.0
100	62.9	62.9	64.4	66.7	67.4	66.7	67.4

Original file No.	Quality value of JPG compression for each frame of target file No. 94						
	0	5	10	15	50	75	100
31	68.7	72.7	70.5	68.2	71.2	71.2	71.2
94	97.0	100	100	100	100	100	100
100	68.9	67.4	67.2	66.7	68.2	68.9	67.4

Original file No.	Quality value of JPG compression for each frame of target file No. 100						
	0	5	10	15	50	75	100
31	64.2	68.2	65.2	68.2	65.9	67.4	66.7
94	68.1	68.9	68.9	70.5	68.9	69.7	71.2
100	94.0	97.0	98.5	100	100	100	100
							(%)

Table 7: Authentication ratios for frames near each selected one

Selected frame No.	Frame distance from selected frame of target file No. 31										
	−5	−4	−3	−2	−1	0	1	2	3	4	5
192	97	97	97	100	100	100	100	99.2	99.2	99.2	98.5
195	98.5	98.5	98.5	98.5	100	100	100	97.7	97.7	97.7	97.7
198	97	99.2	99.2	99.2	100	100	100	100	100	100	100
312	100	100	100	100	100	100	100	100	100	100	100
201	100	100	100	100	100	100	100	100	99.2	99.2	99.2
162	100	100	100	100	100	100	100	100	100	100	99.2
342	99.2	99.2	99.2	100	100	100	100	99.2	99.2	99.2	99.2
299	100	100	100	100	100	100	100	100	100	100	100
222	100	100	100	100	100	100	100	100	100	100	100
282	100	100	100	100	100	100	100	100	100	100	100

Selected frame No.	Frame distance from selected frame of target file No. 47										
	−5	−4	−3	−2	−1	0	1	2	3	4	5
139911	100	100	100	100	100	100	100	100	100	100	100
139926	100	100	100	100	100	100	100	100	100	100	100
139941	100	100	100	100	100	100	100	100	100	100	100
139956	100	100	100	100	100	100	100	100	100	100	100
139971	100	100	100	100	100	100	100	100	100	100	100
140736	100	100	100	100	100	100	100	100	100	100	100
140751	100	100	100	100	100	100	100	100	100	100	100
140766	100	100	100	100	100	100	100	100	100	100	100
140781	100	100	100	100	100	100	100	100	100	100	100
140781	100	100	100	100	100	100	100	100	100	100	100

Selected frame No.	Frame distance from selected frame of target file No. 49										
	−5	−4	−3	−2	−1	0	1	2	3	4	5
17178	78.8	78.8	81.1	100	100	100	78.8	77.3	78.0	77.3	77.3
17188	100	100	100	100	100	100	76.5	76.5	77.3	74.2	73.5
17158	87.1	87.9	84.8	100	100	100	83.3	84.8	85.6	90.9	91.7
17174	81.8	80.3	81.1	100	100	100	100	76.5	76.5	76.5	68.2
17071	100	100	100	100	100	100	92.4	91.7	90.9	90.2	87.9
17183	75.0	74.2	75.8	100	100	100	100	100	100	100	81.1
17168	72.0	72.0	72.7	100	100	100	100	100	100	75.8	73.5
38273	60.6	56.1	56.8	56.1	63.6	100	60.6	52.3	58.3	56.1	52.3
38275	68.9	62.1	56.8	57.6	61.4	100	52.3	49.2	51.5	52.3	53.0
25880	59.1	54.5	57.6	63.6	64.4	100	63.6	57.6	58.3	53.0	55.3

(%)

CONCLUSIONS

We have proposed an authentication method for a moving image by using our previously proposed method for a static image and a newly developed method for selecting several frames in the moving image. No additional information is inserted into the original moving image by the proposed method or in the previously proposed method for the original static image. The experimental results show that the proposed method has high tolerance of authentication to both compressions and vicious attacks. To use the proposed method, we need to store in a database 1) flags used for selective coding, and 2) an original code for several selected frames of each moving image file whose copyright we want to protect. In calculating the authentication ratio for authentication of an original moving image file, we do not need an original moving image file, but we do need 1) the flags, and 2) the original code for several selected frames of the original moving image file.

REFERENCES

1. Cox, I.J., Kilian, J., Leighton, T. and Shamoon, T. (1997) Secure Spread Spectrum Watermarking for Multimedia. IEEE Transactions on Image Process, 6, 1673-1687. http://dx.doi.org/10.1109/83.650120

2. Inoue, H., Miyazaki, A., Miyamoto, A. and Katsura, T. (1988) A Digital Watermark Based on the Wavelet Transform and Its Robustness on Image Compression. 1998 International Conference on Image Processing, 2, 391-395.

3. Kundur, D. and Hatzinakos, D. (1997) A Robust Digital Image Watermarking Method Using Wavelet-Based Fusion. International Conference on Image Processing, 1, 544-547. http://dx.doi.org/10.1109/ICIP.1997.647970

4. Shino, M., Choi, Y. and Aizawa, K. (2000) Wavelet Domain Digital Watermarking Based on Threshold-Variable Decision. Technical Report of IEICE, DSP2000-86, 100, 29-34. (In Japanese)

5. Swanson, M.D., Zhu, B. and Tewfik, A.H. (1996) Transparent Robust Image Watermarking. International Conference on Image Processing, 3, 211-214. http://dx.doi.org/10.1109/ICIP.1996.560421

6. Tsai, M.J., Yu, K.Y. and Chen, Y.Z. (2000) Joint Wavelet and Spatial Transformation for Digital Watermarking. IEEE Transactions on Consumer Electronics, 46, 241-245.

7. Xia, X.G., Boncelent, C.G. and Arce, G.R. (1997) A Multiresolusion Watermark for Digital Image. International Conference on Image Processing, 1, 548-551. http://dx.doi.org/10.1109/ICIP.1997.647971

8. Inoue, D. and Yoshitomi, Y. (2009) Watermarking Using Wavelet Transform and Genetic Algorithm for Realizing High Tolerance to Image Compression. Journal of the IIEEJ, 38, 136-144.

9. Yoshitomi, Y., Asada, T., Kinugawa, Y. and Tabuse, M. (2011) An Authentication Method for Digital Audio Using a Discrete Wavelet Transform. Journal of Information Security, 2, 59-68. http://dx.doi.org/10.4236/jis.2011.22006

10. Asada, T., Yoshitomi, Y. and Tabuse, M. (2010) A Verification Method for a Digital Image File Using a Discrete Wavelet Transform. Journal of IIEEJ, 39, 1088-1094. (In Japanese)

11. MUSCLE-VCD-2007. http://www-rocq.inria.fr/imedia/civrbench/index.html

12. Libjpeg (2015) http://www.ijg.org/

13. FFmpeg (2015) http://ffmpeg.org/

14. Fujii, R., Noguchi, T., Tamura, M., Yoshitomi, Y., Asada, T. and Tabuse, M. (2014) A Verification Method for a Moving Image File Using a Discrete Wavelet Transform. Proceedings of Forum on Information Technology, 3, 195-196. (In Japanese)

CHAPTER 2

KEYBOARD DEPENDENCY OF PERSONAL IDENTIFICATION PERFORMANCE BY KEYSTROKE DYNAMICS IN FREE TEXT TYPING

Yoshitomo Matsubara, Toshiharu Samura, Haruhiko Nishimura

Keywords: Keystroke Dynamics, Biometrics, Information Security, Keyboard Dependency

INTRODUCTION

Timing data for keystrokes follow a fixed pattern, and the biometric approach using such data is called keystroke dynamics. There has been considerable research on keystroke dynamics owing to the advantage of using only a keyboard without requiring special equipment such as a fingerprint scanner [1] -[4] . Most of them have focused on user authentication at the time of log-in, using not only information about a series of input characters for password verification, but also keystroke matching as a part of the authentication process [5] [6] . On the other hand, it is possible to obtain sufficient information for deriving keystroke dynamics statistically by using sentences of a certain length. The keystroke authentication with such long-text input has recently become the subject of academic discussion [7] - [16] and can be used to detect spoofing after log-in process by observing keystroke data when using a system.

In our previous studies [11] - [16] , we have proposed methods for feature extraction and identification that enable identification of individuals through long-text input as an important topic in keystroke dynamics research. We use keystroke timing for single character and paired character sequences when the user is inputting Latin characters. For identification methods, we adopt our previously proposed the Weighted Euclidean Distance (WED) method [11] [12] , the Array Disorder (AD) method proposed by Gunetti et al. [8] [9] , and the WED + AD method which integrates the WED and AD methods [13] - [15] . Through a large-scale study involving 189 participants, it has been confirmed that the WED + AD method stably provides the best recognition accuracy among three methods [15] . Furthermore, we have constructed new profile generation methods, the profile- updating and profile-combining methods, to reinforce the robustness of keystroke dynamics and demonstrated the effectiveness of them through the examinations with subject's practical data [17] - [19] .

As to the robustness in practical circumstances, there exists a question on the keystroke dynamics how much the recognition accuracy is influenced by the change of keyboard. If the influence is significant, users would need to register their profile data keyboard by keyboard they use. Pointed out by many researchers, this point has not been examined yet. In this paper, we investigate dependencies on keyboards for the personal identification by keystroke dynamics in Japanese free text typing. By comparing the performance in the cases of using the same keyboard and different keyboards [20] , the dependencies on keyboards are evaluated through three implemented experiments for subjects.

In Section 2, we briefly introduce the data collection and the feature extraction we have dealt with so far. Next, we present three identification methods in free text typing in Section 3. In Section 4, evaluation procedure for keyboard difference is given, and experimental results are shown in Section 5. Finally, conclusion is given in Section 6.

DATA COLLECTION AND FEATURE EXTRACTION

This section describes keystroke data collection and how to

Citation: Matsubara, Y. , Samura, T. and Nishimura, H. (2015) Keyboard Dependency of Personal Identification Performance by Keystroke Dynamics in Free Text Typing. Journal of Information Security, 6, 229-240. doi: 10.4236/jis.2015.63023.

extract features from the data. Participants input a different text each time for 5 minutes. For each entry, typed key, key pressed time and key released time are recorded as raw data. Figure 1 shows an example of collected keystroke data. The first, second and third fields show typed key, whether the key was pressed (p) or released (r) and UNIX time of the event respectively. For collecting the data, we use a web-based system, and it has typing support software that is familiar to the participants, thereby lowering effects related to unfamiliarity and nervousness. Figure 2 shows a screenshot of the software interface used in this process. Since this experiment focuses only on Latin alphabet input keystroke, conversion into Japanese kanji characters is not designed. Detailed explanation about the interface of this system is described in [20] [21] .

Next, we describe feature extraction from keystroke data. The notation 1pr in Figure 3 indicates the time from press to release of a single key and is referred to below as key press duration. The notation 2rr indicates the time from the release of one key to the release of the following key when typing a consonant-vowel pair.

```
b, p, 1197417770648
a, p, 1197417770733
b, r, 1197417770791
i, p, 1197417770816
a, r, 1197417770823
i, r, 1197417770872
k, p, 1197417770972
k, r, 1197417771039
i, p, 1197417771112
i, r, 1197417771167
```

Figure 1: Example of collected keystroke data (typed key, pressed (p) or released (r), and UNIX time in order from left).

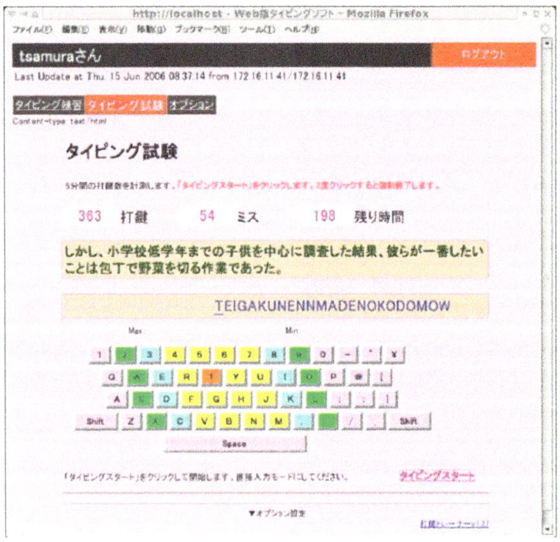

Figure 2: Snapshot of keystroke data collection system.

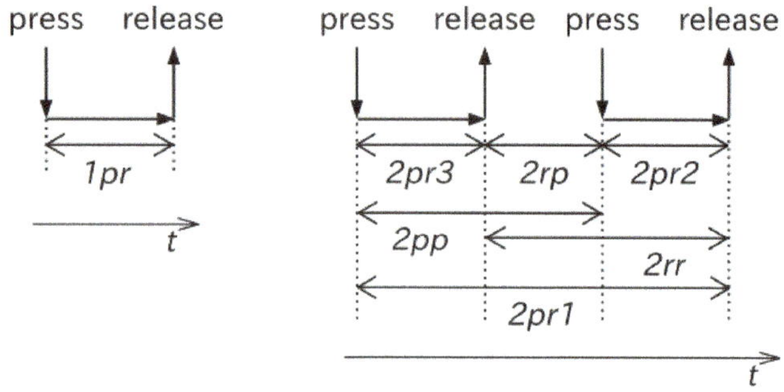

Figure 3: Keystroke measurements of single letter (left) and letter pair (right).

The time from release of the first key to the time of pressing the following key (2rp) and the time from pressing the first key to pressing the second key (2pp) are also considered. Furthermore, 2pr1 indicates the time from pressing the first key to releasing the next key, 2pr2 indicates the key press duration when typing the second (vowel) key, and 2pr3 indicates the key press duration when typing the first (consonant) key.

The average and standard deviation of each of the seven measures described above are used as the feature indices for identification of individuals. For these feature indices, standardization is performed according to the following equation:

$$x' = \frac{x - x_{\min}}{x_{\max} - x_{\min}} \qquad (1)$$

Here, x_{min} and x_{max} respectively refer to the minimum and maximum values obtained from the feature indices of all subjects. It has been confirmed in our previous works [11] [13] - [15] that the standard deviations for six letter pairs (2**) in feature indices have little contribution to improve recognition accuracy. Therefore, we do not adopt them in this study.

IDENTIFICATION METHODS

This section describes identification methods using the Weighted Euclidean Distance (WED) proposed by Samura and Nishimura [11] [12] , the Array Disorder (AD) proposed by Gunetti and Picardi [8] [9] , and the WED + AD proposed by Samura and Nishimura [13] - [15] .

Weighted Euclidean Distance (WED)

Taking the first profiling document of Typist A as docA1, the profiling document of each participant can be represented as docA1, docA2, ···, docAN, docB1, docB2, ···, docBN, docC1, ··· . An unknown document is represented as docUK. The WED(docUK,docA1) used as the identification function is given by the following equation:

$$WED(docUK, docA1) = \sqrt{\frac{1}{m}\sum_{\alpha=1}^{m}\frac{1}{n_\alpha}\sum_{i=1}^{n_\alpha}\left(k_{\alpha(i)} - r_{\alpha(i)}\right)^2} \qquad (2)$$

The index of the feature indices α (=1, 2, ···) is then 1pr.av, 1pr.sd, ··· . Furthermore, m is the number of contributing feature indices, $\alpha(i)$ indicates the feature index α for the i-th character (single letter or letter pair), and n_α is the number of characters therein. n_α will vary greatly with respect to the number of characters compared when, for example, taking the keystroke feature indices for single letters and those for two-letter combinations. $k_{\alpha(i)}$ is the $\alpha(i)$ feature index standardized according to Equation (1) for a profiling document (e.g., docA1), and $r_{\alpha(i)}$ is that for $\alpha(i)$ of an unknown document (docUK). The WED is normalized to 0 - 1 using the weightings $\frac{1}{m}$ and $\frac{1}{n_\alpha}$. Figure 4 illustrates the 2pp.av feature indices for two documents, docUK

and docA1. For five 2pp.av letter pairs common to the two documents, the WED becomes as follows:

$$WED_{2pp.av}(docUK, docA1) = \sqrt{\frac{1}{5}\left(0.33^2 + 0.06^2 + 0.12^2 + 0.22^2 + 0.25^2\right)}. \quad (3)$$

Array Disorder (AD)

The AD, which is called the R-measure in Gunetti and Picardi [9] , but referred to as the Array Disorder in the present study, ranks characters according to their feature index values, and evaluates the disorder of the rankings. Standardized feature indices are sorted in increasing order, the difference in rankings of each is extracted, and the total of each is taken as distance.

$$AD(docUK, docA1) = \frac{1}{m}\sum_{\alpha=1}^{m}\frac{1}{\omega(n_\alpha)}\sum_{i=1}^{n_\alpha}\left|rk_{\alpha(i)} - rr_{\alpha(i)}\right| \quad (4)$$

$$\omega(n_\alpha) = \begin{cases} \dfrac{n_\alpha^2}{2} & (n_\alpha : \text{even}) \\ \dfrac{n_\alpha^2 - 1}{2} & (n_\alpha : \text{odd}) \end{cases} \quad (5)$$

When n_α characters are used to compare a feature index α, if n_α is even then the distance is divided by $\frac{n_\alpha^2}{2}$; if n_α is odd then the distance is divided by $\frac{n_\alpha^2 - 1}{2}$. Finally, the value is normalized to the range 0 - 1 by dividing the value by the number of contributing feature indices m. Figure 5 shows the feature index values rearranged in increasing order from Figure 4.

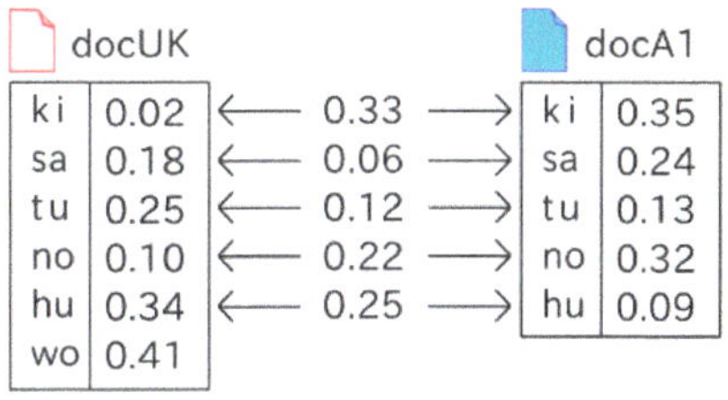

Figure 4: Illustration of the Weighted Euclidean Distance (WED) processing for existing letter pairs and their standardized values of 2pp.av in docUK and docA1, where there are five letter pairs in common between them.

The sum of the difference in rankings of each character is normalized, resulting in the following calculation of the AD value:

$$AD_{2pp.av}(docUK, docA1) = \frac{2}{5^2 - 1}(4 + 2 + 0 + 2 + 4). \quad (6)$$

WED + AD

In contrast to the WED, which evaluates the magnitude of differences in feature index values between documents, the AD focuses on differences between documents in ranking patterns of the feature indices. The WED + AD complementarity incorporates the features of the WED and AD. The distance of the WED + AD is given by the following equation:

$$[WED + AD](docUK, docA1) = WED(docUK, docA1) + AD(docUK, docA1) \quad (7)$$

In this measure, neither WED nor AD dominates because they are normalized to the range 0 - 1. Detailed explanation for the above method is given in [15] .

Identification is performed using the nearest-neighbor rule. In other words, comparisons are performed between the unknown document and each of the profile documents, and the typist of the profile document that gives the lowest value is taken to be the typist of the unknown document. For example, given five profile documents (A1-A5) for a subject (Typist A), we can expect that if Typist A also typed the unknown document then its distance will be close to one of the five states of A1-A5. In the case where the typist of the closest profile document is matched with the typist of the test document, the identification is classified as a success; otherwise, the identification is classified as a failure. Such validation is performed in turn on each document used in this study, and the recognition accuracy is calculated by (the number of successful identifications)/(the number of test documents) ´ 100%.

EVALUATION PROCEDURE FOR KEYBOARD DIFFERENCE

To investigate the influence of keyboard difference, we calculate the recognition accuracy in the following two cases. As shown in Figure 6, one is the case where an extracted unknown document (docUK) typed with keyboard X is identified with profile documents typed with the same keyboard X, and the same for Y. After this process, each recognition accuracy from keyboard X and Y is averaged.

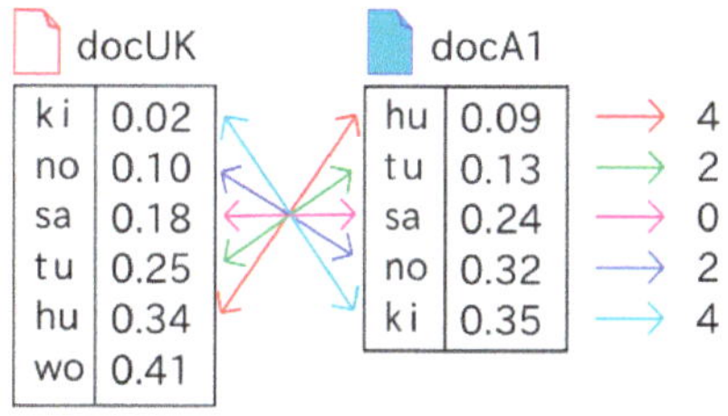

Figure 5: Illustration of the Array Disorder (AD) processing for the example in Figure 4.

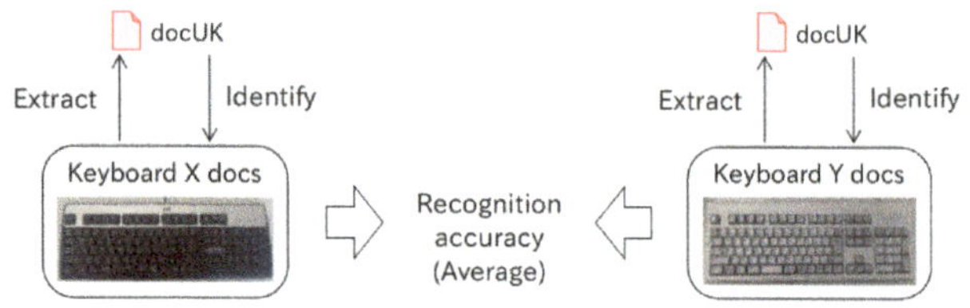

Figure 6: Evaluation procedure in the case where an extracted unknown document (docUK) typed with keyboard X is identified with profiled documents typed with the same keyboard X, and the same for Y (intra-keyboard evaluation).

We call this procedure "intra-keyboard evaluation." The other is the case where an extracted unknown document (docUK) typed with keyboard X is identified with profiled documents typed with the other keyboard Y, and vice versa as illustrated in Figure 7. Each recognition accuracy from keyboard X and Y is averaged as well as the intra-keyboard evaluation. We call this procedure "inter-keyboard evaluation."

We perform experiments for subjects who have 5 or more documents, each of which contains 500 or more letters. Since this criterion has been used as a standard condition in our previous works [11] - [17] , we adopt it in this paper too. As shown in Figure 8, the number of documents from each user is set to 5 by choosing 5 documents at random from those created by a subject who typed an excess number of documents. Analysis is performed taking, as a single set, the number of documents equal to 5× (the number of subjects). Considering possible bias in document selection, analysis is performed five times with 5 different document sets.

EXPERIMENTAL RESULTS

We implemented three experiments exchanging two types of keyboards.

Experiment Using Desktop Keyboards with Low Typing Skill Subjects (Experiment I)

In this experiment, two keyboards were prepared as shown in Figure 9. One is Hewlett-Packard BK-0316 and the other is NEC MT109PSXP.

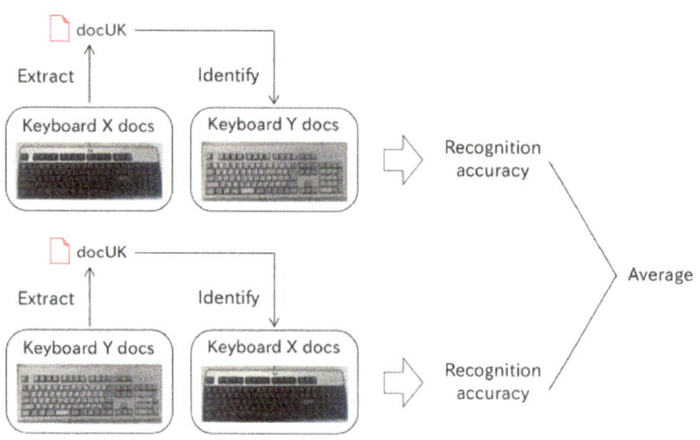

Figure 7: Evaluation procedure in the case where an extracted unknown document (docUK) typed with keyboard X is identified with profiled documents typed with the other keyboard Y, and vice versa (inter-keyboard evaluation).

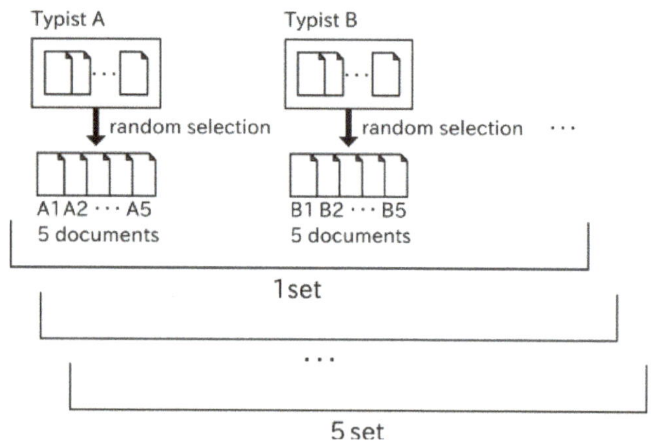

Figure 8: Procedure of preparing 5 document sets for evaluation.

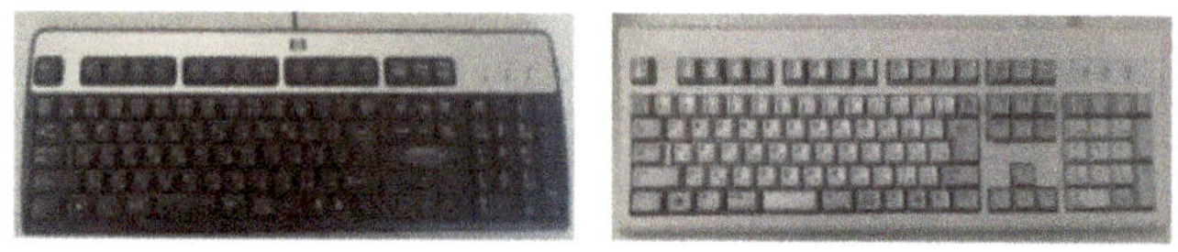

Figure 9: Keyboard 1 [Hewlett-Packard BK-0316] (left) and keyboard 2 [NEC MT-109PSXP] (right) used in Experiment I.

We call these keyboards keyboard 1 and keyboard 2, respectively. Both keyboards belong to the standard desktop keyboards with the keystroke depth of 3.5 - 4.0 mm and the key pitch of 19 mm. The subjects of this experiment were 35 participants who could type 500 or more letters per 5 minutes, and we call this group G500. Figure 10 shows the histogram of percentage of documents on the number of input letters, which indicates the variety of subject's typing skills in G500. The average of input letters per 5 minutes is 866 ± 267 with keyboard 1 and 969 ± 280 with keyboard 2.

The recognition accuracy for G500 is shown in Figure 11. The method using the WED + AD, which is expected to provide the highest recognition accuracy, provides about 96% in the intra-keyboard evaluation and about 86% in the inter-keyboard evaluation. It degrades severely because of changing keyboards and is not adequate level even in the case of using the same keyboard. This seemed to be caused by the existence of low typing skill subjects in G500, and then we left 23 subjects who could type 700 or more letters per 5 minutes with both keyboards (G700) and re-examined. Figure 12 shows the histogram in G700 as well as Figure 10. The average of input letters per 5 minutes becomes 995 ± 237 with keyboard 1 and 1090 ± 238 with keyboard 2, which increase by about 120 from those in G500.

Figure 13 shows the recognition accuracy for G700. Comparing the result with G500 in Figure 11, the recognition accuracy for G700 in the inter-keyboard evaluation increases only 1% - 2%. However, the accuracy for G700 in the inter-keyboard evaluation improves about 8%, and it is found that G500 is more affected by the keyboard difference than G700. Although the numbers of subjects in G500 and G700 are different, it is suggested that low typing skill users are easier to be influenced by the change of keyboards than high typing skill ones. Thus, we can expect that the higher the typing skill is getting, the lesser the influence by the keyboard difference becomes.

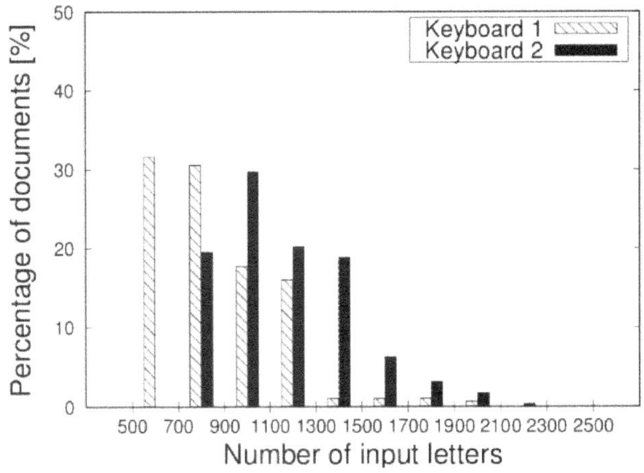

Figure 10: Histogram of percentage of documents on the number of input letters for 35 subjects (G500) in Experiment I.

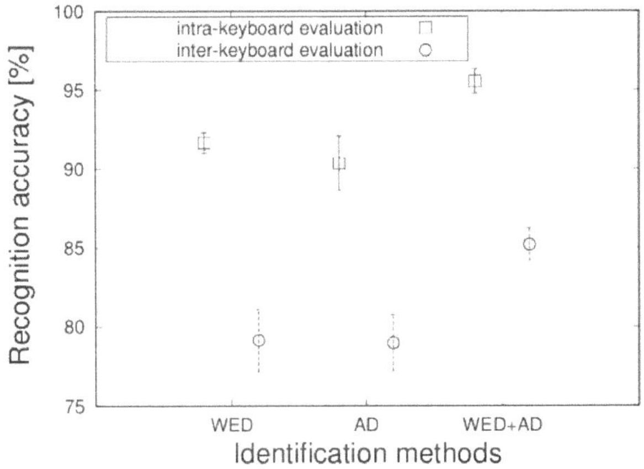

Figure 11: Recognition accuracy in intra-keyboard and inter-keyboard evaluations for G500 in Experiment I, obtained by three identification methods.

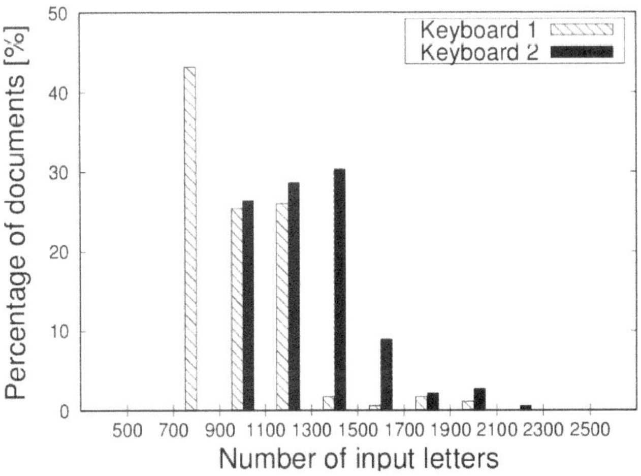

Figure 12: Histogram of percentage of documents on the number of input letters for 23 subjects (G700) in Experiment I.

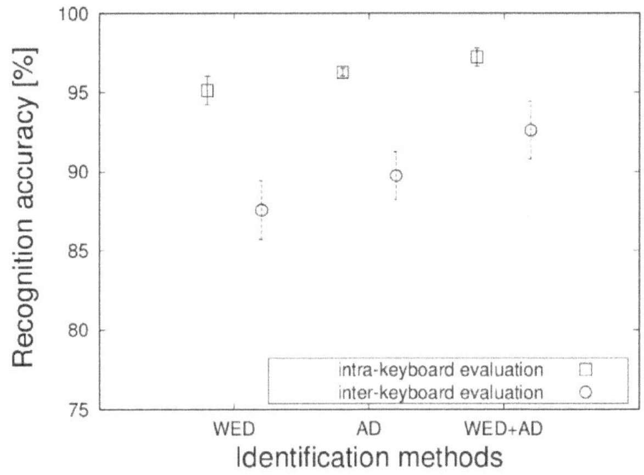

Figure 13: Recognition accuracy in intra-keyboard and inter-keyboard evaluations for G700 in Experiment I.

Experiment Using Desktop Keyboards without Low Typing Skill Subjects (Experiment II)

This experiment was performed on 27 subjects, and they were much more skilled-typists than those in Experiment I. In this experiment, we used two desktop keyboards as shown in Figure 14. One is BTC 5313 classic keyboard of which keystroke depth and key pitch are 3.9 ± 0.2 mm and 19 mm respectively. We call it keyboard 3. The other is Emprex 5211AU keyboard (USB keyboard) of which keystroke depth and key pitch are 3.5 ± 0.5 mm and 19 mm respectively. We call it keyboard 4. Both keyboards belong to the standard desktop keyboards with the keystroke depth and the key pitch are 3.5 - 4.0 mm and 19 mm. Figure 15 shows the histogram of percentage of documents on the number of input letters, which indicates the variety of subject's typing skills in this experiment. The average of input letters per 5 minutes is 1371 ± 313 with keyboard 3 and 1411 ± 301 with keyboard 4. These amounts have no significant difference each other and are about 350 more than those of G700 in Experiment I.

The recognition accuracy in this experiment is shown in Figure 16. High recognition accuracy around 99% is obtained in both cases of intra-keyboard and inter-keyboard evaluations with the WED + AD method. Any influence of the keyboard difference is not seen in the result. It is confirmed that high typing skill users in such a case are not almost influenced by the change of keyboards.

Figure 14: Keyboard 3 [BTC 5313 classic keyboard] (left) and keyboard 4 [Emprex 5211AU keyboard] (right) used in Experiment II.

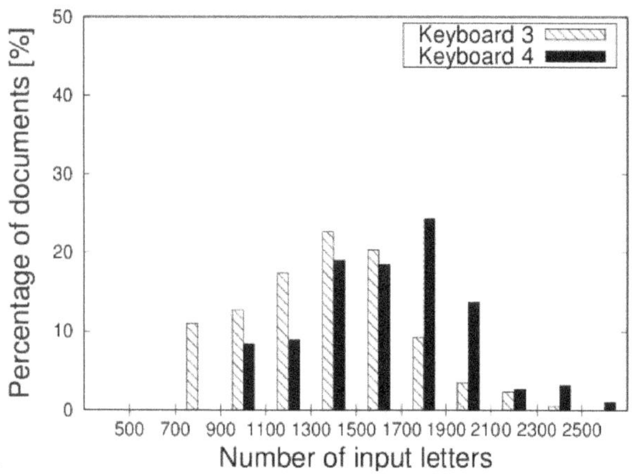

Figure 15: Histogram of percentage of documents on the number of input letters for 27 subjects in Experiment II.

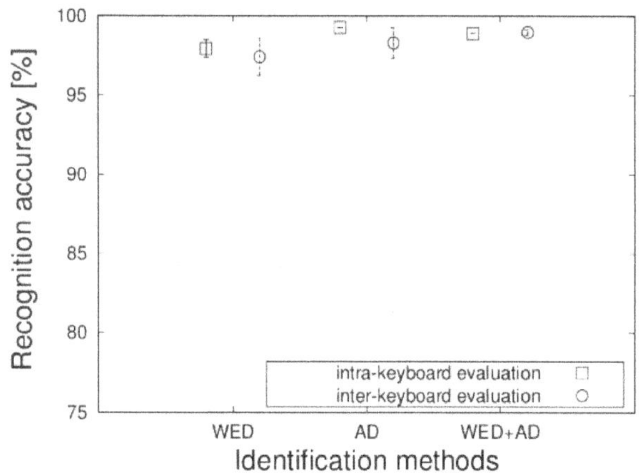

Figure 16: Recognition accuracy in intra-keyboard and inter-keyboard evaluations in Experiment II.

Experiment Using Desktop and Laptop Keyboards without Low Typing Skill Subjects (Experiment III)

This experiment was performed on 21 subjects, and they were also much more skilled-typists than those in Experiment I. Figure 17 shows the desktop and laptop keyboards used in this experiment. As a desktop keyboard, the keyboard 4 adopted in Experiment II was used again. As a laptop keyboard, Hewlett-Packard ProBook 4710s was used, of which keystroke depth and the key pitch are 3.5 ± 0.5 mm and 19 mm respectively. We call it keyboard 5. Figure 18 shows the histogram of percentage of documents on the number of input letters, which indicates the variety of subject's typing skills in this experiment. The average of input letters per 5 minutes is 1464 ± 246 with keyboard 4 and 1427 ± 297 with keyboard 5. There is no significant difference between these amounts as well as in Experiment II, and they are about 400 more than those of G700 in Experiment I.

The recognition accuracy in this experiment is given in Figure 19. The accuracy with the WED + AD method is around 99% and does not suffer the influence of keyboard difference in spite of using a laptop keyboard. Although feels of typing are different between desktop and laptop keyboards, it seems not to be a factor affecting the performance.

Figure 17: Keyboard 4 [Emprex 5211AU keyboard] (left) and keyboard 5 [Hewlett-Packard ProBook 4710s] (right) used in Experiment III.

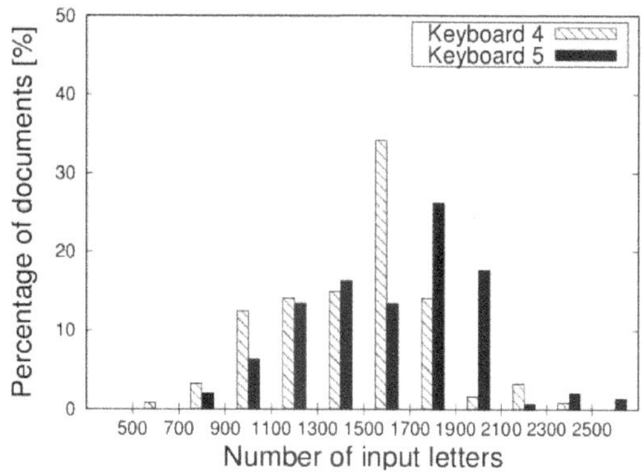

Figure 18: Histogram of percentage of documents on the number of input letters for 21 subjects in Experiment III.

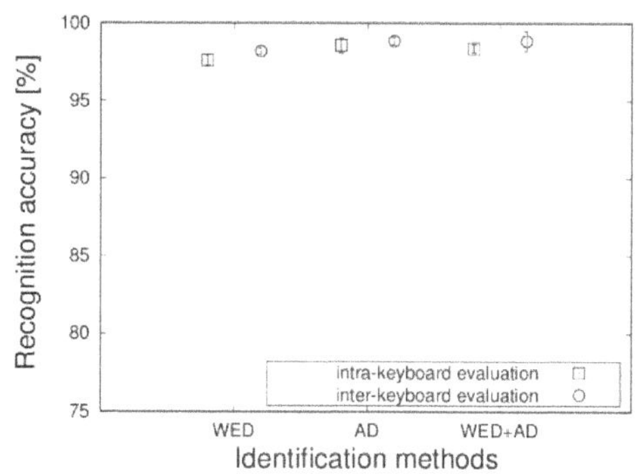

Figure 19: Recognition accuracy in intra-keyboard and inter-keyboard evaluations in Experiment III.

CONCLUSION

In this paper, we have investigated keyboard dependency of the personal identification by keystroke dynamics in Japanese free text typing. In Experiment I, it was confirmed that low typing skill users were easy to be influenced by changing keyboards, and then the recognition accuracy considerably decreased. Through the cases in Experiments II and III for high typing skill users, however, it was found that three identification methods kept high recognition accuracy against the keyboard difference. Especially, even in the situation using desktop and laptop keyboards, the recognition accuracy with the WED + AD method did not become worse. In practice, considering the results in Experiments I, II and III, we do not need to worry about the keyboard difference for users whose typing skills reach high level with about 900 or more letters in 5 minutes, and only for the remaining users it would be necessary to register their profile data with respect to keyboard they use in order to avoid recognition accuracy degradation. Finally, similar tendencies of the keyboard dependency would also be obtained in the cases of other languages, although we have focused only on Japanese text typing.

ACKNOWLEDGEMENTS

This work was supported by the Grant in Aid for Scientific Research (C24500101) from JSPS.

REFERENCES

1. Banerjee, S. and Woodard, D. (2012) Biometric Authentication and Identification Using Keystroke Dynamics: A Survey. Journal of Pattern Recognition Research, 7, 116-139.http://dx.doi.org/10.13176/11.427
2. Killourhy, K.S. (2012) A Scientific Understanding of Keystroke Dynamics. No. CMU-CS-12-100. Ph.D. Thesis, Carnegie Mellon University, Pittsburgh.
3. Alsultan, A. and Warwick, K. (2013) Keystroke Dynamics Authentication: A Survey of Free-Text Methods. International Journal of Computer Science Issues, 10, 1-10.
4. The, P.S., Teoh, A.B.J. and Yue, S. (2013) A Survey of Keystroke Dynamics Biometrics. The Scientific World Journal, 2013, Article ID: 408280.
5. Umphress, D. and Williams, G. (1985) Identity Verification through Keyboard Characteristics. International Journal of Man-Machine Studies, 23, 263-273.http://dx.doi.org/10.1016/S0020-7373(85)80036-5
6. Joyce, R. and Gupta, G. (1990) Identity Authentication Based on Keystroke Latencies. Communications of the ACM, 33, 168-176. http://dx.doi.org/10.1145/75577.75582
7. Monrose, F. and Rubin, A. (2000) Keystroke Dynamics as a Biometric for Authentication. Future Generation Computer Systems, 16, 351-359.http://dx.doi.org/10.1016/S0167-739X(99)00059-X
8. Bergadano, F., Gunetti, D. and Picardi, C. (2002) User Authentication through Keystroke Dynamics. ACM Transactions of Information and Systems Security, 5, 367-397.http://dx.doi.org/10.1145/581271.581272
9. Gunetti, D. and Picardi, C. (2005) Keystroke Analysis of Free Text. ACM Transactions of Information and System Security, 8, 312-347.http://dx.doi.org/10.1145/1085126.1085129
10. Tappert, C.C., Villani, M. and Cha, S. (2009) Keystroke Biometric Identification and Authentication on Long-Text Input. Behavioral Biometrics for Human Identification: Intelligent Applications, IGI Global, 342-367.
11. Samura, T. and Nishimura, H. (2009) Personal Identification by Keystroke Dynamics in Japanese Free Text Typing. Transactions of the Institute of Systems, Control and Information Engineers, 22, 145-153. http://dx.doi.org/10.5687/iscie.22.145
12. Samura, T. and Nishimura, H. (2009) Keystroke Timing Analysis for Individual Identification in Japanese Free Text Typing. Proceedings of ICROS-SICE International Joint Conference 2009, 3166-3170.
13. Samura, T. and Nishimura, H. (2010) A Hybrid Model for Individual Identification Based on Keystroke Data in Japanese Free Text Typing. Transactions of the Society of Instrument and Control Engineers, 46, 676-684. http://dx.doi.org/10.9746/sicetr.46.676
14. Samura, T. and Nishimura, H. (2011) Keystroke Dynamics for Individual Identification in Japanese Free Text Typing. SICE Journal of Control, Measurement, and System Integration, 4, 172-176. http://dx.doi.org/10.9746/jcmsi.4.172
15. Samura, T. and Nishimura, H. (2011) Personal Identification and Authentication Based on Keystroke Dynamics in Japanese Long-Text. Continuous Authentication based on Biometrics, Data, Models, and Metrics, IGI Global, 212-231.
16. Samura, T. and Nishimura, H. (2011) Keystroke Timing Analysis for Personal Authentication in Japanese Long Text Input. Proceedings of the SICE Annual Conference 2011, 2121-2126.
17. Matsubara, Y., Samura, T. and Nishimura, H. (2012) Robustness of Keystroke Dynamics against Changing in Input and Recognition Conditions for Japanese Atypical Text. Proceedings of 2012 International Symposium on Technology for Sustainability, Bangkok, November 2012, 103-106.
18. Samura, T., Matsubara, Y. and Nishimura, H. (2013) Performance Assessment in Keystroke Dynamics by Combined Profile Documents for Free Text Typing. Proceedings of SICE Annual Conference 2013, 265-270.
19. Matsubara, Y., Samura, T. and Nishimura, H. (2015) Profile Generation Methods for Reinforcing Robustness of Keystroke Authentication in Free Text Typing. Journal of Information Security, 6, 131-141. http://dx.doi.org/10.4236/jis.2015.62014
20. Samura, T. and Nishimura, H. (2011) Influence of Keyboard Difference on Personal Identification by Keystroke Dynamics in Japanese Free Text Typing. Proceedings of 6th International Conference on Emerging Trends in Engineering & Technology (ICETET-12), 30-35.
21. Samura, T. (2008) A Web-Based Typing Learning System That Supports Japanese Text. Journal of Education in the College of Technology, 31, 471-476.

CHAPTER 3 ANONYMOUS AUTHENTICATION PROTOCOLS FOR VEHICULAR AD HOC NETWORKS

Hu Xiong, Zhi Guan, Jianbin Hu and Zhong Chen

INTRODUCTION

According to car crash statistics, over six million motor vehicle crashes occur on U.S. highways each year. More than 42,000 people are killed in these accidents which injure three million others, and cost more than $230 billion each year. Astonishingly, five people die every hour in these crashes in the United States which is about one death every 12 minutes IVI (2001). In order to alleviate the threats of these crashes and improve the driving experience, car manufactures and the telecommunication industry have made great efforts to equip each vehicle with wireless devices that allow vehicles to communicate with each other as well as with the roadside infrastructure located in critical points of the road, such as intersections or construction sites. Misener (2005); VII (2011). Technologies built on 802.11p and IEEE 1609 standards, 5.9 GHz Dedicated Short Range Communications (DSRC) protocols 1 DSRC (1999), are proposed to support these advanced vehicle safety applications such as secure and effective vehicle-to-vehicle (V2V) (also known as Inter-Vehicle Communica- tion (IVC)) and vehicle-to-infrastructure (V2I) communications, which are also known as Vehicle Safety Communications (VSC) technologies. As shown in Fig. 1, the wireless communication devices installed on vehicles, also known as onboard units (OBUs), and the roadside units (RSUs), form a self-organized Vehicular Ad Hoc Network (VANET) Lin (2008); Sun (2007). Furthermore, the RSUs are connected to the backbone network via the high speed network connections. In this way, VANETs inherently provide a way to collect traffic and road information from vehicles, and to deliver road services including warnings and traffic information to users in the vehicles. Thus, an increasing interest has been raised recently on the VANETs-based applications Bishop (2000), aiming to improve driving safety and traffic management by the method of providing drivers and passengers with Internet access.

Due to the open broadcasting of wireless communications and the high-speed mobility of the vehicles, extensive research efforts have been launched by academic institutions and industrial research labs several years ago to investigate key issues in VANETs, especially security and privacy preservation for mobile vehicles Calandriello et al. (2007); Chen et al. (2011); Daza et al. (2009); Hubaux et al. (2004); Kamat et al. (2006); Kounga et al. (2009); Li et al. (2008); Lin et al. (2007; 2008a;b); Lu et al. (2008; 2009; 2010); Mak et al. (2005); Plößl & Federrath (2008); Raya & Hubaux (2005; 2007); Sun et al. (2007; 2010a;b); Wasef et al. (2010); Wang et al. (2008); Wu et al. (2010); Xu et al. (2007); Xi et al. (2007; 2008); Xiong et al. (2010a;b); Zhang et al. (2008a;b). Obviously, any malicious behaviors of user, such as injecting beacons with false information, modifying and replaying the previously disseminated messages, could be fatal to the other users. Thus, identifying the message issuer is mandatory to reduce the risk of such attacks. Meanwhile, in order to protect the user-related private information, such as the driver's name, the license plate, speed, position, and travelling routes along with their relationship, authentication in VANETs should be privacy-preserving.

It is natural to observe that achieving privacy and liability simultaneously is conflicting goal. On one aspect, a well-meaning OBU is willing to offer as much local information as possible to RSUs and other OBUs to create a safer driving environment so long as its locations cannot be tracked. And on the other, a misbehaving OBU may abuse the privacy protection mechanism to avoid legal responsibility when it involved in a dispute involving safety messages 2attempts. Therefore, the conditional privacy-preserving authentication should be fulfilled in VANETs where a trusted authority can

Citation: Hu Xiong, Zhi Guan, Jianbin Hu and Zhong Chen (2012). Anonymous Authentication Protocols for Vehicular Ad Hoc Networks, Applied Cryptography and Network Security, Dr. Jaydip Sen (Ed.), InTech, DOI: 10.5772/34675.

reveal the real identity of targeted OBU in case of a traffic event dispute, even though the OBU itself is not traceable by the public.

This chapter surveys the literature on privacy issues in VANETs from different perspectives, and thus provides researchers with a better understanding of this primitive. This chapter does not propose or advocate any specific anonymous authentication mechanisms. Even though some sections might point out vulnerabilities in certain classes of authentication protocols, our purpose is not to criticize, but to draw attention to these problems so that they might be solved.

The remainder of this chapter is organized as follows. Section 2 presents attack model, security requirements and related VANETs network architecture. All previous privacy-preserving protocols for VANETs are classified in Section 3, together with the basic cryptographic primitives. An example of Ring-signature based anonymous authentication protocol based on bilinear pairing are given in Section 4. Section 5 discusses how to use the taxonomies. Section 6 concludes the paper by stating some possible future research directions.

MOTIVATION

Attack Model

According to Lin (2008); Lin et al. (2007); Raya & Hubaux (2005; 2007); Sun et al. (2007), several possible security attacks in VANETs have been defined and listed as follows:

- ***Fake information attack***: The adversary may diffuse bogus messages to affect the behavior of others. For instance, in order to divert traffic from a given road, one may send a fake traffic jam message to the others.
- ***Message replay attack***: The adversary replays the valid messages sent by a legitimate user some time before in order to disturb the traffic.

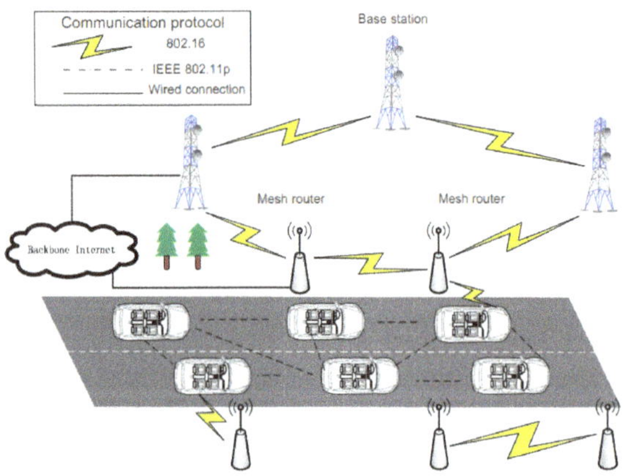

Figure 1: Vehicular Ad Hoc Networks.

- ***Message modification attack***: A message is altered during or after transmission. The adversary may wish to change the source or content of the message in terms of the position and/or time information that had been sent and saved in its device notably in the case of an accident.
- ***Impersonation attack***: The adversary may pretend to be another vehicle or even an RSU by using false identities to fool the others.
- ***RSU preemption/replication attack***: An RSU may be compromised such that the adversary can relocate the compromised RSU to launch any malicious attack, such as broadcasting fake traffic information. Moreover, the adversary may illegally interrupt and manipulate traffic lights which is controlled by the corrupted RSU to get a better traffic condition
- ***Denial of service (DoS) attack***: The adversary injects irrelevant jamming and aggressive dummy messages to take up the channels and consume the computational resources of the other nodes, such as RF interference or jamming or layer 2 packet flooding.
- ***Movement tracking***: Since wireless communication is on an openly shared medium, an adversary can easily eavesdrop on any traffic. After the adversary intercepts a significant amount of messages in a certain region, the adversary may trace a vehicle in terms of its physical position and moving patterns simply through information analysis. Assuming that the attacker does not make use of cameras, physical pursuit, or onboard tracking devices to reveal the identity of his target; otherwise, the tracking problem becomes simpler but also more expensive and limited to few specific targets.

Security Requirements

To countermeasure and mitigate the potential threats in the aforementioned attack models, a security system for safety messaging in a VANET should satisfy the following requirements.

Efficient anonymous authentication of safety messages: The security system should provide an efficient and anonymous message authentication mechanism. First of all, all accepted messages should be delivered unaltered, and the origin of the messages should be authenticated to guard against impersonation attacks. Meanwhile, from the point of vehicle owners, it may not be acceptable to leak personal information, including identity and location, to unauthorized observers while authenticating messages. Therefore, providing a secure yet anonymous message authentication is critical to the applicability of VANETs. Furthermore, considering the limited storage and computation resource of OBUs, the authentication scheme should have low overheads for safety message verification and storage.

Efficient tracking of the source of a disputed safety message: An important and challenging issue in these conditions is enabling a trusted third party (such as police officers) to retrieve a vehicle's real identity from its pseudo identity. If this feature is not provided, anonymous authentication can only prevent an outside attack, but cannot deal with an inside one. Furthermore, the system should not only provide safety message traceability to prevent inside attacks, but also have reasonable overheads for the revealing the identity of a message sender.

Threshold authentication Chen et al. (2011); Daza et al. (2009); Kounga et al. (2009); Wu et al. (2010): A message is viewed as trustworthy only after it has been endorsed by at least n vehicles, where n is a threshold. The threshold mechanism is a priori countermeasure that improves the confidence of other vehicles in a message. In addition, the threshold in the proposed scheme should be adaptive, that is to say, the sender can dynamically change the threshold according to the traffic context and scenarios.

Confidentiality Kamat et al. (2006); Li et al. (2008); Plößl & Federrath (2008); Wang et al. (2008) Some research teams pointed out that the privacy of the communication content should be protected against unauthorized observers. While confidentiality of communicating message can be negligible in most cases, it is e.g. crucial for services subject to costs. Besides application data administrative messages like routing protocol information or messages containing cryptographic material, the cryptographic information held by participants or centralized instances should also be protected against unauthorized access.

Network Model

Similar to previous work Calandriello et al. (2007); Chen et al. (2011); Daza et al. (2009); Hubaux et al. (2004); Kamat et al. (2006); Kounga et al. (2009); Li et al. (2008); Lin et al. (2007; 2008a;b); Lu et al. (2008; 2009; 2010); Mak et al. (2005); Plößl & Federrath (2008); Raya & Hubaux (2005; 2007); Sun et al. (2007; 2010a;b); Wasef et al. (2010); Wang et al. (2008); Wu et al. (2010); Xu et al. (2007); Xi et al. (2007; 2008); Xiong et al. (2010a;b); Zhang et al. (2008a;b), the security system should include at least three types of entities: the top Trusted authority (TA), the immobile RSUs at the roadside, and the moving vehicles equipped with on-board units (OBUs).

- ***OBU***: A vehicle can not join the VANETs unless it registers its own public system parameters and corresponding private key to the TA. The secret information such as private keys to be used generates the need for a tamper-proof device in each vehicle. According to existing works, only the authorized parties can access to this tamper-proof device. OBUs are mobile and moving most of the time. When the OBUs are on the road, they regularly broadcast routine safety messages, such as position, current time, direction, speed, traffic conditions, traffic events. The information system on each vehicle aggregates and diffuses these messages to enable drivers form a better awareness of their environment (Fig. 2). The assumed communication protocol between neighboring OBUs (IVC) or between an OBU and a RSU (V2I) is 5.9 GHz Dedicated Short Range Communication (DSRC) DSRC (1999) IEEE 802.11p.
- ***RSU:*** The RSUs, which are subordinated by the TA, form a wireless multi-hop mesh network (mesh mode in WiMax) aiming to extend the wireless coverage and increase the network robustness and throughput. Some of these RSUs are connected to the backbone networks with wired connections or to the WiMax base stations with wireless connections. Vehicles and passengers can gain access to the Internet for a short moment when passing through any of the RSUs by communicating with it. Thus, the RSUs should be able to perform fast handoff in order to support basic Internet services such as e-mail and TCP applications. We remark that the handoff process should be predictive when the moving pattern and speed of the vehicle are given. In addition, the RSUs should work as gateways which also support the 802.11p protocol and can transform the safety messages broadcasted by the vehicles into IP packets. With the support from RSUs, the workload of the vehicles is reduced. Otherwise, the vehicles need to send multiple copies of safety messages in different formats: one to the other vehicles with 802.11p, and one to the base stations with 802.16e. Different from the vehicles, we assume that RSUs have neither computation and energy constraints nor buffer size constraints.
- ***TA:*** The TA is in charge of the registration of all RSUs and OBUs each vehicle is equipped with. The TA can reveal the real identity of a safety message sender by incorporating with its subordinate RSUs. To the end, the TA requires ample computation and storage capability, and the TA cannot be compromised and is fully trusted by all parties in the system.

The network dynamics are characterized by quasi-permanent mobility, high speed, and (in most cases) short connection times between neighboring vehicles or between a vehicle and a roadside infrastructure network access point.

TAXONOMY OF PRIVACY-PRESERVING AUTHENTICATION PROTOCOL FOR VANETS

RSU-Based Approach

Zhang et al.Zhang et al. (2008a;b) presented a novel RSU-aided message authentication scheme (RSUB), in which the RSUs are responsible for validating the authenticity of messages sent from vehicles and for sending the results back to peer vehicles. Compared to the solutions without support from RSUs, this kind of schemes enables lower computation and communication overheads for each vehicle. Independently, Lu et al. Lu et al. (2008) introduced another anonymous authentication protocol for VANETs based on generating on-the-fly short-lived anonymous keys for the communication between vehicles and RSUs. These keys enable fast anonymous authentication and conditional privacy. All of these schemes employ RSUs to assist vehicles in authenticating messages. To keep a centralized certificate issuer from being a bottleneck, an RSU is allowed to issue certificates for the vehicles. However, it brings a privacy risk when an RSU is compromised by the adversaries. Once the service records of an RSU are leaked, it is easy for the adversary to link the pseudonymous certificates that a vehicle has obtained from the compromised RSU. In particular, when the number of compromised RSUs increases, it possibly provides a solution for the adversaries to revert the mobile trace of the target vehicles. However, relying on the roadside infrastructure for safety message authentication is a precarious solution: while these messages enable critical assisted driving features the roadside infrastructure will likely offer only partial coverage (for example during the deployment stage, for economic considerations, or simply due to physical damage).

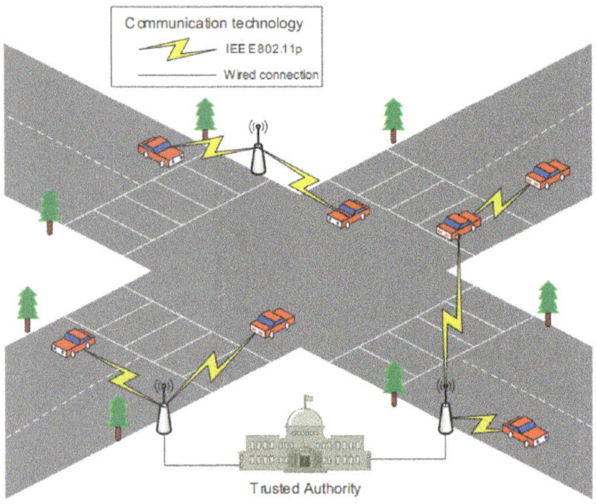

Figure 2: VANETs Architecture.

Group-Oriented Signature-Based Approach

Group Signature-Based Scheme

In Chaum & Hevst (1991), Chaum and Heyst proposed a new type of signature scheme for a group of entities, called group signatures. Such a scheme allows a group member to sign a message on the group's behalf such that everybody can verify the signature but no one can find out which group member provided it. However, there is a trusted third party, called the group manager, who can reveal the identity of the originator of a signature in the case of later dispute. This act is referred to as "opening" a signature or also as revocation of a signer's anonymity. The group manager can either be a single entity or a number of coalitions of several entities (e.g., group members). Dozens of group signature schemes Boneh et al. (2004); Boneh & Shacham (2004); Chaum & Hevst (1991); Nakanishi & Funabiki (2005) have been proposed since 1991 due to its attractive features.

Lin et al. Lin et al. (2007; 2008a); Sun et al. (2007) proposed the group signature based (GSB) protocol, based on the efficient group signature Boneh et al. (2004). With GSB, each vehicle stores only a private key and a group public key. Messages are signed using the group signature scheme without revealing any identity information to the public. Thus privacy is preserved while the trusted authority is able to expose the identity of a sender. However, the time for safety message verification grows linearly with the number of revoked vehicles in the revocation list in the entire network. Hence, each vehicle has to spend additional time on safety message verification. Furthermore, when the number of revoked vehicles in the revocation list is larger than some threshold, the protocol requires every remaining vehicle to calculate a new private key and group public key based on the exhaustive list of revoked vehicles whenever a vehicle is revoked. Lin et al. Lin et al. (2007; 2008a); Sun et al. (2007) do not explore solutions to effectively updated the system parameters for the participating to vehicles in a timely, reliable and scalable fashion. This issue is not explored and represents an important obstacle to the success of this scheme.

Ring Signature-Based Scheme

Ring signature scheme, introduced by Rivest, Shamir and Tauman Rivest et al. (2001), offers two main properties: anonymity and spontaneity. In practice, anonymity in a ring signature means 1-out-of-n signer verifiability, which enables the signer to keep anonymous in these "rings" of diverse signers. Spontaneity is a property which makes the distinction between ring signatures and group signatures Boneh et al. (2004); Chaum & Hevst (1991). Different from group signatures which allow the anonymity of a real signer in a group can be revoked by a group manager, the ring signature only gives the group manager the absolute power to control the formation of the group, and does not allow anyone to revoke the signer anonymity, while allowing the real signer to form a ring arbitrarily without being controlled by any other party. Since Rivest el al.'s scheme, many ring signature schemes have been proposed Abe et al. (2002); Bresson et al. (2002); Dodis et al. (2004); Wong et al. (2003); Xiong et al. (2009; 2011). In 2007, Liu et al. Liu et al. (2007) have introduced a new variant for the ring signature, called revocable ring signature. This scheme allows a real signer to form a ring arbitrarily while allowing a set of authorities to revoke the anonymity of the real signer. In other words, the real signer will be responsible for what has signed as the anonymity is revocable by authorities while the real signer still has full freedom on ring formation.

To address the scalability concern in Lin et al. (2007), Xiong et al. Xiong et al. (2010a) proposed a spontaneous protocol based on the revocable ring signature Liu et al. (2007), which allows the vehicle to generate the message without requiring online assistance from the RSUs or the other vehicles. In this solution, the remaining vehicles are not required to update their system parameters regardless of the number of revoked vehicles. However, this protocol suffers larger communication overhead than that of other protocols because the length of ring signature depends on the size of the ring. Furthermore, Xi et al. Xi et al. (2007; 2008) also introduced a random key-set-based authentication protocol to preserve the vehicle's privacy based on ring signature. However, this solution only provides unconditional anonymity without an effective and efficient mechanism to reveal message sender's identities when necessary.

k-TAA-Based Scheme

In a k-times anonymous authentication (k-TAA) system Teranisi et al. (2004), participants are a group manager (GM), a number of application providers (AP) and a group of users. The GM registers users into the group and each AP independently announces the number of times a user can access his application. A registered user can then be anonymously authenticated by APs within their allowed numbers of times (k times) and without the need to contact the GM. Dishonest users can be traced by anyone while no one, even the GM or APs, can identify honest users or link two authentication executions performed by the same user. Finally no one, even the GM, is able to successfully impersonate an honest user to an AP. In dynamic k-TAA Nguyen & Safavi-Naini (2005), APs have more control over granting and revoking access to their services and so have the required control on their clients.

Sun et al. Sun & Fang (2009); Sun et al. (2010c) proposed a new misbehavior defense technique leveraging the idea of dynamic revocation, to provide a means of limiting the impact of misbehavior by adjusting it to an acceptable level during the vulnerable period existing in the automatic revocation technique based on dynamic k-TAA. However, the downside of Sun et al.'s scheme is obviously the lack of capability to trace misbehaving users.

Pseudonyms-Based Approach

Basic Scheme

Raya et al.Raya & Hubaux (2005; 2007) introduced the large number of anonymous key based (LAB) protocol. Their key idea is to install on each OBU a large number of private keys and their corresponding anonymous certificates. To sign each launched message, a vehicle randomly selects one of its anonymous certificates and uses its corresponding private key. The other vehicles use the public key of the sender enclosed with the anonymous certificate to authenticate the source of the message. These anonymous certificates are generated by employing the pseudo-identity of the vehicles, instead of taking any real identity information of the drivers. Each certificate has a short life time to meet the drivers'privacy requirement. Although LAB protocol can effectively meet the conditional privacy requirement, it is inefficient and may become a scalability bottleneck. The reason is that a sufficient numbers of certificates must be issued to each vehicle to maintain anonymity over a significant period of time. (Raya et al.Raya & Hubaux (2005; 2007) suggest using large pseudo certificates for each vehicle). As a result, the certificate database to be searched by the TRC in order to match a compromised certificate to its owner's identity is huge. In addition, the protocols of Raya & Hubaux (2007) are extended for providing confidentiality in specific scenarios of VANET implementations in Wang et al. (2008).

TESLA-Based Scheme

TESLA is an efficient and message-loss tolerant protocol for broadcast authentication with low communication and computation overhead Perrig et al. (2002a). It is widely used in areas of sensor networks Perrig et al. (2002b). It uses one-way hash chain where the chain elements are the secret keys to compute message authentication code (MAC). With TESLA, a sender sends data packets at a predefined schedule, which has been known in advance to the receivers as well as the commitment to a hash chain as a key commitment. Each hash chain element as a MAC key corresponds to a certain time interval. For each packet, the sender attaches a MAC tag to it. This MAC tag is derived using the next corresponding MAC key in the hash chain based on negotiated key disclosure delay schedule between the sender and the receiver. Obviously, upon receiving the packet, the receiver can ¸a´rt verify the authenticity of the packet yet. After key disclosure delay, the sender discloses MAC key, and then the receiver is able to authenticate the message after verifying the released MAC key is indeed the corresponding element of the chain. One requirement for TESLA scheme is the loose synchronization among the nodes. The disadvantage is the delayed message authentication.

Lin et al. Lin et al. (2008b) developed the 'time-efficient and secure vehicular communication' scheme (TSVC) based on the Timed Efficient Stream Loss-tolerant Authentication (TESLA) standard (RFC 4082) Perrig et al. (2002a). With TSVC, a vehicle first broadcasts a commitment of hash chain to its neighbors and then uses the elements of the hash chain to generate a message authentication code (MAC) with which other neighbors can authenticate this vehicles' following messages. Because of the fast speed of MAC verification, the computation overhead of TSVC is reduced significantly. However, TSVC also requires a huge set of anonymous public/private key pairs as well as their corresponding public key certificates to be preloaded in each vehicle. Furthermore, TSVC may not be robust when the traffic becomes extremely dynamic as a vehicle should broadcast its key chain commitment much more frequently.

Proxy re-Signature-Based Scheme

Proxy re-signature schemes, introduced by Blaze, Bleumer, and Strauss Blaze et al. (1998), and formalized later by Ateniese and Hohenberger Ateniese & Hohenberger (2005), allow a semi-trusted proxy to transform a delegatee ¸a´rs signature into a delegator ¸a´rs signature on the same message by using some additional information. Proxy re-signature can be used to implement anonymizable signatures in which outgoing messages are first signed by specific users. Before releasing them to the outside world, a proxy translates signatures into ones that verify under a system's public key so as to conceal the original issuer's identity and the internal structure of the organization. Recently, Libert et al. Libert & Vergnaud (2008) have introduced the first multi-hop unidirectional proxy re-signature scheme wherein the proxy can only translate signatures in one direction and messages can be resigned a polynomial number of times.

The size of the certificate revocation list (CRL) and the checking cost are two important performance metrics for the revocation mechanism in VANETs. Unfortunately, the pseudonymous authentication schemes are prone to generating a huge CRL, whereas the checking cost in the group-signature-based schemes is unacceptable for the vehicles with limited computation power. Since the CRL is usually transmitted by vehicle-to-vehicle communication, the quick increase of the CRL in the pseudonymous authentication schemes brings large communication cost. Moreover, the larger the CRL size, the longer the transmission delay to all vehicles, and during this period, the misbehaving vehicles can compromise VANETs continually. Sun et al. Sun et al. (2010a;b) proposed an efficient authentication protocol which supports RSU-aided distribution certificate service that allows a vehicle to update its certificate set from an RSU on the road based on the proxy re-signature Libert & Vergnaud (2008). In their scheme, the vehicle only needs to request the re-signature keys from an RSU and re-sign numbers of the certificates issued by the TA to be the same as those issued by the RSU itself, and thus significantly reduces the revocation cost and the certificate updating overhead. However, their scheme also rely on the RSUs which only cover partial high-way or city roads during the deployment stage.

Confidentiality-Oriented Scheme

The need for confidentiality in specific scenarios of VANET implementations has also been discussed in recent works Kamat et al. (2006); Li et al. (2008); Plößl & Federrath (2008); Wang et al. (2008). Specifically in Wang et al. (2008), the protocols of Raya & Hubaux (2007) are extended: session keys for pairs of vehicles are established by using the Diffie-Hellman key agreement protocol while group session keys are established using the key transfer approach. These keys are used for both message authentication and confidentiality Wang et al. (2008). A lightweight authenticated key establishment scheme with privacy preservation and confidentiality to secure the communications in VANET is proposed by Li et al. Li et al. (2008). Meantime, two security frameworks for VANETs to provide authentication, confidentiality, non-repudiation and message integrity have also been proposed by Plößl & Federrath (2008) and Kamat et al. (2006) independently. Nevertheless, all of these works Kamat et al. (2006); Li et al. (2008); Plößl & Federrath (2008); Wang et al. (2008) suffer from the same criticism in LAB, in other words, each OBU has to take a large storage space to store a huge number of anonymous key pairs.

Priori-Based Approach

By taking strict punitive action, a posteriori countermeasures can exclude some rational attackers, but they are ineffective against irrational attackers such as terrorists. Even for rational attackers, damage has already occurred when punitive action is taken. To reduce the damage to a bare minimum, the priori countermeasures have been proposed to prevent the generation of fake messages. In this approach, a message is not considered valid unless it has been endorsed by a number of vehicles above a certain threshold.

Basic Scheme

Most recently, Kounga et al. Kounga et al. (2009) proposed a solution that permits vehicles to verify the reliability of information received from anonymous origins. In this solution, each vehicle can generate the public/private key pairs by itself. However, the assumption in this solution is very restricted in that additional hardware is needed on the OBU. However, Chen and Ng Chen & Ng (2010) showd that the Kounga et al.'s scheme does not achieve the goals of authenticity of a message, privacy of drivers and vehicles, reliability of distributed information, and revocation of illegitimate vehicles.

After that, a proposal is also presented following the priori protection paradigm based on threshold signature by Daza et al. Daza et al. (2009). Nevertheless, to obtain the anonymity, this protocol assumes that the OBU installed on the vehicle can be removable and multi OBUs could alternatively be used with the same vehicle (like several cards can be used within a cell phone in the same time). Thus, this assumption may enable malicious adversary to mount the so-called Sybil attack: vehicles using different anonymous key pairs from corresponding OBUs can sign multiple messages to pretend that these messages were sent by different vehicles. Since multi OBUs can be installed on the same vehicle, no one can find out whether all of these signatures come from the same vehicle or not.

Table 1: Summary of related protocols

	Anonymous authentication	Traceability	Confidentiality	GSBS	RSUS	*Priori* -based	PBS
Zhang *et al.* (2008a;b)	✓	✓			✓		
Lu *et al.* (2008)	✓	✓			✓		
Lin *et al.* (2007; 2008a)	✓	✓		✓			
Sun *et al.* (2007)	✓	✓		✓			
Xiong *et al.* (2010a)	✓	✓		✓			
Xi *et al.* (2007; 2008)	✓			✓			
Sun & Fang (2009)	✓			✓			
Sun *et al.* (2010c)	✓			✓			
Raya & Hubaux (2005; 2007)	✓	✓					✓
Lin *et al.* (2008b)	✓	✓					✓
Sun *et al.* (2010a;b)	✓	✓		✓			✓
Li *et al.* (2008)	✓	✓	✓				✓
Plößl & Federrath (2008)	✓	✓	✓				✓
Kamat *et al.* (2006)	✓	✓	✓				✓
Wang *et al.* (2008)	✓	✓	✓				✓
Kounga *et al.* (2009)[3]						✓	
Daza *et al.* (2009)	✓	✓				✓	
Wu *et al.* (2010)	✓	✓		✓		✓	

GSBS: Group-oriented signature based scheme; RSUS: RSU based scheme; PBS: Pseudonyms-based scheme

Group Signature-Based Scheme

A linkable group signature Nakanishi et al. (1999) is a variant of group signatures. In a linkable group signature, it is easy to distinguish the group signatures produced by the same signer, even though the signer is anonymous. Linkable group signatures can thwart the Sybil attack but are not compatible with vehicle privacy due to the linkability of signer identities, i.e., the various message endorsements signed by a certain vehicle can be linked. Wu et al. Wu et al. (2010) proposed a novel protocol based on linkable group signature, which is equipped with both priori and posteriori countermeasures. However, they face the same adverse conditions in GSB protocol in which the verification time grows linearly with the number of revoked vehicles and every remaining vehicle need to update its private key and group public key when the number of revoked vehicles is larger than some threshold.

AN EXAMPLE OF RING-SIGNATURE BASED ANONYMOUS AUTHENTICATION PROTOCOLS

In order to be self-contained, we give an example of Ring-signature based authentication protocol along with the notion of bilinear pairing Xiong et al. (2010a) as follows.

Bilinear Pairing

Note that the publication of an identity based encryption scheme Boneh & Franklin (2001) built on bilinear pairings has triggered a real upsurge in the popularity of pairings among cryptographers. Following Boneh and Franklin, a lot of cryptosystems based on pairings have been proposed which would be hard to construct using more conventional cryptographic primitives. At this moment, pairing-based cryptography is a highly active field of research, with several hundreds of publications.

Let $\mathbb{G}_1$ denote an additive group of prime order q and $\mathbb{G}_2$ be a multiplicative group of the same order. Let P be a generator of $\mathbb{G}_1$, and $\hat{e}$ be a bilinear map such that $\hat{e}: \mathbb{G}_1 \times \mathbb{G}_1 \rightarrow \mathbb{G}_2$ with the following properties:

1. Bilinearity: For all

$$P, Q \in \mathbb{G}_1, \text{and } a, b \in \mathbb{Z}_q, \hat{e}(aP, bQ) = \hat{e}(P, Q)^{ab}.$$

2. Non-degeneracy: $\hat{e}(P, P) \neq 1_{\mathbb{G}_2}$

3. Computability: It is efficient to compute $\hat{e}(P, Q)$ for all $P, Q \in \mathbb{G}_1$

Ring-Signature Based

System Initialization

Firstly, as described in section 2.3, we assume each vehicle is equipped with a tamper-proof device, which is secure against any compromise attempt in any circumstance. With the tamper-proof device on vehicles, an adversary cannot extract any data stored in the device including key material, data, and codes. We assume that there is a trusted Transportation Regulation Center (TRC) which is in charge of checking the vehicle's identity, and generating and pre-distributing the private keys of the vehicles. Prior to the network deployment, the TRC sets up the system parameters for each OBU as follows:

- Let $\mathbb{G}_1$, $\mathbb{G}_2$ be two cyclic groups of same order q. Let $\hat{e}: \mathbb{G}_1 \times \mathbb{G}_1 \rightarrow \mathbb{G}_2$ be a bilinear map.
- The TRC first randomly chooses $x_{TRC} \in_R \mathbb{Z}_q$ as its private key, and computes $y_{TRC} = x_{TRC}P$ as its public key. The TRC also chooses a secure cryptographic hash function H : $\{0,1\}^* \rightarrow \mathbb{Z}_q$.
- Each vehicle V_i with real identity RID_i generates its public/private key pair as follows:
  - The vehicle V_i first chooses $x_{TRC} \in_R \mathbb{Z}_q$ as its private key, and computes $y_i = x_iP$ as its public key.
  - V_i randomly selects an integer ti ∈R Zq to determine the verification information of y_i : $a_i = H(t_iP \| RID_i)$ and $b_i = (t_i + x_i \cdot a_i)$. Then Vi sends $\{y_i, RID_i, a_i, b_i\}$ to TRC.
  - After receiving $\{y_i, RID_i, a_i, b_i\}$, TRC checks whether the following equation holds:

$$a_i \stackrel{?}{=} \mathcal{H}((b_iP - a_iy_i) \parallel RID_i)$$

If it holds, then $\{y_i, RID_i\}$ is identified as the valid public key and identity. Otherwise, it will be rejected. In the end, the TRC stores the (y_i, RID_i) in its records.

- Each vehicle is preloaded with the public parameters $\{\mathbb{G}_1, \mathbb{G}_2, q, y_{TRC}, \mathcal{H}\}$. In addition, the tamper-proof device of each vehicle is preloaded with its private/public key pairs (x_i, y_i) and corresponding anonymous certificates (these certificates are generated by taking the vehicle's pseudo-identity ID_i). Finally, the vehicle will preload the revocation list (RL) from the TRC.

OBU Safety Message Generation

Vehicle V_π signs the message M before sending it out. Suppose $S = \{y_1, \cdots, y_n\}$ is the set of public keys collected by vehicle V_π and it defines the ring of unrevoked public keys. Note that the public key set S, collected and stored temporarily by V_π, is dynamic. We assume that all public keys y_i, $1 \leq i \leq n$ and their corresponding private keys x_i's are generated by TRC, and π ($1 \leq \pi \leq n$) is the index of the actual message sender. In other words, as V_π travels through the road network, the set of public keys collected by it keeps changing over time. Otherwise, a unique set of public keys used by a vehicle may enable the adversary to infer its traveling trajectory. The signature generation algorithm Sig(S, x_π, y_{TRC}, M) is carried out as follows.

1. Randomly select $r \in_R \mathbb{Z}_q$ and compute R = rP.

2. For y_{TRC}, compute $E_{TRC} = \hat{e}(y_\pi, y_{TRC})^r$.

3. Generate a non-interactive proof SPK(1) as follows: $SPK\{\alpha : \{E_{TRC} = \hat{e}(R, y_{TRC})^\alpha\} \wedge \{\bigvee y_i = \alpha P\}\}(M)$. The signature σ of M with respect to S and y_{TRC} is (R, E_{TRC}) and the transcript of SPK(1).

For clear presentation, we divide SPK(1) into two components:

$$SPK\{\alpha : E_{TRC} = \hat{e}(R, y_{TRC})^\alpha\}(M), \tag{ba}$$

$$SPK\{\alpha : \bigvee_{i \in [1,n]} y_i = \alpha P\}(M). \tag{1b}$$

To generate a transcript of SPK(1a), given E_{TRC}, R, y_{TRC}, the actual message sender indexed by π proves the knowledge of xπ such that $E_{TRC} = \hat{e}(R, y_{TRC})^{x_\pi}$ by releasing (s, c) as the transcript such that

$$c = \mathcal{H}(y_{TRC} \parallel R \parallel E_{TRC} \parallel \hat{e}(R, y_{TRC})^s E_{TRC}^c \parallel M)$$

This can be done by randomly picking $l \in_R \mathbb{Z}_q$ and computing

$$c = \mathcal{H}(y_{TRC} \parallel R \parallel E_{TRC} \parallel \hat{e}(R, y_{TRC})^l \parallel M)$$

and then setting $s = l - cx_\pi \bmod q$.

To generate the transcript of SPK(1b), given S, the actual message sender indexed by π, for some $1 \leq \pi \leq n$, proves the knowledge of $x\pi$ out of n discrete logarithms x_i, where $y_i = x_iP$, for $1 \leq i \leq n$, without revealing the value of π. This can be done by releasing $(s_1, \cdots, s_n, c_1, \cdots, c_n)$ as the transcript such that $c_0 = \sum_{i=1}^{n} c_i$ mod q and

$$c_0 = \mathcal{H}(S \parallel s_1P + c_1y_1 \parallel \cdots \parallel s_nP + c_ny_n \parallel M).$$

To generate this transcript, the actual message sender first picks randomly $l \in_R \mathbb{Z}_q$ and $s_i, c_i \in_R \mathbb{Z}_q$ for $1 \leq i \leq n, i \neq \pi$, then computes

$$c_0 = \mathcal{H}(S \parallel s_1P + c_1y_1 \parallel \cdots \parallel s_{\pi-1}P + c_{\pi-1}y_{\pi-1} \parallel lP \parallel s_{\pi+1}P + c_{\pi+1}y_{\pi+1} \parallel \cdots \parallel s_nP + c_ny_n \parallel M)$$

Table 2: Message Format for OBU

Payload	Timestamp	Signature	Public Key Sets
100 bytes	4 bytes	40n+60 bytes	20n bytes

and finds $c\pi$ such that $c_0 = c_1 + \cdots + c_n$ mod q. Finally the actual message sender sets $s_\pi = l - c_\pi x_\pi$ mod q.

Now we combine the constructions of SPK(1a) and SPK(1b) together. First, the actual message sender randomly picks $l_1, l_2 \in_R \mathbb{Z}_q$ and $s_i, c_i \in_R \mathbb{Z}_q$ for $1 \leq i \leq n, i \neq \pi$, then computes

$$c = \mathcal{H}(S \parallel y_{TRC} \parallel R \parallel E_{TRC} \parallel \hat{e}(R, y_{TRC})^{l_1} \parallel s_1P + c_1y_1 \parallel \cdots \parallel s_{\pi-1}P + c_{\pi-1}y_{\pi-1} \parallel l_2P \parallel s_{\pi+1}P + c_{\pi+1}y_{\pi+1} \parallel \cdots \parallel s_nP + c_ny_n \parallel M).$$

After that, the actual message sender sets $s = l_1 - cx_\pi$ mod q, finds $c\pi$ such that $c = c_1 + \cdots + c_n$ mod q, and sets $s_\pi = l_2 - c_\pi x_\pi$ mod q. The transcript of SPK(1) is therefore $(s, s_1, \cdots, s_n, c_1, \cdots, c_n)$.

According to DoT (2006), the payload of a safety message is 100 bytes. The first two fields are signed by the vehicle, by which the "signature" field can be derived. A timestamp is used to prevent the message replay attack. The last field is the public key sets, which records the public key pairs employed by the OBU. The format of messages in our protocol is defined in Table 2.

Message Verification

Once a message is received, the receiving vehicle first checks if the $RL \cap S \stackrel{?}{=} \emptyset$. If so, the receiver performs signature verification by verifying of SPK(1) as follows:

$$\sum_{i=1}^{n} c_i \stackrel{?}{=} \mathcal{H}(S \parallel y_{TRC} \parallel R \parallel E_{TRC} \parallel \hat{e}(R, y_{TRC})^s E_{TRC}^{\sum_{i=1}^{n} c_i} \parallel s_1P + c_1y_1 \parallel \cdots \parallel s_nP + c_ny_n \parallel$$

After that, the receiving vehicle updates its own public key set by randomly choosing public keys from S.

OBU Fast Tracing

A membership tracing operation is performed when solving a dispute, where the real ID of the signature generator is desired. The TRC first checks the validity of the signature and then uses its private key x_{TRC} and determines if

$$E_{TRC} \stackrel{?}{=} \hat{e}(y_i, R)^{x_{TRC}}$$

for some i, $1 \leq i \leq n$.

If the equation holds at, say when $i = \pi$, then the TRC looks up the record (y_π, RID_π) to find the corresponding identity RID_π meaning that vehicle with identity RID_π is the actual message generator. The TRC then broadcasts the (y_π, RID_π) to all OBUs and each OBU adds the y_π into his local revocation list (RL).

Message Verification

Once a message is received, the receiving vehicle V_j, one of the group G_{GNO}, uses his group's shared secret key κ_{GNO} to do the following with ciphertext (C_1, C_2):

1. Recover the session key $k_s \leftarrow b_1/(b_0)^{\kappa_{GNO}}$.
2. Decrypt $D_{k_s}(C_2) = M\|\sigma\|GNO$ with the session key k_s, where $D_{k_s}(\cdot)$ denotes a symmetric decryption with key k_s and $\sigma = (c, s_1, s_2, s_3, s_4, T_1, T_2, T_3)$.
3. Check whether $c \in \{0,1\}^k$, and $s_1 \in_R \pm\{0,1\}^{\epsilon(\gamma_2+k)+1}$, $s_2 \in_R \pm\{0,1\}^{\epsilon(\lambda_2+k)+1}$, $s_3 \in_R \pm\{0,1\}^{\epsilon(\lambda_1+2l_p+k+1)+1}$, and $s_4 \in_R \pm\{0,1\}^{\epsilon(2l_p+k)+1}$ and $T_1, T_2, T_3 \in \mathbb{Z}_n$.
4. Accept the signature if and only if $c = \mathcal{H}(g\|h\|y\|a_0\|a\|T_1\|T_2\|T_3\|d'_1\|d'_2\|d'_3\|d'_4\|M\|C_1)$ where d'_1, d'_2, d'_3, d'_4 are computed by the following equations: $d'_1 = a_0^c T_1^{s_1-c2^{\gamma_1}}/(a^{s_2-c2^{\lambda_1}} y^{s_3}) \mod n$, $d'_2 = T_2^{s_1-c2^{\gamma_1}}/g^{s_3} \mod n$, $d'_3 = T_2^c g^{s_4} \mod n$, $d'_4 = T_3^c g^{s_1-c2^{\gamma_1}} h^{s_4} \mod n$.

OBU Fast Tracing

A membership tracing operation is performed when solving a dispute, where the real ID_i of the signature generator is desired. The MM first decrypts (T_1, T_2) in a decrypted C_2 message to find the membership certificate A_i as follows:

1. Recover $A_i = T_1/T_2^x$.
2. Prove that $log_g y = log_{T_2}(T_1/A_i \mod n)$.

Then the MM looks up the record (A_i, ID_i) to find the corresponding identity ID_i meaning that vehicle with identity ID_i is the actual message generator. The MM then broadcasts the (A_i, ID_i) to all OBUs and each OBU adds the ID_i into his local revocation list (RL).

USING THE TAXONOMIES

In designing the above taxonomies, we selected those components and approach of existing mechanisms that, in our opinion, offer critical information regarding design philosophy and security properties. How can these taxonomies be used?

- A map of anonymous authentication protocols for VANETs. For novice researchers, these taxonomies offer a comprehensive overview for a quick introduction to this field. Experienced researchers can use and extend these taxonomies to structure and organize their knowledge in the field.
- Exploring new strategies. Besides the existing mechanisms, the taxonomy explored a few strategies seen rarely in the wild and some novel methods.
- Understanding solution constrains. The taxonomy highlights common constraints and weaknesses for each class of mechanisms. Understanding these problems will focus research efforts on solving them.
- Identifying unexplored research areas. Examining the effectiveness of different mechanism classes achieving different security properties will highlight unexplored venues for research.

CONCLUSION

The anonymous authentication protocols for VANETs can be constructed based on a multitude of cryptographic primitives, which obscures a global view of this field. This chapter is an attempt to cut through the obscurity and structure the knowledge in this field. The proposed taxonomies are intended to help the community think about the constrains of existing works and the possible countermeasures.

ACKNOWLEDGEMENTS

This work is partially supported by National Natural Science Foundation of China under Grant No. 61003230, China Postdoctoral Science Foundation under Grant No. 20100480130, Chongqing Key Lab of Computer Network and Communication Technology under Grant No. CY-CNCL-2010-01 and National Research Foundation for the Doctoral Program of Higher Education of China under Grant No. 200806140010.

REFERENCES

1. M. Abe, M. Ohkubo, K. Suzuki. (2002). 1-out-of-n signatures from a variety of keys, In Proc. ASIACRYPT 2002, New Zealand, Lecture Notes in Computer Science, 2501, Springer-Verlag, pp.415 432.
2. G. Ateniese, S. Hohenberger. (2005). Proxy Re-Signatures: New Definitions, Algorithms, and Applications, In: ACM Conference on Computer and Communications Security (CCS 2005), pp. 310-319.
3. R. Bishop. (2000). A survey of intelligent vehicle applications worldwide, in Proceedings of the IEEE Intelligent Vehicles Symposium 2000, Dearborn, MI, USA, Oct. pp. 25-30.
4. M. Blaze, G. Bleumer, M.Strauss. (1998). Divertible Protocols and Atomic Proxy Cryptography, In: Nyberg, K. (ed.) EUROCRYPT 1998, LNCS 1403, pp. 127-144. Springer.
5. D. Boneh and M. K. Franklin. (2001). Identity-Based Encryption from the Weil Pairing, in: CRYPTO 2001, LNCS 2139, pp. 213-229. Springer. SIAM Journal of Computing, Vol. 32, No. 3, pp. 586-615, 2003.
6. D. Boneh, X. Boyen, H. Shacham. (2004). Short group signatures, In: Franklin, M.K. (ed.) CRYPTO 2004. vol 3152 of LNCS, pp. 227-242, Springer, Heidelberg.
7. D. Boneh and H. Shacham. (2004). Group signatures with verifier-local revocation, in Proc. ACM CCS' 04,

pp. 168-177.

8. E. Bresson, J. Stern, M. Szydlo. (2002). Threshold ring signatures and applications to ad-hoc groups, In Proc. CRYPTO 2002, USA, Lecture Notes in Computer Science, 2442, Springer-Verlag, pp.465 480.
9. G. Calandriello, P. Papadimitratos, J.-P. Hubaux, A. Lioy. (2007). Efficient and robust pseudonymous authentication in VANET, Vehicular Ad Hoc Networks pp. 19-28.
10. D. Chaum, E. van Hevst. (1991). Group Signature, In EUROCRYPT 1991,volume 547 of LNCS, pp. 257-265.
11. L. Chen and S. Ng. (2010). Comments on "Proving Reliability of Anonymous Information in VANETs" by Kounga et al., IEEE Transactions on Vehicular Technology, Vol. 59, No. 3, pp. 1503-1505.
12. L. Chen, S.-L. Ng and G. Wang. (2011). Threshold anonymous announcement in VANETs. IEEE Journal on Selected Areas in Communications, Vol. 29, No. 3, pp. 605-615.
13. V. Daza, J. Domingo-Ferrer, F. Sebe´, and A. Viejo. (2009). Trustworthy Privacy-Preserving Car-Generated Announcements in Vehicular Ad Hoc Networks", IEEE Transactions on Vehicular Technology, vol. 58, no. 4, pp. 1876-1886.
14. Y. Dodis, A. Kiayias, A. Nicolosi, V. Shoup. (2004). Anonymous identification in ad doc groups, In Proc. EUROCRYPT 2004, Switzerland, LNCS 3027, Springer-Verlag, pp.609 626, Full version: http://www.cs.nyu.edu/nico-lo-si/pa-pers/
15. U.S. Department of Transportation. (2006). National Highway Traffic Safety Administration, Vehicle Safety Communications Project, Final Report. Appendix H: WAVE/DSRC Security.
16. Dedicated Short Range Communications (5.9 GHz DSRC), Available: http://www. leearmstrong.com/DSRC/DSRCHomeset.htm
17. J.P. Hubaux, S. Capkun, L. Jun. (2004). The Security and Privacy of Smart Vehicles, IEEE Security & Privacy Magazine, Vol. 2, No. 3, pp. 49-55.
18. Saving Lives Through Advanced Vehicle Safety Technology: Intelligent Vehicle Initiative Final Report. [Online]. Available: http://www.itsdocs.fhwa.dot.gov/JPODOCS/REPTS PR/14153 files/ivi.pdf
19. P. Kamat, A. Baliga, W. Trappe. (2006). An Identity-Based Security Framework For VANETs, VANET ˛a´r06, pp. 94-95.
20. G. Kounga, T. Walter, and S. Lachmund. (2009). Proving Reliability of Anonymous Information in VANETs, IEEE Transactions on Vehicular Technology, vol. 58, no. 6, pp. 2977-2989.
21. C.-T. Li, M.-S. Hwang, Y.-P. Chu. (2008). A secure and efficient communication scheme with authenticated key establishment and privacy preserving for vehicular ad hoc networks, Computer Communications, Vol. 31, pp. 2803-2814.
22. B. Libert, D. Vergnaud. (2008). Multi-Use Unidirectional Proxy Re-Signatures, ACM Conference on Computer and Communications Security (CCS 2008), Alexandria, Virginia, USA.
23. D. Y. W. Liu, J. K. Liu, Y. Mu, W. Susilo, D.S. Wong. (2007). Revocable Ring Signature, J. Comput. Sci. Technol. 22(6): pp. 785-794.
24. X. Lin. (2008). Secure and Privacy-Preserving Vehicular Communications, PhD thesis, University of Waterloo, Waterloo, Ontario, Canada.
25. X. Lin, X. Sun, P.-H. Ho and X. Shen. (2007). GSIS: A Secure and Privacy-Preserving Protocol for Vehicular Communications, IEEE Transactions on Vehicular Technology, vol. 56(6), pp. 3442-3456, 2007.
26. X. Lin, R. Lu, C. Zhang, H. Zhu, P.-H. Ho and X. Shen. (2008a). Security in Vehicular Ad Hoc Networks, IEEE Communications Magazine, vol. 46, no. 4, pp. 88-95, 2008.
27. X. Lin, X. Sun, X. Wang, C. Zhang, P.-H. Ho and X. Shen. (2008b). TSVC: Timed Efficient and Secure Vehicular Communications with Privacy Preserving, IEEE Transactions on Wireless Communications, vol. 7, no. 12, pp. 4987-4998.
28. R. Lu, X. Lin, H. Zhu, P.-H. Ho and X. Shen. (2008). ECPP: Efficient Conditional Privacy Preservation Protocol for Secure Vehicular Communications, The 27th IEEE International Conference on Computer Communications (INFOCOM 2008), Phoenix, Arizona, USA.
29. R. Lu, X. Lin, H. Zhu, and X. Shen. (2009). SPARK: A New VANET-based Smart Parking Scheme for Large Parking Lots, The 28th IEEE International Conference on Computer Communications (INFOCOM 2009), Rio de Janeiro, Brazil.
30. R. Lu, X. Lin, and X. Shen. (2010). SPRING: A Social-based Privacy-preserving Packet Forwarding Protocol for Vehicular Delay Tolerant Networks, The 29th IEEE International Conference on Computer Communications (INFOCOM 2010), San Diego, California, USA.
31. T. K. Mak, K. P. Laberteaux and R. Sengupta. (2005). A Multi-Channel VANET Providing Concurrent Safety and Commercial Services, in Proceedings of 2nd ACM International Workshop on Vehicular Ad Hoc Networks, Cologne, Germany, Sep. pp. 1-9.
32. J. A. Misener. (2005). Vehicle-infrastructure integration (VII) and safety, Intellimotion, Vol. 11, No. 2, pp. 1-3.
33. T. Nakanishi, T. Fujiwara, and H. Watanabe. (1999). A linkable group signature and its application to secret voting, Transactions of Information Processing Society of Japan, vol. 40, no. 7, pp. 3085-3096.
34. T. Nakanishi and N. Funabiki. (2005). Verifer-local revocation group signature schemes with backward unlinkability from bilinear maps, in Proc. ASIACRYPT' 05, LNCS, vol. 3788, pp. 533-548.
35. L. Nguyen, R. Safavi-Naini. (2005). Dynamic k-times anonymous authentication, in ACNS 2005, LNCS 3531, pp. 318-333.
36. Perrig, R. Canetti, J. D. Tygar, D. Song. (2002). The TESLA Broadcast Authentication Protocol, RSA CryptoBytes, vol. 5, no. 2, pp. 2-13.
37. Perrig, R. Szewczyk, V. Wen, D. Culler, and J. D. Tygar.

(2002). Spins: security protocols for sensor networks, Wireless Networks, vol. 8, no. 11, pp. 521-534.

38. K. Plo¨βl, H. Federrath. (2008). A privacy aware and efficient security infrastructure for vehicular ad hoc networks, Computer Standards & Interfaces, Vol. 30, pp. 390-397.

39. M. Raya, J. P. Hubaux, (2005). The security of vehicular ad hoc networks, 3rd ACM workshop on Security of ad hoc and sensor networks, pp. 11-21.

40. M. Raya and J. P. Hubaux. (2007). Securing Vehicular Ad Hoc Networks, Journal of Computer Security, Special Issue on Security of Ad Hoc and Sensor Networks, Vol. 15, Nr. 1, pp. 39-68.

41. R. L. Rivest, A. Shamir, Y. Tauman. (2001). How to Leak a Secret, In AsiaCrypt 2001, volume 2248 of LNCS, pp. 552-565.

42. X. Sun, X. Lin, P. Ho. (2007). Secure Vehicular Communications Based on Group Signature and ID-Based Signature Scheme, International Communications Conference (ICC 2007), Glasgow, Scotland, June 24-28.

43. X. Sun. (2007). Anonymous, secure and efficient vehicular communications, Master thesis, University of Waterloo, Waterloo, Ontario, Canada.

44. J. Sun, Y. Fang. (2009). Defense against misbehavior in anonymous vehicular ad hoc networks, Ad Hoc Networks (Special Issue on Privacy and Security in Wireless Sensor and Ad Hoc Networks), Vol. 7, No. 8, pp. 1515-1525.

45. Y. Sun, R. Lu, X. Lin, X. Shen, and J. Su. (2010). A Secure and Efficient Revocation Scheme for Anonymous Vehicular Communications, International Communications Conference (ICC 2010), Cape Town, South Africa.

46. Y. Sun, R. Lu, X. Lin, X. Shen, and J. Su. (2010). An Efficient Pseudonymous Authentication Scheme With Strong Privacy Preservation for Vehicular Communications, IEEE Transactions on Vehicular Technology, Vol. 59, No. 7, pp. 3589-3603.

47. J. Sun, C. Zhang, Y. Zhang, Y. Fang. (2010). An Identity-Based Security System for User Privacy in Vehicular Ad Hoc Networks, IEEE Transactions on Parallel and Distributed Systems, Vol. 21, No. 9, pp. 1227-1239.

48. Teranisi, J. Furukawa, and K. Sako. (2004). k-Times Anonymous Authentication, in ASIACRYPT 2004, Springer-Verlag, LNCS 3329, pp. 308-322.

49. Vehicle infrastructure integration. U.S. Department of Transportation, [Online]. Available: http://www.its.dot.gov/index.htm

50. Wasef, Y. Jiang, and X. Shen. (2010). DCS: An efficient distributed certificate service scheme for vehicular networks, IEEE Transactions on Vehicular Technology, vol. 59, no. 2, pp. 533-549.

51. G. Wang. (2004). Security Analysis of Several Group Signature Schemes. [Online]. Available: http://eprint.iacr.org/2003/194

52. N. W. Wang, Y. M. Huang, and W. M. Chen. (2008). A novel secure communication scheme in vehicular ad hoc networks, Computer Communications, Vol. 31, pp. 2827-2837.

53. D. S. Wong, K. Fung, J. Liu, V. Wei. (2003). On the RS-code construction of ring signature schemes and a threshold setting of RST, In Proc. 5th Int. Conference on Infoation and Communication Security (ICICS 2003), China, Lecture Notes in Computer Science, 2836, Springer-Verlag, pp.34 46.

54. Q. Wu, J. Domingo-Ferrer, and U´ rsula Gonza´lez-Nicola´s. (2010). Balanced Trustworthiness, Safety, and Privacy in Vehicle-to-Vehicle Communications, IEEE Transactions on Vehicular Technology, vol. 59, no. 2, pp. 559-573.

55. Q. Xu, T. Mak, J. Ko and R. Sengupta. (2007). Medium Access Control Protocol Design for Vehicle-Vehicle Safety Messages, IEEE Transactions on Vehicular Technology, Vol. 56, No. 2, pp. 499-518.

56. Y. Xi, K. Sha, W. Shi, L. Scnwiebert, and T. Zhang. (2007). Enforcing Privacy Using Symmetric Random Key-Set in Vehicular Networks, Eighth International Symposium on Autonomous Decentralized Systems (ISADS'07), pp. 344-351.

57. Y. Xi, W. Shi, L. Schwiebert. (2008). Mobile anonymity of dynamic groups in vehicular networks, Security and Communication Networks, Vol. 1, No.3, pp. 219-231.

58. H. Xiong, Z. Qin, F. Li. (2011). Identity-based Ring Signature Scheme based on quadratic residues, High Technology Letters, Vol. 15, No.1, pp. 94-100.

59. H. Xiong, K. Beznosov, Z. Qin, M. Ripeanu. (2010). Efficient and Spontaneous Privacy-Preserving Protocol for Secure Vehicular Communication, International Communications Conference (ICC 2010), Cape Town, South Africa.

60. H. Xiong, Z. Qin, F. Li. (2010). Secure Vehicle-to-roadside communication protocol using certificate-based cryptosystem, IETE Technical Review, Vol 27, No 3, pp. 214-219.

61. H. Xiong, Z. Qin, F. Li. (2011). A Certificateless Proxy Ring Signature Scheme with Provable Security, International Journal of Network Security, Vol.12, No.2, pp.113-127.

62. Zhang, X. Lin, R. Lu and P.-H. Ho. (2008). RAISE: An Efficient RSU-aided Message Authentication Scheme in Vehicular Communication Networks. IEEE International Conference on Communications (ICC'08), Beijing, China.

63. Zhang, X. Lin, R. Lu, P.-H. Ho and X. Shen. (2008). An Efficient Message Authentication Scheme for Vehicular Communications, IEEE Transactions on Vehicular Technology, vol. 57, no. 6, pp. 3357-3368.

CHAPTER 4 SECURE AND PRIVACY-PRESERVING AUTHENTICATION PROTOCOLS FOR WIRELESS MESH NETWORKS

Jaydip Sen

INTRODUCTION

Wireless mesh networks (WMNs) have emerged as a promising concept to meet the challenges in next-generation wireless networks such as providing flexible, adaptive, and reconfigurable architecture while offering cost-effective solutions to service providers (Akyildiz et al., 2005). WMNs are multi-hop networks consisting of mesh routers (MRs), which form wireless mesh backbones and mesh clients (MCs). The mesh routers provide a rich radio mesh connectivity which significantly reduces the up-front deployment cost of the network. Mesh routers are typically stationary and do not have power constraints. However, the clients are mobile and energy-constrained. Some mesh routers are designated as gateway routers which are connected to the Internet through a wired backbone. A gateway router provides access to conventional clients and interconnects ad hoc, sensor, cellular, and other networks to the Internet. The gateway routers are also referred to as the Internet gateways (IGWs). A mesh network can provide multi-hop communication paths between wireless clients, thereby serving as a community network, or can provide multi-hop paths between the client and the gateway router, thereby providing broadband Internet access to the clients.

As WMNs become an increasingly popular replacement technology for last-mile connectivity to the home networking, community and neighborhood networking, it is imperative to design efficient and secure communication protocols for these networks. However, several vulnerabilities exist in the current protocols of WMNs. These security loopholes can be exploited by potential attackers to launch attack on WMNs. Absence of a central point of administration makes securing WMNs even more challenging. Security is, therefore, an issue which is of prime importance in WMNs (Sen, 2011). Since in a WMN, traffic from the end users is relayed via multiple wireless mesh routers, preserving privacy of the user data is also a critical requirement (Wu et al., 2006a). Some of the existing security and privacy protection protocols for WMNs are based on the trust and reputation of the network entities (Sen, 2010a; Sen, 2010b). However, many of these schemes are primarily designed for mobile ad hoc networks (MANETs) (Sen, 2006; Sen, 2010c), and hence these protocols do not perform well in large-scale hybrid WMN environments.

The broadcast nature of transmission and the dependency on the intermediate nodes for multi-hop communications lead to several security vulnerabilities in WMNs. The attacks can be external as well as internal in nature. External attacks are launched by intruders who are not authorized users of the network. For example, an intruding node may eavesdrop on the packets and replay those packets at a later point of time to gain access to the network resources. On the other hand, the internal attacks are launched by the nodes that are part of the WMN. On example of such attack is an intermediate node dropping packets which it was supposed to forward. To prevent external attacks in vulnerable networks such as WMNs, strong authentication and access control mechanisms should be in place for practical deployment and use of WMNs. A secure authentication should enable two communicating entities (either a pair of MC and MR or a pair of MCs) to validate the authenticity of each other and generate the shared common session keys which can be used in cryptographic algorithms for enforcing message confidentiality and integrity. As in other wireless networks, a weak authentication scheme can easily be compromised due to several reasons such as distributed network architecture, the broadcast nature of the wireless medium, and dynamic network topology (Akyildiz et al., 2005). Moreover, the behavior of an MC or MR can be easily

Citation: Jaydip Sen (2012). Secure and Privacy-Preserving Authentication Protocols for Wireless Mesh Networks, Applied Cryptography and Network Security, Dr. Jaydip Sen (Ed.), InTech, DOI: 10.5772/39176.

monitored or traced in a WMN by adversaries due to the use of wireless channel, multi-hop connection through third parties, and converged traffic pattern traversing through the IGW nodes. Under such scenario, it is imperative to hide an active node that connects to an IGW by making it anonymous. Since on the Internet side traditional anonymous routing approaches are not implemented, or may be compromised by strong attackers such protections are extremely critical (X. Wu & Li, 2006).

This chapter presents a comprehensive discussion on the current authentication and privacy protection schemes for WMN. In addition, it proposes a novel security protocol for node authentication and message confidentiality and an anonymization scheme for privacy protection of users in WMNs.

The rest of this chapter is organized as follows. Section 2 discusses the issues related to access control and authentication in WMNs. Various security vulnerabilities in the authentication and access control mechanisms for WMNs are first presented and then a list of requirements (i.e. properties) of a secure authentication scheme in an open and largescale, hybrid WMN are discussed. Section 3 highlights the importance of the protection user privacy in WMNs. Section 4 presents a state of the art survey on the current authentication and privacy protection schemes for WMNs. Each of the schemes is discussed with respect to its applicability, performance efficiency and shortcomings. Section 5 presents the details of a hierarchical architecture of a WMN and the assumptions made for the design of a secure and anonymous authentication protocol for WMNs. Section 6 describes the proposed key management scheme for secure authentication. Section 7 discusses the proposed privacy protection algorithm which ensures user anonymity. Section 8 presents some performance results of the proposed scheme. Section 9 concludes the chapter while highlighting some future direction of research in the field of secure authentication in WMNs.

ACCESS CONTROL AND AUTHENTICATION IN WMNS

Authentication and authorization is the first step towards prevention of fraudulent accesses by unauthorized users in a network. Authentication ensures that an MC and the corresponding MR can mutually validate their credentials with each other before the MC is allowed to access the network services. In this section, we first present various attacks in WMNs that can be launched on the authentication services and then enumerate the requirements for authentication under various scenarios.

Security Vulnerabilities in Authentication Schemes

Several vulnerabilities exist in different protocols for WMNs. These vulnerabilities can be suitably exploited by potential attackers to degrade the network performance (Sen, 2011). The nodes in a WMN depend on the cooperation of other nodes in the network for their successful operations. Consequently, the medium access control (MAC) layer and the network layer protocols for these networks usually assume that the participating nodes are honest and well-behaving with no malicious or dishonest intentions. In practice, however, some nodes in a WMN may behave in a selfish manner or may be compromised by malicious users. The assumed trust (which in reality may not exist) and the lack of accountability due to the absence of a central point of administration make the MAC and the network layer protocols vulnerable to various types of attacks. In this sub-section, we present a comprehensive discussion on various types of attacks on the existing authentication schemes of WMNs. A detailed list various attacks on the different layers of WMN communication protocol stack can be found in (Sen, 2011; Yi et al., 2010).

There are several types of attacks that are related to authentication in WMNs. These attacks are: (i) unauthorized access, (ii) replay attack, (iii) spoofing attack, (iv) denial of service attack (DoS), (v) intentional collision of frames, (vi) pre-computation and partial matching attack, and (vi) compromised or forged MRs. These attacks are discussed in detail below.

Unauthorized Access: in this attack, an unauthorized user gets access to the network services by masquerading a legitimate user.

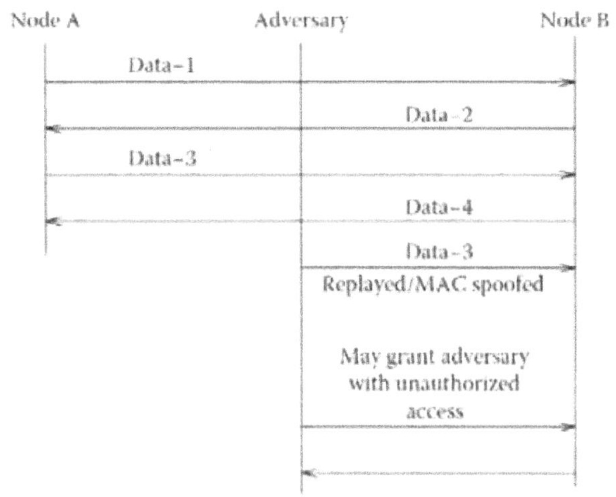

Figure 1: Illustration of MAC spoofing and replay attacks [Source: (Sen, 2011)].

Replay Attack: the replay attack is a type of man-in-the-middle attack (Mishra & Arbaugh, 2002) that can be launched by external as well as internal nodes. An external malicious node can eavesdrop on the broadcast communication between two nodes (A and B) in the network as shown in Fig. 1. It can then transmit legitimate messages at a later point of time to gain access to the network resources. Generally, the authentication information is replayed where the attacker deceives a node (node B in Fig. 1) to believe that the attacker is a legitimate node (node A in Fig. 1). On a similar note, an internal malicious node, which is an intermediate hop between two communicating nodes, can keep a copy of all relayed data. It can then retransmit this data at a later point in time to gain unauthorized access to the network resources.

Spoof Attack: spoofing is the act of forging a legitimate MAC or IP address. IP spoofing is quite common in multi-hop communications in WMNs. In IP spoofing attack, an adversary inserts a false source address (or the address of a legitimate node) from the packets forwarded by it. Using such a spoofed address, the malicious attacker can intercept a termination request and hijack a session. In MAC address spoofing, the attacker modifies the MAC address in transmitted frames from a legitimate node. MAC address spoofing enables the attacker to evade intrusion detection systems (IDSs) that may be in place.

DoS Attack: in this attack, a malicious attacker sends a flood of packets to an MR thereby making a buffer overflow in the router. Another well-known security flaw can be exploited by an attacker. In this attack, a malicious attacker can send false termination messages on behalf of a legitimate MC thereby preventing a legitimate user from accessing network services.

Intentional Collision of Frames: a collision occurs when two nodes attempt to transmit on the same frequency simultaneously (Wood & Stankovic, 2002). When frames collide, they are discarded and need to be retransmitted. An adversary may strategically cause collisions in specific packets such as acknowledgment (ACK) control messages. A possible result of such collision is the costly exponential back-off. The adversary may simply violate the communication protocol and continuously transmit messages in an attempt to generate collisions. Repeated collisions can also be used by an attacker to cause resource exhaustion. For example, a naïve MAC layer implementation may continuously attempt to retransmit the corrupted packets. Unless these retransmissions are detected early, the energy levels of the nodes would be exhausted quickly. An attacker may cause unfairness by intermittently using the MAC layer attacks. In this case, the adversary causes degradation of real-time applications running on other nodes by intermittently disrupting their frame transmissions.

Pre-Computation and Partial Matching Attack: unlike the attacks mentioned above, where the MAC protocol vulnerabilities are exploited, these attacks exploit the vulnerabilities in the security mechanisms that are employed to secure the MAC layer of the network. Precomputation and partial matching attacks exploit the cryptographic primitives that are used at the MAC layer to secure the communication. In a pre-computation attack, or time memory trade-off (TMTO) attack, the attacker computes a large amount of information (e.g., key, plaintext, and the corresponding ciphertext) and stores that information before launching the attack. When the actual transmission starts, the attacker uses the pre-computed information to speed up the cryptanalysis process. TMTO attacks are highly effective against a large number of cryptographic solutions. On the other hand, in a partial matching attack, the attacker has access to some (ciphertext, plaintext) pairs, which in turn decreases the encryption key strength, and improves the chances of success of the brute force mechanisms. Partial matching attacks exploit the weak implementations of encryption algorithms. For example, the IEEE 802.11i standard for MAC layer security in wireless networks is prone to the session hijacking attack and the man-in-the-middle attack that exploits the vulnerabilities in IEEE802.1X. DoS attacks are possible on the four-way handshake procedure in IEEE802.11i.

Compromised or Forged MR: an attacker may be able to compromise one or more MRs in a network by physical tampering or logical break-in. The adversary may also introduce rogue MRs to launch various types of attacks. The fake or compromised MRs may be used to attack the wireless link thereby implementing attacks such as: passive eavesdropping, jamming, replay and false message injection, traffic analysis etc. The attacker may also advertise itself as a genuine MR by forging duplicate beacons procured by eavesdropping on genuine MRs in the network. When an MC receives these beacon messages, it assumes that it is within the radio coverage of a genuine MR, and initiates a registration procedure. The false MR now can extract the secret credentials of the MC and can launch spoof attack on the network. This attack is possible in protocols which require an MC to be authenticated by and MR but not the vice versa (He et al., 2011).

Requirements for Authentication in WMNs

On the basis of whether a central authentication server is available, there are two types of implementations of access control enforcements in WMNs: (i) centralized access control and (ii) distributed access control. For both these approaches, the access control policies should be implemented at the border of the mesh network. In the distributed access control, the access points could act as the distributed authentication servers. The authentication could also be performed in three different places:

- A remote central authentication center
- Local entities such as IGWs or MRs that play the role of an authentication server
- Local MRs

The main benefit of central authentication server is the ease of management and maintenance. However, this approach suffers from the drawback of having a single point of failure. Due to higher round trip time (RTT) and authentication delay, a centralized authentication scheme in a multi-hop WMN is not desirable. Instead, authentication protocols are implemented in local nodes such as IGW or MRs. For ensuring higher level of availability of the network services, the authentication power is delegated to a group of MRs in order to avoid single point of failure.

The objective of an authentication system is to guarantee that only the legitimate users have access to the network services. Any pair of network entities in a WMN (e.g., IGW, MR, and MC) may need to mutually authenticate if required. An MR and MC should be able to mutually authenticate each other to prevent unauthorized network access and other attacks. The MCs and MRs should be able to establish a shared pair-wise session key to encrypt messages. The protocol should have robust key generation, distribution and revocation procedures.

Several requirements have been identified in (Buttyan et al., 2010) for authentication mechanisms between MC and MRs in a WMN. These requirements are summarized below:

- *Authentication should be fast enough to support user mobility*. In order to maintain the quality of service (QoS) of user applications on mobile MCs, the authentication process should be fast. Also, the re-authentication delays should be within the acceptable limit of handoff delay.
- *MCs and MRs should be able to authenticate themselves mutually*. During the authentication process, the MR authenticates the MC, but the MR also should prove its authenticity to the MC.
- *Authentication process should be resistant to DoS attacks*. Since a successful attack against the

central authentication server will lead to a complete compromise of the security system in the network, the authentication process should be robust.

- *Authentication protocols should be compatible with standards.* In a multi-operator environment, it is mandatory that the authentication protocols are standardized so that an MC of one vendor should be able to authenticate with the MR of a different network operator.
- *Authentication protocols should be scalable.* Since the mesh networks have large number of MCs, MRs and IGWs, the authentication protocol should be scalable and must not degrade in performance as the network size increases.

The mutual authentication protocols for MCs and MRs must use several keys for encrypting the credentials. The connection key management should satisfy the following requirements.

- *The connection keys should not reveal long term keys.* The connection keys that the MRs obtain during the authentication of the MCs should not reveal any long-term authentication keys. This requirement must hold because in the multi-operator environment, the MCs may associate to MRs operated by foreign operators.
- *The connection keys should be independent of each other.* As the neighboring MRs may not fully trust each other in a multi-operator environment, the authentication and key generation mechanism have to prevent an MR from deriving connection keys that are used at another MR.
- *The connection keys must be fresh in each session.* It must be ensured that the connection key derived during the authentication protocol for both participants (MC and MR) is fresh.

USER PRIVACY REQUIREMENT IN WMNS

Privacy provision is an important issue to be considered for WMN deployment. However, privacy is difficult to achieve even if messages are protected, as there are no security solutions or mechanisms which can guarantee that data is not revealed by the authorized parties themselves (Moustafa, 2007). Thus, it is important that complementary solutions are in place. Moreover, communication privacy cannot not be assured with message encryption since the attackers can still observe who is communicating with whom as well as the frequency and duration of the communication sessions. This makes personal information susceptible to disclosure and subsequent misuse even when encryption mechanisms are in place. Furthermore, users in WMNs can be easily monitored or traced with regard to their presence and location, which causes the exposure of their personal life. Unauthorized parties can get access to the location information about the MC's positions by observing their communications and traffic patterns. Consequently, there is a need to ensure location privacy in WMNs as well.

To control the usage of personal information and the disclosure of personal data, different types of information hiding mechanisms like anonymity, data masking etc should be implemented in WMN applications. The following approaches can be useful in information hiding, depending on what is needed to be protected:

- ***Anonymity***: this is concerned with hiding the identity of the sender or receiver of the message or both of them. In fact, hiding the identity of both the sender and the receiver of the message can assure communication privacy. Thus, attackers monitoring the messages being communicated could not know who is communicating with whom, thus no personal information is disclosed.
- ***Confidentiality:*** it is concerned with hiding the transferred messages by using suitable data encryption algorithms. Instead of hiding the identity of the sender and the receiver of a message, the message itself is hidden in this approach.
- ***Use of pseudonyms***: this is concerned with replacing the identity of the sender and the receiver of the message by pseudonyms which function as identifiers. The pseudonyms can be used as a reference to the communicating parties without infringing on their privacy, which helps to ensure that the users in the WMNs cannot be traced or identified by malicious adversaries. However, it is important to ensure that there exist no indirect ways by which the adversaries can link the pseudonyms with their corresponding real world entities.

Privacy has been a major concern of Internet users (Clarke, 1999). It is also been a particularly critical issue in context of WMN-based Internet access, where users' traffic is forwarded via multiple MRs. In a community mesh network, this implies that the traffic of a residence can be observed by the MRs residing at its neighbors premises. Therefore, privacy in WMNs has two different dimensions: (i) data confidentiality (or privacy) and traffic confidentiality. These issues are briefly described below:

- Data confidentiality: it is obvious that data content reveals user privacy on what is being communicated. Data confidentiality aims to protect the data content and prevent eavesdropping by intermediate MRs. Message encryption is a conventional approach for data confidentiality.
- Traffic confidentiality: traffic information such as with whom, when and how frequently the users are communicating, and the pattern of traffic also reveal critical privacysensitive information. The broadcast nature of wireless communication makes acquiring such information easy. In a WMN, attackers can conduct traffic analysis as MRs by simply listening to the channels to identify the "ups and downs" of the target's traffic. While data confidentiality can be achieved via message encryption, it is much harder to preserve traffic confidentiality (T. Wu et al., 2006).

SECURE AUTHENTICATION AND PRIVACY PROTECTION SCHEMES IN WMNS

Since security and privacy are two extremely important issues in any communication network, researchers have worked on these two areas extensively. However, as compared to MANETs and wireless sensor networks (WSNs) (Sen, 2009; Sen & Subramanyam, 2007), WMNs have received very little attention in this regard. In this section, we first present a brief discussion on some of the existing propositions for secure authentication and user privacy protection in WMNs. Later on, some of the mechanisms are discussed in detail in the following sub-sections.

In (Mishra & Arbaugh, 2002), a standard mechanism has been proposed for client authentication and access control to guarantee a high-level of flexibility and transparency to all users in a wireless network. The users can access the mesh network without requiring any change in their devices and softwares. However, client mobility can pose severe problems to the security architecture, especially when real-time traffic is transmitted. To cope with this problem, proactive key distribution has been proposed in (Kassab et al., 2005; Prasad & Wang, 2005).

Providing security in the backbone network for WMNs is another important challenge. Mesh networks typically employ resource constrained mobile clients, which are difficult to protect against removal, tampering, or replication. If the device can be remotely managed, a distant hacking into the device would work perfectly (Ben Salem & Hubaux, 2006). Accordingly, several research works have been done to investigate the use of cryptographic techniques to achieve secure communication in WMNs. In (Cheikhrouhou et al., 2006), a security architecture has been proposed that is suitable for multi-hop WMNs employing PANA (Protocol for carrying Authentication for Network Access) (Parthasarathy, 2006). In the scheme, the wireless clients are authenticated on production of the cryptographic credentials necessary to create an encrypted tunnel with the remote access router to which they are associated. Even though such framework protects the confidentiality of the information exchanged, it cannot prevent adversaries to perform active attacks against the network itself. For instance, a malicious adversary can replicate, modify and forge the topology information exchanged among mesh devices, in order to launch a denial of service attack. Moreover, PANA necessitates the existence of IP addresses in all the mesh nodes, which is poses a serious constraint on deployment of this protocol.

Authenticating transmitted data packets is an approach for preventing unauthorized nodes to access the resources of a WMN. A light-weight hop-by-hop access protocol (LHAP) has been proposed for authenticating mobile clients in wireless dynamic environments, preventing resource consumption attacks (Zhu et al., 2006). LHAP implements light-weight hop-by-hop authentication, where intermediate nodes authenticate all the packets they receive before forwarding them. LHAP employs a packet authentication technique based on the use of one-way hash chains. Moreover, LHAP uses TESLA (Perrig et al., 2001) protocol to reduce the number of public key operations for bootstrapping and maintaining trust between nodes.

In (Prasad et al., 2004), a lightweight authentication, authorization and accounting (AAA) infrastructure is proposed for providing continuous, on-demand, end-to-end security in heterogeneous networks including WMNs. The notion of a security manager is used through employing an AAA broker. The broker acts as a settlement agent, providing security and a central point of contact for many service providers. The issue of user privacy in WMNs has also attracted the attention of the research community. In (T. Wu et al., 2006), a light-weight privacy preserving solution is presented to achieve well-maintained balance between network performance and traffic privacy preservation.

At the center of the solution is of information-theoretic metric called traffic entropy, which quantifies the amount of information required to describe the traffic pattern and to characterize the performance of traffic privacy preservation. The authors have also presented a penalty-based shortest path routing algorithm that maximally preserves traffic privacy by minimizing the mutual information of traffic entropy observed at each individual relaying node while controlling the possible degradation of network within an acceptable region. Extensive simulation study proves the soundness of the solution and its resilience to cases when two malicious observers collude. However, one of the major problems of the solution is that the algorithm is evaluated in a single-radio, single channel WMN. Performance of the algorithm in multiple radios, multiple channels scenario will be a really questionable issue. Moreover, the solution has a scalability problem. In (X. Wu & Li, 2006), a mechanism is proposed with the objective of hiding an active node that connects to a gateway router, where the active mesh node has to be anonymous. A novel communication protocol is designed to protect the node's privacy using both cryptography and redundancy. This protocol uses the concept of onion routing (Reed et al., 1998). A mobile user who requires anonymous communication sends a request to an onion router (OR). The OR acts as a proxy to the mobile user and constructs an onion route consisting of other ORs using the public keys of the routers. The onion is constructed such that the inner most part is the message for the intended destination, and the message is wrapped by being encrypted using the public keys of the ORs in the route. The mechanism protects the routing information from insider and outsider attack. However, it has a high computation and communication overhead.

In the following sub-sections, some of the well-known authentication and privacy preservation schemes for WMNs are discussed briefly. For each of the schemes, its salient features and potential shortcomings are highlighted.

Local Authentication Based on Public Key Certificates

In the localized authentication, a trusted third party (TTP) serves as the trusted certificate authority (CA) that issues certificates. In (Buttyan & Dora, 2009), a localized authentication scheme is proposed in which authentication is performed locally between the MCs and the MRs in a hybrid large-scale WMN operated by a number of operators. Each operator maintains its own CA. Each CA is responsible for issuing certificates to its customers. Each CA maintains its own certificate revocation list (CRL). The CAs also issue cross-certificates among each other for enabling entities (MCs or MRs) subscribing to different operators to perform certificate-based authentications and key exchanges. To minimize authentication delay, the provably secure key transport protocol (Blake-Wilson & Menezes, 1998) proposed by Blake-Wilson-Menezes (BWM) has been used.

For authentication in multiple domains in a metropolitan area network, a localized authentication scheme has been proposed in (Lin et al., 2008). In this scheme, an embedded two-factor authentication mechanism is utilized to verify the authenticity of a roaming MC. The authenticity verification does not need any intervention of the home Internet service provider (ISP) of the MC. The two-factor authentication mechanism includes two methods of authentication: password and smart card. To minimize the ping-pong effect, the session key is cached in the current network domain. Whenever the MC requests a handoff into a neighboring MR which has a valid shared session key with the MC, a user-authenticated key agreement protocol with secret key cryptography is performed. Thus an expensive full authentication based on an asymmetric key encryption is avoided. The protocol execution is fast since it involves encryption using only the symmetric key and keyed hash message authentication codes (HMACs).

The localized authentication schemes are based on the assumption that the MRs are trusted and fully protected by robust certificates. In practice, MRs are low cost devices and without extra protection, these devices can easily be compromised. In the event an MR gets compromised, the local authentication schemes will fail. To defend against compromised MRs, a scheme based on local voting strategy (Zhu et al., 2008) is adopted which work on the principle of threshold digital signature mechanism (Cao et al., 2006).

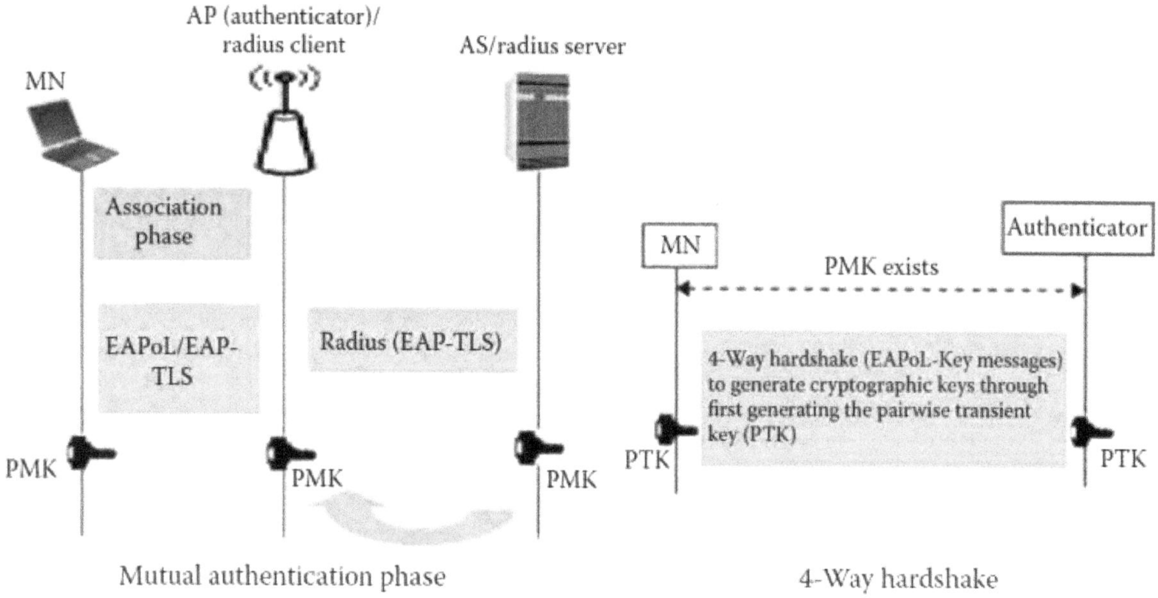

Figure 2: Schematic diagram of IEEE 802.11i authentication protocol [Source: (Moustafa, 2007)].

Authentication Model based on 802.11i Protocol

In most commercial deployments of wireless local area networks (WLANs), IEEE 802.11i (IEEE 802.11i, 2004) is the most common approach for assuring authentication at the layer 2. However, the IEEE 802.11i authentication does not fully address the problem of WLAN vulnerability (Moustafa, 2007). In IEEE 802.11i authentication, as described in Fig. 2, the MC and the authentication server (AS) apply the 802.1X (IEEE 802.1X, 2001) authentication model carrying out some negotiation to agree on pair-wise master key (PMK) by using some upper layer authentication schemes or using a pre-shared secret. This key is generated by both the MC and the AS, assuring the mutual authentication between them. The access point (AP) then receives a PMK copy from the AS, authenticating the MC and authorizing its communication. Afterwards, a four-way handshake starts between the AP and the MC to generate encryption keys from the generated PMK. Encryption keys can assure confidential transfer between the MC and the AP. If the MC roams to a new AP, it will perform another full 802.1X authentication with the AS to derive a new PMK. For performance enhancement, the PMK of the MC is cached by the MC and the AP to be used for later re-association without another full authentication. The features of 802.11i exhibit a potential vulnerability because a compromised AP can still authenticate itself to an MC and gain control over the connection. Furthermore, IEEE 802.11i authentication does not provide a solution for multihop communication. Consequently new mechanisms are needed for authentication and secure layer 2 links setup in WMNs (Moustafa, 2007).

Wireless dual authentication protocol (WDAP) (Zheng et al., 2005) is proposed for 802.11 WLAN and can be extended to WMNs. WDAP provides authentication for both MCs and APs and overcomes the shortcomings of other authentication protocols. The name "dual" implies the fact that the AS authenticates both the MC and the AP. As in the four-way handshake in IEEE 802.11i, this protocol also generates a session key for maintaining confidentiality of the messages communicated between the MC and the AP after a successful authentication. WDAP provides authentication during the initial connection state. For roaming, it has three sub-protocols: an authentication protocol, a de-authentication protocol, and a roaming authentication protocol.

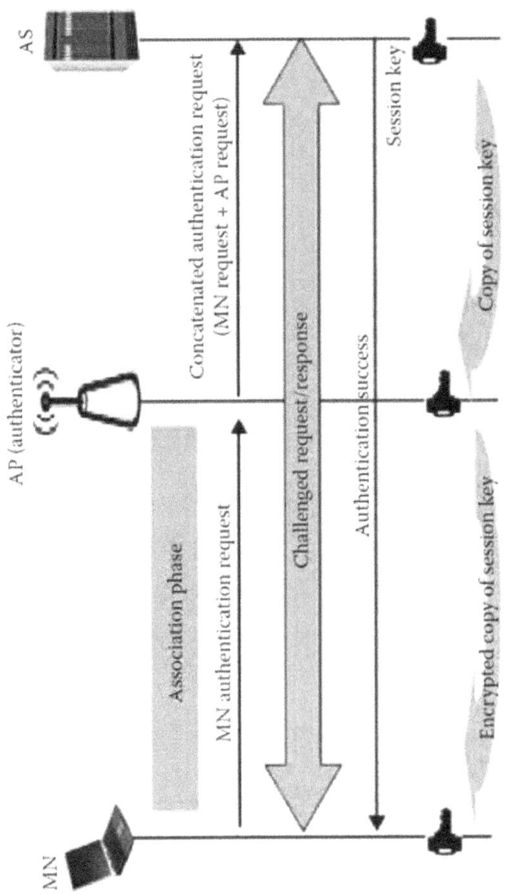

Figure 3: Schematic diagram of the authentication process in WDAP [Source: (Moustafa, 2007)].

Fig. 3 illustrates the WDAP authentication process. In the authentication protocol, the AP receives the authentication request from the MC. It then creates an authentication request for itself and concatenates this request to the received request from the MC. The concatenated request is then sent to the AS. Since both the mobile station and the AP do not trust each other until the AS authenticates both of them, WDAP is a dual authentication protocol. If the authentication is successful, AS generates a session key and sends the key to the AP. The AP then sends this key to the MC encrypting it with the shared key with MC. This key is thus shared between the AP and the MC for their secure communication and secure de-authentication when the session is finished. When an MC finishes a session with an AP, secure de-authentication takes place to prevent the connection from being exploited by an adversary. Use of WDAP in WMN environments ensures mutual authentication of both MCs and MRs. Also, WDAP can be used to ensure authentication between the MRs through authentication requests concatenation. In case of multi-hop communication in WMNs, each pair of nodes can mutually authenticate through the session key generated by the AS. However, a solution is needed in case of open mesh networks scenarios, where the AS may not be present in reality. Another problem arises in case of roaming authentication. WDAP is not ideally suited for use in roaming authentication since it works only for roaming into new APs, and does not consider the case of back roaming in which an MC may need to re-connect with another MC or an AP with whom it was authenticated earlier. As a result, the WDAP session key revocation mechanisms has some shortcomings that makes it unsuitable for deployment in real-world WMNs.

An approach that adapts IEEE 802.11i to the multi-hop communication has been presented in (Moustafa et al., 2006a). An extended forwarding capability in 802.11i is proposed without compromising on its security features to setup authenticated links in layer 2 to achieve secure wireless access as well as confidential data transfer in ad hoc multi-hop environments. The general objective of this approach is to support secure and seamless access to the Internet by the MCs situated near public WLAN hotspots, even when these nodes may move beyond the coverage area of the WLAN. To accomplish the authentication, authorization and accounting (AAA) process for an MC within the WLAN communication range, classical 802.11i authentication and message exchange take place.

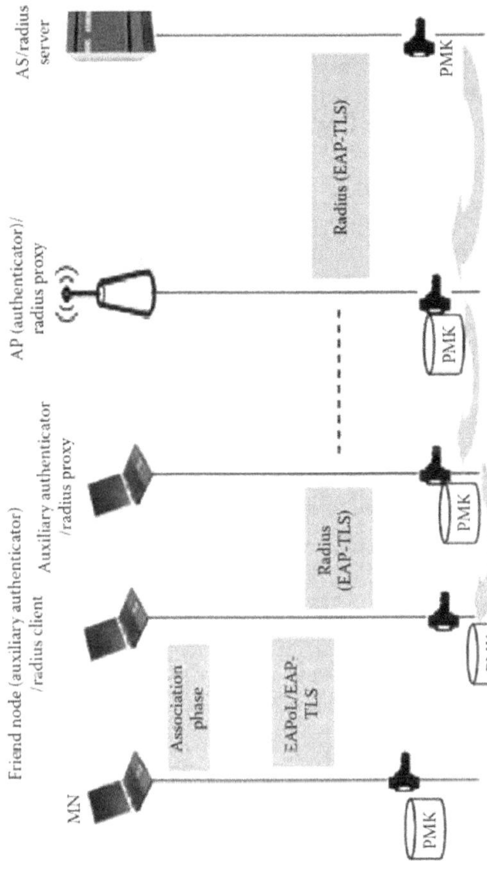

Figure 4: Schematic diagram of adapted 802.11i with EAP-TLS for multi-hop communication [Source: (Moustafa, 2007)].

As shown in Fig. 4, for accomplishing the AAA process for MCs that are beyond the WLAN communication range but belong to the ad hoc clusters, 802.11i is extended to support forwarding capabilities. In this case, the notion of friend nodes is introduced to allow each MC to initiate the authentication process through a selected node in its proximity. The friend node plays the role of an auxiliary authenticator that forwards the authentication request of the MC to the actual authenticator (i.e., the AP). If the friend node is not within the communication range of the AP, it invokes other friend nodes in a recursive manner until the AP is reached. The concept of proxy RADIUS (Rigney et al., 2000) is used for ensuring forwarding compatibility and secure message exchange over multi-hops.

Proxy chaining (Aboba & Vollbrecht, 1999) takes place if the friend node is not directly connected to an AP. To achieve higher level of security on each authenticated link between the communicating nodes, 802.11i encryption is used by invoking the four-way handshake between each MC and its authenticator (AP or friend node). This approach is useful in open mesh network scenarios, since it allows authentication by delegation among the mesh nodes. In addition, since the authentication keys are stored in the immediate nodes, the reauthentication process is optimized in case of roaming of the MCs. However, an adaptation is needed that allows establishment of multiple simultaneous connections to the authenticators - APs and the friend nodes – in a dense mesh topology. Also, a solution is needed to support fast and secure roaming across multiple wireless mesh routers (WMRs). A possible solution is through sharing session keys of authenticated clients among the WMRs (Moustafa, 2007).

Data Packet Authentication

An approach to prevent unauthorized node getting access to the network services in WMNs is to authenticate the transmitted data packets. Following this approach, a lightweight hop-by-hop access protocol (LHAP) (Zhu et al., 2003; Zhu et al., 2006) has been proposed for authenticating MCs for preventing resource consumption attacks in WMNs. LHAP implements light-weight hop-by-hop authentication, where intermediate nodes authenticate all the packets they receive before forwarding them further in the network. In this protocol, an MC first performs some light-weight authentication operations to bootstrap a trust relationship with its neighbors. It then invokes a light-weight protocol for subsequent traffic authentication and data encryption. LHAP is ideally suited for ad hoc networks, where it resides between the data link layer and the network layer and can be seamlessly integrated with secure routing protocols to provide high-level of security in a communication network.

LHAP employs a packet authentication technique based on the use of one-way hash chains (Lamport, 1981). Moreover, it uses TESLA (Perrig et al., 2001) protocol to reduce the number of public key operations for bootstrapping and maintaining trust among the nodes. For every traffic packet received from the network layer, LHAP adds its own header, which includes the node ID, a packet type field indicating a traffic packet, and an authentication tag. The packet is then passed to the data link layer and control packets are generated for establishing and maintaining trust relationships with the neighbor nodes. For a received packet, LHAP verifies its authenticity based on the authentication tag in the packet header. If the packet is valid, LHAP removes the LHAP header and passes the packet to the network layer; otherwise, it discards the packet. LHAP control packets are passed to the network layer with the goal to allow LHAP execution without affecting the operation of the other layers. LHAP is very suitable for WMN applications. For secure roaming, LHAP can be useful in distributing session keys among MCs employing a special type of packet designated for this purpose. However, the focus of this protocol is on preventing resource consumption attack on the network. However, LHAP cannot prevent insider attacks and hence complementary mechanisms are needed for this purpose (Moustafa, 2007).

Proactive Authentication and Pre-Authentication Schemes

In (Pack & Choi, 2004), a fast handoff scheme based on prediction of mobility pattern has been proposed. In this scheme, an MC on entering in the coverage area of an access point performs authentication procedures for multiple MRs (or APs). When an MC sends an authentication request, the AAA server authenticates the all the relevant APs (or MRs) and sends multiple session keys to the MC. A prediction method known as frequent handoff region (FHR) selection is utilized to reduce the handoff delay further. FHR selection algorithm takes into account user mobility pattern, service classes etc. to make a selection of frequent MRs suitable for handoff. To increase the accuracy of the user mobility prediction, a proactive key distribution approach has been proposed in (Mishra et al., 2004). A new data structure – neighbor graphs – is used to determine the candidate MR sets for the MC to associate with.

A reliable re-authentication scheme has been proposed in (Aura & Roe, 2005), in which an MR issues a credential for the MC it is currently serving. The credential can be used later (by the next MR) to certify the authenticity of the MC. A fast authentication and key exchange mechanism to support seamless handoff has been proposed in (Soltwisch et al., 2004). The mechanism uses the context transfer protocol (CTP) (Loughney et al., 2005) to forward session key from the previous router to the new access router.

Extensible Authentication Protocols

IEEE 802.1X has been applied to resolve some of the security problems in the 802.11 standard, where the MC and the AS authenticate each other by applying an upper layer authentication protocol like extensible authentication protocol encapsulating transport layer security (EAP-TLS) protocol (Aboba & Simon, 1999). Although EAP-TLS offers mutual authentication, it introduces high latency in WMNs because each terminal acts as an authenticator for its neighbor to reach the AS. This can lead to longer paths to the AS. Furthermore, in case of high mobility of terminals, re-authentication due to frequent handoffs can make be detrimental to real-time applications. Consequently, variants of EAP have been proposed by researchers to adapt 802.1X authentication model to multi-hop communications in WMNs. Some of these mechanisms are briefly discussed below.

EAP with Token-based Re-Authentication: a fast and secure hand-off protocol is presented in (Fantacci et al., 2006), which allows mutual authentication and access control thereby preventing insider attacks during the re-authentication process. To achieve this, old authentication keys are revoked. Thus, a node should ask for the keys from its neighbors or from the AS when its needs the keys. The mechanism involves a token-based reauthentication scheme based on a two-way handshake between the node that performs the handshake and the AS. The AS is involved in every hand-off to have a centralized entity for monitoring the network. An authentication token, in the form of keying material is provided by the authenticator of the network to the AS to obtain the PMK key. The authenticator can be an AP or a host in the WMN. Initially, the MC performs a full EAP-TLS authentication, generating a PMK key that is then shared between the MC and its authenticator. Whenever the MC performs hand-off to another authenticator, the new authenticator should receive the PMK key to avoid a full re-authentication. The new authenticator issues a request to the AS for the PMK and adds a token to the request. The token is a cryptographic material to prove that the authenticator is in contact with the MC which owns the requested PMK. The token was earlier generated by the MC while performing the hand-off and was transmitted to the new authenticator. The AS verifies the token, and issues the PMK to the new authenticator. This protocol is secure and involves centralized key management. However, the need to involve the AS in each re-authentication is not suitable for scenarios where MCs have random and frequent mobility (Moustafa, 2007). A distributed token verification will be more suitable for open and multi-hop WMN environments.

EAP-TLS over PANA: a security architecture suitable for multi-hop mesh network is presented in (Cheikhrouhou et al., 2006) that employs EAP-TLS over protocol for carrying authentication and network access (PANA) (Parthasarathy, 2006). It proposes an authentication solution for WMNs adapting IEE 802.1X so that MCs can be authenticated by MRs. The authentication between MCs and MRs requires MCs to be directly connected to the MRs. Since PANA enables MCs to authenticate to the access network using IP protocol, it is used in this mechanism to overcome the problem of association between MCs and MRs that can be attached through more than one intermediate node. When a new MC joins the network, it first gets an IP address (pre-PANA address) from a local DHCP server. Then, the PANA protocol is initiated so that the mobile node discovers the PANA access (PAA) router to authenticate itself. After successful authentication, the MC initiates the Internet key exchange (IKE) protocol with the MR for establishing a security association. Finally, IPSec tunnel ensures data protection over the radio link and a data access control by the MR. During the authentication and authorization phases, PANA uses EAP message exchange between the MC and the PAA, where PAA relays EAP messages to the AS using EAP over RADIUS. EAP-TLS message is used in this approach. The protocol is suited for heterogeneous WMNs since it is independent of the technology of the wireless media. However, PANA requires use of IP addresses in the mesh nodes. This puts a restriction in its use since all elements of a WMN may not use IP as the addressing standard.

EAP-TLS using Proxy Chaining: the combinations of (Moustafa et al., 2006a; Moustafa et al., 2006b) propose adaptive EAP solutions for authentication and access control in the multihop wireless environment. In (Moustafa et al., 2006a), an adapted EAP-TLS approach is used to allow authentication of mobile nodes. A delegation process is used among mobile nodes by use of auxiliary authenticators in a recursive manner until the AS is reached. To allow extended forwarding and exchange of EAP-TLS authentication messages, proxy RADIUS is involved using proxy chaining among the intermediate nodes between the MCs requesting the authentication and the AS. This approach permits the storage of authentication keys of the MCs in the auxiliary authenticators. This speeds up the re-authentication process and enhances the performance of the adaptive EAP-TLS mechanism. This solution is applicable for WMNs, especially in multi-hop communications. However, to support secure roaming across different wireless mesh routers (WMRs), communication is required between the old and the new WMRs. This can be done by using central elements or switches that link the WMRs and allow storing of information in a central location and distribution of information among the WMRs.

EAP-Enhanced Pre-Authentication: an EAP-enhanced pre-authentication scheme for mobile WMN (IEEE 802.e) in the link layer has been proposed in (Hur et al., 2008). In this scheme, the PKMv2 (public key management version 2) has been slightly modified based on the key hierarchy in a way that the communication key can be established between the MC and the target MR before hand-off in a proactive way. The modification allows the master session key generated by the authentication server to bind the MR identification (i.e., base station identification) and the MAC address of the MC. In the pre-authentication phase, the authentication server generates and delivers the unique public session keys for the neighbor MRs of the MC. The neighboring MRs are the access points that the MC potentially moves to. These MRs can use the public session key to derive an authorization key of the corresponding MC. In the same way, the MC can derive the public session key and the authorization key for its neighbor MRs, with the MR identification. Once the handoff is complete, the MC only needs to perform a three-way handshake and update the encryption key since the MC and MR already possess the authentication key. Thus a re-authentication with the authentication server is avoided and the associated delay is reduced.

Distributed Authentication: a distributed authentication for minimizing the authentication delay has been proposed in (Lee et al., 2008), in which multiple trusted nodes are distributed over a WMN to act on the behalf of an authentication server. This makes management of the network easy, and it also incurs less storage overhead in the MRs. However, the performance of the scheme will degrade when multiple MCs send out their authentication requests, since the number of trusted nodes acting as the authentication server is limited compared to the number of access routers. In (He et al., 2010), a distributed authenticated key establishment scheme (AKES) has been proposed based on hierarchical multi-variable symmetric functions (HMSF). In this scheme, MCs and MRs can mutually authenticate each other and establish pair-wise communication keys without the need of interaction with any central authentication server. The authors have extended the polynomial-based key generation concept (Blundo et al., 1993) to the asymmetric function for mutual authentication among the MCs and MRs. Based on the symmetric polynomial and an asymmetric function, an efficient and hierarchical key establishment scheme is designed This substantially reduces the communication overhead and authentication delay.

Secure Authentication: an improved security protocol for WMNs has been proposed in (Lukas & Fackroth, 2009). The protocol is named "WMNSec", which is based on the fourway handshake mechanism in 802.11i. In WMNSec, a dedicated station - mesh key distributor (MKD) – generates one single dynamically generated key for the whole network. This key is called the global key (GK). The GK is distributed from the MKD to the authenticated stations (MRs) using the four-way handshake from 802.11i. A newly joined MR would become another authenticator after it is authenticated and become the authenticated part of the WMN. Thus, the iterative authentication forms a spanning tree rooted as the MKD and spanning the whole network. To provide a high level of security, each key has a limited validity period. Periodic re-keying ensures that the keys used in all stations are up-to-date.

Authentication using Identity-Based Cryptography

Identity-based cryptography (IBC) is a public key cryptography in which public key of a user is derived from some publicly available unique identity information about the user, e.g. SSN, email address etc. Although the concept of IBC was first introduced by Shamir (Shamir, 1984), a fully functional IBC scheme was not established till Boneh and Franklin applied Weil pairing to construct a bilinear map (Boneh & Franklin, 2001). Using IBC, an attack-resilient security architecture called "ARSA" for WMNs has been proposed in (Zhang & Fang, 2006). The relationship among three entities in this scheme, e.g., brokers, users and network operators are made analogous to that among a bank, a credit card holder, and a merchant. The broker acts as a TTP that distributes secure pass to each authenticated user. Each secure pass has the ID of the user enveloped in it and the WMN operator grants access to all the users those possess secure passes. The users are not bound to any specific operator, and can get ubiquitous network access by a universal pass issued by a third-party broker. ARSA also provides an efficient mutual authentication and key agreement (AKA) between a user and a serving WMN domain or between users served by the same WMN domain.

Privacy Protection Schemes in WMNs

Traffic privacy preservation is an important issue in WMNs. In a community mesh network, the traffic of mobile users can be observed by the MRs residing at its neighbors, which could reveal sensitive personal information. A mesh network privacy-preserving architecture is presented in (T. Wu et al., 2006). The mechanism aims to achieve traffic confidentiality based on the concept of traffic pattern concealment by controlling the routing process using multipaths. The traffic from the source (i.e., IGW) to the destination (i.e., MR) is split into multiple paths. Hence, each relaying nodes along the path from the source to the destination can observe only a portion of the entire traffic. The traffic is split in a random manner (both spatially and temporally) so that an intermediate node can have little knowledge to figure out the overall traffic pattern. In this way the traffic confidentially is achieved. The mechanism defines an information-theoretic metric, and then proposes a penalty-based routing algorithm to allow traffic pattern hiding by exploiting multiple available paths between a pair of nodes. Source routing strategy is adopted so that a node can easily know the topology of its neighborhood. The protocol can also ensure communication privacy in WMNs, where each destination node is able to consistently limit the proportion of mutual information it shares with the observing node. However, the traffic splitting can increase delay in communication and hence this mechanism may not be suitable for real-time applications in WMNs.

A novel privacy and security scheme named PEACE (Privacy Enhanced yet Accountable seCurity framEwork) for WMNs has been proposed in (Ren et al., 2010). The scheme achieves explicit mutual authentication and key establishment between users (i.e. MCs) and MRs and between the users themselves (i.e., between the MCs). It also enables unilateral anonymous authentication between users and the MRs and bilateral anonymous authentication between a pair of users. Moreover, it enables user accountability by regulating user behaviors and protects WMNs from being abused and attacked. Network communications can be audited in cases of disputes and frauds. The high level architecture of PEACE trust model consists of four kinds of network entities: the network operator, user group managers, user groups and a trusted third party (TTP). Before accessing the WMN services, each user has to enroll in at least one user group whose manager, thus, knows the essential and non-essential attributes of the user. The users do not directly register with the network operator; instead, each group manager subscribes to the network operator on behalf of its group members. Upon registration from a group manager, the network operator allocates a set of group secret keys to this user group. The network operator divides each group secret key into two parts – one part is sent to the requesting group manager and the other part to the TTP. To access network services, each user request one part of the group secret key from his group manager and the other part from the TTP to recover a complete group secret key. The user also needs to return signed acknowledgments to both the group manager and the TTP. PEACE uses a variation of the short group signature scheme proposed in (Boneh & Shacham, 2004) to ensure sophisticated user privacy. The scheme is resistant to bogus data injection attacks, data phishing attacks and DoS attacks (Ren et al., 2010).

A security architecture named "SAT" has been proposed in (Sun et al., 2008; Sun et al., 2011). The system consists of ticket-based protocols, which resolves the conflicting security requirements of unconditional anonymity for honest users and traceability of misbehaving users in a WMN. By utilizing the tickets, self-generated pseudonyms, and the hierarchical identity-based cryptography, the architecture has been demonstrated to achieve the desired security objectives and the performance efficiency. The system uses a blind signature technique from the payment systems. (Brands, 1993; Wei et al., 2006; Figueiredo et al., 2005; Chaum, 1982), and hence it achieves the anonymity by delinking user identities from their activities. The pseudonym technique also renders user location information unexposed. The pseudonym generation mechanism does not rely on a central authority, e.g. the broker in (Zhang & Fang, 2006), the domain authority in (Ateniese et al., 1999), the transportation authority or the manufacturer in (Raya & Hubaux, 2007), and the trusted authority in (Zhang et al., 2006), who can derive the user's identity from his pseudonyms and illegally trace on an honest user. However, the system is not intended for achieving routing anonymity. Hierarchical identitybased cryptography (HIBC) for inter-domain authentication is adopted to avoid domain parameter certification in order to ensure anonymous access control.

THE HIERARCHICAL ARCHITECTURE OF A WMN

In this section, we first present a standard architecture of a typical WMN for which we propose a security and privacy protocol. The architecture is a very generic one that represents majority of the real-world deployment scenarios for WMNs. The architecture of a hierarchical WMN consists of three layers as shown in Fig. 5. At the top layers are the Internet gateways (IGWs) that are connected to the wired Internet.

They form the backbone infrastructure for providing Internet connectivity to the elements in the second level. The entities at the second level are called wireless mesh routers (MRs) that eliminate the need for wired infrastructure at every MR and forward their traffic in a multi-hop fashion towards the IGW. At the lowest level are the mesh clients (MCs) which are the wireless devices of the users. Internet connectivity and peer-to-peer communications inside the mesh are two important applications for a WMN. Therefore design of an efficient and low-overhead communication protocol which ensure security and privacy of the users is a critical requirement which poses significant research challenges.

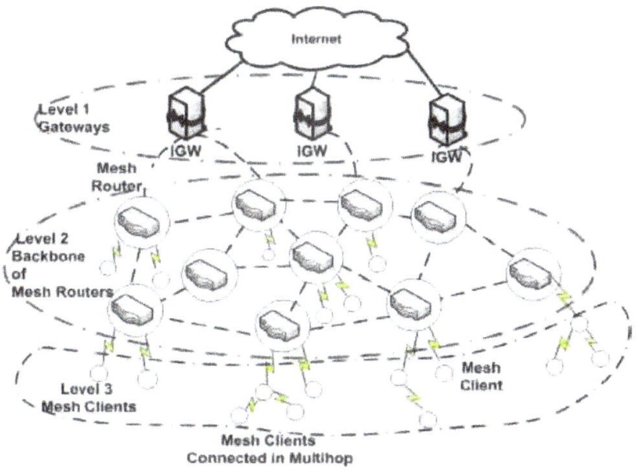

Figure 5: A three-tier architecture of a wireless mesh network (WMN).

For designing the proposed protocol and to specify the WMN deployment scenario, the following assumptions are made.

- Each MR which is authorized to join the wireless backbone (through the IGWs), has two certificates to prove its identity. One certificate is used during the authentication phase that occurs when a new node joins the network. EAP-TLS (Aboba et al., 2004) for 802.1X authentication is used for this purpose since it is the strongest authentication method provided by EAP (Aboba et al., 2004), whereas the second certificate is used for the authentication with the authentication server (AS).
- The certificates used for authentication with the RADIUS server and the AS are signed by the same certificate authority (CA). Only recognized MRs are authorized to join the backbone.
- Synchronization of all MRs is achieved by use of the network time protocol (NTP) protocol (Mills, 1992).

The proposed security protocol serves the dual purpose of providing security in the access network (i.e., between the MCs and the MRs) and the backbone network (i.e., between the MRs and the IGWs). These are described the following sub-sections.

Access Network Security

The access mechanism to the WMN is assumed to be the same as that of a local area network (LAN), where mobile devices authenticate themselves and connect to an access point (AP). This allows the users to the access the services of the WMN exploiting the authentication and authorization mechanisms without installing any additional software. It is evident that such security solution provides protection to the wireless links between the MCs and the MRs. A separate security infrastructure is needed for the links in the backbone networks. This is discussed in Section 5.2.

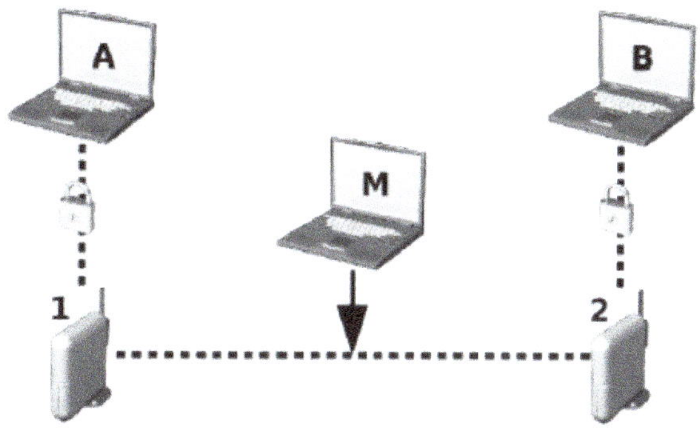

Figure 6: Secure information exchange among the MCs A and B through the MRs 1 and 2.

Fig. 6 illustrates a scenario where users A and B are communicating in a secure way to MRs 1 and 2 respectively. If the wireless links are not protected, an intruder M will be able to eavesdrop on and possibly manipulate the information being exchanged over the network. This situation is prevented in the proposed security scheme which encrypts all the traffic transmitted on the wireless link using a stream cipher in the data link layer of the protocol stack.

Backbone Network Security

For providing security for the traffic in the backbone network, a two-step approach is adopted. When a new MR joins the network, it first presents itself as an MC and completes the association formalities. It subsequently upgrades its association by successfully authenticating to the AS. In order to make such authentication process efficient in a high mobility scenario, the key management and distribution processes have been designed in a way so as to minimize the effect of the authentication overhead on the network performance. The overview of the protocol is discussed as follows.

Fig. 7 shows the three phases of the authentication process that a MR (say N) undergoes. When N wants to join the network, it scans all the radio channels to detect any MR that is already connected to the wireless backbone. Once such an MR (say A) is detected, N requests A for access to network services including authentication and key distribution. After connecting to A, N can perform the tasks prescribed in the IEEE 802.11i protocol to complete a mutual authentication with the network and establish a security association with the entity to which it is physically connected. This completes the Phase I of the authentication process. Essentially, during this phase, a new MR performs all the steps that an MC has to perform to establish a secure channel with an MR for authentication and secure communication over the WMN.

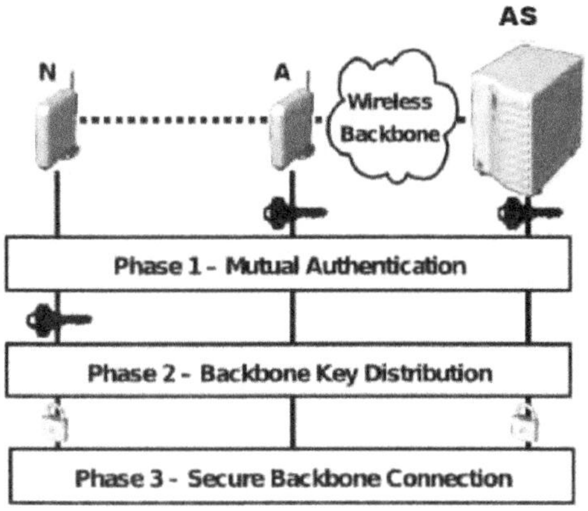

Figure 7: Steps performed by a new MR (N) using backbone encrypted traffic to join the WMN.

During Phase II of the authentication process, the MRs use the transport layer security (TLS) protocol. Only authorized MRs that have the requisite credentials can authenticate to the AS and obtain the cryptographic credentials needed to derive the key sequence used to protect the wireless backbone. In the proposed protocol, an end-to-end secure channel between the AS and the MR is established at the end of a successful authentication through which the cryptographic credentials can be exchanged in a secure way.

To eliminate any possibility of the same key being used over a long time, a server-initiated protocol is proposed for secure key management. The protocol is presented in Section 6. As mentioned earlier in this section, all the MRs are assumed to be synchronized with a central server using the NTP protocol.

Fig. 8 shows a collection of four MRs connected with each other by five wireless links. The MR A is connected with the AS by a wired link. At the time of network bootstrapping, only node A can connect to the network as an MR, since it is the only node that can successfully authenticate to the AS. Nodes B and C which are neighbors of A then detect a wireless network to which can connect and perform the authentication process following the IEEE 802.11i protocol. At this point of time, nodes B and C are successfully authenticated as MCs. After their authentication as MCs, nodes B and C are allowed to authenticate to the AS and request the information used by A to produce the currently used cryptographic key for communication in the network. After having derived such key, both B and C will be able to communicate with each other, as well as with node A, using the ad hoc mode of communication in the WMN. At this stage, B and C both have full MR functionalities. They will be able to turn on their access interface for providing node D a connection to the AS for joining the network.

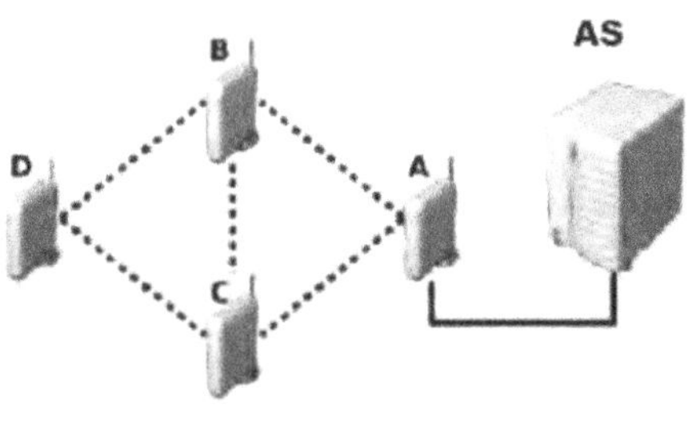

Figure 8: Autonomous configuration of the MRs in the proposed security scheme.

THE KEY DISTRIBUTION PROTOCOL

In this section, the details of the proposed key distribution and management protocol are presented. The protocol is essentially a server-initiated protocol (Martignon et al., 2008) and provides the clients (MRs and MCs) flexibility and autonomy during the key generation.

In the proposed key management protocol delivers the keys to all the MRs from the AS in a reactive manner. The keys are used subsequently by the MRs for a specific time interval in their message communications to ensure integrity and confidentiality of the messages. After the expiry of the time interval for validity of the keys, the existing keys are revoked and new keys are generated by the AS. Fig. 9 depicts the message exchanges between the MRs and the AS during the execution of the protocol.

A newly joined MR, after its successful mutual authentication with a central server, sends its first request for key list (and its time of generation) currently being used by other existing MRs in the wireless backbone. Let us denote the key list timestamp as TS_{KL}. Let us define a session as the maximum time interval for validity of the key list currently being used by each node MR and MC). We also define the duration of a session as the product of the cardinality of the key list (i.e., the number of the keys in the key list) and the longest time interval of validity of a key (the parameter timeout in Fig. 9).

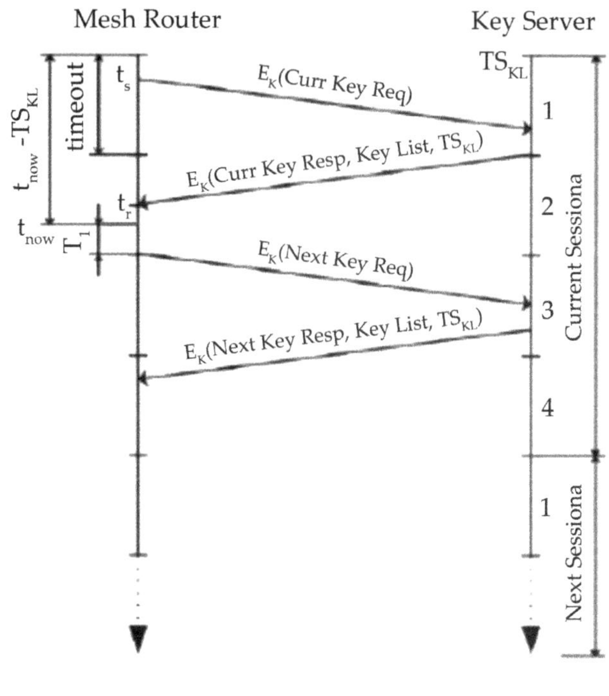

Figure 9: Message exchanges between an MR and the AS in the key management protocol.

The validity of a key list is computed from the time instance when the list is generated (i.e., TS_{KL}) by the AS. An MR, based on the time instance at which it joins the backbone (t_{now} in Fig. 9), can find out the key (from the current list) being used by its peers (key_{idx}) and the interval of validity of the key (T_i) using (1) and (2) as follows:

$$key_{idx} = \left\lfloor \frac{t_{now} - TS_{KL}}{timeout} \right\rfloor + 1 \tag{1}$$

$$T_i = key_{idx} * timeout - (t_{now} - TS_{KL}) \quad (2)$$

In the proposed protocol, each WMN node requests the AS for the key list that will be used in the next session before the expiry of the current session. This is feature is essential for nodes which are located multiple hops away from the AS, since, responses from the AS take longer time to reach these nodes. The responses may also get delayed due to fading or congestion in the wireless links. If the nodes send their requests for key list to the AS just before expiry of the current session, then due to limited time in hand, only the nodes which have good quality links with the AS will receive the key list. Hence, the nodes which will fail to receive responses for the server will not be able to communicate in the next session due to non-availability of the current key list. This will lead to an undesirable situation of network partitioning.

The key index value that triggers the request from the nodes to the server can be set equal to the difference between the cardinality of the list and a correction factor. The correction factor can be estimated based on parameters like the network load, the distance of the node from the AS and the time required for the previous response.

In the proposed protocol, the correction factor is estimated based on the time to receive the response from the AS using (3), where t_s is the time instance when the first key request was sent, t_r is the time instance when the key response was received from the AS, and timeout is the validity period of the key. Therefore, if a node fails to receive a response (i.e., the key list) from the AS during timeout, and takes a time t_{last}, it must send the next request to the AS before setting the last key.

$$c = \left\lceil \frac{t_{last} - timeout}{timeout} \right\rceil \text{ if } t_{last} \geq timeout$$

$$= 0 \text{ if } t_{last} < timeout$$

$$t_{last} = t_r - t_s \quad (3)$$

The first request of the key list sent by the new node to the AS is forwarded by the peer to which it is connected as an MC through the wireless access network. However, the subsequent requests are sent directly over the wireless backbone.

THE PRIVACY AND ANONYMITY PROTOCOL

As mentioned in Section 1, to ensure privacy of the users, the proposed security protocol is complemented with a privacy protocol so as to ensure user anonymity and privacy. The same authentication server (AS) used in the security protocol is used for managing the key distribution for preserving the privacy. To enable user authentication and anonymity, a novel protocol has been designed extending the ring signature authentication scheme in (Cao et al., 2004). It is assumed that a symmetric encryption algorithm E exists such that for any key k, the function E_k is a permutation over b-bit strings. We also assume the existence of a family of keyed combining functions Ck,v(y_1, y_2, …., y_n), and a publicly defined collision-resistant hash function H(.) that maps arbitrary inputs to strings of constant length which are used as keys for $C_{k,v}(y_1, y_2, …., y_n)$ (Rivest et al., 2001). Every keyed combining function $C_{k,v}(y_1, y_2, …., y_n)$ takes as input the key k, an initialization b_{bit} value v, and arbitrary values y_1, y_2, …., y_n. A user U_i who wants to generate a session key with the authentication server, uses a ring of n logged-on-users and performs the following steps.

Step 1. U_i chooses the following parameters: (i) a large prime pi such that it is hard to compute discrete logarithms in GF(p_i), (ii) another large prime q_i such that $q_i \mid p_i - 1$, and (iii) a generator g_i in GF(pi) with order q_i.

Step 2. U_i chooses A $x_{A_i} \in Z_{q_i}$ as his private key, and computes the public key A_i mod $y_{A_i} = g_i^{x_{Ai}}$ mod p_i.

Step 3. U_i defines a trap-door function $f_i(\alpha, \beta) = \alpha . y_{Ai}^{\alpha \bmod q_i} . g_i^{\beta} \bmod p_i$. Its inverse function $f_i^{-1}(y)$ is defined as $f_i^{-1}(y) = (\alpha, \beta)$, where a and b are computed as follows (K is a random integer in Z_{qi} .

$$\alpha = y_{Ai} . g_i^{-K.(g_i^K \bmod p_i) \bmod q_i} \bmod p_i \quad (4)$$

$$\alpha^* = \alpha \bmod q_i \quad (5)$$

$$\beta = K.(g_i^K \bmod p_i) - x_{Ai} . \alpha^* \bmod q_i \quad (6)$$

U_i makes p_i, q_i, g_i and y_{A_i} public, and keeps x_{A_i} as secret.

The authentication server (AS) chooses: (i) a large prime p such that it is hard to compute discrete logarithms in GF(p), (ii) another large prime q such that q | p – 1, (iii) a generator g in GF(p) with order q, (iv) a random integer x_B from Z_q as its private key. AS computes its public key $y_B = g^{x_B} \bmod p$ and publishes (y_B, p, q, g).

Anonymous Authenticated Key Exchange: The key-exchange is initiated by the user U_i and involves three rounds to compute a secret session key between U_i and AS. The operations in these three rounds are as follows:

Round 1: When U_i wants to generate a session key on the behalf of n ring users U_1, U_2, …..U_n, where $1 \leq i \leq n$, U_i does the following:

(i) U_i chooses two random integers $x_1, x_A \in Z_q^*$ and computes the following:

1. $R = g^{x_1} \bmod p$, $Q = y_B^{x_1} \bmod p \bmod q$, $X = g^{x_a} \bmod p$ and $l = H(X, Q, V, y_B, I)$

.

(ii) U_i Chooses a pair of values (α_t, β_t) for every other ring member U_t $(1 \leq t \leq n, t \neq k)$ in a pseudorandom way, and computes $y_t = f_t(\alpha_t, \beta_t) \bmod p_t$.

(iii) U_i randomly chooses a b-bit initialization value v, and finds the value of y_i from the equation $C_{k,v}(y_1, y_2, ... y_n) = v$.

(iv) Ui computes $(\alpha_i, \beta_i) = f_i^{-1}(y_i)$ by using the trap-door information of f_i. First, it chooses a random integer $K \in Z_{q_i}$, computes αi using (6), and keeps K secret. It then computes α_i^* using (5) and finally computes β_i using (6).

(v) $(U_1,U_2.,U_n,v,V,R,(\alpha_1,\beta_1),(\alpha_2,\beta_2),.,(\alpha_n,\beta_n)$ is the ring signature s on X.

Finally, U_i sends s and I to the server AS.

Round 2: AS does the following to recover and verify X from the signatures .

i. AS computes mod mod $Q = R^{x_B}$, recovers $X = V.g^Q \bmod p$ and hashes X, Q, V and y_b to recover I, where $I = H(X,Q,V,y_B,I)$.

ii. AS computes $y_t = f_i(\alpha_t,\beta_t) \bmod p_i$, for $t = 1,2,\ldots..n$.

iii. AS checks whether $C_{k,v}(y_1,y_2,\ldots\ldots.y_n) = v$. If it is true, AS accepts X as valid; otherwise, AS rejects X. If X is valid, AS chooses a random integer x_b from Z_q^*, and computes the following: $Y = g^{x_b} \bmod p$ $K_s = X^{x_b} \bmod p$ and $h = H(K_s,X,Y,I')$. AS sends {h, Y, I'} to U_i.

Round 3: U_i verifies whether K_S' is from the server AS. For this purpose, U_i computes $K_S' = Y^{x_a} \bmod p$, hashes K, X, Y to get $h' = H(K_s',X,Y,I')$. If $h' = h$, U_i accepts Ks as the session key.

Security Analysis: The key exchange scheme satisfies the following requirements.

User Anonymity: For a given signature X, the server can only be convinced that the ring signature is actually produced by at least one of the possible users. If the actual user does not reveal the seed K, the server cannot determine the identity of the user. The strength of the anonymity depends on the security of the pseudorandom number generator. It is not possible to determine the identity of the actual user in a ring of size n with a probability greater than 1/n. Since the values of k and v are fixed in a ring signature, there are $(2^b)^{n-1}$ number of $(x_1,x_2,\ldots x_n)$ that satisfy the equation , $C_{k,v}(y_1,y_2,\ldots y_n) = v$, and the probability of generation of each $(x_1,x_2,\ldots x_n)$ is the same. Therefore, the signature can't leak the identity information of the user.

Mutual Authentication: In the proposed scheme, not only the server verifies the users, but the users can also verify the server. Because of the hardness of inverting the hash function f(.), it is computationally infeasible for the attacker to determine (α_i,β_i), and hence it is infeasible for him to forge a signature. If the attacker wants to masquerade as the AS, he needs to compute $h = H(K_s,X,Y)$. He requires x_B in order to compute X. However, x_B is the private key of AS to which the attacker has no access.

Forward Secrecy: The forward secrecy of a scheme refers to its ability to defend leaking of its keys of previous sessions when an attacker is able to catch hold of the key of a particular session. The forward secrecy of a scheme enables it to prevent replay attacks. In the proposed scheme, since x_a and x_b are both selected randomly, the session key of each period has not relation to the other periods. Therefore, if the session key generated in the period j is leaked, the attacker cannot get any information of the session keys generated before the period j. The proposed protocol is, therefore, resistant to replay attack.

PERFORMANCE EVALUATION

The proposed security and privacy protocols have been implemented in the Qualnet network simulator, version 4.5 (Network Simulator, Qualnet). The simulated network consists of 50 nodes randomly distributed in the simulation area forming a dense WMN. The WMN topology is shown in Fig. 10, in which 5 are MRs and remaining 45 are MCs. Each MR has 9 MCs associated with it. To evaluate the performance of the security protocol, first the network is set as a full-mesh topology, where each MR (and also MC) is directly connected to two of its neighbors. In such as scenario, the throughput of a TCP connection established over a wireless link is measured with the security protocol activated in the nodes. The obtained results are then compared with the throughput obtained on the same wireless link protected by a static key to encrypt the traffic.

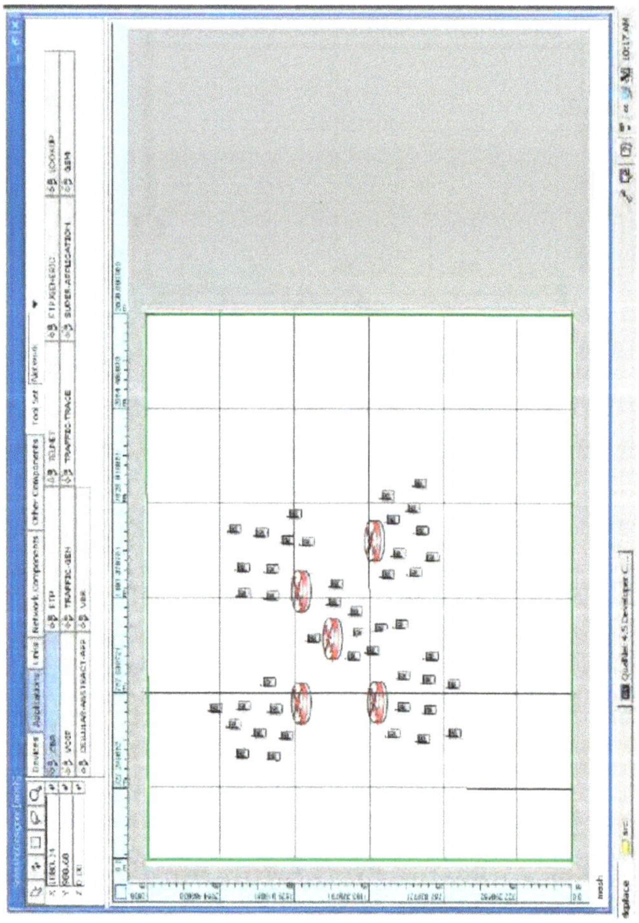

Figure 10: The simulated network topology in Qualnet Simulator.

After having 10 simulation runs, the average throughput of a wireless link between a pair of MRs was found to be equal to 30.6 MBPS, when the link is protected by a static key. However, the average throughput for the same link was 28.4 MBPS when the link was protected by the proposed security protocol. The results confirm that the protocol does not cause any significant overhead on the performance of the wireless link, since the throughput in a link on average decreased by only 7%. The impact of the security protocol for key generation and revocation on packet drop rate in real-time applications is also studied in the simulation. For this purpose, a VoIP application is invoked between two MRs which generated UDP traffic in the wireless link. The packet drop rates in wireless link when the link is protected with the proposed security protocol and when the link is protected with a static key. The transmission rate was set to 1 MBPS. The average packet drop rate in 10 simulation runs was found to be only 4%. The results clearly demonstrate that the proposed security scheme has no adverse impact on packet drop rate even if several key switching (regeneration and revocation) operations are carried out.

The performance of the privacy protocol is also analyzed in terms of its storage, communication overhead. Both storage and communication overhead were found to increase linearly with the number of nodes in the network. In fact, it has been analytically shown that overhead due to cryptographic operation on each message is: 60n + 60 bytes, where n represents the number of public key pairs used to generate the ring signature (Xiong et al., 2010). It is clear that the privacy protocol has a low overhead.

CONCLUSION AND FUTURE WORK

WMNs have become an important focus area of research in recent years owing to their great promise in realizing numerous next-generation wireless services. Driven by the demand for rich and high-speed content access, recent research has focused on developing high performance communication protocols, while security and privacy issues have received relatively little attention. However, given the wireless and multi-hop nature of communication, WMNs are subject to a wide range of security and privacy threats. This chapter has provided a comprehensive discussion on the current authentication, access control and user privacy protection schemes for WMNs. It has also presented a novel security and key management protocol that can be utilized for secure authentication in WMNs. The proposed security protocol ensures security in both the access and the backbone networks. A user privacy protection algorithm has also been presented that enables anonymous authentication of the users. Simulation results have shown the effectiveness of the protocol. Future research issues include the study of a distributed and collaborative system where the authentication service is provided by a dynamically selected set of MRs. The integration with the current centralized scheme would increase the robustness of the proposed protocol, maintaining a low overhead since MRs would use the distributed service only when the central server is not available. Authentication on the backbone network in a hybrid and open WMN is still an unsolved problem. In addition, authentication between MRs and IGWs from different operators in a hybrid WMN environment is another challenge. Authentication and key distribution in a mobile WMN such as mobile WiMAX or LTE networks is another open problem. High mobility users make the challenge even more difficult. Owing to very limited coverage IEEE 802.11-based MRs (e.g., 100 meters), the high-mobility users (e.g. a user on a fast moving car) will migrate from the coverage area of an MR to that of another. It is not acceptable for the user to authenticate and negotiate the key with each MR. Novel solutions possibly using group keys are needed for this purpose. The requirements of user anonymity and privacy of users should be integrated to most of the applications in WMNs.

REFERENCES

1. Aboba, B.; Bluk, L.; Vollbrecht, J.; Carlson, J. & Levkowetz, H. (2004). Extensible Authentication Protocol (EAP). RFC 3748, June 2004.
2. Aboba, B. & Simon, D. (1999). PPP EAP TLS Authentication Protocol. RFC 2716, 1999.
3. Aboba, B. & Vollbrecht, J. (1999). Proxy Chaining and Policy Implementation in Roaming, RFC 2607, October 1999.
4. Akyildiz, I. F.; Wang, X. & Wang, W. (2005). Wireless Mesh Networks: A Survey. Computer Networks, Vol 47, No 4, pp. 445–487, March 2005.
5. Ateniese, G.; Herzberg, A.; Krawczyk, H. & Tsudik, G. (1999). Untraceable Mobility or How to Travel Incognito. Computer Networks, Vol 31, No 8, pp. 871–884, April 1999.
6. Aura, T. & Roe, M. (2005). Reducing Reauthentication Delay in Wireless Networks. Proceedings of the 1st IEEE International Conference on Security and Privacy for Emerging Areas in Communications Networks (SecureComm'05), pp. 139-148, Athens, Greece, September 2005.
7. Ben Salem, N. & Hubaux, J.-P. (2006). Securing Wireless Mesh Networks. IEEE Wireless Communication, Vol 13, No 2, pp. 50-55, April 2006.
8. Blake-Wilson, S. & Menezes, A. (1998). Entity Authentication and Authenticated Key Transport Protocols Employing Asymmetric Techniques. Proceedings of the 5th International Workshop on Security Protocols, Lecture Notes in Computer Science, Vol 1361, pp. 137–158, Christianson et al. (eds.), Springer-Verlag, Heidelberg, Germany, 1998.
9. Blundo, C.; Santis, A. D.; Herzberg. A.; Kutten, S.; Vaccaor, U. & Yung, M. (1993). PerfectlySecure Key Distribution for Dynamic Conferences. Proceedings of the 12th Annual International Cryptology Conference on Advances in Cryptology (CRYPTO'92). Lecture Notes in Computer Science, Brickell (ed.), Vol 740, pp. 471-486, 1993.
10. Boneh, D. & Franklin, M. (2001). Identity-Based Encryption from the Weil Pairing. Proceedings of the Annual International Cryptology Conference (CRYPTO'01). Lecture Notes in Computer Science, Vol 2139, pp. 213–229, Springer-Verlag, Berlin, Germany, August 2001.
11. Boneh, D. & Shacham, H. (2004). Group Signatures with Verifier-Local Revocation. Proceedings of the 11th ACM Conference on Computer and Communication Security (CCS), pp. 168-177, Washington DC, USA, October 2004.
12. Brands, S. (1993). Untraceable Off-Line Cash in Wallets with Observers. Proceedings of the Annual International Cryptology Conference (CRYPTO'93). Lecture Notes in Computer Science Vol 773, pp. 302–318, August 1993.
13. Buttyan, L. & Dora, L. (2009). An Authentication

Scheme for QoS-Aware Multi-Operator Maintained Wireless Mesh Networks. Proceedings of the 1st IEEE WoWMoM Workshop on Hot Topics in Mesh Networking (HotMESH '09), Kos, Greece, June 2009.

14. Buttyan, L.; Dora, L; Martinelli, F. & Petrochhi, M. (2010). Fast Certificate-based Authentication Scheme in Multi-Operator Maintained Wireless Mesh Networks. Journal of Computer Communications, Vol 33, Issue 8, May 2010.
15. Cao, T.; Lin, D. & Xue, R. (2004). Improved Ring Authenticated Encryption Scheme. Proceedings of 10th Joint International Computer Conference (JICC), International Academic Publishers World Publishing Corporation, pp. 341-346, 2004.
16. Cao, Z; Zhu, H. & Lu, R. (2006). Provably Secure Robust Threshold Partial Blind Signature. Science in China Series F: Information Sciences, Vol 49, No 5, pp. 604–615, October 2006.
17. Chaum, D. (1982). Blind Signatures for Untraceable Payments. Proceedings of the Annual International Cryptology Conference (CRYPTO'82). Advances in Cryptology, pp. 199– 203, Plenum Press, New York, USA, August 1983.
18. Cheikhrouhou, O.; Maknavicius, M. & Chaouchi, H. (2006). Security Architecture in a MultiHop Mesh Network. Proceedings of the 5th Conference on Security Architecture Research (SAR 2006), Seignosse-Landes, France, June 2006.
19. Clarke, R. (1999). Internet Privacy Concerns Confirm the Case for Intervention. Communications of the ACM, Vol 42, No 2, pp. 60–67, February 1999.
20. Fantacci, R.; Maccari, L.; Pecorella, T. & Frosali, F. (2006). A Secure and Performant TokenBased Authentication for Infrastructure and Mesh 802.1X Networks. Proceedings of the 25th IEEE International Conference on Computer Communications (INFOCOM'06), Poster Paper, Barcelona, Spain, April 2006.
21. Figueiredo, D.; Shapiro, J. & Towsley, D. (2005). Incentives to Promote Availability in Peerto-Peer Anonymity Systems. Proceedings of the 13th IEEE International Conference on Network Protocols (ICNP'05), pp. 110–121, November 2005.
22. He, B.; Xie, B.; Zhao, D. & Reddy, R. (2011). Secure Access Control and Authentication in Wireless Mesh Networks. Security of Self-Organizing Networks: MANET, WSN, WMN, WANET, Al-Sakib Khan Pathan (ed.), CRC Pres, USA, 2011.
23. He, B.; Joshi, S.; Agrawal, D. P. & Sun, D. (2010). An Efficient Authenticated Key Establishment Scheme for Wireless Mesh Networks. Proceedings of IEEE Global Telecommunications Conference (GLOBECOM'10), pp. 1-5, Miami, Florida, USA, December 2010.
24. Hur, J.; Shim, H.; Kim, P.; Yoon, H. & Song, N.-O. (2008). Security Consideration for Handover Schemes in Mobile WiMAX Networks. Proceedings of IEEE Wireless Communications and Networking Conference (WCNC '08), Las Vegas, NV, March, 2008.
25. IEEE Standard 802.11i (2004). Medium Access Control Security Enhancements, 2004.
26. IEEE Standard 802.1X (2001). Local and Metropolitan Area Networks Port-Based Network Access Control, 2001.
27. Kassab, M.; Belghith, A.; Bonnin, J.-M. & Sassi, S. (2005). Fast Pre-Authentication Based on Proactive Key Distribution for 802.11 Infrastructure Networks. Proceedings of the 1st ACM Workshop on Wireless Multimedia Networking and Performance Modeling (WMuNeP 2005), pp. 46–53, Montreal, Canada, October 2005.
28. Lamport, L. (1981). Password Authentication with Insecure Communication. Communications of the ACM, Vol. 24, No. 11, pp. 770-772, November 1981.
29. Lee, I.; Lee, J.; Arbaugh, W. & Kim, D. (2008). Dynamic Distributed Authentication Scheme for Wireless LAN-Based Mesh Networks. Proceedings of International Conference on Information, Networking, Towards Ubiquitous Networking and Services (ICOIN '07), Estril, Portugal, January, 2007. Lecture Notes in Computer Science, Vazao et al. (eds.), Vol. 5200, pp. 649–658, Springer-Verlag, Heidelberg, Germany, 2008.
30. Lin, X.; Ling, X.; Zhu, H.; Ho, P.-H. & Shen, X. (2008). A Novel Localised Authentication Scheme in IEEE 802.11 Based Wireless Mesh Networks. International Journal of Security and Networks, Vol. 3, No. 2, pp. 122–132, 2008.
31. Loughney, L.; Nakhjiri, M.; Perkins, C. & Koodli, R. (2005). Context Transfer Protocol (CXTP). IETF RFC 4067, July 2005.
32. Lukas, G. & Fackroth, C. (2009). WMNSec: Security for Wireless Mesh Networks. Proceedings of the International Conference on Wireless Communications and Mobile Computing: Connecting the World Wirelessly (IWCMC'09), pp. 90–95, Leipzig, Germany, June, 2009, ACM Press, New York, USA.
33. Martignon, F.; Paris, S. & Capone, A. (2008). MobiSEC: A Novel Security Architecture for Wireless Mesh Networks. Proceedings of the 4th ACM Symposium on QoS and Security for Wireless and Mobile Networks (Q2SWinet'08), pp. 35-42, Vancouver, Canada, October 2008.
34. Mills, D.L. (1992). Network Time Protocol, RFC 1305, March 1992.
35. Mishra, A. & Arbaugh, W. A. (2002). An Initial Security Analysis of the IEEE 802.1X Standard. Computer Science Department Technical Report CS-TR-4328, University of Maryland, USA, February 2002.
36. Mishra, A.; Shin, M.H.; Petroni, N. I.; Clancy, J. T. & Arbauch, W. A. (2004). Proactive Key Distribution Using Neighbor Graphs. IEEE Wireless Communications, Vol. 11, No. 1, pp. 26–36, February 2004.
37. Moustafa, H. (2007). Providing Authentication, Trust, and Privacy in Wireless Mesh Networks, pp. 261-295. Security in Wireless Mesh Networks. Zhang et al. (eds.), CRC Press, USA, 2007.
38. Moustafa, H.; Bourdon, G. & Gourhant, Y. (2006a). Authentication, Authorization and Accounting (AAA) in Hybrid Ad Hoc Hotspot's Environments. Proceedings of the 4th ACM International Workshop on Wireless

Mobile Applications and Services on WLAN Hotspots (WMASH'06), pp. 37-46, Los Angeles, California, USA, September 2006.

39. Moustafa, H.; Bourdon, G. & Gourhant, Y. (2006b). Providing Authentication and Access Control in Vehicular Network Environment. Proceedings of the 21st IFIP TC-11 International Information Security Conference (IFIP-SEC'06), pp. 62-73, Karlstad, Sweden, May 2006.

40. Network Simulator QUALNET. URL: http://www.scalable-networks.com. Pack, S. & Choi, Y. (2004). Fast Handoff Scheme Based on Mobility Prediction in Public Wireless LAN Systems. IEEE Communications, Vol. 151, No. 5, pp. 489–495, October 2004.

41. Parthasarathy, M. (2006). Protocol for Carrying Authentication and Network Access (PANA) Threat Analysis and Security Requirements. RFC 4016, March 2005.

42. Perrig, A.; Canetti, R.; Song, D. & Tygar, J. (2001). Efficient and Secure Source Authentication for Multicast. Proceedings of the Network and Distributed System Security Symposium (NDSS 2001), pp. 35-46, San Diego, California, USA, February 2001.

43. Prasad, N. R.; Alam, M. & Ruggieri, M. (2004). Light-Weight AAA Infrastructure for Mobility Support across Heterogeneous Networks. Wireless Personal Communications, Vol 29, No 3–4, pp. 205–219, June 2004.

44. Prasad, A. R. & Wang, H. (2005). Roaming Key Based Fast Handover in WLANs. Proceedings of IEEE Wireless Communications and Networking Conference (WCNC 2003), Vol 3, pp. 1570–1576, New Orleans, Louisiana, USA, March 2005.

45. Raya, M. & Hubaux, J.-P. (2007). Securing Vehicular Ad Hoc Networks. Journal of Computer Security, Special Issue on Security of Ad Hoc and Sensor Networks, Vol 15, No 1, pp. 39– 68, January 2007.

46. Reed, M.; Syverson, P. & Goldschlag, D. D. (1998). Anonymous Connections and Onion Routing. IEEE Journal on Selected Areas in Communications, Vol 16, No 4, pp. 482-494, May 1998.

47. Ren, K.; Yu, S.; Lou, W. & Zhang, Y. (2010). PEACE: A Novel Privacy-Enhanced Yet Accountable Security Framework for Metropolitan Wireless Mesh Networks. IEEE Transactions on Parallel and Distributed Systems, Vol 21, No 2, pp. 203–215, February 2010.

48. Rigney, C.; Willens, S.; Rubins, A. & Simpson, W. (2000). Remote Authentication Dial in User Service (RADIUS), RFC 2865, June 2000.

49. Rivest, R.; Shamir, A. & Tauman, Y. (2001). How to Leak a Secret. Proceedings of the 7th International Conference on the Theory and Applications of Cryptology and Information Security: Advances in Security (ASIACRPT'01). Lecture Notes in Computer Science, Vol 2248, pp. 552-565, Boyd, C. (ed.), Springer, Heidelberg, December 2001.

50. Sen, J.; Chowdhury, P. R. & Sengupta, I. (2006). Proceedings of the International Symposium on Ad Hoc and Ubiquitous Computing (ISAHUC'06), pp. 62-67, Surathkal, Mangalore, India, December, 2006.

51. Sen, J. & Subramanyam, H. (2007). An Efficient Certificate Authority for Ad Hoc Networks. Proceedings of the 4th International Conference on Distributed Computing and Internet Technology (ICDCIT'07), Bangalore, India, December 2007. Lecture Notes in Computer Science, Janowski & Mohanty (eds.), Vol 4882, pp. 97-109, 2007.

52. Sen, J. (2009). A Survey on Wireless Sensor Network Security. International Journal of Communication Networks and Information Security (IJCNIS), Vol 1, No2, pp. 59-82, August 2009.

53. Sen, J. (2010a). A Distributed Trust and Reputation Framework for Mobile Ad Hoc Networks. Recent Trends in Network Security and its Applications, Meghanathan et al. (eds.), pp. 528–537, Communications in Computer and Information Science (CCIS), Springer- Verlag, Heidelberg, Germany, July 2010.

54. Sen, J. (2010b). Reputation- and Trust-Based Systems for Wireless Self-Organizing Networks, pp. 91-122. Security of Self-Organizing Networks: MANET, WSN, WMN, VANET, A-S. K. Pathan (ed.), Aurbach Publications, CRC Press, USA, December 2010.

55. Sen, J. (2010c). A Robust and Efficient Node Authentication Protocol for Mobile Ad Hoc Networks. Proceedings of the 2nd International Conference on Computational Intelligence, Modelling and Simulation (CIMSiM'10), pp. 476-481, Bali, Indonesia, September 2010.

56. Sen, J. (2011). Secure Routing in Wireless Mesh Networks, pp. 237-280. Wireless Mesh Networks, Nobuo Funabiki (ed.), InTech, Croatia, January 2011.

57. Shamir, A. (1984). Identity-Based Cryptosystems and Signature Schemes. Proceedings of the International Cryptology Conference (CRYPTO'84). Lecture Notes in Computer Science, Vol. 196, pp. 47–53, Springer-Verlag, Berlin, Germany, August 1984.

58. Soltwisch, R.; Fu, X.; Hogrefe, D. & Narayanan, S. (2004). A Method for Authentication and Key Exchange for Seamless Inter-Domain Handovers. Proceedings of the 12th IEEE International Conference on Networks (ICON '04), pp. 463–469, Singapore, November 2004.

59. Sun, J.; Zhang, C. & Fang, Y. (2008). A Security Architecture Achieving Anonymity and Traceability in Wireless Mesh Networks. Proceedings of the 27th IEEE International Conference on Computer Communications (IEEE INFOCOM'08), pp. 1687–1695, April 2008.

60. Sun, J.; Zhang, C. ; Zhang, Y. & Fang, Y. (2011). SAT: A Security Architecture Achieving Anonymity and Traceability in Wireless Mesh Networks. IEEE Transactions on Dependable and Secure Computing, Vol 8, No 2, pp. 295–307, March 2011.

61. Wei, K.; Chen, Y. R.; Smith, A. J. & Vo, B. (2006). WhoPay: A Scalable and Anonymous Payment system for Peer-to-Peer Environments. Proceedings of the 26th IEEE International Conference on Distributed Computing Systems (ICDCS'06), July 2006.

62. Wood, A. D. & Stankovic, J. A. (2002). Denial of Service in Sensor Networks. IEEE Computer, Vol 35, No. 10, pp. 54–62, October 2002.

63. Wu, T.; Xue, Y. & Cui, Y. (2006). Preserving Traffic Privacy in Wireless Mesh Networks. Proceedings of the International Symposium on a World of Wireless, Mobile and Multimedia Networks (WoWMoM'06), pp. 459-461, Buffalo-Niagara Falls, NY, USA, June 2006.

64. Wu, X. & Li, N. (2006). Achieving Privacy in Mesh Networks. Proceedings of the 4th ACM Workshop on Security of Ad Hoc and Sensor Networks (SASN), pp. 13-22, October 2006.

65. Xiong, H.; Beznosov, K.; Qin, Z. & Ripeanu, M. (2010). Efficient and Spontaneous PrivacyPreserving Protocol for Secure Vehicular Communication. Proceedings of IEEE International Conference on Communications (ICC'10), pp. 1-6, Cape Town, South Africa, May 2010.

66. Yi, P.; Wu, Y.; Zou, F. & Liu, N. (2010). A Survey on Security in Wireless Mesh Networks. IETE Technical Review, Vol 27, No 1, pp. 6-14.

67. Zhang, Y. & Fang, Y. (2006). ARSA: An Attack-Resilient Security Architecture for Multihop Wireless Mesh Networks. IEEE Journal of Selected Areas in Communication, Vol. 24, No. 10, pp. 1916–1928, October 2006.

68. Zhang, Y.; Liu, W.; Lou, W. & Fang, Y. (2006). MASK: Anonymous On-demand Routing in Mobile Ad Hoc Networks. IEEE Transactions on Wireless Communications, Vol. 5. No. 9, pp. 2376–2385, September 2006.

69. Zheng, X.; Chen, C.; Huang, C.-T.; Matthews, M. & Santhapuri, N. (2005). A Dual Authentication Protocol for IEEE 802.11 Wireless LANs. Proceedings of the 2nd IEEE International Symposium on Wireless Communication Systems, pp. 565–569, September 2005.

70. Zhu, S.; Xu, S.; Setia, S. & Jajodia, S. (2003). LHAP: A Lightweight Hop-by-Hop Authentication protocol for Ad-hoc Networks. Proceedings of the 23rd IEEE International Conference on Distributed Computing Systems Workshops (ICDCSW'03), pp. 749–755, May 2003.

71. Zhu, S.; Xu, S.; Setia S. & Jajodia, S. (2006). LHAP: A Lightweight Network Access Control Protocol for Ad Hoc Networks. Ad Hoc Networks, Vol 4, No 5, pp. 567-585, September 2006.

72. Zhu, H.; Lin, X.; Lu, R.; Ho, P.-H. & Shen, X. (2008). SLAB: A Secure Localized Authentication and Billing Scheme for Wireless Mesh Networks. IEEE Transactions on Wireless Communications, Vol 7, No. 10, pp. 3858–3868, October 2008.

SECTION II: INTRUSION DETECTION AND PREVENTION

CHAPTER 5 FEATURE SELECTION FOR INTRUSION DETECTION USING RANDOM FOREST

Md. Al Mehedi Hasan, Mohammed Nasser, Shamim Ahmad, Khademul Islam Molla

Keywords: Feature Selection, KDD'99 Dataset, RRE-KDD Dataset, Random Forest, Permuted Importance Measure

INTRODUCTION

The internet and local area networks are growing larger in recent years. As a great variety of people all over the world are connecting to the Internet, they are unconsciously encountering the number of security threats such as viruses, worms and attacks from hackers [1] . Now firewalls, anti-virus software, message encryption, secured network protocols, password protection and so on are not sufficient to assure the security in computer networks, when some intrusions take advantages of weaknesses in computer systems to threaten. Therefore, Intrusion Detection Systems (IDSs) have become a necessary addition to the security infrastructure of most organizations [2] .

Deploying highly effective IDS systems is extremely challenging and has emerged as a significant field of research, because it is not theoretically possible to set up a system with no vulnerabilities [3] . Several machine learning (ML) algorithms, for instance Neural Network [4] , Genetic Algorithm [5] , Support Vector Machine [2] [6] , Clustering Algorithm [7] and more have been extensively employed to detect intrusion activities from large quantity of complex and dynamic datasets.

Current Intrusion Detection Systems (IDS) examine all data features to detect intrusion or misuse patterns [8] . Since the amount of audit data that an IDS needs to examine is very large even for a small network, therefore their analysis is difficult even with computer assistance because extraneous features can make it harder to detect suspicious behavior patterns [8] - [10] . As a result, IDS must reduce the amount of data to be processed. This is very important if a real-time detection is desired. Reduction can be performed by data filtering, data clustering or feature selection. In our work, we investigate feature selection to reduce the amount of data directly handled by the IDS.

Literature survey showed that, most of the researchers used randomly generated records or a portion of record from the KDD'99 dataset to develop feature selection method and to build intrusion detection system [1] [8] [10] [11] without using the whole train and test dataset. Yuehui Chen et al. [8] , Srilatha et al. [10] [11] present a reduced number of features by using a randomly generated dataset containing only 11,982 records [8] [10] [11] , therefore, the number of features reduced to 12 or 17 [10] [11] is in question if the property of whole dataset is considered. So, those findings do not indicate the actual relevant features for classification. Although some researcher use the whole dataset but do not remove redundant records, which implies a limitation of having a chance of redundant record used for the same feature selection and because of that, classification methods may be biased toward to the class that has redundant records [12] . These limitations have motivated us to find out the actual relevant features for classification based on the whole train and test dataset of KDD'99 by removing redundant record.

Feature selection also known as variable selection, feature reduction, attribute selection or variable subset selection, is a widely used dimensionality reduction technique, which has been the focus of much research in machine learning and data mining and has found applications in text classification, web mining, and so on [1] . It allows faster model building by reducing the number of features, and also helps removing irrelevant, redundant and noisy features. This begets simpler and more comprehensible classification models with classification performance. Hence, selecting relevant attributes are a critical

Citation: Hasan, M. , Nasser, M. , Ahmad, S. and Molla, K. (2016) Feature Selection for Intrusion Detection Using Random Forest. Journal of Information Security, 7, 129-140. doi: 10.4236/jis.2016.73009.

issue for competitive classifiers and for data reduction. Feature Selection can fall into two approaches: filter and wrapper [13] . The difference between the filter model and wrapper model is whether feature selection relies on any learning algorithm. The filter model is independent of any learning algorithm, and its advantages lies in better generality and low computational cost [13] . It ranks the features by a metric and eliminates all features that do not achieve an adequate score (selecting only important features). The wrapper model relies on some learning algorithm, and it can expect high classification performance, but it is computationally expensive especially when dealing with large scale data sets [14] like KDDCUP99. It searches for the set of possible features for the optimal subset. In this paper, we adapt Random Forest to rank the features and select a subset feature, which can bring to a successful conclusion of intrusion detection.

Random Forest directly performs feature selection while a classification rule is built. The two commonly used variable importance measures in RF are Gini importance index and permutation importance index (PIM) [15] . In this paper, we have used two steps approach to feature selection. In first step, permutation importance index are used to rank the features and then in second step, Random Forest is used to select the best subset of features for classification. This reduced feature set is then employed to implement an Intrusion Detection System. Our approach results in more accurate detection as well as fast training and testing process.

The remainder of the paper is organized as follows. Section 2 provides the description of KDD'99 dataset. We outline mathematical overview of RF and calculation procedure of variable importance in Section 3. Experimental setup is presented in Section 4 and RF model selection is drawn in Section 5. Measurement of Variable Importance and Variable Selection are discussed in section 6. Finally, Section 7 reports the experimental result followed by conclusion in Section 8.

KDDCUP'99 DATASET

Under the sponsorship of Defense Advanced Research Projects Agency (DARPA) and Air Force Research Laboratory (AFRL), MIT Lincoln Laboratory has collected and distributed the datasets for the evaluation of researches in computer network intrusion detection systems [16] . The KDD'99 dataset is a subset of the DARPA benchmark dataset prepared by Sal Stofo and Wenke Lee [17] . The KDD data set was acquired from raw tcpdump data for a length of nine weeks. It is made up of a large number of network traffic activities that include both normal and malicious connections.

Attack and Feature Description of KDD'99 Dataset

The KDD'99 data set includes three independent sets; "whole KDD", "10% KDD", and "corrected KDD". Most of researchers have used the "10% KDD" and the "corrected KDD" as training and testing set, respectively [18] . The training set contains a total of 22 training attack types and one type for normal. The "corrected KDD" testing set includes an additional 17 types of attack and excludes 2 types (spy, warezclient) of attack from training set, so therefore there are 37 attack types that are included in the testing set, as shown in Table 1 and Table 2. The simulated attacks fall in one of the four categories [2] [18] : 1) Denial of Service Attack (DoS), 2) User to Root Attack (U2R), 3) Remote to Local Attack (R2L), 4) Probing Attack.

A connection in the KDD'99 dataset is represented by 41 features, each of which is in one of the continuous, discrete and symbolic forms, with significantly varying ranges [19] (Table 3). The description of various features is shown in Table 3. In Table 3, C is used to denote continuous and D is used to donate discrete and symbolic type data in the Data Type field.

Inherent Problems and Criticisms against the KDD'99

Statistical analysis on KDD'99 dataset found important issues which highly affects the performance of evaluated systems and results in a very poor evaluation of anomaly detection approaches [20] . The most important deficiency in the KDD data set is the huge number of redundant records. Analyzing KDD train and test sets, Mohbod Tavallaee found that about 78% and 75% of the records are duplicated in the train and test set, respectively [21] . This large amount of redundant records in the train set will cause learning algorithms to be biased towards the more frequent records.

As a result, this biasing prevents the system from learning infrequent records which are usually more harmful to networks such as U2R attacks.

Table 1: Attacks in KDD'99 training dataset

Classification of Attacks	Attack Name
Probing	Port-sweep, IP-sweep, Nmap, Satan
DoS	Neptune, Smurf, Pod, Teardrop, Land, Back
U2R	Buffer-overflow, Load-module, Perl, Rootkit
R2L	Guess-password, Ftp-write, Imap, Phf, Multihop, Spy, Warezclient, Warezmaster

Table 2: Attacks in KDD'99 testing dataset

Classification of Attacks	Attack Name
Probing	Port-sweep, IP-sweep, Nmap, Satan, Saint, Mscan
DoS	Neptune, Smurf, Pod, Teardrop, Land, Back, Apache2,Udpstorm, Processtable, Mail-bomb
U2R	Buffer-overflow, Load-module, Perl, Rootkit, Xterm, Ps, Sqlattack.
R2L	Guess-password, Ftp-write, Imap, Phf, Multihop, Warezmaster, Snmpget attack, Named, Xlock, Xsnoop, Send-mail, Http-tunnel, Worm, Snmp-guess

Table 3: List of Features with their descriptions and data types

S. No	Feature	Description	Data Type	S. No	Feature	Description	Data Type
1	Duration	Duration of the connection.	C	22	Is guest login	1 if the login is a "guest" login; 0 otherwise	D
2	Protocol type	Connection protocol	D	23	Count	Number of connections to the same host as the current connection in the past two seconds	C
3	Service	Destination service	D	24	Srv count	Number of connections to the same service as the current connection in the past two seconds	C
4	Flag	Status flag of the connection	D	25	Serror rate	% of connections that have "SYN" errors	C
5	Source bytes	Bytes sent from source to destination	C	26	Srv serror rate	% of connections that have "SYN" errors	C
6	Destination bytes	Bytes sent from destination to source	C	27	Rerror rate	% of connections that have "REJ" errors	C
7	Land	1 if connection is from/to the same host/port; 0 otherwise	D	28	Srv rerror rate	% of connections that have "REJ" errors	C
8	Wrong fragment	Number of wrong fragments	C	29	Same srv rate	% of connections to the same service	C
9	Urgent	Number of urgent packets	C	30	Diff srv rate	% of connections to different Services	C
10	Hot	Number of "hot" indicators	C	31	Srv diff host rate	% of connections to different hosts	C
11	Failed Login	Logins number of failed logins	C	32	Dst host count	Count of connections having the same destination host	C
12	Logged in	1 if successfully logged in; 0 otherwise	D	33	Dst host srv count	Count of connections having the same destination host and using the same service	C
13	Compromised	Number of "compromised" conditions	C	34	Dst host same srv rate	% of connections having the same destination host and using the same service	C
14	Root shell	1 if root shell is obtained; 0 otherwise	C	35	Dst host diff srv rate	% of different services on the current host	C
15	Su attempted	1 if "su root" command attempted; 0 otherwise	C	36	Dst host same src port rate	% of connections to the current host having the same src port	C
16	Root	Number of "root" accesses	C	37	Dst host srv diff host rate	% of connections to the same service coming from different hosts	C
17	File creations	Number of file creation operations	C	38	Dst host serror rate	% of connections to the current host that have an S0 error	C
18	Shells	Number of shell prompts	C	39	Dst host srv serror rate	% of connections to the current host and specified service that have an S0 error	C
19	Access files	Number of operations on access control files	C	40	Dst host rerror rate	% of connections to the current host that have an RST error	C
20	Outbound cmds	Number of outbound commands in an ftp session	C	41	Dst host srv rerror rate	% of connections to the current host and specified service that have an RST error	C
21	Is hot login	1 if the login belongs to the "hot" list; 0 otherwise	D				

The existence of these repeated records in the test set, on the other hand, will cause the evaluation results to be biased by the methods which have better detection rates on the frequent records.

To solve these issues, we have derived a new data set RRE-KDD by eliminating redundant record from KDD'99 train and test dataset (10% KDD and corrected KDD), so the classifiers will not be biased towards more frequent records. This RRE-KDD dataset consists of KDD99Train+ and KDD99Test+ dataset for training and testing purposes, respectively. The numbers of records in the train and test sets are now reasonable, which makes it affordable to run the experiments on the complete set without the need to randomly select a small portion.

VARIABLE SELECTION AND CLASSIFICATION

Consider the problem of separating the set of training vectors belong to two separate classes, (x_1, y_1), (x_2, y_2), …, (x_n, y_n) where $x_i \in R^p$ and $y_i \in \{-1, +1\}$ is the corresponding class label, $1 \leq i \leq n$. The main task is to find a classifier with a decision function $f(x, \theta)$ such that $y = f(x, \theta)$, where y is the class label for x, θ is a vector of unknown parameters in the function.

Random Forest

The random forest is an ensemble of unpruned classification or regression trees [15] . Random forest generates many classification trees and each tree is constructed by a different bootstrap sample from the original data using a tree classification algorithm. After the forest is formed, a new object that needs to be classified is put down each of the tree in the forest for classification. Each tree gives a vote that indicates the tree's decision about the class of the object. The forest chooses the class with the most votes for the object. The random forests algorithm (for both classification and regression) is as follows [22] [23] :

1) From the Training of n samples draw n_{tree} bootstrap samples.

2) For each of the bootstrap samples, grow classification or regression tree with the following modification: at each node, rather than choosing the best split among all predictors, randomly sample m_{try} of the predictors and choose the best split among those variables. The tree is grown to the maximum size and not pruned back. Bagging can be thought of as the special case of random forests obtained when m_{try} = p, the number of predictors.

3) Predict new data by aggregating the predictions of the n_{tree} trees (i.e., majority votes for classification, average for regression).

There are two ways to evaluate the error rate. One is to split the dataset into training part and test part. We can employ the training part to build the forest, and then use the test part to calculate the error rate. Another way is to use the Out-of-Bag (OOB) error estimate. Because random forests algorithm calculates the OOB error during the training phase, therefore to get OOB error, we do not need to split the training data. In our work, we have used both ways to evaluate the error rate.

There are three tuning parameters of Random Forest: number of trees (n_{tree}), number of descriptors randomly sampled as candidates for splitting at each node (m_{try}) and minimum node size [23] . When the forest is growing, random features are selected at random out of the all features in the training data. The number of features employed in splitting each node for each tree is the primary tuning parameter (m_{try}). To improve the performance of random forests, this parameter should be optimized. The number of trees should only be chosen to be sufficiently large so that the OOB error has stabilized. In many cases, 500 trees are sufficient (more are needed if descriptor's importance or intrinsic proximity is desired). In contrast to other algorithms having a stopping rule, in RF, there is no penalty for having "too many" trees, other than waste in computational resources. Another parameter, minimum node size, determines the minimum size of nodes below which no split will be attempted. This parameter has some effect on the size of the trees grown. In Random Forest, for classification, the default value of minimum node size is 1, ensuring that trees are grown to their maximum size and for regression, the default value is 5 [23] .

Variable Important Measure and Selection Using Random Forest

The high dimensional nature of many tasks in pattern recognition has created an urgent need for feature selection techniques. The goal of feature selection in this field is manifold, where the two most important are: 1) to avoid over fitting and improve model performance, and 2) to gain a deeper insight into the underlying processes that generated the data [24] . The interpretability of machine learning models is treated as important as the prediction accuracy for most life science problems.

Unlike most other classifiers, Random Forest directly performs feature selection while a classification rule is built [25] . The two commonly used variable important measures in RF are Gini importance index and permutation importance index (PIM) [15] . Gini importance index is directly derived from the Gini index when it is used as a node impurity measure. A feature's importance value in a single tree is the sum of the Gini index reduction over all nodes in which the specific feature is used to split. The overall variable importance for a feature in the forest is defined as the summation or the average of its importance value among all trees in the forest. Permutation importance measure (PIM) is arguably the most popular variable's importance measure used in RF. The RF algorithm does not use all training samples in the construction of an individual tree. That leaves a set of out of bag (OOB) samples, which can be used to measure the forest's classification accuracy. In order to measure a specific feature's importance in the tree, randomly shuffle the values of this feature in the OOB samples and compare the classification accuracy between the intact OOB samples and the OOB samples with the particular feature permutated. In this work, we have used permutation importance measure (PIM) and developed two algorithms to measure PIM and select an important subset of feature among all features, as shown in Algorithm 1 and Algorithm 2.

Algorithm 1 (Step One): Measure of Variable Importance

1) Build 50 Random Forest. For each Random Forest, k = 1 to 50, repeat Steps 2 to 4.

2) For each tree t of the k-th Random Forest, Consider the associated OOB_t sample.

3) Denoted by $errOOB_t$ the error of a single tree t on this OOB_t sample.

4) Randomly permute the values of X_j in OOB_t to get a perturbed sample denoted by OOB_t^j After that, compute $errOOB_t$ and the difference of the error between the intact OOB samples and the OOB samples with the permutated feature X_j. Finally, find out permutation importance measure (PIM) for the permuted feature X_j using the following equation:

$$PIM_k\left(X^j\right)=\frac{1}{n_{tree}}\sum_t\left(errOOB_t^j-errOOB_t\right)$$

5) Find out the average permutation importance measure (APIM) of each variables from the 50 Random Forest using following equation

$$APIM\left(X^j\right)=\frac{1}{50}\sum_{k=1}^{50}PIM_k\left(X^j\right)$$

Algorithm 2 (Step Two): Variable Selection:

1) Rank the variables by sorting the APIM score (averaged from the 50 runs of RF using Algorithm 1) in descending order.

2) Perform a sequential variable introduction with testing: a variable is added only if the error gain exceeds a threshold. The variables of the last model are selected.

DATASET AND EXPERIMENTAL SETUP

Investigating the existing papers on the feature selection and anomaly detection which have used the KDD data set, we found that a subset of KDD'99 dataset has been used for training, testing and selecting feature instead of using the whole KDD'99 dataset [1] [8] [10] [11] . Existing papers on the feature selection and anomaly detection mainly used two common approaches to apply KDD'99 [21] . In the first, KDD'99 training portion is employed for sampling both the train and test sets. However, in the second approach, the training samples are randomly collected from the KDD train set, while the samples for testing are arbitrarily selected from the KDD'99 test set. The basic characteristics of the original KDD'99 and RRE-KDD (KDD'99Train+ and KDD99Test+) intrusion detection datasets in terms of number of samples is given in Table 4. Although the distribution of the number of samples of attack is different on different research papers, in our previous work, we have found out the distribution of attack given in Table 4 [2] [6] . In our experiment, whole train (KDD99Train+) dataset has been used to train our classifier and the test (KDD99Test+) set has been used to test the classifier. All experiments were performed using Intel core i52.27 GHz processor with 4 GB RAM, running Windows 7.

To select the best model in model selection phase, we have drawn 10% samples from the training set (KDDTrain+) to tune the parameters of all kernel and another 10% samples from the training set (KDDTrain+) to validate those parameters, as shown in Table 4.

MODEL SELECTION OF RF

In order to generate highly performing classifiers capable of dealing with real data an efficient model selection is required. In this section, we present the experiments conducted to find efficient model for RF. To improve the detection rate, we optimize the number of the random features (m_{try}) which is used to build the RF. We build the forest with different m_{try} (5, 6, 7, 10, 15, 20, 25, 30, 35, and 38) over the train set (TrainSet) with keeping n_{tree} = 100, then plot the OOB error rate and the time required to build the classifier RF versus different values of m_{try}. As Figure 1 shows, the OOB error rate reaches its minimum when the value of m_{try} is 7. Besides this, it is obvious that increasing in m_{try} increases the time required to build the classifier. Thus, we choose the value of m_{try} = 7 as the optimal value, which reaches at the minimum value of the OOB error rate and does cost moderately the least time among these values.

There are two other parameters in Random Forest: number of trees and minimum node size. In order to find out the value of the number of trees of (n_{tree}) Random Forest, we use TrainSet and ValidationSet for training and testing, respectively and then compare the OOB error rate and train error rate with the independent test set (ValidationSet) error rate as shown in Figure 2. The plot shows that the OOB error rate follows the test set error rate fairly and closely, when the number tress are more than 100, therefore sufficient number of tree is found around 100. In addition to it,Figure 2 also shows an interesting phenomenon which is the characteristic of Random Forest: the test and OOB error rates do not increase after the training error reaches zero; instead they converge to their "asymptotic" values, which is close to their minimum.

Table 4: Number of samples of each attack in dataset

Dataset	Various Independent Sets	Normal	DoS	Probing	R2L	U2R	Total
Original KDD'99 Dataset	WholeKDD	972,780	3,883,370	41,102	1126	52	4,898,430
	10% KDD	97,278	391,458	4107	1126	52	494,021
	KDD corrected	60,593	229,853	4166	16,347	70	311,029
RRE-KDD Dataset	KDD99Train+	87,832	54,572	2130	999	52	145,585
	KDD99Test+	47,913	23,568	2678	3058	70	77,287
	Train Set (For Model Selection)	8784	5458	213	100	6	14,561
	Validation Set (For Model Selection)	8784	5458	213	100	6	14,561

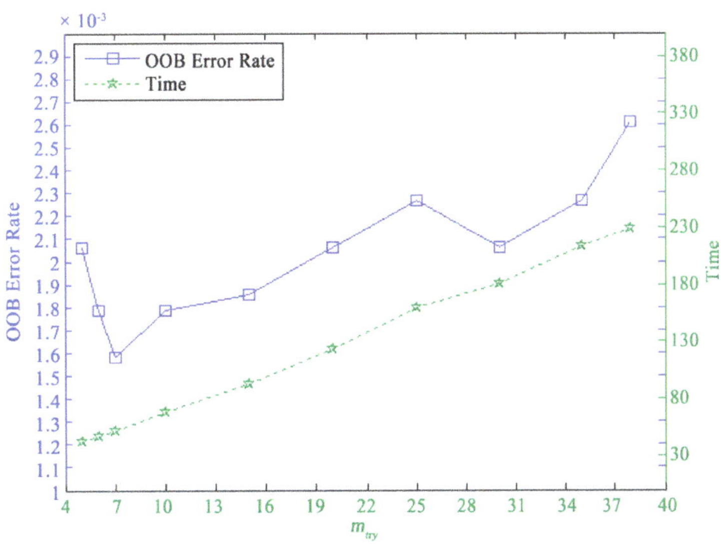

Figure 1: OOB error rates and required time to train for random forest vs the number of m_{try}.

To determine the minimum node size, we use TrainSet for training and compare the OOB error rate with varying the number of node size with keeping $n_{tree} = 100$ and $m_{try} = 7$, as shown in Figure 3. The plot shows that default value 1 (one) for classification gives the lowest OOB error rate.

MEASURE OF VARIABLE IMPORTANCE AND VARIABLE SECTION

We run the Algorithm 1 to find out the APIM score of each feature and, also to analyze the feature relevancy in the training set. To run the Algorithm 1 (step one), we use the whole train dataset (KDD99Train+) with the value of $n_{tree} = 100$ and $m_{try} = 7$ those have been found in Section 5.Table 5 shows the details of the importance of each feature based their APIM score. The feature having higher APIM score is ranked high as shown in Table 5.

After getting the sorted 41 features according to the APIM score, we run Algorithm 2 to select the best subset among 41 features. For every subset according to sorted order,, the whole train dataset (KDD99Train+) are used for RF and finally, we test the model by using the test dataset (KDD99Test+). As shown in Figure 4, where the test error rates for each of the subset selected from the sorted 41 variables are calculated for various choices of m_{try} and a fixed choice of $n_{tree} = 100$. The four different choices of m_{try} those we examined here are m_{try} = P, P/2, P/4, and $P^{1/2}$, where the value of P is the number of features for each subset.

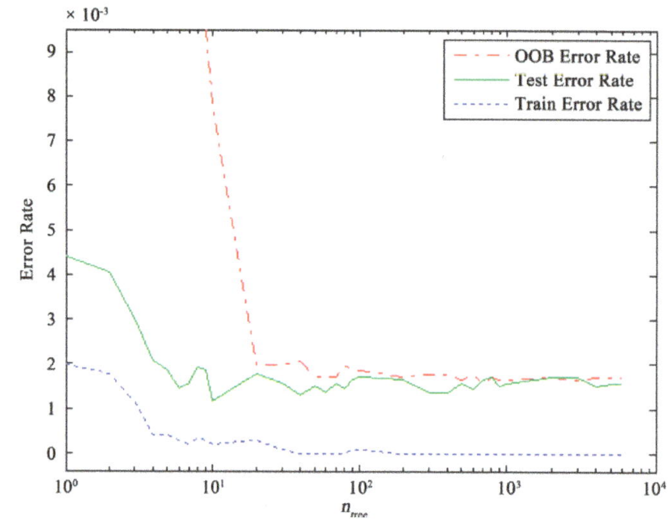

Figure 2: Comparison of training, Out-of-Bag, and independent test set error rates for random forest vs the number of trees.

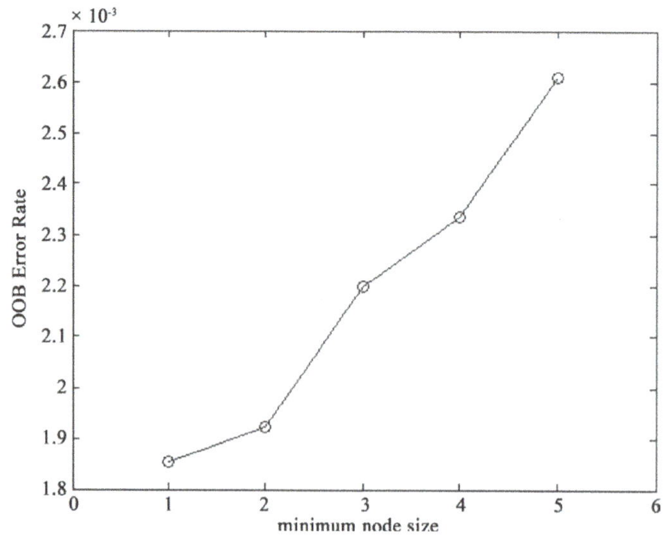

Figure 3: OOB error rates for random forest vs the number of minimum node size.

Table 5: APIM scores are sorted for all the 41 features

S. No	Name of Feature	APIM	S. No	Name of Feature	APIM
8	Wrong fragment	1.796	34	Dst host same srv rate	0.575
10	Hot	1.377	35	Dst host diff srv rate	0.574
5	Source bytes	1.203	30	Diff srv rate	0.563
3	Service	1.194	38	Dst host serror rate	0.542
2	Protocol type	1.069	39	Dst host srv serror rate	0.529
23	Count	1.034	33	Dst host srv count	0.483
36	Dst host same src port rate	1.019	19	Access files	0.454
32	Dst host count	1.006	18	Shell	0.441
4	Flag	0.946	41	Dst host srv rerror rate	0.428
24	Srv count	0.915	25	Serror rate	0.419
22	Is guest login	0.897	31	Srv diff host rate	0.416
14	Root Shell	0.858	16	Root	0.412
6	Destination Bytes	0.833	7	Land	0.385
13	Compromised	0.754	17	File Creations	0.375
11	Failed logins	0.664	28	Srv rerror rate	0.371
29	Same srv rate	0.660	26	Srv serror rate	0.358
40	Dst host rerror rate	0.649	9	Urgent	0.337
1	Duration	0.639	15	Su attempted	0.103
37	Dst host srv diff	0.616	20	Outbound cmds	0
12	Logged in	0.586	21	Is hot login	0
27	Rerror rate	0.579			

From Figure 4, it is clear that the test error rate remains roughly constant, if, at least, 25 descriptors are considered, however, this figures also shows that consideration of descriptors more than 25 do not have significant effect on test error rate. Therefore, in our work, we select 25 variables which are listed in Table 6. Besides this, it is observed that the performance of various m_{try}, the default (sqrt(P)) one is usually the best, and bagging is the worst. Although, the default value of m_{try} is doing better, we again tune m_{try} for newly selected 25 variables by following the approach described in section 5 and we got the best performance at m_{try} = 8 and got the value of n_{tree} = 100.

Finally, we take m_{try} = 8 and n_{tree} = 100 for the selected 25 variables to train the whole train dataset (KDD99 Train+) as well as test the test dataset (KDD99Test+).

RESULTS AND DISCUSSION

The final training/test phase is concerned with the development and evaluation on a test set of the final RF model that is created based on the optimal hyper-parameters set found so far from the model selection phase [26] . After getting the parameters of RF with 41 features and selected 25 features as described in section 5 and 6 respectively, we build the model by using the whole train dataset (KDD99Train+) for the RF classifier and finally, we test the model by using the test dataset (KDD99Test+). The training and testing results are given in Table 7 according to the classification accuracy. From this Table 7, it is observed that the test accuracy for RF with 25 features is better than RF classifier with 41 variables. It is expected that reducing feature requires less time to train than to train with the whole feature, in our case, RF with 25 variables took less time than RF with 41 variables.

For the test case, the confusion matrix for each of the classifier is given in Table 8 and Table 9respectively.

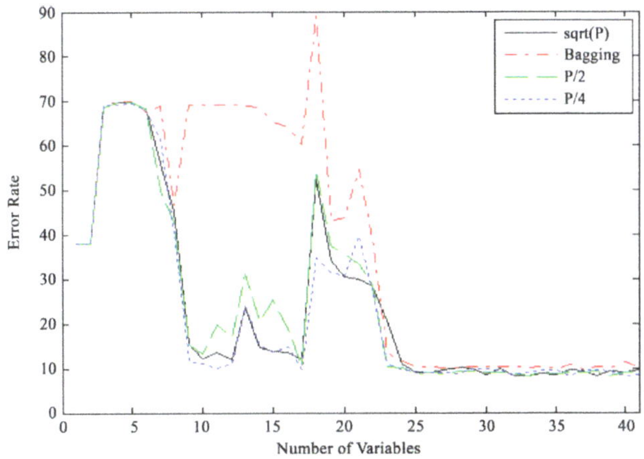

Figure 4: Test error rates versus the number of important variables, using different m_{try}.

Table 6: Selected 25 variables according to the APIM score

Selected Feature According to Serial Number
1, 2, 3, 4, 5, 6, 8, 10, 11, 12, 13, 14, 22, 23, 24, 27, 29, 30, 32, 34, 35, 36, 37, 38, 40

Table 7: Training and testing accuracy

Classifier	Training Accuracy	Testing Accuracy	Train Time (min)
RF with 41 Features	100	91.41	10.62
RF with 25 Features	100	91.90	7.98

Table 8: Confusion matrix for random forest with 41 variables

		Actual					
		Dos	Normal	Probing	R2L	U2R	%
Prediction	Dos	21795	55	185	0	0	98.91
	Normal	1609	46585	231	2649	67	91.09
	Probing	164	1272	2262	405	1	55.12
	R2L	0	1	0	4	1	66.67
	U2R	0	0	0	0	1	100
	%	92.48	97.22	84.47	0.13	1.43	

Table 9: Confusion matrix for random forest with 25 variables

		Actual					
	Dos	Normal	Probing		R2L	U2R	%
Prediction	Dos	22196	56	181	0	0	98.94
	Normal	1145	46424	213	2681	63	91.88
	Probing	227	1344	2284	258	0	55.53
	R2L	0	60	0	119	1	66.11
	U2R	0	29	0	0	6	17.14
	%	94.18	96.89	85.29	3.89	8.57	

Table 10: False positive rate (%) of random forest for each of the attack types including normal

Classifier	Dos	Normal	Probing	R2L	U2R	Average False Positive Rate
RF with 41 Variables	7.52	2.77	15.53	99.87	98.57	44.85
RF with 25 Variables	5.82	3.1	14.71	96.11	91.43	42.23

Table 11: Precision (%) of random forest for each of the attack types including normal

Classifier	Dos	Normal	Probing	R2L	U2R	Average Precision
RF with 41 Variables	98.91	91.09	55.11	66.67	100	82.36
RF with 25 Variables	98.94	91.88	55.53	66.11	17.14	65.92

Going into more detail of the confusion matrix, it can be seen that RF with 25 variables performs better on all types of attack detection.

We also consider the false positive rate and precision for each of classifier and these are shown inTable 10 and Table 11, respectively. The RF with 41 variables gives high precision and on the other hand RF with 25 variables gives lower false positive rate.

CONCLUSION

In this paper, we presented a Random Forest model for Intrusion Detection Systems (IDS) with a focus on improving the intrusion detection performance by reducing the input features. From the context of real-world applications, smaller numbers of features are always advantageous in terms of both data management and processing time. The obtained results indicate that the ability of the RF classification with reduced features (25 features) produces more accurate result than that of found from Random Forest classification with all features (41 features). Moreover, time required to process 25 features with RF is smaller than the processing time of RF with 41 features. The research in intrusion detection and feature selection using RF approach is still an ongoing area due to its good performance. The findings of this paper will be very useful for research on feature selection and classification. These findings can also be applied to use RF in more meaningful way in order to maximize the performance rate and minimize the false positive rate.

REFERENCES

1. Suebsing, A. and Hiransakolwong, N. (2011) Euclidean-Based Feature Selection for Network Intrusion Detection. International Conference on Machine Learning and Computing, 3, 222-229.
2. Hasan, M.A.M., Nasser, M. and Pal, B. (2013) On the KDD'99 Dataset: Support Vector Machine Based

Intrusion Detection System (IDS) with Different Kernels. IJECCE, 4, 1164-1170.

3. Adebayo, O.A., Shi, Z., Shi, Z. and Adewale, O.S. (2006) Network Anomalous Intrusion Detection Using Fuzzy-Bayes. Intelligent Information Processing III, 525-530.

4. Cannady, J. (1998) Artificial Neural Networks for Misuse Detection. National Information Systems Security Conference, 368-381.

5. Pal, B. & Hasan, M.A.M. (2012) Neural Network & Genetic Algorithm Based Approach to Network Intrusion Detection & Comparative Analysis of Performance. 15th International Conference on Computer and Information Technology (ICCIT), Chittagong, 22-24 December 2012, 150-154. http://dx.doi.org/10.1109/iccitechn.2012.6509809

6. Hasan, M.A.M., Nasser, M., Pal, B. and Ahmad, S. (2014) Support Vector Machine and Random Forest Modeling for Intrusion Detection System (IDS). Journal of Intelligent Learning Systems and Applications, 6, 45. http://dx.doi.org/10.4236/jilsa.2014.61005

7. Wang, Q. and Megalooikonomou, V. (2005) A Clustering Algorithm for Intrusion Detection. Defense and Security, International Society for Optics and Photonics, 31-38.

8. Chen, Y., Abraham, A. and Yang, J. (2005) Feature Selection and Intrusion Detection Using Hybrid Flexible Neural tree. Advances in Neural Networks—ISNN 2005, 3498, 439-444. http://dx.doi.org/10.1007/11427469_71

9. Lee, W., Stolfo, S.J. and Mok, K.W. (1999) A Data Mining Framework for Building Intrusion Detection Models. Proceedings of the 1999 IEEE Symposium on Security and Privacy, 120-132.

10. Chebrolu, S., Abraham, A. and Thomas, J.P. (2004) Hybrid Feature Selection for Modeling Intrusion Detection Systems. Neural Information Processing, 3316, 1020-1025. http://dx.doi.org/10.1007/978-3-540-30499-9_158

11. Chebrolu, S., Abraham, A. and Thomas, J.P. (2005) Feature Deduction and Ensemble Design of Intrusion Detection Systems. Computers & Security, 24, 295-307. http://dx.doi.org/10.1016/j.cose.2004.09.008

12. Takkellapati, V.S. & Prasad, G.V.S.N.R.V. (2012) Network Intrusion Detection System Based on Feature Selection and Triangle Area Support Vector Machine. International Journal of Engineering Trends and Technology, 3, 466-470.

13. Chou, T.S., Yen, K.K. and Luo, J. (2008) Network Intrusion Detection Design Using Feature Selection of Soft Computing Paradigms. International Journal of Computational Intelligence, 4, 196-208.

14. Lee, W., Stolfo, S.J. and Mok, K.W. (2000) Adaptive Intrusion Detection: A Data Mining Approach. Artificial Intelligence Review, 14, 533-567. http://dx.doi.org/10.1023/A:1006624031083

15. Breiman, L. (2001) Random Forests. Machine learning, 45, 5-32. http://dx.doi.org/10.1023/A:1010933404324

16. (2010) MIT Lincoln Laboratory, DARPA Intrusion Detection Evaluation. https://www.ll.mit.edu/ideval/data/

17. (2010) KDD'99 Dataset. http://kdd.ics.uci.edu/databases

18. Bahrololum, M., Salahi, E. and Khaleghi, M. (2009) Anomaly Intrusion Detection Design Using Hybrid of Unsupervised and Supervised Neural Network. International Journal of Computer Networks & Communications (IJCNC), 1, 26-33.

19. Singh, S. and Silakari, S. (2009) An Ensemble Approach for Feature Selection of Cyber Attack Dataset. arXiv preprint arXiv:0912.1014.

20. Eid, H.F., Darwish, A., Hassanien, A.E. and Abraham, A. (2010) Principle Components Analysis and Support Vector Machine Based Intrusion Detection System. 10th International Conference on Intelligent Systems Design and Applications (ISDA), 363-367.

21. Tavallaee, M., Bagheri, E., Lu, W. and Ghorbani, A.A. (2009) A Detailed Analysis of the KDD CUP 99 Data Set. Proceedings of the Second IEEE Symposium on Computational Intelligence for Security and Defence Applications 2009, Ottawa, 8-10 July 2009, 1-6. http://dx.doi.org/10.1109/CISDA.2009.5356528

22. Liaw, A. and Wiener, M. (2002) Classification and Regression by Random Forest. R News, 2, 18-22.

23. Svetnik, V., Liaw, A., Tong, C., Culberson, J.C., Sheridan, R.P. and Feuston, B.P. (2003) Random Forest: A Classification and Regression Tool for Compound Classification and QSAR Modeling. Journal of Chemical Information and Computer Sciences, 43, 1947-1958. http://dx.doi.org/10.1021/ci034160g

24. Sandri, M. and Zuccolotto, P. (2006) Variable Selection Using Random Forests. In: Zani, S., Cerioli, A., Riani, M. and Vichi, M., Ed., Data Analysis, Classification and the Forward Search, Springer, Berlin Heidelberg, 263-270. http://dx.doi.org/10.1007/3-540-35978-8_30

25. Qi, Y. (2012) Random Forest for Bioinformatics. In: Zhang, C. and Ma, Y.Q. Ed., Ensemble Machine Learning, Springer, US, 307-323. http://dx.doi.org/10.1007/978-1-4419-9326-7_11

26. Yao, J., Zhao, S. and Fan, L. (2006) An Enhanced Support Vector Machine Model for Intrusion Detection. Rough Sets and Knowledge Technology, 4062, 538-543. http://dx.doi.org/10.1007/11795131_78

CHAPTER 6

MOBILE PHISHING ATTACKS AND MITIGATION TECHNIQUES

Hossain Shahriar, Tulin Klintic, Victor Clincy

Keywords: Mobile Application, Phishing, Smishing, Vishing

INTRODUCTION

Mobile phishing is an emerging threat in today's connected world. In a mobile phishing attack, an attacker usually sends an SMS message containing links to phishing web pages or applications which, if visited, ask for credential information [1] . Attacks can also be initiated via email messages loaded in the browser of mobile devices.

A report finds that the number of mobile phishing attacks has been increasing over the last few years for various mobile device platforms [2] . For example, the number of unique phishing attempts blocked by Microsoft Windows Phone 8 devices doubled from February to June 2013, and the volume of phishing attempts and online phishing websites doubled in the first half of 2013.

Compared with traditional desktop software users, mobile application users are more vulnerable to phishing attacks (at least three times [3]). Experts agree on some of the common, well-known reasons for this vulnerability:

1) Within a small devise, it is rather difficult for a user to check whether a page is legitimate, as is confirming the actual pointed hyperlinks, as URLs are not often displayed within mobile browsers.
2) Mobile users are less aware of security options to stop or prevent phishing attacks.
3) Most legitimate mobile applications require users to enter their credentials with very simple user interfaces, making the job of an attacker rather easy to come up with fake apps or plain websites mimicking legitimate user interfaces.
4) Surveys find that 40% of mobile application users enter passwords into their phones at least once.

The information provided by victims is harvested by attackers within the first 60 minutes. A phishing campaign typically takes at least one hour to be identified by IT security administrators before it can take down the phishing site (this is described as the "golden hour") [4] . Phishing attacks target commonly popular financial organizations. A survey found that 71% of phishing attacks were related to spoofed financial organizations, compared with 67% in 2012. Phishing attacks on organizations in the Information Services sector accounted for 22% of phishing attacks in 2013 [5] .

The scope of phishing attacks is vast, and the consequences can be severe. On the other hand, there is limited knowledge among users on how to avoid phishing attacks. Symantec's Norton Report shows that 44% of adults are unaware that security solutions exist for mobile devices. This clearly shows not only the lack of awareness, but also the danger posed by mobile application phishing attacks [5] .

A phishing (or fraudulent) mobile application potentially can grab victim's account information and data stored on mobile devices [6] . Recently, Google pulled 50 applications from its Android Market app store in response to concerns that they may be malicious. All the apps were uploaded by the same developer and claimed to offer access to bank accounts from a wide variety of institutions such as J. P. Morgan Chase, HSBC, USAA and ING Group. As Google's Android Market relies on its community to flag fraudulent applications, the likelihood of being vulnerable to mobile phishing attacks via fraudulent Android application is more likely than in Apple applications [6] . Given that it is important to be aware of various avenues of mobile phishing attacks and mitigation approaches for Android applications. In this paper, we describe various types

Citation: Shahriar, H. , Klintic, T. and Clincy, V. (2015) Mobile Phishing Attacks and Mitigation Techniques. Journal of Information Security, 6, 206-212. doi: 10.4236/jis.2015.63021.

of mobile phishing attacks. We also discuss some mitigation approaches and best practices to avoid phishing attacks and future research directions. The work is intended to bring more awareness among mobile application users.

The paper is organized as follows. Section 2 discusses various techniques for phishing attacks. In Section 3, some mitigation approaches are discussed. Finally, Section 4 draws the conclusions and discusses future work.

MOBILE PHISHING ATTACK TECHNIQUES

Small Screen and Partial Display of URLs

Mobile devices and smart phones mostly have a small screen. Those small screens make it harder to see the full URLs when users click to the links. Also, the companies keep their mobile web sites simple to be able to use the small screen more efficiently. Moreover, some of them cannot even put their own logo due to limited screen size. Therefore, many users are not aware when they are not at official web sites while browsing on the Internet.

When a fake site URL and a legitimate site URL are compared, the differences in URL can be hidden due to small size of the screen and URL bar. Figure 1 shows a sample of fake PayPal page (left[1]) and its URL address compared to the legitimate one (right[2]) [7] . While legitimate address has secure protocol, HTTPS, the fake site does not. In addition, the fake page has some additional text which may not be visible at all to users at some browsers. Besides the URL address, the fake-site does not display the original PayPal logo. In addition, they pull the attention to the other images to trick the users.

Accessibility to App Store

Another channel to reach to the end users is via application stores, called application phishing. Android 09Droid phishing application is one good example that was intended to gather users' banking credentials [8] . It has been reported that the 09Droid phishing application was uploaded to potential victims through the Android market app store, where most of the other apps are legitimate. Figure 2 shows a snapshot of a set of fake mobile banking applications uploaded in Android marketplace (the picture taken from a mobile device) with pricing information. Note that the targeted companies are mostly from North America, and the pricing was in GBP, leaving the prospective North American customers in the dark.

It is unknown what the application performed behind the scene. However, it opens a login web page. It is likely that the application's goal was to steal user credentials. Banking apps that were developed by 09Droid have been pulled from Android market ever since. The targeted companies include Sun Trust, Chase, Wachovia, Bank of America, and Wells Fargo [8] .

Phishing attacks are applicable for Apple app that runs on iPad and may have larger screen size. Marble Security implemented a fake iTunes App to show how phishing works on an iOS iPad. First, a phishing email is sent to users informing them they need to install a "mandatory" SpamArrest page and enter university credentials (see Figure 3 for an example of email) [9] .

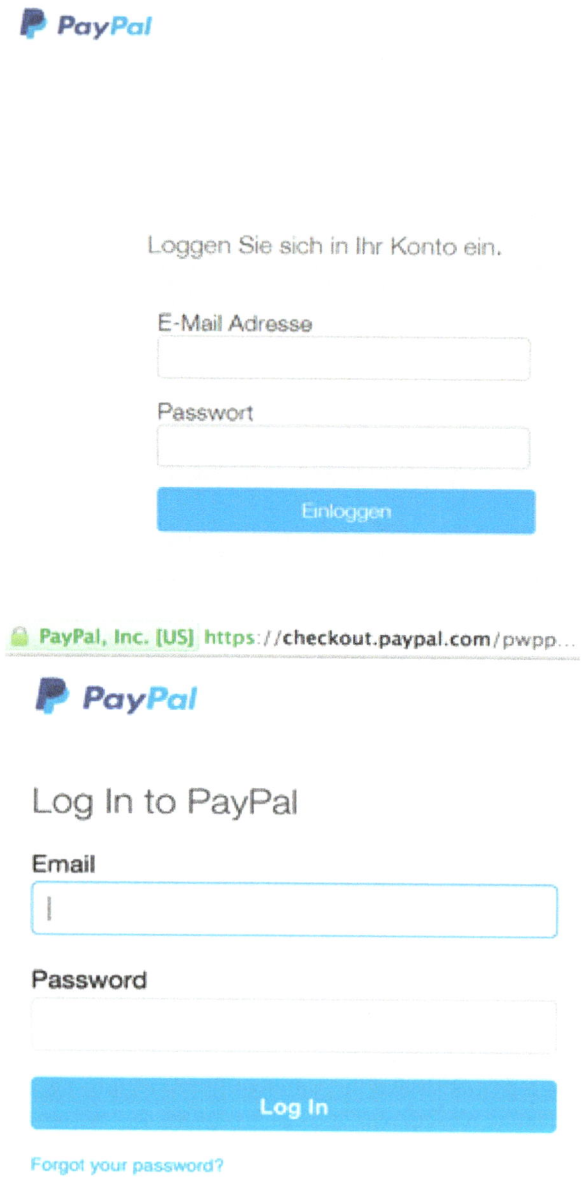

Figure 1: Fake paypal web page and URL (left) vs. real paypal web page and URL (right).

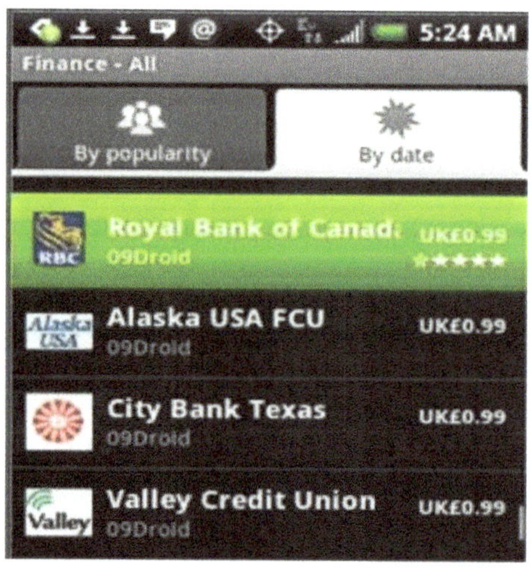

Figure 2: Screenshot of 09Droid banking applications with price information uploaded to Android App market.

Once the user follows the instruction, believing that it is legitimate, the application sets a new user profile. iOS allows applications to create unsigned and unverified profiles (as shown in Figure 4). Then, a user enters the password of the device if it has been set earlier. The last step is to delete the original iTunes app, and install the new fake one (see Figure 5). At this point, the fake iTunes app can be used to steal login credentials to the iTunes store easily.

Smishing

Another popular phishing method is using SMS messages; this method is called "smishing" [10] . It works the same way as phishing, but instead of an email, a victim receives a text message that asks for banking credentials or to claim a prize.

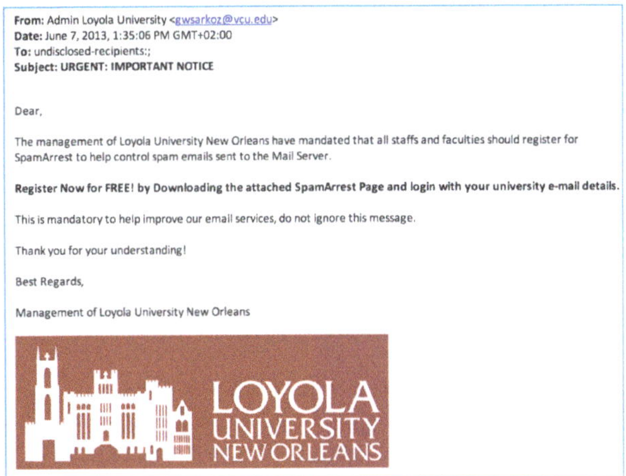

From: Admin Loyola University <gwsarkoz@vcu.edu>
Date: June 7, 2013, 1:35:06 PM GMT+02:00
To: undisclosed-recipients:;
Subject: URGENT: IMPORTANT NOTICE

Dear,

The management of Loyola University New Orleans have mandated that all staffs and faculties should register for SpamArrest to help control spam emails sent to the Mail Server.

Register Now for FREE! by Downloading the attached SpamArrest Page and login with your university e-mail details.

This is mandatory to help improve our email services, do not ignore this message.

Thank you for your understanding!

Best Regards,

Management of Loyola University New Orleans

LOYOLA UNIVERSITY NEW ORLEANS

Figure 3: Screenshot of a phishing email targeting university employees.

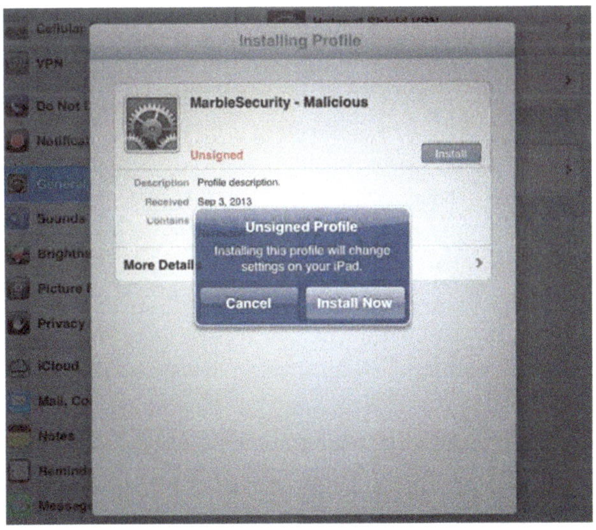

Figure 4: Screenshot of iOS allowing unsigned and unverified profile.

Once the user receives the smishing message from a phone number, it is recommended to inform the cell phone carrier. If the number presents as 5000, it means it has been sent from an email instead of a cell phone. Figure 6 shows a snapshot of a smishing attack where a spoofed link is provided as part of SMS with an alluring message to a potential victim (winning a lottery).

Figure 5: Original iTunes app removed and fake iTunes app installed.

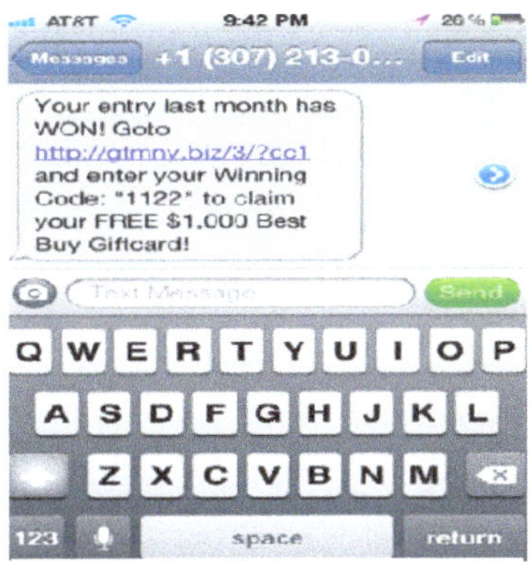

Figure 6: Screenshot of smishing.

Wi-Fi and Vishing

Wi-Fi phishing occurs when a user connects to the Internet via Wi-Fi hotspots. Evil twin is an example where attackers set up a Wi-Fi to eavesdrop on wireless communications where there is a legitimate Wi-Fi hotspot, such as at a Starbucks [12] .

Vishing, voice mail phishing, is a phishing attack on mobile devices into Bluetooth phishing or Voice over IP phishing to reach users' identification or financial information [11] . Other vishing schemes may play a message about a local or regional bank in the area by recording the greeting message of a real bank. Scammers attempt to greet victims and lure them into providing credentials for online banking [12] .

MITIGATION APPROACHES AND BEST PRACTICES

Mitigation Approaches

Common phishing detection systems for mobile devices include content-based filtering, blacklisting, and whitelisting [11] . We discuss them below briefly. We also show the extent to which they can be applied to detect smishing, vishing, and Wi-Fi attacks.

Content Based Filtering: In this technique, content is examined for suspected URLs and matches the context of the URLs [13] - [16] . The approach supplements traditional spam filtering techniques. Content-Based filtering can be performed based on a set of rules or based on identifying statistical differences between benign and suspected phishing contents. It can effectively detect smishing, vishing, and Wi-Fi phishing attacks.

Blacklisting: In this approach, based on human verification, a set of websites is explicitly listed as known phishing URLs [17] . This approach leads to very low false positive rates and is currently supported by various browsers that communicate with trusted servers to obtain a list of blacklisted URLs. Though this approach can possibly identify suspected websites, it may not be able to detect smishing, vishing, and Wi-Fi phishing attacks.

Whitelisting: In this method, users specify websites they trust and access frequently so that other websites are examined for suspected phishing attacks. The approach can be applied to detect smishing where a set of legitimate numbers can be provided to stop receiving unwanted SMS containing fake web addresses [15] .

Best Practices

Although it is hard to detect fake mobile applications, there are several methods to reduce phishing attacks on mobile devices.

- Using official apps: Users should only download official apps from the app stores.
- User training: User training is very important to prevent users clicking unknown links.
- Safer browsers: Browsers with security features installed (such as Chrome mobile) eliminates malware and phishing sites to protect users.
- Bookmarks: Bookmarks eliminate typos when typing URLs. Since it is hard to see the URL bar completely, bookmarking is a good solution to eliminate landing on unwanted pages.
- More controls by app stores: Vendors should take more steps before letting developers uploading their apps for the public.
- Security solutions: Just as security companies have anti-virus programs for desktops, now many also have mobile security solutions. Those programs eliminate malicious activity on mobile devices. An example is COMODO app [18] for Android device available in Google play store.

CONCLUSION

Hossain Shahriar, Tulin Klintic, Victor Clincy Mobile devices have small screens, so users are not able to see the whole URLs and are very likely to click on the links without enough forethought of possible phishing attacks. Moreover, users download and install applications without realizing that installed applications may not be a copy of legitimate official applications, a problem which overwhelmingly targets financial institutions. This paper provides an overview of various types of mobile phishing attacks. We also discuss some mitigation approaches and their limitations. We suggest some best practices. Our approach would enable users to be more careful when downloading apps and running on their devices to avoid fake interfaces designed by phishers. There is a broad scope of further research to be done to develop novel mitigation approaches, especially considering the variation of devices and accessibility of application market.

REFERENCES

1. CAPEC-164: Mobile Phishing. https://capec.mitre.org/data/definitions/164.html
2. Ashford, W. (2014) Phishing Attacks Track Mobile Adoption, Research Shows.http://www.computerweekly.com/news/2240215873/Phishing-attacks-track-mobile-adoption-research-shows
3. Kessem, L. (2012) Rogue Mobile Apps, Phishing, Malware and Fraud.https://blogs.rsa.com/rogue-mobile-apps-phishing-malware-and-fraud
4. Klein, A. (2010) The Golden Hour of Phishing Attacks. http://www.trusteer.com/blog/golden-hour-phishing-attacks
5. Symantec Internet Security Threat Report 2014, Vol. 19.http://www.symantec.com/content/en/us/enterprise/other_resources/b-istr_main_report_v19_21291018.en-us.pdf
6. Todorova, A. (2010) "Phishing" Scams Cast Net on Mobile Banking.http://online.wsj.com/news/articles/SB10001424052748704343104575033380555965818
7. Trend Micro eBook (2013) Trend Micro. http://about-threats.trendmicro.com/ebooks/protecting-yourself-against-mobile-phishing/files/assets/downloads/protecting-yourself-against-mobile-phishing.pdf
8. Morrison, D. (2010) Mobile Phishing Highlights Need for Greater Security.http://www.cutimes.com/2010/01/20/mobile
9. Jevan, D. (2012) Latest Threats against Mobile Devices. Information Systems Security Association.http://sfbay.issa.org/comm/presentations/2014/ISSA%20Marble%20Security_2014_0114.pptx
10. Wilson, S. (2014). Smishing, Yes It Is All Bad. http://www.zcorum.com/smishing-yes-its-all-bad/
11. Foozy, C.F.M., Ahmad, R. and Abdollah, M.F. (2013) Phishing Detection Taxonomy for Mobile Device. International Journal of Computer Science, 10, 338-344.
12. (2014) Hackers Target Wi-Fi Hotspots in New Phishing Attack.https://johnib.wordpress.com/2007/05/06/hackers-target-wi-fi-hotspots-in-new-phishing-attack
13. Johnston, S. (2013) How to Protect Yourself from Smishing and Vishing.http://money.usnews.com/money/personal-finance/articles/2013/09/19/how-to-protect-yourself-from-smishing-and-vishing
14. Yoon, J.W., et al. (2010) Hybrid Spam Filtering for Mobile Communication. Computers & Security, 29, 446-459. http://dx.doi.org/10.1016/j.cose.2009.11.003
15. Mahmoud, T.M. and Mahfouz, A.M. (2012) SMS Spam Filtering Technique Based on Artificial Immune System. International Journal of Computer Science, 9, 589-597.
16. Zhang, Y., Hong, J. and Cranor, L. (2007) Cantina: A Content-Based Approach to Detecting Phishing Web Sites. Proceedings of the 16th International Conference on World Wide Web, Banff, May, 639-648. http://dx.doi.org/10.1145/1242572.1242659

17. Sheng, S., Wardman, B., Warner, G., Cranor, L., Hong, J. and Zhang, C. (2009) An Empirical Analysis of Phishing Blacklists. 6th Annual Conference on Email and AntiSpam (CEAS), Mountain View.

18. COMODO Security Solutions. https://play.google.com/store/apps/developer?id=Comodo+Security+Solutions&hl=en

CHAPTER 7

AN ENHANCED DRAGONFLY KEY EXCHANGE PROTOCOL AGAINST OFFLINE DICTIONARY ATTACK

Eman Alharbi, Noha Alsulami, Omar Batarfi

Keywords: Password Authenticated Key Exchange (PAKE), Original Dragonfly, Patched Dragonfly, Enhanced Dragonfly, Two-Pre-Shared Password

INTRODUCTION

Nowadays, information is increasing at a faster rate and it needs to be secured when exchanging it over insecure networks. The most efficient way to secure this information is Cryptology which is the science of building and analyzing secret code. It consists of cryptography and cryptanalysis. Cryptography is the science that builds secret codes and cryptanalysis is the science that analyzes those codes [1] . There are two types of cryptography: Symmetric and Asymmetric key cryptography. Symmetric key cryptography has a shared key that is used by the sender and receiver in encryption and decryption processes, while Asymmetric key cryptography has a public key which is used in encryption processes and private key which is used in decryption processes [2] .

One of the symmetric cryptography protocols is key exchange protocol, which allows two parties who share non-secret information to compute a shared key via public communication. Authenticated Key Exchange (AKE) is a symmetric protocol that not only allows parties to compute the shared key but also ensures the identity of the parties where a party can compute a shared key only if he/she is the one who claims to be [3] . Another example of symmetric protocols is the Two-party Password-based Authenticated Key Exchange (2PAKE) protocol that permits two parties to generate a session key based on a pre-shared password and authenticates each other [4] . In general, PAKE protocols are exposed to different types of attacks, mainly passive and active attacks. Passive attacks are difficult to detect and are used to get information that is sent between parties without modifying the information or harming the resources. Active attacks enable the attacker to modify the encrypted message or change the meaning of the decrypted message by creating false streams [5] . However, the most complicated type of attack is the dictionary attack regardless of whether it is offline or online. Offline dictionary attack enables the attacker to record information from successful execution of the protocol by eavesdropping on the communication between parties. Then the attacker goes offline to find the required password by trying all passwords and choosing the correct password depending on the recorded information. The interaction with the server is not required in an offline dictionary attack. Online dictionary attacks enable the attacker to find the required password by trying all passwords during the interaction with the server [6] .

2PAKE protocol has various types of protocols. In 1992, the first 2PAKE protocol (called the Encrypted Key Exchange (EKE)) was proposed by Bellovin and Merritt [7] . Since then, many other 2PAKE protocols have been proposed (e.g. [8] -[12]). One of these protocols was Dragonfly which was defined by Dan Harkins who claimed that this protocol had resistance to passive attacks, active attacks and offline dictionary attacks without security proofs [12] . In 2013, Dylan and Feng analyzed this protocol and proved that this protocol had weakness points in its security properties against active attack and offline dictionary attacks. They proposed to patch Dragonfly as a solution to verify its security properties by adding a public key validation [12] .

The main problem in the patched dragonfly protocol was that it consumed an increased computation cost during the execution of the protocol when public key was used, which involved a large bit operation. In this paper, we introduced another enhancement for the Dragonfly protocol without using a public key. The proposed solution is based on using two-pre-shared secret passwords instead of one and the number of

Citation: Alharbi, E. , Alsulami, N. and Batarfi, O. (2015) An Enhanced Dragonfly Key Exchange Protocol against Offline Dictionary Attack. Journal of Information Security, 6, 69-81. doi: 10.4236/jis.2015.62008.

rounds between parties has been reduced to two instead of four. This step adds more security to the original Dragonfly protocol while the attacker will require more than 1.5 days to perform the off-line attack in case the shared password is extracted from a dictionary with the size 1000. This result has been approved through a simulation project which was developed by the java programming language. The simulation project has been used to find out the required execution time by both parties who are sharing the communication. The execution time is found to be less than the time required in the use of public key validation. We also approved the efficiency of Enhanced-Dragonfly protocol by using the Scyther tool to analyze its security properties and its structure.

The paper is organized into sections: Section 2 presents the related work; Section 3 presents review of the Dragonfly protocol; the proposed solution is presented in Section 4, while discussion is presented in Section 5. Finally, the conclusion is in Section 6. It is focused towards those who are interested in cryptography and cryptanalysis domain.

RELATED WORK

Password Authenticated Key Exchange (PAKE) protocols have been playing an essential role in providing secure communications. As is usual in cryptography, with each new release of a protocol, attempts to attack this protocol have also been released in order to measure resistance against these attacks.

In research [13] , analysis of the security weaknesses of SPAKE1 and SPAKE2 protocols has been introduced. It was found that these protocols are vulnerable against password compromises, impersonation and Denial- of-Service (DoS) attacks. Additionally, it was proved that the Hitchcock protocol [14] , which uses public key encryptions, is insecure against momentary key compromise masquerades, Key Compromise Impersonation (KCI) attacks and off-line dictionaries. To remove these disadvantages, a new efficient protocol has been designed which relies on two-party PAKE protocols based on symmetric key exchange protocol and multiple hash function calculations. The public key scheme has been replaced here with the symmetric encryption because the latter requires fewer bit operations. Many theories have been explained to prove that the proposed scheme is secure against various attacks. It provides the mutual authentication and forward secrecy attributes with many other security attributes. However, there is a little increase in computational costs that was caused by the extra hash calculations. This may be deemed negligible when considering the efficiency of the extra security attributes and lower number of rounds.

Moreover, another research [15] introduced the vulnerabilities of SPEKE and EKE protocols and analyzed them due to theoretical practices. In addition, a new PAKE protocol was proposed and was called Password Authenticated Key Exchange by Juggling (J-PAKE). It depends on shared secret-password between two entities and it has two rounds to create a strong shared key. It is based on well-established primitive in cryptography called Zero-Knowledge Proof (ZKP) that allows a person to prove his knowledge of a discrete logarithm without revealing it. The analysis of this protocol proved that it prevents off-line dictionary attacks, limits an active attacker to guess only one password per protocol execution and provides forward secrecy. It has advantages like: protection of users from leaking passwords and it does not require PKI deployments. This protocol is very efficient according to the use of well-established primitives.

Recent researches in the field of PAKE protocols are moving towards using Public Key Infrastructure (PKI) in the authentication process. In recent years, PAKE has been used with RSA encryption method to provide the appropriate secrecy between two parties. In [16] a new proposed protocol named as E3PAKE-RSA, which is based on RSA scheme with the three-party model that enables two entities to only need to remember a human- memorable password to authenticate each other and agree on a large session key with the assistance of the trusted server. The public/private key parameters are selected by the clients rather than a trusted distribution center, which makes the process of on-line authentication obsolete. It was predicted that the computation cost for this protocol would be respectively high according to the two-party RSA-PAKE. However, during the testing phase, which applied to the generic constructions, the computation cost of E3PAKE-RSA protocol was found to be as much as the two-party RSA-PAKE and the number of total rounds are less than this. Actually, this protocol requires more time to execute due to the use of the RSA encryption method and the long bit operations, while the other PAKE protocols (which do not use PKI) work faster.

OVERVIEW ON DRAGONFLY PROTOCOL

Dragonfly is a PAKE protocol that is used to exchange session keys between two parties with mutual authentication inside mesh networks. It was defined by Dan [12] . Finite cyclic groups are required to implement dragonfly such as Finite Field Cryptography (FFC) or Elliptic Curve Cryptography (ECC) [17] . This paper implements this protocol by using FFC. A finite field is "a field F that contains a finite number of elements which is the order of F" [18] . More details about finite field are presented in [19] [20] .

In this section, we will explain the Dragonfly protocol in detail, with the discovered attack on it followed by the solution which is suggested in [12] .

Original Dragonfly Protocol

Notations

The meanings of different notations that occur in this paper are listed in Table 1.

Message Exchange

There are two types of message exchanges in Dragonfly which are [12] [17] [21] :

1) Commit Exchange is the message that is sent by both parties who commit to a single guess of the shared password.
2) Confirm Exchange occurs when both the parties confirm knowledge of the shared password.

Operations

There are three operations in Dragonfly protocol which are [12] [17] [21] :

- Operation: is the modular multiplication that takes two elements as inputs and the output will be a new element, e.g. C = A.B mod p (A, B and C are elements and p is a prime number).
- Scalar operation takes one element and one scalar as input and the output will be a new element, e.g. C = Ab mod p (for scalar b, elements A, C and p a prime number).

Table 1. Notations of original/enhanced dragonfly protocol

Notation	Definition	Notation	Definition
IDA	Initiator's identifier	EA	Initiator's element operation
IDB	Responder's identifier	EB	Responder's element operation
Q	Finite cyclic group	E'A	Initiator's element operation after hashing
K	Shared session key	E'B	Responder's element operation after hashing
ss	Shared secret code	A	Initiator's scalar and element operations
N	New password element	B	Responder's scalar and element operations
P	Password element	rA	Random number generated by initiator.
q	the order of Q	rB	Random number generated by responder.
p	The group prime	H()	Hash function
sA	Initiator's scalar operation	mA	2nd random number generated by initiator.
sB	Responder's scalar operation	mB	2nd random number generated by responder.

- Inverse operation: There is an inverse of elements if the result of the multiplication of that element with its inverse is 1, e.g. (A*inverse (A)) mod p = 1 (for elements A and p which is a prime number).

Protocol Execution

Suppose Alice and Bob are parties who want to execute Dragonfly protocol, they should follow some sequential steps in order to implement this protocol as shown in Figure 1 [12] [17] [21] :

- Before sending any message, Alice and Bob share a password that is a string which includes their identities and they also choose FFC or ECC to use. Then the password is mapped into an element of Q which is a generator (P) by using an algorithm.
- Both parties produce scalar and element operations based on choosing two scalars that belong to Q randomly (r, m). Then each party sends his/her scalar and element operations to another party (s, E).
- After that each party calculates the shared secret depending on element and scalar operations for them ss.
- Both parties send a hash function that contains scalar and element operations of both parties and ss.
- Each party verifies the hash; if it is valid then the authentication succeeds. Then they create a shared key K = H(ss|EA·EB|(sA + sB) mod q), but if it is invalid then the authentication fails and all messages must be destroyed.

Attack on Original Dragonfly Protocol

An attacker was able to impersonate the identity of Bob by following specific algorithm which has been defined in [12] which makes him accessible to the pre-shared password that is P. There are two cases when the attacker can do such attack:

1) If the algorithm takes a long time to run and Alice terminates the communication, then the attacker can get P and he can impersonate the identity of Alice or Bob in the next run of the Dragonfly protocol.
2) If the algorithm is completed quickly, then the attacker impersonates the identity of Bob during the run of protocol by sending his hash function and sends it to Alice to compute the shared key K.

Patched Dragonfly Protocol

This solution was used to secure the Dragonfly protocol against the off-line attack. This was developed by [12] , which relies on using public key validation. However, the execution time, which was examined through the introduced simulated project, was relatively high. Generally, the use of public key validation causes an increase in the computation cost to the execution of the protocol because a large number of bit operations will be required.

This research is conducted to find a better solution for this protocol without consuming more time in order to keep it efficient and compete with other PAKE protocols. This will be discussed in the following sections.

	Alice		Bob
	$P \in Q$		$P \in Q$
1.	$r_A, m_A \in \{1,\cdots,q\}$		$r_B, m_B \in \{1,\cdots,q\}$
2.	$s_A = r_A + m_A$		$s_B = r_B + m_B$
3.	$E_A = P^{-m_A}$	$\xrightarrow{s_A, E_A}$	$E_B = P^{-m_B}$
4.		$\xleftarrow{s_B, E_B}$	
5.	$ss = \left(P^{s_B} E_B\right)^{r_A} = P^{r_B r_A}$	$\xrightarrow{A = H\left(ss\vert E_A\vert s_A\vert E_B\vert s_B\right)}$	Verify A
6.	Verify B	$\xleftarrow{B = H\left(ss\vert E_B\vert s_B\vert E_A\vert s_A\right)}$	$ss = \left(P^{s_A} E_A\right)^{r_B} = P^{r_A r_B}$
7.	Compute the shared key: $K = H\left(ss\vert E_A \cdot E_B\vert\left(s_A + s_B\right) \bmod q\right)$		

Figure 1: Steps of dragonfly protocol.

THE PROPOSED SOLUTION

This paper proposes a solution to secure the original Dragonfly protocol without the addition of public key in order to keep the execution time as fast as possible. It relies on using two pre-shared passwords instead of one. Here the attacker must search for each N, P in the dictionary. The first password P will be generated in the same way as in the original Dragonfly protocol. This is done by extracting a string from the dictionary and using the identities of both parties. It has a length of 1024 bits. The generation of the second password N is the same as P but with two minor changes; which are based on the extraction of another word from the same dictionary and the use of the identity of the respondent and it has a length of 160 bits instead of 1024.

The enhanced Dragonfly protocol will work according to the following steps:

- Two passwords will be generated, which are P and N, and will be shared between both parties.
- Both parties produce scalar and element operations based on choosing one scalar that belongs to Q randomly (r). Then each party will compute his/her scalar (A,B) = r(A,B) + N and element operations E = P ? N.
- Both parties will compute the hash value of E which is E' = H (E).
- The first party will compute the hash value A for the parameters E' and s_A. Then A will be sent to the second party with the scalar value of the first party. The second party will verify the hash value A to ensure the authentication process. Here if the hash value is verified then the second party will compute the hash value B and send it to the first party with his/her scalar value S_B, otherwise it will be declined. The first party in turn will verify the hash value B. If it is valid then the authentication succeeds.
- After that each party will calculate the shared secret which is ss = $(P^{sB} E)^{rA}$
- Then they create a shared secret key which is K = $H(ss|E|(s_A + s_B) \bmod q)$.

The benefits of this solution are: firstly, the attacker will never be able to guess the hash value which includes the hash of the element value that uses the exponent of two-secret values. Secondly, the authentication process occurs in two rounds rather than four rounds as in the original protocol. This elimination makes the execution process go faster. The steps of enhanced Dragonfly protocol have been displayed in Figure 2.

Methodology over Protocol Testing

A simulation project has been developed to test the time needed to execute the protocol compared to the patched dragonfly protocol. It was written in Java and maintained in Net Beans. This project has been handled by using 64 bits Windows 8.1 pro-operating system and a processor with the speed 2.38 GHz. This project includes three various classes:

1)Dragonfly: is the main class that has objects from the other two classes and it also has some local variables such as:

- ID_A, ID_B are identities of initiator and respondent. The identity is the Mac address. For example ID_A = 001CB3098515, ID_B = 001AB3008600.

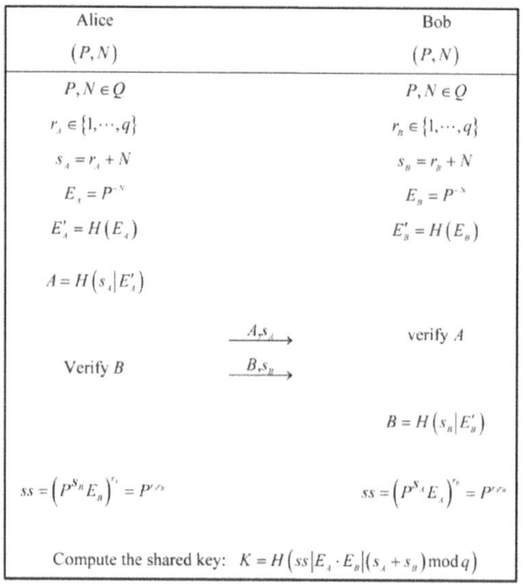

Figure 2: The enhanced dragonfly protocol.

- p_modular with the length of 1024 bits.
- Q is the order of subgroup whose length is 160 bits.
- secret_password: it is the first shared word from the dictionary (English word dictionary) that is used to generate P, while secret_password_2 is the second shared string word from the dictionary that is used to generate N. for example Password 1 = aardvark, Password 2 = aback, and the result of the generation process is located in Table 2.

2) Password: is the class to convert two shared string words that are taken from the dictionary into elements in Q subgroup and using two Mac addresses as identities for Alice and Bob to generate P and N. It has three methods which are:

- Password_Generator: the constructor that takes p_modular and q as parameters.
- pass1_ToGenerator: which takes the first word and generates the first shared password with the identities of Alice and Bob, which is P. The generated password will be 1024 bits long.
- pass2_ToElement: which takes the second word and generates the second shared password with the identity of Bob only, which is N. The generated password will be 160 bits long.

3) EnhancedDragonfly: is the class that implements the proposed solution. It works as the initiator agent, which is Alice. The respondent agent which is Bob will follow the same steps that are provided by this class. First, a random value rA will be selected from {1,...,q} while q is a Subgroup Order as shown in Table 2. The passed P and N will be used with rA to calculate Scalar sA, Element E and hash value A. Then these values will be used to calculate the shared secret key. We use MD5 for hash function.

This class includes seven methods:

- Enhanced Dragonfly is the constructor that takes p_modularandq as parameters.
- scalar_operation: it is calculating scalar operation that is sA = rA + N

- element_operation: it is calculating element operation that is E = P N
- sending_operation: it is used to calculate and send the hash value A
- verifying_operation: It returns true or false according to the verification of the hash value of the other party.
- sharedsecret_computation: used to calculate the shared secret key ss, which will be used later in the next equation.
- sharedkey_computation: returns the secret key in the form of hash value.

Table 2: Values of important parameters of enhanced dragonfly protocol simulation

Parameter	Value
p (prime modulus) Length = 1024 bit	1585042373501172182576940404078584628912009633935915161416345300195000735766689114843202366912302727008296966278353005282688125899457108929153123878719154776399812996991995088020542026387125639386947983208903598717587142959933164297906661669496372032914301994232528383208758588903518754761707263729117491635 31
P (shared password 1) Generator of subgroup Length = 1024 bit	2458360507494950257907169557213565949220290741575434138792655296081464061030904277466496859919479502796763367775099503299271500392133319453219695664779197506465865994961311816897923419532301337447539348533358115278382718938317040492955705861894330613420032023903964025700499474450889991172178764572215861074
q (subgroup order) Length = 160 bit	1067173368745944614404811917041803739479862559381
N (shared password 2) Length = 160 bit	1000000000067898284897661991820474501459056843147
r_A Length = 160 bit	7315915602211222684006538355559825803482213175 61
Shared key in hash value with length 128 bits	843770100120502117178769103307912571

The class diagram of this project is displayed in Figure 3, while Figure 4 presents the input and output of Enhanced Dragonfly protocol simulation. The values of important parameters of Enhanced Dragonfly protocol simulation are listed in Table 2.

By applying this simulation, the execution time for one participant was found to be 19 minutes only. This experiment was applied 15 times in order to measure the total execution time of the enhanced Dragonfly protocol and the average of the total time is almost 38 minutes. This result works as a proof for the efficiency of the proposed solution, and the use of two-shared passwords will not affect the time of exchanging the secret keys.

Testing and Analysis of the Enhanced Dragonfly Protocol

Any protocol should be analyzed in order to see if there are any possible attacks that can occur and find how secure it is. The automatic analysis is the most recent approach which is used in analysis of security protocols and it is more efficient than the manual one. The required time to write the protocol description depends on the learning of its language. All possible attacks will be tested by the used tool. The automatic analysis will be used in this research.

Various tools are used to analyze the security protocols and to check the possibility of any attack can happen when protocol is put to use. An example for this is the Scyther tool which supports the evaluation of protocols with respect to these corruption models which have led to the automatic detection of many attacks that previously could only be found by manual analysis [22] .

Description of Scyther Tool and SPDL

Scyther [23] is one of the most efficient analyzing tools compared with other tools [24] . It was found that this tool can discover attacks more efficiently than others and it can also verify protocols with an unlimited number of sessions. Its run time is also less than others. There are many protocols that have been analyzed by this tool such as IKEv1, IKEv2 protocol suits, ISO/IEC 9798 family of authentication protocols and MQV family of protocols.

The Scyther tool takes the protocol description as input, and outputs a summary report stating whether the claim was true or false, whether any attack was found or not, and optionally, visual graph descriptions in the dot language from the GraphVizlibrary or representations of trace patterns in XML which describe the trace pattern [25] . Additionally, there are a set of Python bindings for the Scyther command-line tool, which provide a convenient means to script Scyther experiments.Figure 5 displays how this tool works.

Security Protocol Description Language (SPDL) is a language that is used in Scyther for writing a protocol [26] . This language is just expressive enough to capture the most relevant security protocols in an abstract way. It allows us to develop high-level reasoning methods and tools, which can be applied to a large class of protocols. SPDL is used to create a definition for existing protocols that use symmetric or asymmetric encryption. It includes three scopes; global scope (the largest scope), protocol scope (smaller than global) and role scope (the smallest one). Furthermore, it includes the initial knowledge required to execute a role (each agent's role includes sequence of events, such as sending or receiving a message), the declaration of functions, global constants and variables.

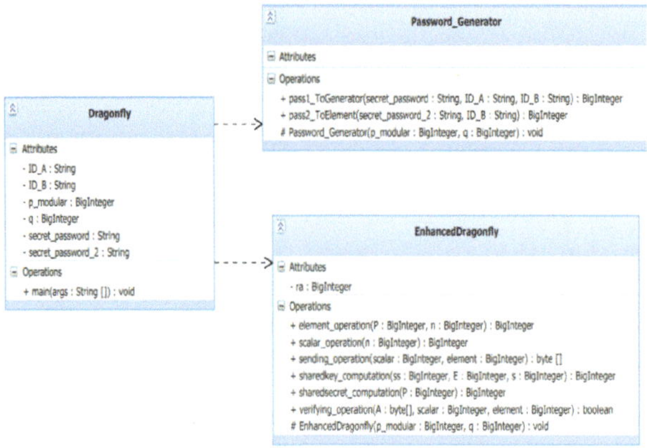

Figure 3: Enhanced dragonfly class diagram.

```
run:
p=
1585042373501172182576940404078584628912009633935915161416345
3001950007357866891148432023669123027270082969662783530052826
8812589945710892915312387871915477639981299699199508802054202
6387125639386947983208903598717587142959933164297906661669496
3720329143019942325283832087585889035187547617072637291174916
3531
q= 10671733687459446144048119170418037394798625593 81
Enter a secret password:
aardvark
Enter The Identity of the Initiator:
001CB3098515
Enter The Identity of the Respondent:
001AB3008600
P=
2458360507494950257907169557213565949220290741575434138792655
2960814640610309042774664968599194795027967633677750995032992
7150039213331945321969566477919750646586599496131181689792341
9532301337447539348533358115278382718938317040492955705861894
3306134200320239039640257004994744508899911721787645722158610
74
Enter a second secret password:
aback
Enter The Identity of the Respondent:
001AB3008600
n= 1000000000067898284897661991820474501459056843147
ra = 7315915602211222684006538355559825803482213175 61
hash value of shared key
84 - 37 70 100 120 50 2 117 - 17 87 69 - 103 - 30 79 125 - 71
Execution time of protocol in millisecond= 11
```

Figure 4: Input and output of the enhanced dragonfly simulation project.

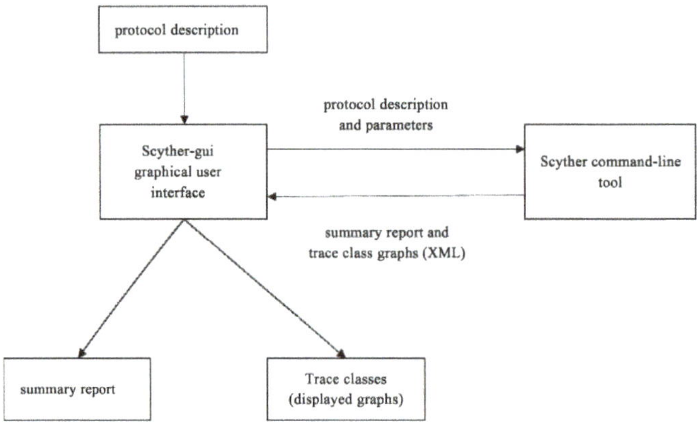

Figure 5: The syther tool.

SPDL of Enhanced Dragonfly Protocol and Analysis Result

In this sub-section, the SPDL representation of Enhanced Dragonfly protocol will be explained in detail. After that, the findings from this analysis will be discussed. The SPDL code of the enhanced dragonfly is displayed in Figure 6. First of all, a global hash function H1 & H2 has been defined (outside the protocol definition) to make it available to be accessed by all rolls in the protocol. Also, the functions of multiplication mult, addition add, exponential exp and the inverse inv were defined globally. Function is a special type which defines a function term that can take a list of variables. By default, it behaves like a hash function: given the term H1(x) where H1 is of type Function, it is impossible to derive x. These functions are defined in an abstract way in SPDL, which doesn't support any real equations.

Next, the protocol description starts with the keyword protocol which takes the role names as parameters. There are three rolls, namely; the key generator center (role KGC), the initiator (role A) and the respondent (role B):

- Key generator center role KGC [27] : Used here to pass the shared secret password P and N to role A and B. The way of generation, which is used to generate these shared passwords, doesn't take a place here in the tool because the tool depends on the structure of the protocol only. The shared secret passwords P&N have been identified as constants and their scope is within the protocol because they should be used inside all roles.
- Initiator role A:
  - This role represents the start of the communication to compute the shared secret key. The selection of random value r_A, which is the first step in the protocol structure (see Figure 2) by Alice (initiator), has been clarified by using the fresh declaration which is used by SPDL to get random values. Nonce is a standard data type that is often used in Scyther tool.
  - The calculation of S_A (Scalar value), E (element value), and A1 (hash value) occurs by using the predefined functions, and then S_A and A1 will be sent to role B.
  - Note: labels in recv and send need to disambiguate similar occurrences of events in a protocol specification. In addition, they are used to link each send event with its recv one [28] .
  - In the received event of role A, the hash value of B and the Scalar value S_B will be saved in a Ticket variable, which can be substituted by any term.
  - Role A will verify if these values are from Role B or not by using the match function. The definition of match [29] ensures the new variable assignment equivalent to the old one and it returns true or false. If the returned value is true then the next steps computed, otherwise Role A will conclude that this value is not from the honest agent, and it closes the session.
  - The calculation of the secret key needs to be kept in secrecy, so that a claim with the type secret is used. The main idea behind claim events is locality [28] [29] : that a term is not in the adversary knowledge, or any certain role in run. Secrecy means that if an agent communicates with non-compromised agents, the term should be secret in every trace of the protocol. Secrecy expresses that certain information is not revealed to an adversary, even though this data is communicated over an un-trusted network. Here, claim event has been used to keep session's key secret and is known to role A only. When the tool runs, it tries to find the corresponding attack to each claim.
- Respondent Role B:
  - Generates the random value r_B by fresh declaration.
  - Calculates the scalar S_B, Element E and hash value B1 and sends it to Role A.
  - Verifies the received hash value from Role A and compares it by using match function.

If the output of matching is true, then B will calculate the secret session key and claim it with secret type.

The SPDL of the protocol is inserted into the Scyther tool to see if any attack could occur or if there is any structural weak point in this proposed protocol. The result of this analysis brings out that there is NO attack found. All roles are verified, which means that no impersonation can occur during the connection and the characteristics of the protocol structure are verified. This means that the way of exchanging the data is totally secure. This result is printed in Figure 7 and Figure 8.

```
// Hash functions
hashfunction H1,H2;
// Addition, multiplication, exponent, inverse
function mult,add,exp,inv;
// The protocol description
protocol dragonfly(A,B,KGC)
{
const N,P;
role KGC // Key Generation Center
{
send_1(KGC,A,P,N); // Publish public parameters
send_2(KGC,B,P,N);
}
role A
{
fresh ra:Nonce;
var B1,SB:Ticket;
recv_1(KGC,A,P,N);
send_3(A,B,add(ra,N), H1(exp(P,inv(N)),add(ra,N))); // Send SA and A1

recv_4(B,A,SB,B1);
match(H1(add(ra,N),H1(exp(P,inv(N)))),B1);
claim_A1(A,Secret,(H2(exp(exp(P,SB), mult (exp(P,inv(N))),ra),H1(exp(P,inv(N))), add(ra,N))));
};
role B
{
fresh rb:Nonce;
var A1,SA:Ticket;
recv_2(KGC,B,P,N);
recv_3(A,B,SA,A1);
match(A1,H1(SA,H1(exp(P,inv(N)))));
send_4(B,A,H1(add(rb,N),H1(exp(P,inv(N)))),add(rb,N));// Send SB and B1
claim_B1(B,Secret,(H2(exp(exp(P,SA), mult(exp(P,inv(N))),rb),H1(exp(P,inv(N))), add(SA,add(rb,N)))));
};
}
```

Figure 6: SPDL of enhanced dragonfly protocol.

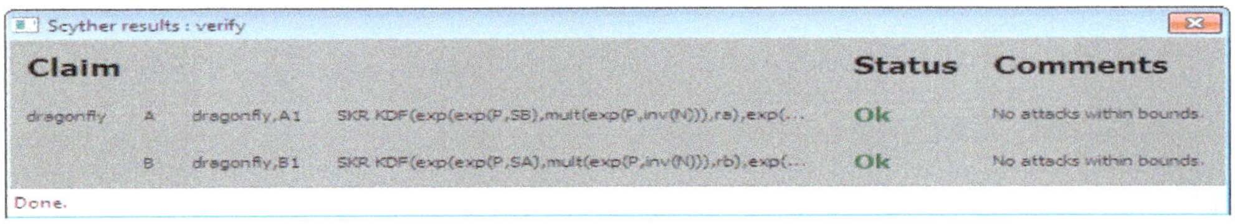

Figure 7: Scyther result of the enhanced dragonfly.

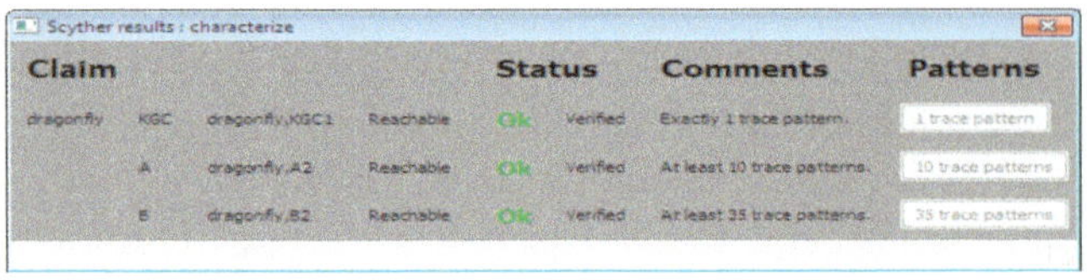

Figure 8: Verification of the enhanced dragonfly structure.

DISCUSSION

This study has revealed that the enhanced Dragonfly protocol is secure against off-line dictionary attacks and it's approved for efficiency due to its execution speed. In this section, the off-line attack will be developed within the simulation project in order to analyze the time which is required for the attacker to perform his/her search against the two-shared passwords. Then, a comparison between the efficiency of the enhanced Dragonfly protocol and the original/patched Dragonfly protocol is introduced.

Off-Line Attack Simulation

Attack class has been applied to previous simulation projects. This class works by measuring the time taken to check all possible passwords, as dictionary size varies from 100, 1000 to 100,000 words. Each experiment was performed 5 times to find the search time by attack class and the average value was taken. As a result, the average time of this search within the enhanced protocol increased linearly as with increase in the dictionary size. The average time of off-line search when the dictionary length is 10,000 is more than 1.5 days, and with the original Dragonfly protocol [12] the off-line search algorithm took an average of 25 seconds to find the correct password with the same dictionary length. This is because the enhanced protocol has an exponential relationship between the two-secret passwords in the computation of the element variable. Therefore, the attacker will be forced to search for two words instead of one. As a comparison between the time that is required for searching one password and the time required for searching two passwords, this experiment found that the time increased exponentially. The search of such an attack on the patched Dragonfly protocol requires few days to be successful. However, here the execution time will have an impact on the efficiency of Key exchange technique. Table 3 shows a linear relationship between dictionary size and the time taken to try all passwords.

Comparison between Enhanced Dragonfly and Patched Dragonfly Protocols

The enhanced Dragonfly protocol is very similar to the patched Dragonfly protocol except for two minor changes. Firstly, the patched protocol uses only one shared password and a public key, while the enhanced protocol uses two-shared passwords. Second, the rounds between the initiator and the respondent are only two rounds in the enhanced protocol while it is four rounds in the patched protocol. However, the patched dragonfly involves some computational cost because it is uses a public key validation which creates large bit operations due to its large size. This can decrease the protocol efficiency and make it less appealing than its competitors [12] . Otherwise, in the enhanced dragonfly protocol, the execution of the protocol will take less time. In order to measure the execution time of the enhanced Dragonfly protocol we used the simulation project to compute the time required by the key generation center that uses dictionary size 10,000 plus the time which required by the initiator party when execute the required computation of the protocol. The cost of both patched and enhanced Dragonfly protocol for each participant has been placed into Table 4, and based on these time measurements we have observed that the efficiency of using two-shared passwords is more than using the public key.

Table 3: Time average of off-line search on enhance dragonfly protocol

Dictionary size	Average of the first attempt to find P	Average of the first attempt to find P & N	The time of the dictionary attack
100	20 ms	40 ms	5.1 minutes
1000	135 ms	269 ms	4.8 hours
10,000	141 ms	282 ms	More than 1.5 days

Table 4: Computation cost for dragonfly and enhanced protocol

Protocol	Execution time/participant
Public key Dragonfly	64.0 ms
Two-shared password Dragonfly	19.0 ms

The limitation of this research is that these results are based on a normal speed machine with the 64 bits Windows 8.1 pro-operating system and a processor with the speed of 2.38 GHz which is not the case in the real time attack. Furthermore, the attacker is likely to significantly shorten the time of exhaustive search by distributing the calculation over several high performance machines.

CONCLUSION

Eman Alharbi, Noha Alsulami, Omar Batarfi In this research we proved that the Dragonfly protocol can be enhanced in a way, other than the public key validation, to make it secure against off-line dictionary attacks. The proposed solution that has been introduced to the original Dragonfly protocol relies on the use of two-shared secret passwords P and N. This solution works by the use of an exponential relationship between these passwords and performing the authentication process in two rounds only instead of four, which positively affects its efficiency. The use of public key validation, which is proposed in the patched protocol, is causing a computational cost to its execution that makes it less efficient. However, the execution time of the enhanced Dragonfly protocol and the time of an off-line dictionary attack were measured in the developed simulation project. As a result of this simulation, the required time to execute the enhanced protocol for one of the parties was 19 ms, while it was 64 ms in the patched protocol. Respectively, the time to perform an off-line dictionary attack was very close to the time to attack the patched protocol for the dictionary size 10,000, which meant that the resistance of the enhanced protocol against off-line dictionary attack was proved. The enhanced protocol has been analyzed by using Scyther analysis tool and it was found to be secure and did not have any structural failure. We can say that, the enhanced dragonfly protocol can be executed in a very short time while the off-line dictionary attack is a time consuming search for the attacker and it needs a few days to complete it.

REFERENCES

1. Stamp, M. (2007) Classic Ciphers in Applied Cryptanalysis: Breaking Ciphers in the Real World. Wiley-IEEE Press, Canada, 25. http://dx.doi.org/10.1002/9780470148778.ch2
2. Kendhe, A.K. and Agrawal, H. (2013) A Survey Report on Various Cryptanalysis Techniques. International Journal of Soft Computing and Engineering (IJSCE), 3, 287-293.
3. Lauter, K. and Mityagin, A. (2006) Security Analysis of KEA Authenticated Key Exchange Protocol. International Association for Cryptologic Research.
4. Saeedetal, M. (2012) An Enhanced Password Authenticated Key Exchange Protocol without Server Public Keys. ICTC, 2012.
5. Ali, R., Kumar, A. and Narayan, E. (2013) Encryptioan/Decryption Tool with Cryptanalysis. International Journal of Computer Science & Engineering Technology (IJCSET), 4, 1043-1050.
6. Goyal, V., et al. (2005) CompChall: Addressing Password Guessing Attacks. ITCC 1, IEEE Computer Society.
7. Bellovin, S.M. and Merritt, M. (1992) Encrypted Key Exchange: Password-Based Protocols Secure against Dictionary Attacks. Proceedings of IEEE Symposium on Security and Privacy, Oakland, 4-6 May 1992, 72-84. http://dx.doi.org/10.1109/RISP.1992.213269
8. Kobara, K. and Imai, H. (2002) Pretty-Simple Password-Authenticated Key Exchange under Standard Assumptions. IEICE Transactions, E85-A(10), 2229-2237.
9. Bellare, M., Pointcheval, D. and Rogaway, P. (2000) Authenticated Key Exchange Secure against Dictionary Attacks. Proceedings of the 2000 Advances in Cryptology (EUROCRYPT'2000). Springer-Verlag, Berlin, 139-155. http://dx.doi.org/10.1007/3-540-45539-6_11
10. Bresson, E., Chevassut, O. and Pointcheval, D. (2004) New Security Results on Encrypted Key Exchange. In: Proc. PKC 2004, Lecture Notes in Computer Science, Vol. 2947, Springer-Verlag, Berlin, 145-158.
11. Abdalla, M. and Pointcheval, D. (2005) Simple Password-Based Encrypted Key Exchange Protocols. Proceedings of Topics in Cryptology—CT-RSA, Lecture Notes in Computer Science, Vol. 3376, Springer-Verlag, Berlin, 191-208.
12. Clarke, D. and Hao, F. (2013) Cryptanalysis of the Dragonfly Key Exchange Protocol.
13. Saeed, M., Shahriar Shahhoseini, H. and Mackvandi, A. (2011) An Improved Two-Party Password Authenticated Key Exchange Protocol without Server's Public Key. IEEE 3rd International Conference on Communication Software and Networks, Xi'an, 27-29 May 2011, 90-95.
14. Hitchcock, Y., Tin, Y.S.T., Boyd, C., Nieto, J.M.G. and Montague, P. (2003) A Password-Based Authenticator: Security Proof and Applications. INDOCRYPT'03, Lecture Notes in Computer Science, Vol. 2904, Springer-Verlag, Berlin, 388-401.
15. Hao, F. and Ryan, P. (2010) J-PAKE: Authenticated Key Exchange without PKI. In: Transactions on Computational Science XI, Springer, Berlin, 192-206.
16. Ma, C.G., Wei, F.S. and Gao, F.X. (2013) Efficient Client-to-Client Password Authenticated Key Exchange Based on RSA. IEEE 5th International Conference on Intelligent Networking and Collaborative Systems, Xi'an, 9-11 September 2013, 233-238.
17. Harkins, D. (2008) Simultaneous Authentication of Equals: A Secure, Password-Based Key Exchange for Mesh Networks. 2nd International Conference on Sensor Technologies and Applications (SENSORCOMM), Cap Esterel, 25-31 August 2008, 839-844.
18. http://cacr.uwaterloo.ca/hac/about/chap14.pdf
19. Stalling, W. (2006) Chapter 4: Finite Fields. In: Cryptography and Network Security, 4th Edition, Pearson Education International, Upper Saddle River, 97-109.
20. Saeed, M., Mackvandi, A., Naddafiun, M. and Karimnejad, H. (2012) An Enhanced Password Authenticated Key Exchange Protocol without Server Public Keys. 2012 International Conference on ICT Convergence (ICTC), Jeju Island, 15-17 October 2012, 87-91.
21. Harkins, D. (2012) Dragonfly Key Exchange. Internet Research Taskforce Internet Draft Version 00. http://tools.ietf.org/html/draft-irtf-cfrg-dragonfly-00
22. Basin, D., Cremers, C. and Meadows, C. (2009) LTL Model Checking Security Protocols. Journal of Applied Non- Classical Logics, 194, 403-429.
23. http://www.cs.ox.ac.uk/people/cas.cremers/scyther/index.html
24. Cremers, C.J.F., Lafourcade, P. and Nadeau, P. (2009) Comparing State Spaces in Automatic Security Protocol Analysis.
25. Franciscus, C.J. (2006) Scyther—Semantics and Verification of Security Protocols. Eindhoven University of Technology, Eindhoven.
26. Dalal, N., Shah, J., Hisaria, K. and Jinwala, D. (2010) A Comparative Analysis of Tools for Verification of Security Protocols.

27. Farouk, A., Fouad, M. and Abdelhafez, A. (2014) Analysis and Improvement of Pairing-Free Certificate-Less Two- Party Authenticated Key Agreement Protocol for Grid Computing. International Journal of Security, Privacy and Trust Management, IJSPTM, 3, 23-36.

28. Cremers, C. and Mauw, S. (2012) Chapter 4: Security Properties. In: Operational Semantics and Verification of Security Protocols, Information Security and Cryptography, Springer-Verlag, Berlin, 37-65.

29. Cremers, C. (2014) Scyther User Manual. 18 February 2014.

CHAPTER 8

HARDWARE REALIZATION OF ARTIFICIAL NEURAL NETWORK BASED INTRUSION DETECTION & PREVENTION SYSTEM

Indraneel Mukhopadhyay, Mohuya Chakraborty

Keywords: Artificial Neural Network, Feed Forward Multilayer ANN, Intrusion Detection & Prevention System, FPGA, VHDL, Virtex 7

INTRODUCTION

Intrusion prevention is the process of performing intrusion detection and attempting to stop detected possible incidents. Intrusion Detection & Prevention Systems (IDPS) [1] are primarily focused on identifying possible incidents, logging information about them, attempting to stop them, and reporting them to security administrators. IDPS perform extensive logging of data that is related to detected events in the network. These data can then be used to confirm the validity of alerts, investigate incidents, and correlate events between the IDPS and other logging sources. Artificial neural networks (ANN) have found widespread deployment in a broad spectrum of classification, perception, association and control applications [2] . The aspiration to build intelligent systems complemented with the advances in high speed computing has proved through simulation the capability of ANN to map, model and classify nonlinear systems. Real time applications are possible only if low cost high-speed neural computation is made realizable. Towards this goal numerous works on implementation of ANN have been proposed [2] .

ANNs have been mostly implemented in software. However, a disadvantage in real-time applications of software-based ANNs is slower execution compared to hardware-based ANNs. Hardware-based ANNs have been implemented as both analogue and digital circuits. Recent advances in reprogrammable logic enable implementing large ANNs on a single field-programmable gate array (FPGA) device. The main reason for this is the miniaturization of component manufacturing technology, where the data density of electronic components doubles every 18 months [3] . ANNs are biologically inspired and require parallel computations in their nature. Microprocessors and Digital Signal Processors (DSPs) are not suitable for parallel designs. Designing fully parallel modules may be possible with Application Specific Integrated Circuits (ASICs) for which the best example is Vertex 7 FPGA boards. In addition the design results in an ANN suited only for one target application. FPGAs not only offer parallelism but also flexible designs, savings in cost and design cycle [4] . Our idea is to realize an IDPS based on feed forward ANN on FPGA.

The organization of the paper is as follows. After the introduction in Section 1, Section 2 provides an overview of the proposed architecture of ANN based IDPS. Theoretical background study of feed forward ANN and IDPS implementation in FPGA have been described in Section 3. Section 4 describes the MATLAB implementation and simulation of the proposed ANN based IDPS model. Simulation environment of the proposed design followed by its performance analysis using VHDL XILINX ISE 13.2 design suite have been presented in Section 5. In Section 6 the hardware implementation of the proposed architecture on Virtex7 FPGA board followed by results are presented. Section 7 concludes the paper with some highlights on future work.

PROPOSED ARCHITECTURE OF ANN BASED IDPS

The idea is to design an IDPS based on feed forward ANN on FPGA. The proposed IDPS architecture consists of two blocks—an Intrusion Detection System (IDS), which classifies the attack and the Intrusion Prevention System (IPS), which takes the classified signature and decides which signatures to be propagated. The block diagram shown in Figure 1 represents the architecture of our proposed IDS. The data

Citation: Mukhopadhyay, I. and Chakraborty, M. (2014) Hardware Realization of Artificial Neural Network Based Intrusion Detection & Prevention System. Journal of Information Security, 5, 154-165. doi: 10.4236/jis.2014.54015.

collected from the Internet is fed into the pre-processing unit where the raw data is formatted to make it compatible with the intrusion detection system under consideration. Subsequently data is classified as normal or attack. Normal data is allowed to pass through while on the other hand attack data is classified to the type of attack, saved in the database (Db) and an alert is raised [5] . The proposed IDS architecture may be divided into four sub-processes whose functionalities are briefly described below.

1. Data Collector: KDD 99 data set based on the DARPA intrusion detection programme, which is publicly accessible via MIT Lincoln Lab is first of all collected at this block.
2. Pre-processor: This block takes the original data from the MIT Lincoln Lab, extracts the required features, and converts the data set into Matlab compatible format. This basically performs the data cleaning procedure.
3. Encoder: The attributes given in the data set are converted into double data type to make it compatible with the ANN Tool box of Matlab. The authors have converted the feature variables “protocol type” with values like tcp = 0, udp = 1, icmp = 2; “error flag” with values S0 = 0, SF = 1, S1 = 2, REJ = 3, S2 = 4. The attacks in the data set have been categorized as normal = 0, DoS = 1, probe = 2, r2l = 3, u2r = 4, others = 5. The details of all 41 attributes are given in Appendix.
4. Neural Network Classifier: The data at the output of the encoder stage is fed into the neural network with following experimental criteria to properly classify attack types.

IPS on the other hand is a software programme that stops possible attack signatures. Therefore once the classification is done by the IDS the IPS takes the classified signature and decides which signatures to be propagated. If the signature is classified as an attack signature then the network traffic is not allowed otherwise if the signature is classified as normal then the signature is propagated as shown in Figure 2.

THEORETICAL BACKGROUND

Feed Forward ANN

ANNs are inspired by the biological neural systems. The transmission of signals in biological neurons through synapses is a complex chemical process in which specific transmitter substances are released from the sending side of the synapse. The effect is to raise or lower the electrical potential inside the body of the receiving cell. If this potential reaches a threshold, the neuron fires. It is this characteristic of the biological neurons that the artificial neuron model proposed by McCulloch Pitts attempts to reproduce [6] . Following neuron model shown in Figure 3 is widely used in artificial neural networks with some variations. The artificial neuron given in this figure has N inputs, denoted as $x_1, x_2, \ldots, x_N$. Each line connecting these inputs to the neuron is assigned a weight, denoted as $w_1, w_2, \ldots, w_N$ respectively. The activation a, which determines whether the neuron is to be fired or not is given by Equation (1).

$$a = \left(\sum_{j=1}^{N} ww_j x_j\right) \quad (1)$$

A negative value for a weight indicates an inhibitory connection while a positive value indicates excitatory connection. The output, y of the neuron is given by Equation (2).

$$y = f(a) \quad (2)$$

Originally the neuron output function $f(a)$ in McCulloch Pitts model was proposed as threshold function, however linear, ramp, and sigmoid functions are also used in different situations. The vector notation as shown in Equation (3) may be used for expressing the activation of a neuron.

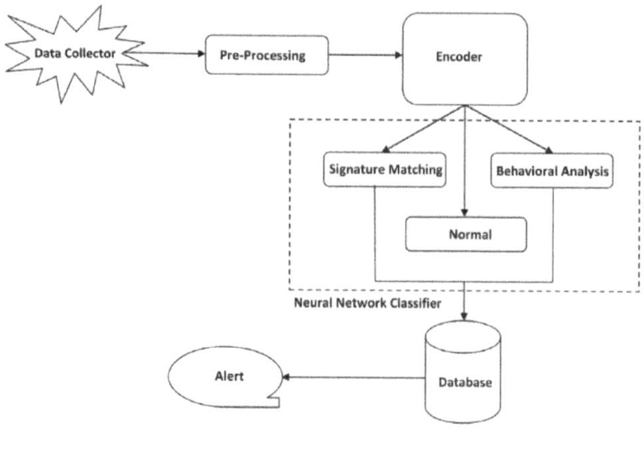

Figure 1: Architecture of intrusion detection system.

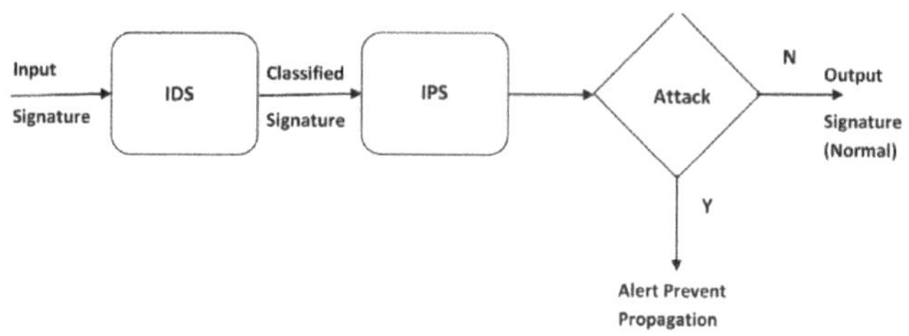

Figure 2: Proposed intrusion detection and prevention system architecture.

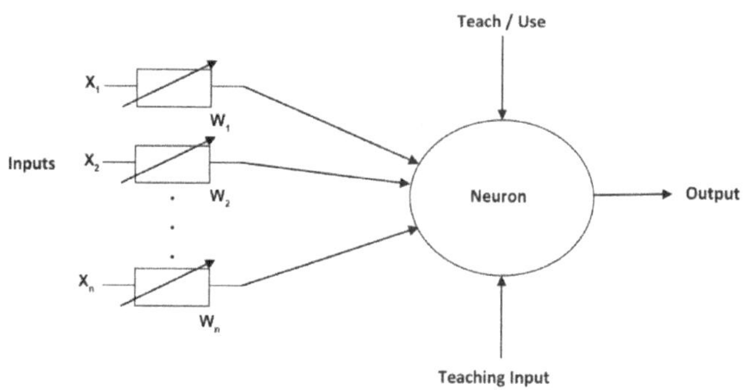

Figure 3: Artificial neural network.

$$a = w^T x \quad (3)$$

Here, the j_{th} element of the input vector x is x_j, the j_{th} element of the weight vector of w is w_j. Both of these vectors are of size N. A Neuro-computing system is made up of a number of artificial neurons and a huge number of interconnections between them. Figure 4 shows architecture of feed forward neural network. In layered neural networks, the neurons are organized in the form of layers [7] . The neurons in a layer get inputs from the previous layer and feed their output to the next layer. These types of networks are called feed forward networks.

Output connections from a neuron to the same or previous layer neurons are not permitted. The input layer is made up of special input neurons, transmitting only the applied external input to their outputs. The last layer is called the output layer, and the layers other than input and output layers are called the hidden layers. A single layer network consists of solely input and output layers without a hidden layer. Networks with one or more hidden layers are called multilayer networks. Multilayer perceptron is a well-known feed forward layered network, on which the Back propagation learning algorithm is widely implemented. The structures, where connections to the neurons are to the same layer or to the previous layers are called recurrent networks. Hopfield and Boltzmann Machine are examples of widely used recurrent networks [8] .

IDPS Implementation on FPGA

The field of network security guarantees the prevention and monitoring of unauthorized access, misuse, modification as well as denial of network accessible resources. The major goals of network security include confidentiality, data integrity, authentication and non repudiation. In the same context, intrusion detection is a security management tool which monitors network traffic for detecting possible security breaches. These security breaches attempt to compromise the confidentiality, integrity or availability of network resources and can be either from outside or inside the network concerned. In traditional networks, firewalls are used to monitor and filter incoming and outgoing packets but they cannot eliminate all security threats, nor can they detect attacks when they happen. It is like a locked gate to a treasure house that prevents the entry of thieves.

IDPS is another network processing application, which is either a software application (example Snort) [9] or a hardware device that monitors network for malicious activities such as denial of service attacks, port scans etc. These IDPS are essential network security appliances that help in maintaining the security goals in a network to a great extent. IDPS are primarily focused on identifying possible incidents, logging information about them, attempting to stop them, and reporting them to security administrators. As the main work of such systems is to monitor network traffics for suspicious activities or patterns, they can be regarded as a multiple pattern matching module. Pattern matching algorithm is thus one of the most critical in such systems and the detection of intruders is performed based on this module. At the higher level, there are management software's that configure log and display alarms. A database for a number of malicious patterns is maintained at the back end. Whenever any packet containing such malicious patterns is found during packet monitoring, the detector engine of IDPS raises an alert call to the administrator for taking necessary action against the target packet. Although the decisive factor for an IDPS is a pattern matching algorithm, it is a highly challenging task to implement.

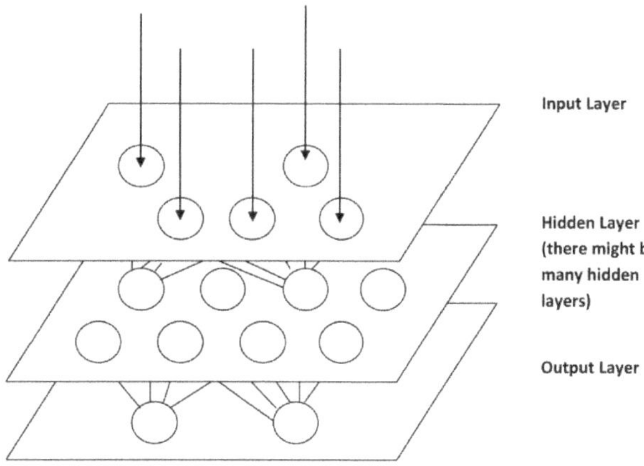

Figure 4: Feed forward neural network.

It is because the operation of a typical IDPS involves deep packet inspection [10] . Checking every byte of an incoming packet in a network to see if it is matching with one of a set of thousands of patterns becomes a computationally intensive task. Moreover if it is a high speed network, packet inspection needs to be performed in line speed which is more challenging. Software based approach is not efficient in terms of speed and moreover parallelism cannot be exploited in case of multiple pattern matching.

So specialized hardware approaches are required to maintain match-up with the network speed and to maintain a tight bound on worst case performance. Here, a new architecture for a pattern matching based IDPS is presented. The aim of our work is to design the ANN-based IDPS and implement it on Virtex 7 FPGA board.

MATLAB IMPLEMENTATION OF THE PROPOSED IDPS ARCHITECTURE

The processing element of an ANN is the neuron. A neuron can be viewed as processing data in three steps; the weighting of its input values, the summation of them all and their filtering by sigmoid function. The summation can be calculated by a serial accumulation. For the weighted inputs to be calculated in parallel using conventional design techniques, a large number of multiplier units would be required. To avoid this, Multiplier/ Accu- mulator architecture has been selected [11] .

It takes the input serially, multiplies them with the corresponding weight and accumulates their sum in a register. The processes are synchronized to clock signal. The number of clock cycles for a neuron to finish its work, equals to the number of connections from the previous layer. The accumulator has a load signal, so that the bias values are loaded to all neurons at start-up.

To implement our proposed architecture we have selected MATLAB SIMULINK version 2010b as an environment as it supports multi-domain simulation and model-based design for dynamic and embedded systems. It provides an interactive graphical environment and a customizable set of block libraries that allows to design, simulate, implement, and test a variety of time-varying systems, including communication, control, signal processing, video processing, image processing etc. Two architectures were built in MATLAB: single layer and double layer. We have used 6 and 10 neurons to train the system for single layer and double layer architectures respectively. During training of the ANN we have specified some values to detect attacks e.g., Normal 0; DoS 1; Probe 2; U2R 3; R2L 4; Other 5 (yet to be discovered attacks). After training our ANN with the given KDD CUP dataset we have generated the SIMULINK ANN Attack classifier model to classify the attack and the normal data separately. Figure 5 shows the architecture and simulation of ANN based IDPS indicating an U2R attack. Here the input signature consists of the 41 attributes of our dataset and the IDPS block consists of 5 classified attack outputs along with the normal signature output [12] .

The proposed IDPS architecture consists of two blocks—the ANN based Intrusion Detection System (IDS), which classifies the attack and the Intrusion Prevention System (IPS) designed using embedded MATLAB function, which takes the classified signature and decides which signatures to be propagated as indicated by the binary values of Intrusion Prevention (IP) status. Figure 5 shows the simulation result for U2R attack signature. After classification by the IDS as U2R attack, the IPS prevents the signatures to be propagated indicated by the IP status of "0". For normal input signature the IPS allows the input to be propagated indicated by the IP status of "1".

The performance of the system was found to be satisfactory. We had tested the system taking 10% of the data from the KDD Cup dataset [13] . Figure 6 shows the False Positive Graph taking into account number of Input Signature (Normal) vs. Number of False positives generated. It is clear from the graph that false positive is within the expected range of 10% to 13%. It however increased to 16% on increasing the number of normal signatures beyond 100.

VHDL MODELING OF THE PROPOSED IDPS

The ANN-based IDPS model designed in MATLAB was transformed into VHDL model from MATLAB environment and was simulated using Xilinx ISE 13.2 ISim (ISE Simulator). ISim provides a complete, full-featured HDL simulator integrated within Xilinx ISE. HDL simulation now will be a fundamental step within our design flow with the tight integration of the ISim within our design environment. After the initial setup we passed a normal packet through the design to check the behavior of the model.

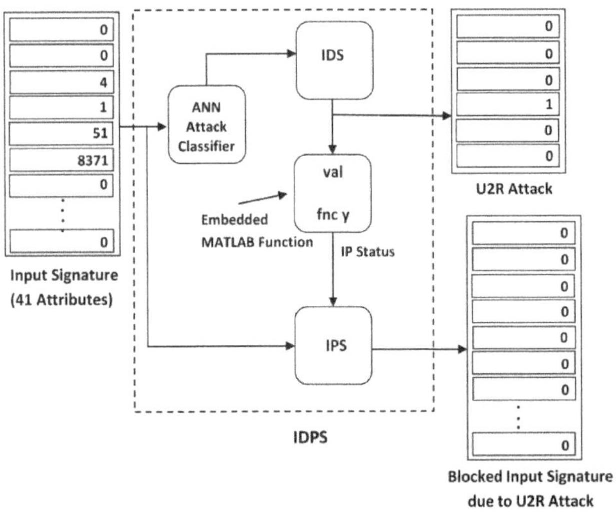

Figure 5: Proposed architecture and simulation of ANN based IDPS showing U2R attack.

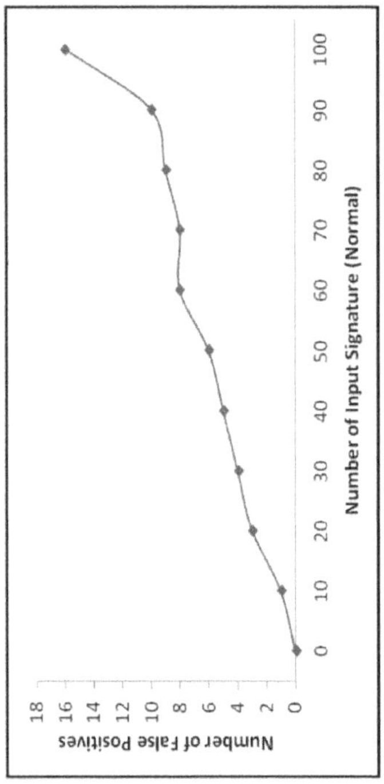

Figure 6: False positive graph.

As predicted the output was same as the result obtained using MATLAB SIMULINK. We then passed different signatures and recorded the behavior of the design. Based on attack signatures we got different simulation results which have been presented in Table 1 with respect to the kind of attack that was detected and subsequently prevented.

We used two types of models for your simulation. Model 1 takes in floating point input values, the actual values as obtained from KDD CUP dataset as signature of an attack. The result is depicted inTable 1(a). In Model 2 we had rounded off the floating point input values to its nearest integer values so as to implement the proposed design on FPGA. Keeping that in mind we trained our ANN model and then executed our simulation output, which has been depicted in Table 1(b). For both the simulations we have used the same set of input data. Due to the conversion of floating point values to integer values there was some loss of precision in the case of simulation results.

As per the model that was simulated the result has been shown with respect to the highest value in the simulation column. According to our simulation environment that was set up classifier detects the signature with the highest value in the simulation and based on the highest value the signature is classified into either Normal, DoS, Probe, U2R, R2L or Other.

If we look deeply into Table 1(a) we can see that simulation 1 and simulation 3 show the corresponding values for DoS signature, simulation 2 show the corresponding values for R2L attack signature, simulation 4 and simulation 5 show the corresponding values for normal signature as designed in our model, and simulation 6 shows the corresponding value for Probe attack signature.

When we execute the same dataset after converting the data to integer we have the following observations. Simulation 1 and simulation 3 show the corresponding values for DoS signature (same as Table 1(a)), simulation 2 shows the corresponding values for a normal signature which denotes false positive, and simulation 4 and simulation 5 show the corresponding values for normal signature. However simulation 4 also shows Probe attack which means false negative as designed in our model, and simulation 6 shows the corresponding value for Probe attack signature. The discrepancy in the values of Table 1(a) and Table 1(b) has been further discussed in this paper.

For comparison purpose we have designed, simulated and implemented the proposed architecture both as a single layer and as a double layer ANN model. Comparison of the both is shown in Table 2. When comparing single layer with double layer ANN model with same set of signatures using floating point as well as integer values we got 100% correct result for double layer ANN model in floating point mode as against 83.33% in integer mode. Similarly for single layer ANN model in floating point mode we got 96.66% correct result as against 70% for integer mode. This discrepancy is due to precision error while rounding off the floating point values to integer ones. Similarly there has been discrepancy between single and double layer ANN model with respect to False Positives and False Negatives as given in Table 2.

Table 1: (a) Simulation results for floating point values. (b) Simulation results for integer values

	Simulation 1	Simulation 2	Simulation 3	Simulation 4	Simulation 5	Simulation 6
Normal	0	0	0	1	1	0
DoS	1	0	1	0	0	0
Probe	0	0	0	0	0	1
R2L	0	1	0	0	0	0
U2R	0	0	0	0	0	0
Others	0	0	0	0	0	0

	Simulation 1	Simulation 2	Simulation 3	Simulation 4	Simulation 5	Simulation 6
Normal	0	1	0	1	1	0
DoS	1	0	1	0	0	0
Probe	0	0	0	1	0	1
R2L	0	0	0	0	0	0
U2R	0	0	0	0	0	0
Others	0	0	0	0	0	0

The proposed architecture allows only the packets of normal signature to pass through the system and stops any other attack signature [14] . Intrusion prevention is the process of performing intrusion detection and attempting to stop detected possible incidents. Intrusion detection and prevention systems (IDPS) are primarily focused on identifying possible incidents, logging information about them, attempting to stop them, and reporting them to security administrators. In our proposed architecture once the attack signature has been detected by the IDS, the IPS comes into play and the signature is stored in our database, compared with a reference value and IP status is set as binary value of "1" to pass the normal signature and a binary value of "0" to block the attack signature. Figure 7 shows the simulation result for a normal signature where IP status is set to "1" to pass the traffic between 1 ps and 2 ps interval. The figure also shows dos attack during the interval 2 ps to 3 ps where IP Status goes low to block the traffic.

FPGA IMPLEMENTATION OF THE PROPOSED ANN BASED ARCHITECTURE

After simulation of the proposed architecture in ISim we have synthesized, implemented and tested the model onto Virtex-7 2000T FPGA device. The system requirement is Intel Core 2 Duo at 2.5 GHz with 4 GB RAM. Virtex-7 2000T combines four smaller FPGAs into a single package by placing them on a special silicon interconnection pad to deliver 6.8 billion transistors in a single large chip. The interposer provides 10,000 data pathways between the individual FPGAs—roughly 10 to 100 times more than would usually be available on a board to create a single FPGA [15] . We have done a comparative analysis between single layer and double layer ANN implementation on Virtex7 2007 T with respect to resource parameters as shown in Table 3.

Table 2: Comparison between single & double layer ANN based IDPS

	Single Layer ANN		Double Layer ANN	
	Floating Point Values	Integer Values	Floating Point Values	Integer Values
Dataset Result (%)	96.66	70	100	83.33
False Positive (%)	10	6	3	10
False Negative (%)	10	10	23	10

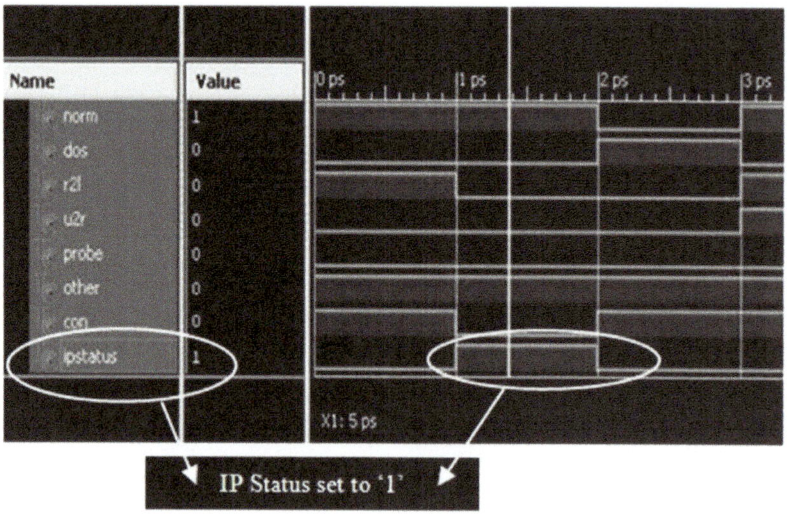

Figure 7: Simulation of normal signature.

The register-transfer level (RTL) schematics sub-part for the single layer and double layer ANN models of IDS are shown in Figure 8 and Figure 9 respectively. RTL abstraction is used in hardware description languages (HDLs) like Verilog and VHDL to create high-level representations of a circuit, from which lower-level representations and ultimately actual wiring can be derived. Design at the RTL level is a typical practice in modern digital design [16] .

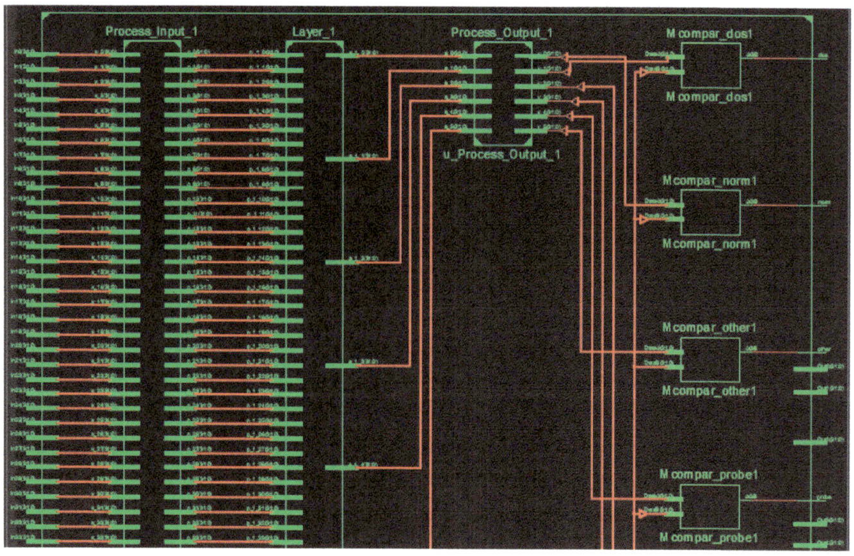

Figure 8: RTL schematic sub-part of single Layer ANN Model.

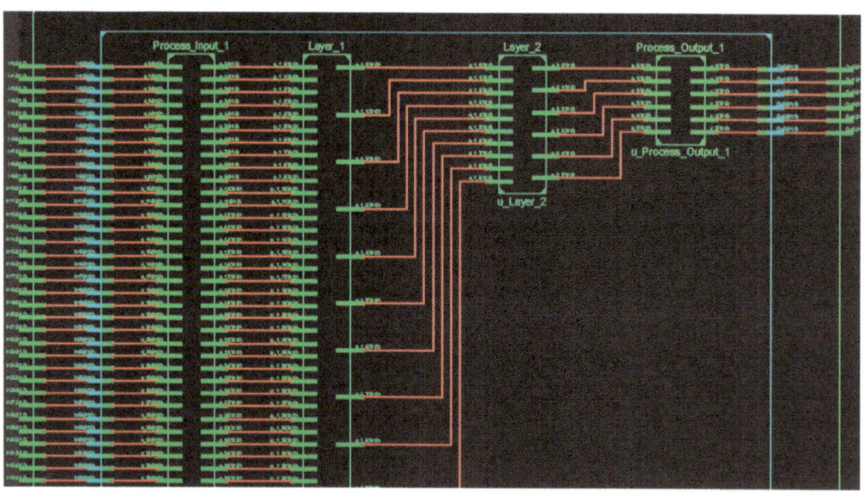

Figure 9: RTL schematic sub-part of double layer ANN Model.

Table 3: Comparative analysis between Single & Double Layer ANN based IDPS Model with respect to Resources used on a Virtex7 FPGA board

	Single Layer Integer ANN Model	% Age of Resources Used	Double Layer Integer ANN Model	% Age of Resources Used	Resources Available in Virtex 7 FPGA
Memory Usage	120 MB		194 MB		
Time Required	24 sec		2 min, 21 sec		
No. of Slice LUT's	8337	0	14169	1	1221600
Number of Fully Used LUT-FF Pair	0	0	0	0	8336
Number of Bonded IOB's	793	66	989	83	1200
Number of DSP48E1's	6	0	865	40	2160

SUMMARY AND FUTURE WORK

The proposed IDPS model using artificial neural network was verified in MATLAB environment using Simulink. The design was later converted to VHDL environment using Xilinx Project Navigator 13.2 and simulated using ISim. In the next step the proposed design was implemented on Virtex-7 2000T FPGA. In all the cases the performance of the design was within the acceptable range.

Future work will include further classification of different types of attacks to further subtypes as and when signatures are available and then integrate it to the proposed architecture so that the model can be robust in nature. Next step will be to evaluate the performance of the proposed architecture in real-time environment.

Indraneel Mukhopadhyay, Mohuya Chakraborty (e.g., military, defense etc.,) in today's world of network defenselessness.

REFERENCES

1. Scarfone, K. and Mell, P. (2007) Guide to Intrusion and Prevention System (IDPS). Department of Commerce, National Institute of Standard and Technology, Technology Administration. http://csrc.nist.gov/publications/nistpubs/800-94/SP800-94.pdf
2. Widrow, B., Rumelhart, D.E. and Lehr, M.A. (1994) Neural Networks: Applications in Industry, Business and Science. Communications of the ACM, 37, 93-105. http://dx.doi.org/10.1145/175247.175257
3. Muthuramalingam, A., Himavathi, S. and Srinivasan, E. (2008) Neural Network Implementation Using FPGA: Issues and Application. The International Journal of Information Technology, 4, 86-92.
4. Tommiska, M.T. (2003) Efficient Digital Implementation of the Sigmoid Function for Reprogrammable Logic. IEEE Proceedings of Computers and Digital Techniques, 150, 403-411.
5. Mukhopadhyay, I., Chakraborty, M. and Chakarbarti, S. (2011) A Comparative Study of Related Technologies of Intrusion Detection & Prevention Systems. Journal of Information Security, 1, 28-38. http://dx.doi.org/10.4236/jis.2011.21003
6. Savran, A. and Ünsal, S. (1999) Hardware Implementation of a Feed forward Neural Network Using FPGAs'. Department of Electrical and Electronics Engineering, Ege University.
7. Haykin, S. (1999) Neural Networks—A Comprehensive Foundations. Prentice-Hall International, New Jersey.
8. Rai, C.S. and Singh, A.P. (2006) A Review of Implementation Techniques for Artificial Neural Networks. University School of Information Technology, GGS Indraprastha University, Delhi.
9. (2014) SNORT User Manual. http://www.snort.org/
10. Chang, R.-I, Lai, L.-B., Su, W.-D., Wang, J.-C. and Kouh, J.-S. (2007) Intrusion Detection by Back Propagation Neural Networks with Sample-Query and Attribute-Query. International Journal of Computational Intelligence Research, 3, 6-10.
11. Dharmapurikar, S., Krishnamurthy, P., Sproull, T., Lockwood, J. and Speeds, L. (2004) Deep Packet Inspection Using Parallel Bloom Filters.
12. Mukhopadhyay, I., Chakraborty, M., Chakrabarti, S. and Chatterjee, T. (2011) Back Propagation Neural Network Approach to Intrusion Detection System. The Proceeding of International Conference on Recent Trend in Information System (ReTIS-11), Kolkata, 21-23 December 2011, 303-308.
13. KDD Cup (1999) Computer Network Intrusion Detection. http://www.sigkdd.org/kdd-cup-1999-computer-network-intrusion detection
14. Mukhopadhyay, I., Chakraborty, M. and Chatterjee, T. (2012) Artificial Neural Network Modeling of Intrusion Detection & Prevention System. IEM International Journal of Management & Technology, 2.
15. Manners, D. (2011) Electronics Weekly. Xilinx Launches 20m ASIC Gate Stacked Silicon FPGA.
16. Vahid, F. (2010) Digital Design with RTL Design, Verilog and VHDL. 2nd Edition, John Wiley and Sons, 247.

CHAPTER 9 DETECTION OF SOPHISTICATED NETWORK ENABLED THREATS VIA A NOVEL MICRO-PROXY ARCHITECTURE

Andrew Blyth

Keywords: Network Security, Firewalls, Proxies and Intrusion Detection

INTRODUCTION

Organizations today seek to utilize information technology as part of their business processes. Networks allow for organizations to communicate with other organizations and people across the globe in real-time. This allows organizations to integrate their supply chains and perform just in time supply-chain management. However this level of connectivity and dependency on information technology can be viewed as a risk as it has the potential to allow an adversary to access confidential/sensitive information and act upon it. Thus organizations have a requirement to protect and defend their information technology so as to maximize their business utility. Over the past three years the following high profile sophisticated computer network attacks have functioned to illustrate how Computer Network Attack (CNA) has moved into the area of information acquisition and intelligence gathering via the application of zero-day exploits. This indicates that the nature and capabilities of threats and threat agents continues to evolve.

- Ghostnet: This the name given to the cyber spying operation discovered in March 2009. It infiltrated highvalue political, economic and media locations in 103 countries, and in total 1295 computer systems were compromised.
- Operation Aurora: This is a cyber attack, which began in mid-December 2009 and continued into February 2010. Google first publicly disclosed the attack on January 12, 2010, when Google stated that over 20 other companies had been attacked.
- Stuxnet: Stuxnet is a Windows-specific computer worm first discovered in June 2010. It is the first discovered worm that spies on and reprograms industrial systems.
- Red October: This cyber espionage network discovered in 2012 focused upon diplomatic, governmental and scientific research organizations in different countries mostly within the region of Eastern Europe, former USSR members and countries in central Asia.

The traditional approach to proxies says that they are placed at the main ingress and egress points on a network. Due to bandwidth requirements this approach fails to fully protect network services at the interaction level. Instead, it focuses upon the utilization of signatures and statistical analysis of data flows. What is required is a proxy approach targeted at the application layer within which a service functions and focused on the nature of the discourse that a server engages in with a client.

UNIVERSE OF DISCOURSE

We can analyze the search spaces required by various cyber attacks from a logical perspective with a view to identifying the complexity of the search spaces. So let the set of all possible inputs to a program be denoted as the set I_p. We will define two further sets: let I_a be the input set of all possible attacks, and let I_v be the input set of all possible valid inputs that are not an attack. Thus we may assert that $I_p = I_a \cup I_v$. As was observed in [1] , the size and complexity of this search is to all intents and purposes infinity. The challenge for an intrusion detection system is to identify all malicious input from this set. Misuse Intrusion Detection Systems such assume that the input space is benign and that the set of valid attacks is finite, and thus $|I_a| < |I_v|$. If this statement is true then a logical deduction is that it

Citation: Blyth, A. (2014) Detection of Sophisticated Network Enabled Threats via a Novel Micro-Proxy Architecture. Journal of Information Security, 5, 37-45. doi: 10.4236/jis.2014.52004.

is possible to express via a formal grammar and a set of rules by which the membership of I_v can be completely defined. In taking such a view, the implicit assumption is to allow all input except that which can be shown to be malicious. However, this assumption is now being challenged and event correlation models are being proposed that view the set of all possible attacks as being infinitely large and the set of all possible valid inputs being finite. Thus $|I_a| > |I_v|$. If this is true then we would assert that the logical approach to take to intrusion detection is to specify the set of allowable inputs and define all other non-valid input to be attacks, hence $I_v = I_p - I_a$. In taking such a view the implicit assumption is to deny all inputs except that which can be shown to be non-malicious. Consequently this project seeks to explore this novel approach to intrusion detection via the profiling of code artifacts to construct/derive a rule-set that defines the set I_v. In defining $|I_a| < |I_v|$ we are constraining the freedom of movement of our adversary and thus controlling the cyber battle space. Thus the challenge is to define the allowable inputs that can occur between a remote user and a service executing on a computer system. In defining this interaction a detailed model of the communication that can occur at the application (OSI level 7) must be constructed, hence the need to examine the service at the binary, and code, artifact level to determine the precise structure of the interaction.

STATE OF THE ART

Static Analysis of Assembly Code

Understanding what an executable does is paramount to the analysis of computer systems and networks in predicting accurately their behaviour, and to the discovery of critical vulnerabilities that have a devastating effect on our global computing infrastructure. Static approaches have also been applied to virus and worm detection, as well as polymorphic worm detection. Static analysis has also been applied to rootkit detection and to identifying spyware-like behaviour.

In addition we can also further classify these approaches based on the following [2] :

- Testing-based approaches try to trigger vulnerability by exercising an application with random or malicious inputs, [2] .
- Monitoring-based approaches instead of examine the execution of an application during normal use look for anomalous behaviours. In particular, a whole area of research has focused on ways to detect attacks on the basis of the analysis of the system call invocations performed by a program [3] .
- Slicing is a widely used technique for program analysis, debugging, and comprehension [4] . Software slice analysis attempts to approximate the state of an application during execution via the construction of cohesion and coupling metrics.
- Shape analysis attempts to construct a directed graph construct that represents the execution of a program [5] . Various topological transformation functions can be applied to identify sub-graphs, where each sub-graph corresponds to a known function call implementation.
- Alias analysis is a method for the identification of possible security flaws due to the conversion of one type or another, such as type conversation/casting in the C programming language.

Automated static analysis (ASA) identifies probable source code anomalies early in the soft ware development lifecycle that could lead to vulnerabilities. Automated static analysis (ASA) can identify common coding problems early in the development process via a tool that automates the inspection of source code [6] . Automated static analysis reports potential source code anomalies, which we call alerts, like null pointer dereferences, buffer over flows, and style inconsistencies [7] . Developers inspect each alert to determine if the alert is an indication of an anomaly important enough for the developer to fix. If a developer determines the alert is an important, fixable anomaly, then we call the alert an actionable alert [8] . When an alert is not an indication of an actual code anomaly or the alert is deemed unimportant to the developer (e.g. the alert indicates a source code anomaly inconsequential to the program's functionality as perceived by the developer), we call the alert an un actionable alert [8] .

Improving ASA's ability to generate predominantly actionable alerts through the development of tools that are both sound and complete can be said to be an intractable problem [9] . Additionally, the development of algorithms underlying ASA requires a trade-off between the level of analysis and execution time [9] . Methods proposed for improving static analysis include annotations, which could be specified incorrectly and require developer overhead, and allowing the developer to select ASA properties, such as alert types, specific to their development environment and project [10] . Another way to increase the number of actionable alerts identified by static analysis is to use the alerts generated by ASA with other information about the software under analysis to prioritize or classify alerts.

Static analysis techniques attempt to identify the presence of a vulnerability, or the ways in which a vulnerability can be exploited. Thus in terms of search spaces they define $|I_A| < |I_V|$ to be true.

Dynamic Analysis

Dynamic analysis is the ability to observe and examine code as it executes in real-time, and thus it has become a central tool in computer security and vulnerability research. Dynamic analysis is attractive because it provides us with the ability to perform deductive reasoning about actual executions, and thus the ability to perform precise security analysis based upon run-time data.

Two of the most commonly employed dynamic analysis techniques in security research are dynamic taint analysis and forward symbolic execution. Dynamic taint analysis runs a program and observes which computations are affected by predefined taint sources such as user input. Symbolic execution refers to the analysis of programs by tracking symbolic rather than actual values, a case of abstract interpretation. Dynamic forward symbolic execution automatically builds a logical formula describing a program execution path, which reduces the problem of reasoning about the execution to the domain of logic. The two analyses can be used in conjunction to build formulas representing only the parts of an execution that depend upon tainted values [11] . The purpose of dynamic taint analysis is to track information flows [12] . Any program value whose computation depends on data derived from a taint source is considered tainted. Any other value is considered untainted. Symbolic execution maintains a symbolic state, which maps variables to symbolic expressions. Forward symbolic execution allows us to reason about the behaviour of a program on many different inputs at one time by building a logical formula that represents a program execution. Thus, reasoning about the behaviour of the program can be reduced to the domain of logic. The advantages of forward symbolic execution include [13] :

- Multiple inputs. One of the advantages of forward symbolic execution is that it can be used to reason about more than one input at once.
- The primary difference between forward symbolic execution and regular execution is that when a function is executed it is evaluated symbolically; it returns a symbol instead of a concrete value. When a new symbol is first returned, there are no constraints on its value; it represents any possible value.
- Creating a forward symbolic execution engine is conceptually a very simple process: take the operational semantics of the language and change the definition of a value to include symbolic expressions.
- The number of security applications utilizing these two techniques is enormous. Examples of security research areas employing either dynamic taint analysis of forward symbolic executions are:
- Unknown Vulnerability Detection. Dynamic taint analysis can look for misuses of user input during an execution. For example, dynamic taint analysis can be used to prevent code injection attacks by monitoring whether user input is executed [14] .
- Automatic Input Filter Generation. Forward symbolic execution can be used to automatically generate input filters that detect and remove exploits from the input stream [15] . Filters generated in response to actual executions are attractive because they provide strong accuracy guarantees [17] .
- Malware Analysis. Taint analysis and forward symbolic execution are used to analyse how information flows through a malware binary, explore trigger-based behaviour, and detect emulators [16] .
- Test Case Generation. Taint analysis and forward symbolic execution are used to automatically generate inputs to test programs [17] , and can generate inputs that cause two implementations of the same protocol to behave differently [17] .
- Abstract Interpretation [18] using numerical domains, such as intervals, octagons, and convex polyhedrals necessitates the use of widening and narrowing operators to guarantee termination over loops in the program.

It should be noted that taint analysis as a technique for malware detection suffers from a variety of evasion techniques that allow an intruder to avoid detection of the malicious software. Dynamic analysis techniques attempt to identify the presence of a vulnerability, or the ways in which a vulnerability can be exploited. Thus in terms of search spaces they define $|I_A| < |I_V|$ to be true.

Intrusion Detection

In terms of the analysis of software artifacts various Intrusion Detection Systems have been developed that attempt to detect the presence of software artifacts, such as malicious software, at the TCP/IP packet level. Examples of such approaches include:

- The Snort intrusion detection system is a host/network rule based expert system approach to misuse detection. It operates by monitoring all TCP/IP traffic targeted at a host/network. Consequently, the rule based expert system approach to misuse detection is incapable of detecting new forms of malicious software due to its lack of prior knowledge.
- Process monitoring approaches such as [19] monitor software processes with a view to identifying malicious activity based on pre-defined norms of behaviour. This type of approach is based on user-defined levels of normality and has a computational impact on the performance of the process being monitored. Anomaly detection approaches such as [20] , attempt to learn user behaviour via Markov Chains based analysis engines. However such approaches suffer from generating false positive results and the time taken to learn behaviour.
- A proxy functions as the man-in-the-middle of an information flow, allowing for the information stream to be inspected and rules governing malicious behaviour applied [21] . Such approaches either make use of user defined rules to identify malicious activity, or else make use of learning algorithms to identify abnormal behaviour. In addition, proxies implement a white-list/black-list access control mechanism governing access to remote systems. Due to the volume of network traffic that the network-based proxy solutions support security checks governing malicious behaviour are computationally and time/resource bounded. The net effect of this is that the complexity and sophistication of the rule set/language is constrained. Proxies' function to protect systems from attacks at the application/content layer. The challenges facing this type of approach is that a rule specification is required to define malicious behaviour, and that learning algorithms suffer from generating false positive results and the time taken to learn behaviour. As a rule application/content layer proxies implement a default allow rule. Thus proxies fail to detect novel sophisticated attacks.

All of the above attempt to define rules/algorithms by which erroneous behaviour can be identified and thus in terms of search spaces they define $|I_A| < |I_V|$ to be true. Therefore they attempt to codify all of the ways in which a threat agent can exploit vulnerability in order to gain unauthorized access to a system. The aim of the proposed architecture is to limit the access space within which an adversary can manoeuvre by assuming that all input is malicious unless it meets a goodness function. Hence in terms of search spaces they define $|I_A| < |I_V|$ to be false and $|I_A| > |I_V|$ to be true. Thus the default access rule is to deny access from a remote user to a server/service.

CONCEPTAL ARCHITECTURE

The basic principle underpinning the micro proxy conceptual

architecture is to assume that all input are malicious unless proved otherwise, in effect to implement a default deny policy at the application level. In making such an assumption we are constraining the way in which an adversary can interact with a system. For any interaction to succeed it must pass a series of tests that define the goodness of the interaction. Hence in terms of search spaces we define $|I_A| > |I_V|$. The challenge can thus be reshaped to the analysis of software artifacts so as to define/impose the rules governing the acceptance of valid input.

Figure 1 Defines the Conceptual Architecture. The role and function of Figure 1 is to define the various components by which a binary/software artifact is analyzed and a proxy configuration is constructed. The basic ontological constructs contained in Figure 1 are that arrows represent data flows and, squares represent processes, ovals represent remote agents (either a user or a service) and rounded squares represent data sources. At the heart of the conceptual architecture is a control flow graph.

The Service Analysis Engine

The service analysis engine takes a set of Service Area Artifacts as input and produces a service area profile. For example, suppose that the remote/legacy service is a web server and that the files in the home directory of the web server are as follows:

1) /index.html 2) /search.php 3) /images/logo.jpeg The service area artifacts listed above function to specify the allowable set of valid file requests that can be contained in a HTTP request.

The Reverse Analysis Engine

The role and function of the reverse analysis engine is to take either binary artifacts such as PE/ELF, or source code artifacts such as C, and to produce a control flow graph. A control flow graph is a directed graph that represents all of the possible execution paths that can occur during the execution of a program [22] . Certain compliers such as GCC and disassemblers already possess a limited capability to construct control flow graphs in a simple text based format [23] .

The Control Flow Graph (CFG)

The role and function of a control flow graph is to allow for the easy constructing and reasoning about the control flow of an artifact. Traditional control flow models are no more than type-less directed graphs where each node is either a collection of commands or a conditional statement. The control flow model presented, and utilized, in this project draws upon socio-linguistic constructs to create a richer and more structured syntactic/semantic representation of the execution of an artifact. Figure 2 is a simple example of a C program and a control flow graph that determines if the character typed at the keyboard is a space or not. A control flow graph is a directed graph that consists of a number of nodes and arcs. There are a number of rules governing the consistency of a control flow graph.

- Every arc in a control flow graph must have a conditional associated with it.
- Every node is either an atomic action or a function that can be decomposed. In Figure 2, we can see one atomic action that is assigned the result value of a function to a variable, and three functional actions.
- The logical conjugation of all of the conditions on the output arcs from a node is logically true. So for example in Figure 2 we can observe that the following logical condition is true: $a = 31 \wedge a \neq 32$.
- Every arc must have a source and a destination. The source of an arc is called the point from which the arc originates and the destination of an arc is the point at which the arc terminates.

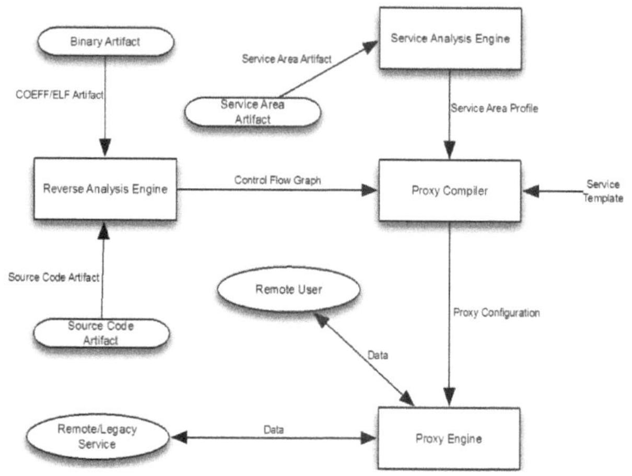

Figure 1: Conceptual architecture.

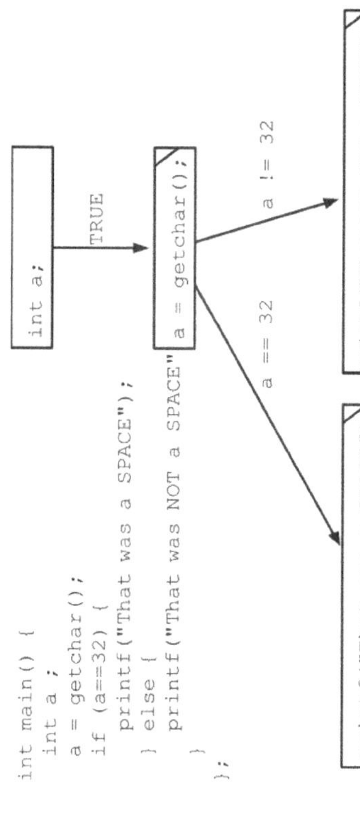

Figure 2: A simple control flow graph.

- Only one node in the graph can function solely as the source for arcs and that node is called the root node and is the logical start of the control flow graph.
- In constructing a socio-linguistic model of a control flow graph it is necessary to map a computer programming language construct into a series of speech acts. A speech act is an action that when combined within a series of rules allows for the expression of a conversation. Thus

when viewing the following program/server we may observe that it presents a conversation in content and structure [24] . In expressing this content and structure in accordance with the formal definition of a speech act we map certain types of structures to program constructs.

- A propositional act is a statement which can be evaluated to be true or false, such as "is x + y < z" or "does this file exist". People or machines can meaningfully utter propositional acts. Thus in terms of a control flow graph propositional acts are viewed as directed arcs that link nodes together.
- An illocutionary act is always performed when a person utters certain expressions with an intention. Thus we can view a function invocation as an illocutionary act that can be seen as an expression of intent to perform some behaviour. Types of illocutionary act are:
- Assertive: speech acts that commit a speaker to the truth of the expressed such as assigning a value to a variable (x = x + y).
- Directive: speech acts that are to cause the agent to take a particular action, e.g. the expression of a conditional statement such as an if, case, repeat or while statement.
- Commissive: speech acts that commit an agent to some future action, e.g. a function innovation (max(a,b)).
- Declaration: speech acts that change the reality in accordance with the proposition of the declaration, e.g. the termination of a loop, or the return value of a function.
- Expressive: speech acts that express the agent's positions towards the proposition. In programming terms it can be viewed as the creation of a variable, e.g. int a.
- A perlocutionary act is an act that produces an effect on the behaviour of an agent. For example in control flow graph terms a perlocutionary act can be seen as an action such as input or output.

The output of the reverse analysis engine is a control flow graph such as the one described inFigure 2, but encoded in XML.

The Proxy Compiler

The proxy compiler functions to take the following as input and to produce an executable configuration as output.

- Service Area Profile (SAP)
- Control Flow Graph (CFG)

The executable configuration is produced via the concurrent execution of a series of defined constraints on a distributed cloud environment. This configuration is then executed on the proxy engine. The proxy compiler checks that the structure provided by the control flow graph matches the parameter provided via the analysis of the file/directory structures (the service area profile), and the application interaction patterns/behaviours specified by the service template.

The Proxy Engine

The role of the proxy engine is to function as a guard ensuring that all data passing to/from the remote service is protected and meets the goodness criteria as defined in the proxy configuration. Thus the proxy takes the input data stream from the user of the service and executes the configuration of proxy to ensure that the input data stream adheres to the rules governing the goodness of the input. If the goodness conditions are adhered to then the data is passed onto the remote service.

EVALUATION

The test methodology to evaluate the utility of the proxy architecture is to take all of the Microsoft Security Bulletins published from 1st Jan 2011 to 31st Dec 2011 and examine via inspection of each bulletin whether the proxy architecture could detect the attack. The role and function of the Microsoft Security Bulletins is to provide an independent data set from which an impartial and repeatable assessment of the utility of the proxy architecture could be conducted. From Jan 2011 to Dec 2011 Microsoft published 100 security bulletins numbered MS11-001 to MS11-100. These security bulletins cover every type of Microsoft technology, operating system and application. In board terms we can classify these security bulletins via two dimensions:

- How the exploit code is delivered. Typically there are two ways that exploit code is delivered to a target either via a remote connection of some description or locally.
- The target of the exploitation. Typically this can be divided down into four elements.
    - Applications such as IE, Word, PowerPoint, etc.
    - Middle-ware such as .NET, JavaScript, OLE etc.
    - Services such as HTTP, DNS, WINS etc.
    - Kernel Executive, Host Operating System, Device Drivers, TCP/IP Stack etc.
- The test data contained in the Microsoft Security Bulletins is broken down as follows (Table 1).

Table 1: Evaluation data

	Application	Middleware	Services	Kernel
Remote exploitation	32	24	19	7
Local exploitation	0	0	0	18

- Thus from the data contained in Table 1 we can observe for all of 2011 Microsoft issues:
- 18 security bulletins regarding kernel level vulnerabilities that could be exploited locally and 7 security bulletins regarding kernel vulnerabilities that could be exploited remotely;
- 19 security bulletins regarding service level vulnerabilities that could be exploited remotely;
- 24 security bulletins regarding middleware level vulnerabilities that could be exploited remotely;
- 32 security bulletins regarding application level vulnerabilities that could be exploited remotely.
- From the analysis of the data we can observe for all

Microsoft Security Bulletins published in 2011 (MS 001 to MS 100), that the proxy could have detected 29 of these vulnerabilities, and have their exploitation prevented by our proxy architecture. Of these 29 vulnerabilities that could have been detected detailed breakdown is as follows:

- 19 of these vulnerabilities relate to remote exploitation of services;
- 2 of the vulnerabilities relate to remote exploitation of the kernel;
- 8 of these vulnerabilities relate to remote exploitation of the middleware.
- It should be noted that our proposed micro-proxy architecture;
- Did detect 100% of the vulnerabilities targeted at a service running on a server. Key services include: DNS, WINS, IIS and FTP.
- Could only detect the middleware vulnerabilities when the middle-ware technology was deployed within a server environment;
- Did not detect any of the Microsoft Security Bulletins relating to applications such as Microsoft Office and Internet Explorer.

ACKNOWLEDGEMENTS

My thanks go to the following people for their help: Dr. Gaius Mulley and Mr. Konstantinos Xynos. This research has been funded by DSTL.

REFERENCES

1. Bass, T. (2000) Intrusion Detection Systems and Multi-Sensor Data Fusion. Communications of the ACM, 43, 4. http://dx.doi.org/10.1145/332051.332079
2. Cova, M., Felmetsger, V., Banks, G. and Vigna, G. (2006) Static Detection of Vulnerabilities in x86 Executables. ACSAC '06 Proceedings of the 22nd Annual Computer Security Applications Conference, Miami Beach, December 2006, 269-278.
3. Mutz, D., Valeur, F., Vigna, G. and Kruegel, C. (2006) Anomalous System Call Detection. ACM Transactions on Information and System Security, 9, 1.http://dx.doi.org/10.1145/1127345.1127348
4. Wang, T. and Roychoudhury, A. (2007) Hierarchical Dynamic Slicing. Proceedings of the 2007 International Symposium on Software Testing and Analysis, 228-238.
5. Zhang, X. and Gupta, R. (2004) Whole Execution Traces. 37th International Symposium on Microarchitectures. IEEE Press.
6. Zheng, J., Williams, L., Nagappan, N., Snipes, W., Hudepohl, J. and Vouk, M. (2006) On the Value of Static Analysis for Fault Detection in Software. IEEE Transactions on Software Engineering, 32, 240-253. http://dx.doi.org/10.1109/TSE.2006.38
7. Hovemeyer, D. and Pugh, W. (2004) Finding Bugs Is Easy. Proceedings of the 19th ACM Conference on ObjectOriented Programming, Systems, Languages, and Applications, Vancouver.
8. Heckman, S. and Williams, L. (2009) A Model Building Process for Identifying Actionable Static Analysis Alerts. Proceedings of the 2nd IEEE International Conference on Software Testing, Verification and Validation, Denver, 1-4 April 2009, 161-170.
9. Chess, B. and McGraw, G. (2004) Static Analysis for Security. IEEE Security & Privacy, 2, 76-79. http://dx.doi.org/10.1109/MSP.2004.111
10. Yi, K., Choi, H., Kim, J. and Kim, Y. (2007) An Empirical Study on Classification Methods for Alarms from a BugFinding Static C Analyzer. Information Processing Letters, 102, 118-123. http://dx.doi.org/10.1016/j.ipl.2006.11.004
11. Schwartz, E.J., Avgerinos, T. and Brumley, D. (2010) All You Ever Wanted to Know about Dynamic Taint Analysis and Forward Symbolic Execution (but Might Have Been Afraid to Ask). Proceedings of the 2010 IEEE Symposium on Security and Privacy, Oakland, 16-19 May 2010, 317-331. http://dx.doi.org/10.1109/SP.2010.26
12. Cavallaro, L., Saxena, P. and Sekar, R. (2008) On the Limits of Information Flow Techniques for Malware Analysis and Containment. Proceedings of the 5th International Conference on Detection of Intrusions and Malware, and Vulnerability Assessment (DIMVA), Springer.
13. Pasareanu, C.S. and Visser, W. (2009) A Survey of New Trends in Symbolic Execution for Software Testing and Analysis. International Journal of Tools Technology Transfer, 11, 339-353. http://dx.doi.org/10.1007/s10009-009-0118-1
14. Crandall, J., Su, Z., Wu, S.F. and Chong, F. (2005) On Deriving Unknown Vulnerabilities from Zero-Day Polymorphic and Metamorphic Worm Exploits. Proceedings of the ACM Conference on Computer and Communications Security, 235-248.http://dx.doi.org/10.1145/1102120.1102152
15. Brumley, D., Newsome, J., Song, D., Wang, H. and Jha, S. (2008) Theory and Techniques for Automatic Generation of Vulnerability Based Signatures. IEEE Transactions on Dependable and Secure Computing, 5, 224-241.http://dx.doi.org/10.1109/TDSC.2008.55
16. Sharif, M., Lanzi, A., Giffin, J. and Lee, W. (2009) Automatic Reverse Engineering of Malware Emulators. Proceedings of the IEEE Symposium on Security and Privacy, 94-109.
17. Cadar, C., Dunbar, D. and Engler, D. (2008) Klee: Unassisted and Automatic Generation of High-Coverage Tests for Complex Systems Programs. Proceedings of the USENIX Symposium on Operating System Design and Implementation, 209-224.
18. Mine, A. (2001) A New Numerical Abstract Domain Based on Difference-Bound Matrices. PADO II, 2053, 155-172.
19. Yin, H., Poosankam, P., Hanna, S. and Song, D. (2010) HookScout: Proactive Binary-Centric Hook Detection. Proceedings of the Detection of Intrusions and Malware, and Vulnerability Assessment, Springer, 1-20.
20. Frossi, A., Maggi, F., Rizzo, G.L. and Zaneo, S. (2009)

Selecting and Improving System Call Models for Anomaly Detection. Proceedings of the Detection of Intrusions and Malware, and Vulnerability Assessment, Springer.

21. Bockermann, C., Apel, M. and Meier, M. (2009) Learning SQL for Databasc Intrusion Detection Using Context-Sensitive Modelling. Proceedings of the Detection of Intrusions and Malware, and Vulnerability Assessment, Springer.

22. Tanenbaum, A.S. (2007) Modern Operating Systems, Pearson Education.

23. Abadi, M., Budiu, M., Erlingsson, U. and Ligatti, J. (2009) Control Flow Integrity Principles, Implementations and Applications. ACM Transactions on Information and Systems Security (TISSEC), 13, 1. http://dx.doi.org/10.1145/1609956.1609960

24. Searle, J.R. (1969) Speech Acts: An Essay in the Philosophy of Language. Cambridge Press, Cambridge. http://dx.doi.org/10.1017/CBO9781139173438

SECTION III: CLOUD SECURITY METHODS

CHAPTER 10 ANOMALY DETECTION SYSTEMS IN CLOUD NETWORKS AND SURVEY OF CLOUD SECURITY MEASURES IN CLOUD STORAGE APPLICATIONS

Arif Sari

Keywords: Anomaly Detection Systems, Cloud Computing, Cloud Environment, Intrustion Detection Systems, Cloud Security

INTRODUCTION

Cloud computing is not a promise but a fulfillment in the IT world. The benefits of cloud computing have no infinite end as to what can't be done using the cloud environment due to a variety of deployment model such as Software as a Service, Platform as a Service, and Infrastructure as a Service. The cloud computing technology allows for much more efficient computing by centralizing storage, memory, processing and bandwidth. This allows flexibility in accessing of data over the cloud network.

Network traffic analysis in cloud environments is one of the most important tasks in cloud management to guarantee the quality of services, validate performance of new applications and services, build accurate network models and detect anomalies in the cloud. The flow of network that is been created by cloud computing systems shows users' behavior in service operation or use. Traffic analysis and the recognition of all significant application flows are important tools for modeling service usage, building up patterns for identifying normal system operations [1] .

The cloud computing environment has faced numbers of security challenges. Most of them have been fixed up to an extent, other security aspects spring up and it's vital to know before organizations switch fully. Intrusion detection system in cloud networks plays a very important role as the active security defense against intruders. IDS needs to be employed properly in the cloud networks, because it requires scalability, efficiency and virtualized-based approach in implementation. Sabastian Roschke et al. proposed that the users of cloud computing have a limited control over its data and resources that have been hosted on a cloud service provider remote servers [2] . Due to this proposed theory, it automatically becomes the responsibility of the cloud service provider to oversee the IDS in the cloud environment. Additionally, network communication between cloud provider and its customers affects significantly the performance of most cloud-based applications [3] . Analyzing the flow of network traffic provides insights on how applications behave and also their performance in cloud environment. Therefore, it is necessary to develop network traffic measurement and analysis techniques to improve availability, performance and security in cloud computing environments.

On the other hand, managing and analyzing network traffic of large scale cloud systems is a challenging task. The techniques used to monitor and analyze traffic in conventional distributed systems differ from cloud computing systems. In conventional approaches, assumptions are made that network flows follow some patterns, which is acceptable for corporate applications, but cloud applications may have significant changes in traffic patterns [4] .

In the first section of this paper the concept of anomaly detection is described and taxonomies of anomalies are discussed broadly. Additionally, separate sections discuss security measures and comparison among basic cloud storage applications such as Google Drive, ICloud and Dropbox to highlight their security preferences and mechanisms.

CONCEPT OF ANOMALY DETECTION SYSTEMS

Anomaly Detection System (ADS) is a technique of the Intrusion Detection System which identifies activities that are

Citation: Sari, A. (2015) Anomaly Detection Systems in Cloud Networks and Survey of Cloud Security Measures in Cloud Storage Applications. Journal of Information Security, 6, 142-154. doi: 10.4236/jis.2015.62015.

not normal among the normality of a system behavior as it is illustrated on Figure 1 as N represents malicious nodes, R represents routers, G represents anomaly guard modules and "n" represents nodes.

Whenever such anomaly occurs an alert is generated to the administrators that shows the occurrence of an anomaly in the system, this makes a suitable supposition that the anomaly or changes are caused by either malicious or disrupting activities, and the IDS is also capable of suspending or blocking the connection where the anomaly is originating from. The ADS identifies intrusions by classifying activities as either anomalous or normal, and also a training phase needs to be done for the ADS to recognize "new" attacks. The ADS generates more false alarms than the Misuse based IDS systems. The Intrusion Detection System technique is split into two forms or categories which are the Misuse Detection System and the Anomaly Detection System [5] .

Misuse Detection System

Most IDS that are well known make use of the Misuse Detection System approach in the IDS algorithm. The misuse detection system has a pre-defined rules because it works based on the previous or known attacks, that's how intrusion is been detected in the system. It's like the database of an antivirus signature, if it's not up to date it cannot detect new attack signature because such virus signature it's not in its database. The effectiveness of the Misuse Detection System is in detecting only "Know Attacks", because the rules or pattern of the Misuse Detection System are stored in the database of the system. The main downside in the Misuse Detection System is that it doesn't detect new attacks because it's not in its pre-defined rules.

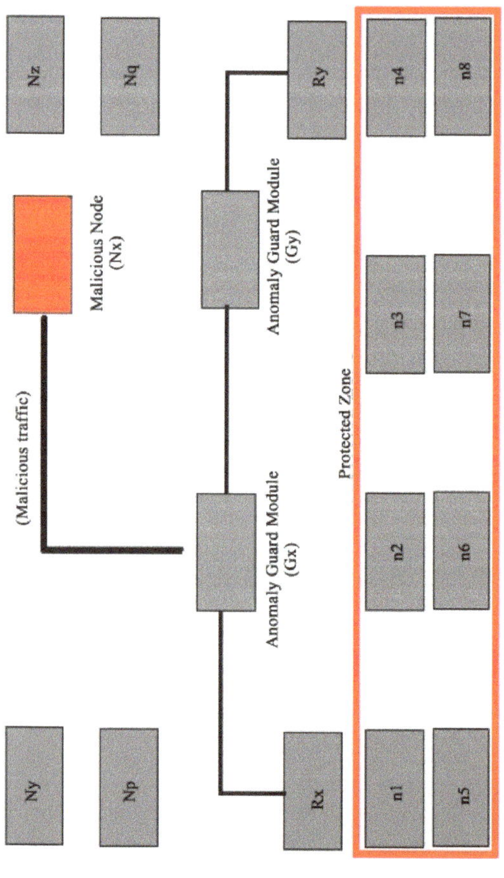

Figure 1: Illustration of anomaly detection.

Anomaly Detection Systems

There have been studies or research in the Anomaly Detection System in different problem domain, but in the cloud environment it has not been widely researched on. The Anomaly Detection technique in cloud based computing is still in view and evolving because it provides challenges that's still in the cooking pot. Anomaly Detection Systems in cloud based networks detects unwanted traffic in the network and this can be caused by loss of packets, unwanted behavior of application etc.

In a traditional network, IDS monitor detects, and alert the administrative user by deploying IDS on important points on the user site. But in the cloud network IDS has to be managed by the service providers [6] . The data that the intrusion communicates through is passed through the cloud service provider, this makes it only possible for the service provider to be the administrator and the user just has to depend on the service provider. Most times the user is not aware of such activities so as to keep the reputation and image of the cloud service provider. A solution was proposed by Roschke and et al. [2] that combines and integrates various IDS sensor output reports on a single interface. The communication between different IDS has been with the Intrusion Detection Message Exchange Format (IDMEF) standards. The positioning of IDS sensors on various layers of the cloud environment like the application layer, system layer, and platform layer can create better communication between the IDS sensors and also increases the detection process within the cloud environment. Generated pro- mpts or alerts are sent to the "Event Gatherer" program. The Event Gatherer program acts as a collector of alerts that spring up as a result of intrusion in the cloud based network. The alert received by the Event Gatherer is converted in the IDMEF standard and is stored in the Event Gatherer database with the help of a plug-in known as the Sender and Receiver Handler plug-in [7] .

TAXONOMY OF ANOMALIES

Anomaly detection aspires at finding the presence of anomalous patterns in network traffic and usual detection of such outline can provide network administrator with extra information source to identify network behavior or tracing and locating the root cause of faults in a network [8] . Anomalies can be classified into three categories: as Point Anomalies, Contextual Anomalies and Collective Anomalies [9] [10] .

Point Anomalies

This is when an individual data instance deviates from its normal activity or form it is said to be anomalous, because other data are normal. This shows that the anomalous activity lies outside the boundaries of the normal region. This is the easiest type of anomaly amongst the 3 types or categories and it is the strength or importance of anomaly detection. Figure 2 illustrates the point anomalies.

From Figure 2, N_1 and N_2 are regions of normal behavior, Points O_1 and O_2 are anomalies and Points in region O_3 are anomalies.

Contextual Anomalies

The contextual anomalies occur when the occurrence of

information is or shows traces of anomalous character in an exact or precise context, which is the unwanted behavior of activities that surrounds an individual data instance. Figure 3 illustrates the Contextual Anomaly.

As it is shown on Figure 3, when this occurs it is characterized as a related anomaly. This requires an idea or notion of context in the data instance. It is also referred to as conditional anomalies.

Collective Anomaly

This is when related data instances collected acts as anomalous or show unwanted activities related to the entire data set. In collective anomaly, the individual data instance with collective anomaly are not otherwise said to be anomalous on their own because the collective anomaly requires a relationship between or among data instances; Sequential, Spatial, and Graph data to cause a collective anomaly. But their occurrence as a whole or collection is or can be anomalous. Figure 4illustrates the Collective anomaly.

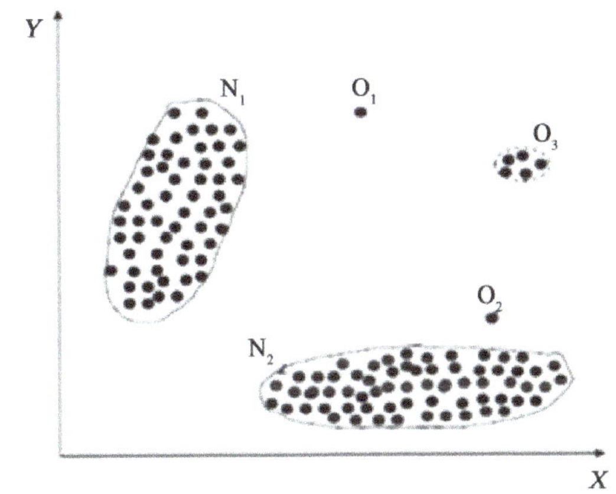

Figure 2: Illustration of point anomaly.

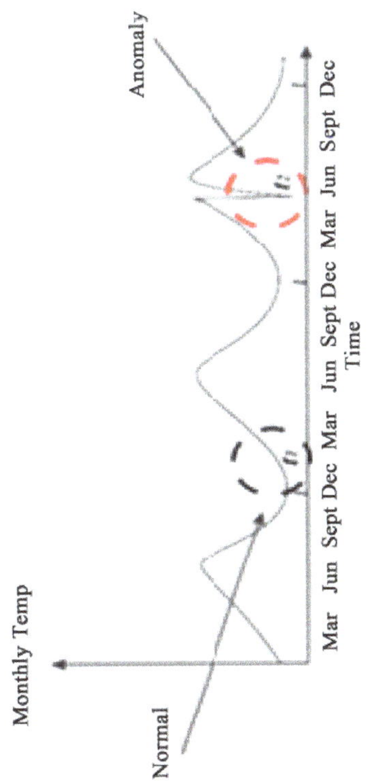

Figure 3: Illustration of contextual anomaly.

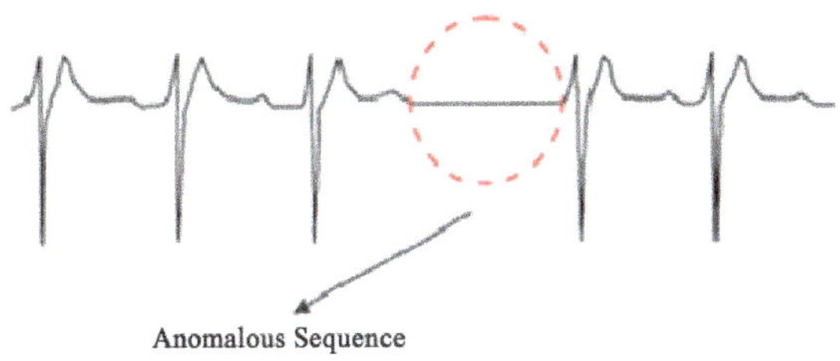

Figure 4: Collective anomaly.

ANOMALY DETECTION IN CLOUD NETWORKS

In cloud networks, traffic or flow of packets comes from more than one domain. There's a rapid change that occurs in the cloud environment due to the patterns or behavior of clients/tenants using the cloud infrastructure and the state of the unprotected services. In cloud environment, various challenges of identifying anomaly detection such as misconfiguration or high volumes of legitimate traffic in the network. The importance of the anomaly detection in cloud networks is the unwanted activities in data that brings the importance of reason for such anomaly in the information. Generally, the commercial off-the-shelf systems (COTS) for detecting intrusions are based on signatures or rules [11] [12] .

Signature based IDS can be used to detect known attacks in the cloud network, although the point of deploy can be before the cloud to detect external or incoming attacks or at the back end of the cloud to detect both external and internal attacks.

Methods and Techniques of Anomaly Detection in Cloud Based Networks

In the cloud networks, there are different techniques or methods that have been used in the detection of anomalous activities; these include Threshold detection, statistical analysis, Rule-based measures, neural networks, genetic algorithms, data mining and machine learning [13] . This section exposes a comparative view of the different method of anomaly detection in cloud networks. A comparison between the three main methods or techniques and others would be researched on namely; Statistical, data mining and machine learning.

Statistical Anomaly Detection Systems

This method of anomaly detection in cloud base network detects anomaly by observing computations in the network and creates a profile which keeps or stores the generated value in resenting their behavior. In identification of anomaly using this technique, there are two profiles created; the first one stores the normal or anomaly rules or signatures while the second one updates at regular intervals. During the update anomaly scores are calculated. If the threshold value is lower than the current anomaly profile generated, then it is known to be anomalous and detected. There's high probability of occurrence of normal data instances in dense regions of the model, while irregularities is seen in the low possibility regions [14] . Some proposed model of Statistical Anomaly Detection Systems are: Cloud Diag [15] , EbAT (Entropy based Anomaly Testing) [16] etc. The benefits of using this technique are that there is no previous or prior knowledge or training of security risks or knowledge domain required. Additionally, it has the capability of detecting even recent anomaly generated in the network or data and there's accurate notification of anomalies that have occur over extended time frame.

Data Mining Based Anomaly Detection Systems

The analyzing or extracting knowledge of large data set to fine patterns that are useful to the data owner is known as Data Mining [17] [18] . This technique uses the classification, clustering and association rule mining methods in the detection of anomalies in cloud environment. An analyst mechanism is in the data mining technique that detects anomaly by differentiating between normal and abnormal activities within the cloud. This is accomplished by stating or delineating some boundaries for valid and normal activities in the cloud network. There's also an added level of focus in this technique for anomaly detection. Data mining techniques are more flexible and easily to deploy at any point. Putting data mining into effect in the cloud network makes available the opportunity to extract meaningful information from data warehouse that are integrated into the cloud, this reduces the infrastructure storage costs. Customers or users of a cloud service only have to pay for the data mining tool that's been used [19] .

Data mining is typically used by Cloud Service Providers to provide a much better service for their users or clients using their cloud service [19] . The downside in this is that if the clients are not informed of the information that's been collected and used for mining, there's a violation of their privacy and it's illegal. There are varieties of issues available in data mining detection in cloud based networks which are the priority replacement of preserving privacy and setting the wrong parameters of these privacy settings while using different rules and strategy to enhance cloud network security.

Machine Learning Based Anomaly Detection Systems

The ability for programs or software to improve performance of their task over time by learning is an important technique in the detection of anomaly. Verified values or normal behavior of data are stored, when anomaly occurs or is being detected the machine learns its behavior, stores the new sequence or rule. This technique creates a system that can improve on performance of the program by leaning from the previous results. The interesting part in this technique is that upon improving of performance from previous results, new information are extracted and if it requires a change in the strategy of execution to improve performance it is done on the basis of the new information from the previous results. There are various categories of Machine leaning based anomaly detection such as; Bayesian Network, Genetic Algorithm, Neural Network etc.

Bayesian Network has the ability to include in its process both the old knowledge or signature and the data in detecting of anomalies. This technique is combining with the statistical mechanism which is highly advantageous in anomaly detection [20] .

Neural Networks has the capability to improve on data that is not complete to create a potential to detect and understand patterns that are not visible. The Neural network does not only detect previous attacks but also unseen behavior or patterns [21] . Genetic Algorithms employs the evolutionary algorithm techniques such as mutation, selection etc. their different process is based on collected rules from the information on the network analysis carried out by the IDS.

Adaptive Anomaly Detection Systems

The Adaptive Anomaly Detection Systems (AAD) employs data description using hyper-sphere for adaptive failure detection. In cloud networks, possible failures or anomaly which are detected by cloud operators are detected by the AAD using the performance data of the cloud service. The AAD detection systems utilize or capitalize on the log of the detected failure records that have been sent in by the cloud operators to identify new types of failures subsequently. The AAD detection algorithm changes its behavior by repeatedly learning from the new certified results or detection from the cloud provider so as to be prepared for future detections. According to Husanbir S. Pannu et al. [22] a prototype of AAD system was built and experiment was conducted in it testing the prototype in a 362-node cloud computing environment.

It was noted that the prototype was lightweight, and it took couple of seconds to startup the detector and couple of seconds more for the set adaptation and the failure detection to be up and running. 518 metrics were profiled every minute, the profiling covered or circled through the entire statistics of a typical cloud server, its Central Processing Unit usage, task switching processes, memory and swap space utilization, paging and page faults, input and output data transfer, interrupts, and more. Failure detector such as subspace regularization was used in comparing the ADD algorithm. The failure detector in [23] achieves 67.8% sensitivity in the experiments. The Bayesian sub-models and decision tree classifiers that were proposed only have 72.5% detection sensitivity. In the AAD the failure detector could get up to 92.1% and 83.8% detection sensitivity and detection specificity [22] .

As shown on Figure 5, to make failure detection it takes 7.26 seconds on an average control node in the cloud network, to extract the performance metrics, create the hyper sphere and make failure detections. It is even more lightweight in updating of the hyper sphere and identifies failures in about 2.17 seconds.

COMPARATIVE SURVEY OF CLOUD SECURITY MEASURES IN CLOUD STORAGE APPLICATIONS

Cloud storage is a useful way of storing data and also sharing of information online. The important question asked is "is it safe to store sensitive information on the cloud?" well that's a question we are trying to evaluate and answer if possible. Security in the cloud is not all that 100% guarantee. Files maybe encrypted in transmission, and at the final destination, the CSP might decrypt the file to gain access because the encryption algorithm used is provided by them. Access to your account can be gotten by anyone and your sensitive files can be compromised. In this case encryption on the client or the cloud user side is important and also using of a strong encryption key is advised.

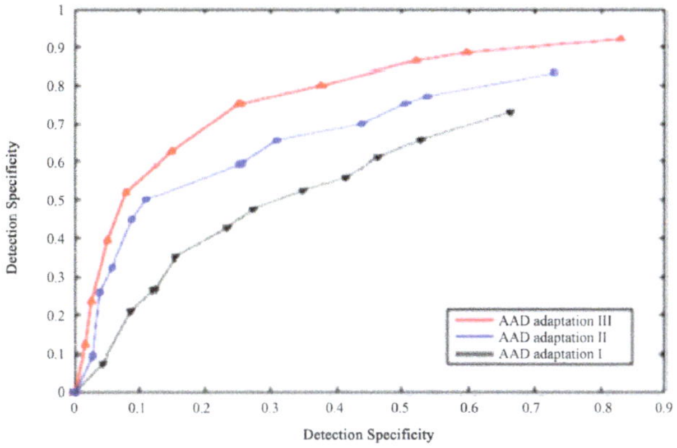

Figure 5: Illustration of failure detection with AAD.

In cloud computing, the usability of the computing capabilities have been moved from the users side to that of the CSP end; meaning users can access their files from anywhere at any time even using of multiple devices such as laptops, tablets, smart phones etc. this gives the user a sense of data mobility than just storing the data in a computer at home only [20] .

Dropbox

Dropbox is a public cloud storage, which was developed by 2 graduate of MIT who always forget or misplace their USB devices holding information that they need to use momentarily. Due to this Dropbox was brought to light in the IT world. In 2007 Dropbox Inc. was founded, it provides cloud storage, client software and file synchronization [21] . Dropbox allows it users to upload their files or folders into the Dropbox folder where it can be viewed or shared on any device at any time as long as the device has Dropbox installed along with a username and password and also internet connection for synchronization.

Dropbox was developed for personal use that was the intention of the two MIT graduate, but as of 2011 the cloud application have housed over 50 million users worldwide storing over 20 billion files and occupying petabyte of storage. Dropbox gives a 2 GB cloud storage space for free, but additional space can be purchased. Dropbox application is available for windows, Apple OS X, Android, and Linux [21] .

Figure 6 illustrates the example of working mechanism of Dropbox protocol. The basic mechanism is working based on so called hand-shaking process of basic networking standards.

Dropbox Security Measures

The cloud computing environment has many security issues affecting its usability. Dropbox being a cloud application or storage has several security measures put in place to ensure the data integrity and data security is in check. Dropbox saves all deleted and earlier versions of files for thirty days; this feature is supported by both the free and the premium (that's the paid account) account. In the free account the "save earlier version of files" feature only apply for 30 days, while in the paid or premium account the features saves the files indefinitely. The

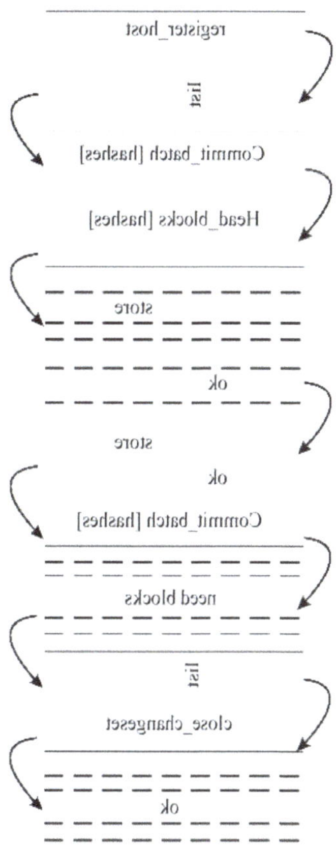

Figure 6: Illustration of Dropbox protocol.

Amazon S3 (Simple Storage Service) is used in the Dropbox cloud computing environment for their file storage. This is done for high integrity and data availability, and multiple data center replication is also used [14] .

An AES-256 encryption is used for ensuring privacy of data in the Dropbox cloud environment. In Dropbox, encryption is machine-protected that is the encryption key is stored in the machine not in the cloud storage [14] . Additionally the Dropbox encryption algorithm uses a TEA symmetric encryption [15] .

The SSL secure tunnel protocol is utilized for data in transit, and it's also an AES-256 encryption standard. Two-step verification process is used for or to increase security measures and it is recommended [15] [16] . Availability of third-party applications in the Dropbox cloud environment also adds another form of security in data encryption [15] [16] . Additionally Dropbox uses SQLite 3 database for ensuring data integrity and no data redundancy when users communicate with the database. The network traffic is fully transported over HTTPS, Proper certificate checking is done during the authentication process and OpenSSL is used to tackle with security issues in Dropbox services [17] .

The usage of OpenSSL increase security for authentication and authorization of Dropbox users. NCrypt wrapper is used by the Dropbox. The NCrypt wrapper creates security where there's none. The NCrypt is a file encyptor/decryptor and uses AES as its encryption algorithm [17] [18] .

It minimizes the exposure of plaintext password in memory and converts the plaintext to a SHA-1 hash before erasing the plaintext from hard drive immediately, and once the SHA-1 is used to make a key for encryption it is wiped form the memory too [17] -[19] . RSYNC (Remote Synchronization) Protocol is used, which allows a user to synchronize files between two or more computer device making sure that the same file is available in all connected device. Remote device unlinking is another technology used in Dropbox [24] .

Google Drive

The "Google Drive" is the Google version of cloud storage, and it is one of the popular cloud services. It supports photos, videos, documents and other files. There's a 15 GB free storage given that can be increased at any time by the user. Google drive provides generic applications for viewing of more than 30 file types without having to install the corresponding application into your computer system for viewing the corresponding file type. The Google drive provides unlimited file size upload quotation for uploading files into corresponding user drive.

Google Drive Security Measures

The Google Drive is integrated into Gmail services and once user owns a Gmail account can automatically have a Google drive account setup. Since Google drive uses a 2 step verification feature, the data security becomes one of the important obstacles for the corresponding technology users since 3-tier security architectures are more important and enhance data security for users [25] -[27] .

Additionally, "Cloud lock" feature is used to improve personal security of information and this also ensures PCI compliance. Files in Google drive are encrypted using AES-256 and RSA-4096 standards and in addition to his, there is an automatic data encryption on Google drive and server-side encryption mechanisms are used [28] [29] .

iCloud

iCloud is cloud storage from Apple Inc. It was launched on October 12, 2011 [30] . iCloud offers its users with the means to store data such as; documents, images, videos, etc. users can also backup their iOS devices directly to the iCloud wirelessly. As of July 2013, the iCloud service had 320 million users [31] [32] . The iCloud was first branded as iTools in 2000, Mac in 2002, and MobileMe in 2008 [32] .

iCloud Security Measures

iCloud keeps data of its users secure by encrypting it when it is sent over the Internet or in transition which also contains 2 step verification processes [33] . Secure tokens are used for authentication, this creates a secure and unauthorized access both in transit and while it is stored in the iCloud. For the messages transferred over the network, iCloud introduced iCloud Keychain, which uses a 256-bit AES encryption to store password and also to store credit card information. It uses elliptic curve asymmetric cryptography and key wrapping. The iCloud Keychain encryption keys are created and stored on the user's device not on the iCloud server [34] [35] . iCloud sessions are encrypted with SSL protocol to enhance security for login information and a minimum of 128-bit AES encryption is used for encrypting documents in iCloud. The files that will be transferred are encrypted in transition using 128-bit AES encryption algorithm [36] .

COMPARISON OF CLOUD SERVICES: ICLOUD, DROPBOX AND GOOGLE DRIVE

The various cloud services that this paper is characterized on, having their various service requirements to their clients as well as their cost. In Table 1, a detailed comparison was carried out to determine which among the three cloud services has a better security feature. We'd find out that the Dropbox cloud service incorporate more security measure compared to the Google Drive and iCloud.

Dropbox cloud storage service accounts for about 100 GB of traffic daily in one of their networks that was monitored [37] . A deduplication mechanism was developed to help avoid the duplication of data [38] [39] . Dropbox has the sharing of content ability and the percentage of files or folder shared amongst home users is about 70%, while linked devices is about 30%. Amongst students in campus about 40% of them share 5 folders or more. Dropbox uses delta encoding mechanism when transferring or transmitting chunks, "a chunk is a split large file". In Dropbox, a file larger than 4 MB is split into chunks which are identified by a SHA256 hash value, which is included in the meta-data description of files [40] .

The two major components in the Dropbox architecture that can be identified are the control and data storage [37] . In Dropbox cloud service, each linked device has a unique identifier (host_int), these unique identifier are also used for each shared folder in Dropbox. The various devices that belong to a single user are deduced by relating namespace lists [40] .

Table 1: Secuirty comparison between Dropbox, Google drive, and iCloud

Security Measures	Google Drive	Dropbox	iCloud
Secure Connection	YES	YES	YES
Files Stored Encryption	YES	YES	YES
SSL Protocol	YES	YES	YES
Open SSL	NO	YES	NO
128-bit AES encryption Algorithm	NO	NO	YES
2-step Authentication process	YES	YES	YES
HTTPS protocol	YES	YES	YES
Remote Device Unlinking	NO	YES	NO
AES-256 Encryption	NO	YES	YES
RSYNC (Remote Synchronization)	YES	YES	YES
NCrypt Wrapper	NO	YES	NO

Contents that are stored in Dropbox can be viewed and accessed using a web interface like a browser. Different set of domain names are used to identify public and private operations; URLs that contain dl-web.dropbox.com are associated with the private contents, while the dl.dropbox.com is associated with the public shared files [37] .

Google Drive is best for creating of documents and sharing of files. You can create spreadsheets, presentations, drawing, a new document etc. and stored files can be accessed anywhere with smartphones having Google Drive apps installed and desktop applications are available for PCs and Mac. Synchronization of files between PC and Google Drive is done automatically [37] .

As it is shown on Figure 7, Google Drive supports Microsoft Word documents, PowerPoint presentations, Adobe InDesign, Adobe Illustrator, Microsoft Excel, Adobe Photoshop, Wave Audio files, Adobe Reader, etc. with these applications installed in the Google Drive by the cloud service provider, it makes it may easy for users to edit, create and view respective documents without having to install corresponding application on every device.

In Table 1 shown, the various security measures of the Dropbox, Google Drive, and iCloud shows that the security infrastructure of various cloud services differs in the perspective of data security, availability, and control.

In Table 2, Dropbox gives 2 GB of free storage to a subscribed user of its cloud services; additional storage space can be added by buying a premium package. Google Drive gives 15 GB free storage space to its users, also additional storage can be purchased to increase the storage capacity, finally iCloud gives 5 GB free storage to its users and additional storage is available to users for a price. For users going for a free large storage capacity Google Drive has a better offer. Dropbox, Google Drive and iCloud allow any file type to be stored in their cloud server by their clients. Offline feature is also available so users can download a file to view later even when there's no internet connection.

Dropbox, Google Drive and iCloud allow any file type to be stored in their cloud server by their clients. Offline feature is also available so users can download a file to view later even when there's no internet connection.

As it is shown in Table 3, the cloud services differ also in terms of price, storage and performance.Table 3 shows the price difference in services of Dropbox, Google Drive, and iCloud. However, it depends on the user and its choice of product.

Table 4 indicates the overall capability of Cloud storage applications. As it can be seen from the table, the Dropbox is the only cloud storage application that allows all features while iCloud and Google Drive does not.

Figure 7: Generic applications of Google drive.

Table 2: Storage comparison between Dropbox, Google drive, and iCloud

	Dropbox	Google Drive	iCloud
Storage Space	2 GB	15 GB	5 GB
Maximum File Space	N/A	250 MB	N/A
File Type	Anything	Anything	Anything
Offline Services	YES	YES	YES

Table 3: Service cost of Dropbox, Google drive, and iCloud

Storage	Dropbox	Google Drive	iCloud
100 GB	$99	$60	N/A
200 - 250 GB	N/A	$120 (200 GB)	$3.99 (200 GB)/month
400 - 500 GB	$499 (500 GB)	$240 (400 GB)	$9.99 (500 GB)/month
1 TB	$119.99	$600	$19.99/month
2 - 16 TB	N/A	$1200 - 7600	N/A

Table 4: Capability measures of Dropbox, Google drive, and iCloud

Capability	Dropbox	Google Drive	iCloud
Chunking	YES (4 MB)	YES (8 MB)	NO
Bundling	YES	NO	NO
Client-Side Deduplication	YES	NO	NO
Data Encoding	YES	NO	YES
Data Compression	YES	YES	NO

CONCLUSION

Arif Sari Anomaly detection in could networks is a wide area of research, and it holds a good number of developments and proposing of detection systems. Anomalous activities occur always in our networks cloud based or non- cloud based. With the different types of methods or techniques in anomaly detection in cloud based network, detection of unwanted behavior can be traced, detected, stopped. These techniques have their limitations that create a gap between their performance metrics. In cloud based network hybrid anomaly detection system or method should be used so as to have a more efficient and high performance system. In this paper, we have discussed the importance of anomaly detection system in cloud environment, its types, methods, and the limitations that each method is faced with such as, false alarm being created; detection accuracy is hinged on the basis of previous collected information on anomalous behavior; more time is needed in the identification of attacks etc. These limitations can create inaccuracy in anomaly detection. A wide study should be conducted to develop a more reliable and efficient model that would encompass and try to improve on the limitations that are associated to the anomaly detection systems. Security in the cloud computing environment is very important as individuals and companies utilize their services. In this paper we have compared the security measures of Dropbox, Google Drive, and iCloud; we have found that most of the cloud service providers have similar security measures while few are different. Some of their similarities are the use of AES encryption algorithm, the communication over HTTPS, the use of SSL protocol, and the 2-step authentication process. This helps to secure data both in transit and in the cloud storage. Dropbox security measures tend to be intense in protecting the information of its cloud users; it incorporates Ncrypt wrapper and the Remote Device Unlinking mechanism. From the security measures, I'd say that for a more secured cloud service the Dropbox is a best choice although you can increase the storage by going for the premium offer which is costly, but for storage and application variety the Google Drive is a take.

REFERENCES

1. Oliveira, A.C., Chagas, H., Spohn, M., Gomes, R. and Duarte, B.J. (2014) Efficient Network Service Level Agreement Monitoring for Cloud Computing Systems. 2014 IEEE Symposium on Computers and Communications (ISCC), Funchal, 23-26 June 2014, 1-6.
2. Roschke, S., Cheng, F. and Meinel, C. (2009) Intrusion Detection in Cloud. Eight IEEE International Conference on Dependable Automatic and Secure Computing, Liverpool, 729-734.
3. Zhang, Q., Cheng, L. and Boutaba, R. (2010) Cloud Computing: State-of-the-Art and Research Challenges. Journal of Internet Services and Applications, 1, 7-18. http://www.springerlink.com/index/10.1007/s13174-010-0007-6
4. Wang, C. (2009) Ebat: Online Methods for Detecting Utility Cloud Anomalies. Proceedings of the 6th Middleware Doctoral Symposium, ser. MDS '09. New York, ACM, 4:1-4:6.http://doi.acm.org/10.1145/1659753.1659757
5. Hussain, M. (2011) Distributed Cloud Intrusion Detection Model. International Journal of Advanced Science and Technology, 34, 71-82.
6. Gul, I. and Hussain, M. (2011) Distributed Cloud Intrusion Detection Model. International Journal of Advanced Science and Technology, 34, 71-81.
7. Shelke, P.K., Sontakke, S. and Gawande, A.D. (2012) Intrusion Detection System for Cloud Computing. International Journal of Scientific & Technology Research, 1, 67-71.
8. Denning, D.E. (1987) An Intrusion Detection Model. IEEE Transactions on Software Engineering, Vol. SE-13, 222- 232.
9. Marhas, M.K., Bhange, A. and Ajankar, P. (2012) Anomaly Detection in Network Traffic: A Statistical Approach. International Journal of IT, Engineering and Applied Sciences Research (IJIEASR), 1, 16-20.
10. Gu, Y., McCallum, A. and Towsley, D. (2005) Detecting Anomalies in Network Traffic Using Maximum Entropy Estimation. Proceedings of Internet Measurement Conference, October 2005.
11. IBM Security Network Intrusion Prevention System. Technical Report. http://www-01.ibm.com/software/tivoli/products/security-network-intrusion-prevention/
12. Cisco Intrusion Prevention System. Technical Report, Cisco.
13. Cisco Network Solutions, 2015. http://www.cisco.com/go/ips
14. Hand, D.J., Mannila, H. and Smyth, P. (2001) Principles of Data Mining. The MIT Press, Cambridge.
15. Wu, X., Kumar, V., Ross Quinlan, J., Ghosh, J., Yang, Q., Motoda, H., et al. (2008) Top 10 Algorithms in Data Mining. Knowledge and Information Systems, 14, 1-37. http://dx.doi.org/10.1007/s10115-007-0114-2
16. Pannu, H.S., Liu, J.G. and Fu, S. AAD: Adaptive Anomaly Detection System for Cloud Computing Infrastructures.
17. Garcia Teodora, P., Diaz Verdejo, J., Macia Farnandez, G. and Vazquez, E. (2009) Anomaly-Based Network Intrusion Detection: Techniques, Systems and Challenges. Computers & Security, 28, 18-28. http://dx.doi.org/10.1016/j.cose.2008.08.003
18. Zhang, Y.M., Hou, X., Xiang, S. and Liu, C.L. (2009) Subspace Regularization: A New Semi-Supervised Learning Method. Proceedings of European Conference on Machine Learning and Knowledge Discovery in Databases (PKDD), Bled, 7-11 September 2009, 586-601. http://dx.doi.org/10.1007/978-3-642-04174-7_38
19. Alsafi, H.M., Abduallah, W.M. and Khan Pathan, A. (2012) IDPS: An Integrated Intrusion Handling Model for Cloud Computing Environment. International Journal of Computing and Information Technology (IJCIT).
20. Mi, H.B., Wang, H.M., Zhou, Y.F., Lyu, M.R.T. and Cai, H. (2013) Toward Fine-Grained, Unsupervised, Scalable Performance Diagnosis for Production Cloud Computing Systems. IEEE Transactions on Parallel and Distributed Systems, 24, 1245-1255.http://dx.doi.

org/10.1109/TPDS.2013.21

21. Wang, C.W., Talwar, V., Schwan, K. and Ranganathan, P. (2010) Online Detection of Utility Cloud Anomalies Using Metric Distributions. IEEE Network Operations and Management Symposium (NOMS), Osaka, 19-23 April 2010, 96- 103.
22. Chandola, V., Banerjee, A. and Kumar, V. (2009) Anomaly Detection: A Survey. ACM Computing Surveys, 41, 1-58.
23. Han, S.J. and Cho, S.B. (2006) Evolutionary Neural Networks for Anomaly Detection Based on the Behavior of a Program. IEEE Transaction on Systems, Man, and Cybernetics, Part B: Cybernetics, 36, 559-570.
24. Buyya, R., Yeo, C.S., Venugopal, S., Broberg, J. and Brandic, I. (2009) Cloud Computing and Emerging IT Platforms: Vision, Hype, and Reality for Delivering Computing as the 5th Utility. Future Generation Computer Systems, 25, 599- 616.http://dx.doi.org/10.1016/j.future.2008.12.001
25. Sara, T., Vance, C., Fenger, T., Brunty, J. and Price, J. (2013) Forensic Analysis of Dropbox Application File Artifacts Recovered on Android and iOS Mobile Devices.
26. Bermudez, I., Mellia, M., Munafo, M.M., Keralapura, R. and Nucci, A. (2012) DNS to the Rescue: Discerning Content and Services in a Tangled Web. Proceedings of the 12th ACM SIGCOMM Conference on Internet Measurement, IMC'12, Boston, 14-16 November 2012, 413-426. http://dx.doi.org/10.1145/2398776.2398819
27. Ruff, N. and Ledoux, F. A Critical Analysis of Dropbox Software Security.
28. Wallen, J. (2014) Easy Steps for Better Google Drive Security.www.techrepublic.com/article/easy-steps-for-better-google-drive-security
29. www.hongkiat.com/blog/dropbox-gdrive-skydrive/
30. Singh, J. and Jha, A. (2014) Cloud Storage Issues and Solutions. International Journal of Engineering and Computer Science, 3, 5499-5506.
31. Barth, D. (2013) Google Cloud Storage now Provides Server-Side Encryption.www.googlecloudplatform.blogspot.com/2013/08/google-cloud-storage-now-provides.html
32. GBacom News. http://GBaom.com/apple/apple-may-have-snapped-up-icloud-com
33. CNET News. http://news.cnet.com/8301-13579_3-20068165-37.html
34. Computerworld Report Articles, on iCloud.http://www.computerworld.com/s/article/9216301/Reports_Apple_acquires_icloud.com_domain
35. Voo, B. (2014) Cloud Storage Face-Off: Dropbox vs Google Drive vs SkyDrive.http://www.hongkiat.com/blog/dropbox-gdrive-skydrive/
36. http://www.whois.net/whois/icloud.de
37. Marshall, G. (2014) Best Cloud Services Compared: Google Drive vs OneDrive vs Amazon vs iCloud vs Dropbox. http://www.techradar.com/news/internet/cloud-services/best-cloud-storage-dropbox-vs-skydrive-vs-google-drive-vs-icloud-1120024/2#articleContent
38. Drago, I., Mellia, M., Munafo, M.M., Sperotto, A., Sadre, R. and Pras, A. (2012) Inside Dropbox: Understanding Personal Cloud Storage Services. Proceedings of the 12th ACM Internet Measurement Conference, IMC'12, Boston, 14-16 November 2012, 481-494.http://dx.doi.org/10.1145/2398776.2398827
39. Halevi, S., Harnik, D., Pinkas, B. and Shulman-Peleg, A. (2011) Proofs of Ownership in Remote Storage Systems. Proceedings of the 18th ACM Conference on Computer and Communications Security, CCS'11, Chicago, 17-21 October 2011, 491-500.http://dx.doi.org/10.1145/2046707.2046765
40. Harnik, D., Pinkas, B. and Shulman-Peleg, A. (2010) Side Channels in Cloud Services: Deduplication in Cloud Storage. IEEE Security and Privacy, 8, 40-47. http://dx.doi.org/10.1109/MSP.2010.187

CHAPTER 11

GENERATION OF LABELLED DATASETS TO QUANTIFY THE IMPACT OF SECURITY THREATS TO CLOUD DATA CENTERS

Sai Kiran Mukkavilli, Sachin Shetty, Liang Hong

Keywords: Amazon Web Services, Anomaly Detection, Cloud Computing, Datasets, Intrusion Detection, Network Traces

INTRODUCTION

Intrusion detection is a very interesting topic among the researchers. In particular, anomaly detection is of high interest since it helps in detecting many novel attacks. However, there has not been a proper application of this system in the real world due to the complexity of these systems, as these require continuous testing and evaluation and proper tuning prior to deployment [1] . The most ideal methodology for running these systems is to train them with real labeled network traces which consist of comprehensive set of intrusions and abnormal behavior. Anomaly-based network intrusion detection systems (IDS) model patterns of normal activity and detect novel network attacks [2] [3] . However, these systems depend on the availability of normal profile pattern. But these patterns can change over a period of time due to various changes [2] [3] . This is a major challenge in itself as the availability of such datasets is very rare and the systems have to depend on one or more available datasets which lack understanding as they are heavily anonymized.

Another challenge is the comparison of IDS systems against one another. The lack of appropriate public dataset severely affects the evaluation of IDSs mainly affecting anomaly based detectors. Many existing datasets (KDD & DARPA etc.) [4] - [6] are static making them obsolete, unmodifiable, and irreproducible, despite being used widely. As with any other emerging internet technology, security is a major challenge for clouds especially for the migrating organizational data. These security risks can be well understood if we have access to the network traces in the cloud. To the best of our knowledge; there is no publicly available dataset which captures the normal and anomalous network traces in the interactions between cloud users and cloud data centers. Due to the ubiquity of cloud computing environments in commercial and government internet services; there is a need to assess the impacts of network attacks in cloud data centers. A systematic approach has been devised to design and develop an experimental platform designed to represent a practical interaction between cloud users and cloud services and collect network traffic traces resulting from this interaction to conduct anomaly detection. These network traces from the cloud are readily sharable and can be interchanged among collaborators and researchers without major privacy issues. This work has been geared towards reaching the aforementioned vision. This paper is organized as follows: Section 2 provides an insight into the related work; Section 3 emphasizes on cloud datacenter and its services; Section 4 & 5 talk about the execution and collection of normal and attack traces in detail; Section 6 emphasizes on ethics when performing experiments. And the paper concludes in Section 7 with details on future work and improvements to the dataset.

RELATED WORK

Cloud security issues have recently gained traction in the research community where the focus has primarily been on protecting servers on cloud providers (securing the low level operating systems or virtual machine implementations). Unsecured cloud servers have been proven to be crippled with novel denial-of-service attacks. Most existing work on network traffic generation has not focused on applicability in the area of network security and evaluation of anomaly based techniques. The authors in Sommer and Paxson [7] have made observations on anomaly based network intrusion detection

Citation: Mukkavilli, S. , Shetty, S. and Hong, L. (2016) Generation of Labelled Datasets to Quantify the Impact of Security Threats to Cloud Data Centers. Journal of Information Security, 7, 172-184. doi: 10.4236/jis.2016.73013.

mechanisms and have provided recommendations to further improve research in this field [7] . They indicate that in order to improve the intrusion detection systems, datasets play a crucial role to know the system behavior. They also acknowledge that to obtain these datasets is very difficult and to do so it must be done with some collaboration with network operators. We have tried to implement the same in our work.

DHS Predict is a distributed repository of many hosts and providers at major universities and other institutions. Datasets mainly include Domain Name System (DNS) data, Internet Traffic Flow, Border Gateway Protocol (BGP), Internet Topology Data, Intrusion Detection System (IDS) and Firewall Data, and Botnet Behavior. Access to this dataset is available to certain verified accounts at some locations. Despite the major contributions by DARPA (Lincoln laboratory) [6] and KDD (UC Irvine) [4] datasets, they have not been able to reproduce the real world scenarios which is criticized in McHugh (2000) [8] and Brown et al. (2009) [9] . All these datasets are static making them obsolete, unmodifiable, and irreproducible, despite being used widely. Also the authors of the ISCX (2011) [10] dataset suggest a dynamic approach for generating the dataset, but this does not reflect the real world scenarios as the target servers they use are within the lab under the human assistance. Also, not much research has been done on the implication of vulnerabilities on the datacenter connecting the cloud user. In order to do so, datasets play a key role in demonstrating how well a system behaves. To the best of our knowledge, there is no publicly available dataset which captures the normal and anomalous network traces in the interactions between cloud users and cloud data centers. The systematic approach in this work addresses the flaws in the ISCX [10] dataset for generating a dataset dynamically and also shows the need for addressing the security issues in the cloud.

OVERVIEW OF CLOUD DATA CENTER & DATACENTER SERVICES

Cloud computing is a general term for anything that involves delivering hosted services over the Internet. It is a nascent technology. These services are broadly divided into three categories: Infrastructure-as-a-Service (IaaS), Platform-as-a-Service (PaaS) and Software-as-a-Service (SaaS). Supplying all those services at that scale requires can be achieved by expanding the hardware which makes up the datacenter. These services are delivered in various means (like private, public or hybrid cloud) by the cloud service providers (CSP) [11] - [16] . Examples include Amazon, Google, and Microsoft as shown in Table 1. A datacenter is usually a house of computers, and other components such as storage and network systems with other environmental supplies, backup power supplies and other security devices. Cloud Data centers are generally very huge, almost the size of multiple football fields (like Microsoft Azure datacenter). And maintaining them is a big issue too which costs millions of dollars [17] . So many companies lease space in large coalition facilities. Also many cloud regions are actually comprised of two or more distinct data centers (such as AWS in Sydney) [17] .

Amazon Datacenters

AWS is located in 9 geographical regions : US East (Northern Virginia), US West (Northern California), US West (Oregon), AWS GovCloud (US) Region, Sao Paulo (Brazil), Ireland, Singapore, Tokyo and Sydney [17] as shown in Figure 1 [18] . There is a dedicated GovCloud region located at Oregon, USA for US Government customers. All the data and the services stay within a designated region. When the user launches an instance the user can select an Availability zone or it is provided to him by Amazon. In order to prevent power outages within the zones they are isolated from each other. Our rented instances are located in the US-East (Northern Virginia) Region. We have chosen Amazon over other cloud providers for several reasons since Amazon's carriers (routers) security risks are lower compared to other carriers like Microsoft Azure [19] . Also Amazon has better pricing scheme (le carte pricing), where the users pay for what they use. There is couple of other benefits such as deployment speed, flexibility & performance.

Amazon Web Services (AWS)

Amazon web services (AWS) is an evolving and comprehensive cloud computing platform provided by Amazon.com. The first AWS was launched in 2006 to provide online services for websites. Sometimes web services are also known as remote or cloud services. AWS is distributed geographically into regions to ensure robustness and minimize the outages impact. The AWS offers many services like cloud drive, cloud search etc. [18] . These regions have central hubs located at Eastern USA, Western USA (two locations) Ireland, Australia, Singapore, Japan, and Brazil. Each region is divided into availability zones. Users of Amazon Web Services range from individual users (like students, professors etc.) to University research groups and small startup companies to large corporate businesses like Dropbox, Netflix. Etc. One of the main users of Amazon web service is the popular online storage service Dropbox which uses the IAAS (Infrastructure as a service) of the AWS.

Table 1: Table showing cloud datacenter locations of Amazon, Google, Microsoft

PROVIDER	REGION & SUBREGION
AWS US	US East (N Virginia)
AWS US	US West (N California)
AWS US	US West (Oregon)
AWS	GovCloud (Oregon)
AWS	South America (Sao Paulo)
AWS	EU (Ireland)
AWS	Asia Pacific (Singapore)
AWS	Asia Pacific (Tokyo)
AWS	Asia Pacific (Sydney)
Google	Central US (Council Bluffs, IA)
Google	Central US (Pryor Creek, OK)
Google	Europe (Europe)
Microsoft	Azure North-central US (Chicago, IL)
Microsoft	Azure South-central US (San Antonio, TX)
Microsoft	Azure West US (California)
Microsoft	Azure East US (Boydton, Virginia)
Microsoft	Azure East Asia (Hong Kong, China)
Microsoft	Azure South East Asia (Singapore)
Microsoft	Azure Northern Europe (Dublin, Ireland)
Microsoft	Azure West Europe (Amsterdam, Netherlands)

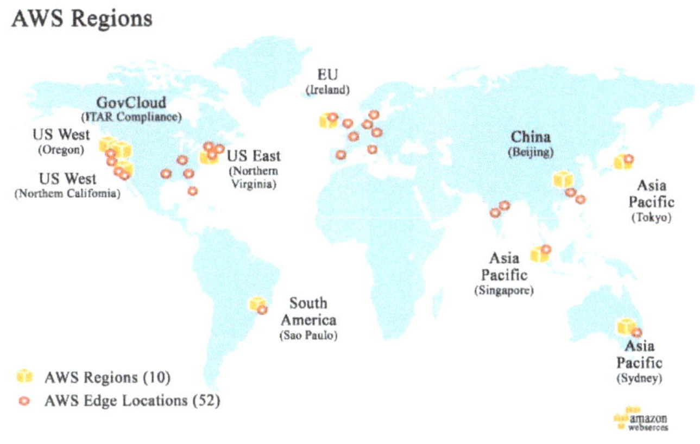

Figure 1: Map showing the location of Amazon cloud datacenters.

Once a file is added to Dropbox the file is transferred to Amazon S3 after encryption to various datacenters across USA. Similarly the download process is also the same. All AWS offerings are billed according to usage from service to service.

Cloud Users

Users access cloud computing using networked client devices, such as smartphones, desktop computers, laptops, tablets. The users are classified into two categories: Mobile cloud user's & Stationary cloud users. Mobile cloud users are the clients with access to mobile devices like smartphone, tablet etc. which use the resources of the cloud provider. Stationary users are the ones like desktop computers for accessing the cloud and also for performing research related to it. There are two main examples of stationary cloud users that are used for the research: PlanetLab, EmuLab. For our experiments we use PlanetLab nodes which mimic stationary cloud users. PlanetLab is a group of computers available as a test bed for computer networking and distributed systems research. PlanetLab is a great tool for performing large-scale Internet studies. Its power lies in that it runs over the common routes of the Internet and spans nodes across the world, making it far more realistic than a simulation. PlanetLab nodes utilize virtualization software, allowing applications to have full access to the system kernel [20] .

Network Traffic Datasets

During the last decade, anomaly detection has attracted the attention of many researchers to overcome the weakness of signature-based IDSs in detecting novel attacks. There are often limitations to test and evaluate a novel network concept/ solution on a real network. Hence, most researchers rely on captured network traffic data to evaluate the performance of their proposed network concept/solution. Also there is a scarce commodity among network research community for a real network traffic dataset. Various network problems have been analyzed, evaluated & validated based on captured network traffic. Hence it is important to maintain the completeness and quality of the network traffic dataset. There are many examples of network datasets like KDD CUP-99 [4] , DARPA [6] , and LBNL [21] etc.

Signature Based IDS

Intrusion detection systems (IDS) are classified into Anomaly based & Signature based. Signature based detection involves searching the traces (packets & bytes) for malicious traffic. The advantage of this technique is that if you know the network behavior you are trying to identify it is easy to develop and understand the signatures.

GENERATION OF NORMAL CLOUD TRACES

One of the highest priorities of this work is to generate realistic background traffic. The main concern is to accurately reproduce the quantity and time distribution of flows for HTTP protocol (since majority of the traffic using the web is based on HTTP). To achieve this we have generated series of time instances which send web requests from the planet lab nodes to the EC2 server as shown in Figure 2. Table 2 shows the nodes that are used to generate the requests. Each node has JDK installed in it which runs the java script for the requests.

To model HTTP requests, several approaches are available. The majority of work in literature is based on well-known statistical distributions. These probability distributions are analytically well described and have the advantage of being compact and easy to evaluate. We have generated series of random time instances using mean (μ) and standard deviation (σ) which follow both normal and uniform distributions separately. These are used to generate series of web requests from the PlanetLab nodes to the EC2 server. Algorithm 1 explains in detail the mechanism for generating the web requests from normal nodes.

The algorithm (Algorithm 1) is executed in the PlanetLab nodes which are used as the clients for generating the web requests. For our experiments we chose 4 nodes for generating normal instances. Initially the start time (t{1}) of the node is calculated and then a time sequence (t) is read from the file. Then the thread is made to sleep for some time and then again the current system time (t{2}) is calculated. The time difference (d) between current time (t{2}) and start time (t{1}) is calculated. Then the difference (d) is compared with the time sequence (t). If (d) is more than (t), this is the time to start the web request (t{3}). The node generates a request to the EC2 server to which the server responds. There is a TCP Handshake taking place between the node and the server. Then the file is downloaded onto the node. The end time (t{4}) is calculated after the web request response is completed. The web response time (WRT) is the difference between the end time (t{4}) and start time (t{3}). In this way WRT is calculated for one sequence. If (d) is less than (t) then the new time sequence is read from the file. Figure 2 shows the time instances generated using the normal distribution. These time instances are generated with a mean of 2.0216 and standard deviation of 0.3423. Similarly we generate time instances based on uniform distribution with a mean of 3.9209 and Standard deviation of 2.3446. The entire traffic is captured using the WIRESHARK running on the EC2 server.

GENERATION OF ATTACK CLOUD TRACES

Since the proposed dataset is intended for network security and intrusion detection purposes [8] , it would not be complete without a diverse set of attack scenarios.

Table 2: PlanetLab nodes for generating normal traces

PlanetLab Nodes IP Address
pl2.eecs.utk.edu 160.36.57.173
pli1-pa-6.hpl.hp.com204.123.28.57
planetlab2.unl.edu129.93.229.139
planetlab2.cesnet.cz195.113.161.83

Algorithm 1: HTTP wget request logic

```
begin:
Get current system time t1
t ← Get time instance from the file
thread.sleep()
Get current system time t2
while t.hasnext() do
    index i ← 0
    diff of time d ← t2-t1
    if d>t then
        time t3← start the wed request
        wget file from EC2
        time t4 ←end the web request
        Web Response time d ← t4-t3
    else
        thread.sleep()
    end if
end while
```

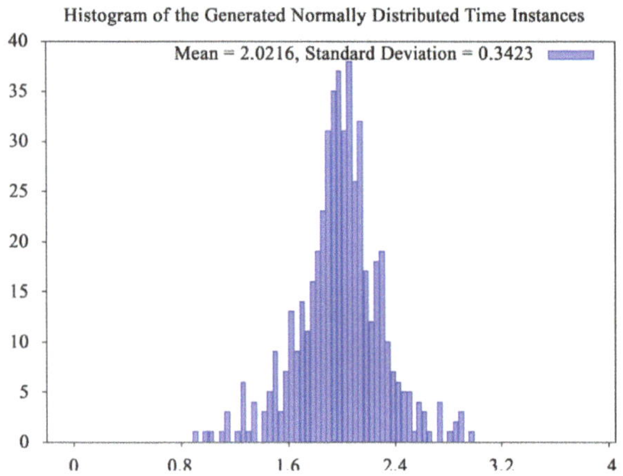

Figure 2: Time Instances based on normal distribution.

Attack traffic represents an attack scenario in an unambiguous manner. In the simplest case humans can carry out these attacks, and in the ideal case the autonomous agents can be used along with the compilers to carry out these attacks. Today, cloud computing systems are providing a wide variety of services and interfaces to the customers. There are various threats to these services which are explained in this paper. Our aim here is to mimic the actions of malicious hackers by performing multi-stage attack scenarios, each carefully crafted toward achieving a predefined set of goals [1] . The following are the common attacks that take place in the network. Denial-of-Service attack, Man-in-the-Middle Attack, Sniffer Attack, Portscan Application-Layer Attack etc. Out of these attacks we use the following three for the attacks in the cloud and for capturing traffic since these attacks deal with the Application layer protocols in the cloud and these best describe them and in capturing traffic.

- DDoS (Distributed denial of service)
- Man-in-the-Middle attack or ARP spoof
- Portscan

DDoS in Cloud

Distributed denial of service (DDoS) is an attack which many nodes systems attack one node all at the same time with a flood of messages. A distributed denial-of-service (DDoS) attack is one in which a multitude of compromised systems attack a single target, thereby causing denial of service for users of the targeted system [22] [23] . There are two types of DDoS attacks: a network-centric attack which overloads a service by using up bandwidth and an application-layer attack which overloads a service or database with application calls. For our experiments we use H-DOS in which we exploit seemingly-legitimate HTTP GET or POST requests to attack a web server. On July 17th 2013 a Distributed Denial-of-Service attack crippled the servers at hosting services firm Network Solutions, disrupting thousands of websites for several hours. DDoS attackers overwhelm servers by flooding a company's pipeline with unwanted network packets. Herndon, Va.-based Network Solutions, which manages more than 6 million domains, said on Facebook that its network security team was forced to respond to the attack. The outage is one of at least a dozen outages at cloud hosting providers impacting users in 2013. DDoS attacks are a common occurrence at hosting providers, e-commerce businesses and financial institutions [24] . In June, Network Solutions had its DNS servers hijacked and reconfigured to a malicious website after it botched efforts to thwart a DDoS attack.

Testbed Network Architecture for DDoS

The testbed network architecture for DDoS as shown in Figure 3 consists of 8 PlanetLab nodes which are distributed globally but are interconnected. They are loaded with fedora operating systems. Out of these few nodes are used to launch the attacks and few to generate normal traces. To perform the experiments we have rented an Amazon EC2 instance with Windows server 2008 as the operating system. Amazon provides various instances which vary based on price, performance etc. There are various kinds like General, Compute, Memory, Storage & GPU. Out of this we have selected the General category. In the general category we chose t1.micro for our experiments. T1 Micro instances (t1.micro) provide a small amount of consistent CPU resources and allow you to increase CPU capacity in short burst when additional cycles are available. They are well suited for lower throughput applications and websites that require additional compute cycles periodically [18] . The rented instance is located in US-east region. The instance has the following configuration: Processor: Intel(R) Xeon(R) CPU E5430 @ 2.66 GHz RAM: 595 MB Cache: 6MB Address sizes: 38 bits physical, 48 bits virtual. Operating System: Windows Server 2008. The instance was launched and then an Apache Server 2.0 was setup to host our website. The website has a public IP of 72.44.46.206. We install and launch WIRESHARK in the same instance for capturing and storing the network traces. These traces are then moved to another system for monitoring and intrusion detection. The PlanetLab nodes used for the attack are shown in the Table 3 and for generating normal traces are shown in Table 2.

Security Groups in EC2

When launching an Amazon EC2 instance we need to specify its security group. The security group acts as a firewall allowing us to choose which protocols and ports are open to computers over the internet. We can choose to use the default security group and then customize it, or can create our own security group. Configuring a security group can be done with code or using the Amazon EC2 management console [25] [26] . The default security group allows all the incoming traffic and leaves most of the ports open. In order to make the experiment more realistic we have customized the security group in the following way. We have allowed the following protocols from the following ports as shown in Table 4.

SSH was used so that remote hosts could communicate with the EC2 server, HTTP was used for the website to be accessible; RDP was used so that the server could be launched from our system, DNS so that the server could be accessed with a DNS. All the other protocols were blocked.

Load Balancing & Round-Robin DNS in EC2

Load balancing is when the processes and communications are distributed evenly across a network. When it's difficult to predict the number of requests that will be issued to a server we use load balancing.

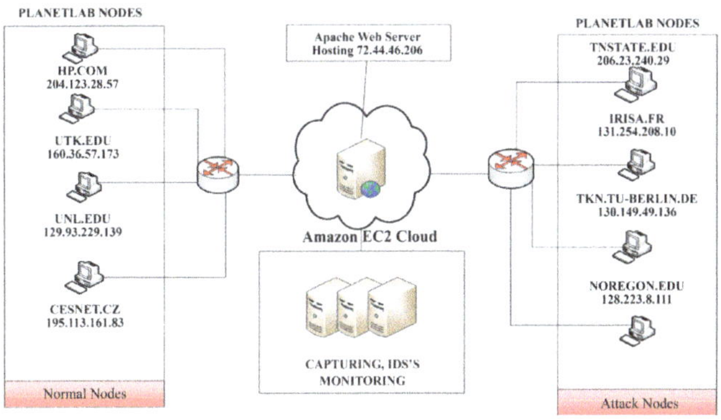

Figure 3: Testbed network architecture for DDoS [5.2].

Table 3: PlanetLab nodes for generating attack traces

PlanetLab Nodes IP Address
peeramide.irisa.fr 131.254.208.10
planetlab01.tkn.tu-berlin.de 130.149.49.136
planetlab2.tsuniv.edu 206.23.240.29
planetlab1.cs.uoregon.edu 195.113.161.83

Table 4: Protocols allowed to communicate through EC2

Protocols	Port
SSH	22
HTTP	80
RDP	3389
DNS	53

Busy Web sites typically employ more than one web server in a load balancing scheme. If one server is full of requests, the requests are forwarded to another server with more capacity [27] . We use a popular tool available online 'lbd.sh' [28] to determine whether the web server is load balanced or not. Lbd (load balancing detector) detects if a given domain uses DNS and/or HTTP Load-Balancing (via Server: and Date: headers and differences between server answers). After running the script on EC2, it was shown that EC2 does load balancing. Also we have tested whether the EC2 uses the Round robin DNS scheme, wherein the server has one domain name but multiple IP addresses. After testing it was found that the EC2 has only one IP linked to one domain name.

Implementing DDOS on EC2

This attack is designed toward performing a stealthy, low bandwidth distributed denial of service attack without flooding the network. We will be using "slowloris" [29] as the main tool in this scenario as it has proven to make web servers completely inaccessible using a single machine. The slowloris starts by making a full TCP connection to the remote server. The connection is held open by the tool by sending valid & incomplete requests to the server at the regular intervals to keep the socket from closing. Since the web server capacity is limited, in a certain amount of time all the sockets are used up and no other connection is made. We start the attack by deploying the "slowloris" script in the attack nodes. The attack is planned in such a way that all the machines start the attack within the same time window with a minimum lag. The attack nodes start running the script with each script sending 110 numbers of requests and with a "tcpto" 5 to port 80 of the EC2 server. The attack takes place at random intervals while the normal behavior (traffic) keeps on running continuously. The attack is a stealthy one since the magnitude and the frequency of requests are made to look similar to the normal behavior.

The attack slowly overwhelms the server thereby bringing down the service completely. When the attack stops the server starts automatically again. Figure 4 & Figure 5 show the attack and normal behavior of the network traces following different distributions. The traffic is captured using the wireshark on the EC2 and then is moved to another system for monitoring and IDS (Intrusion detection system).

ARP Spoofing in EC2

ARP spoofing is a technique where spoofed messages are sent by the attacker into the LAN (Local area network). The attacker machine sits anonymized in between the host and the gateway and captures the traffic both ways. The technique it uses for capturing the traffic is IP forwarding. Many of today's networks are built on what is called the eggshell principle: hard on outside and soft on the inside. This means that if an attacker gains access to a host on the inside, she can then use the compromised host as a pivot to attack systems not previously accessible via the Internet such as a local intranet server or a domain controller. In our case we host two machines in the same virtual private cloud (VPC) in Amazon EC2, one machine acts as host and the second machine will be the attacker. The attacker machine will capture the traffic between the host and the gateway as shown in the Figure 6.

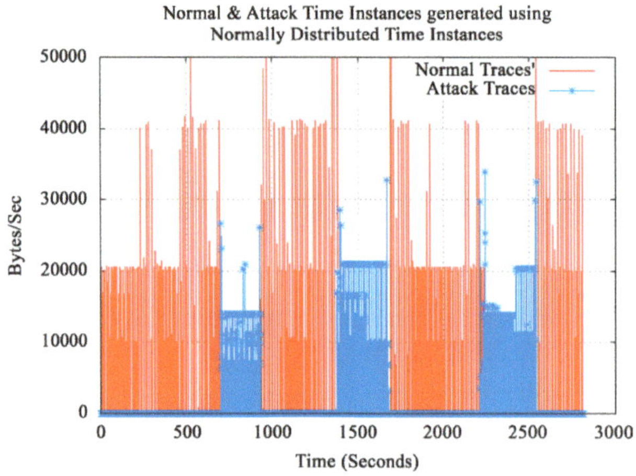

Figure 4: Network traces generated using normal time instances.

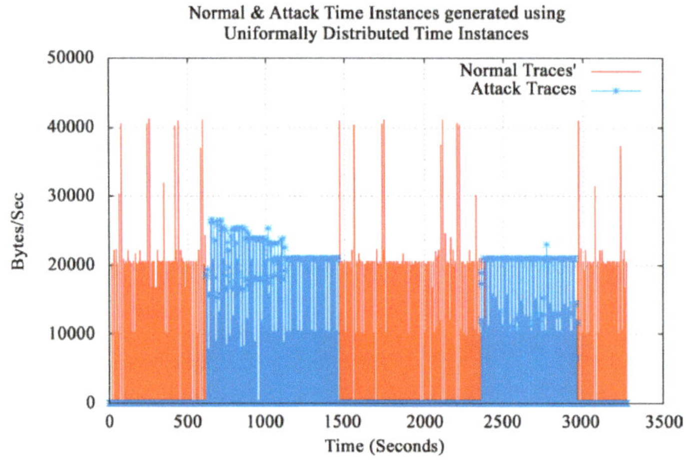

Figure 5: Network traces generated using uniform time instances.

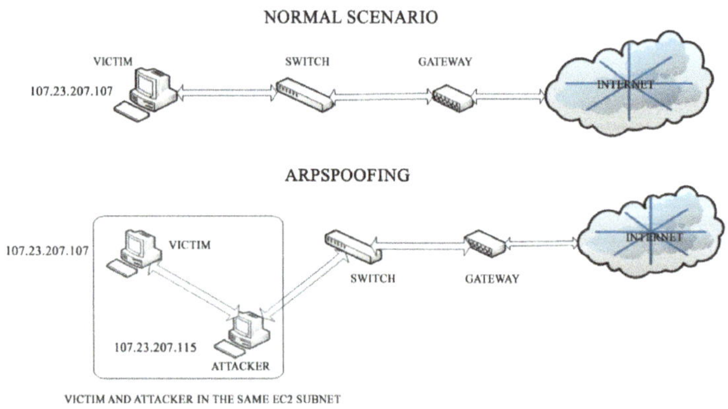

Figure 6: ARP spoofing in EC2.

For this experiment we consider the following: Two Windows 2008 server EC2 instances in the same subnet, Wire-shark, Ettercap-NG. We rent two instances with following configuration as shown inTable 5. The two instances are selected such that both are in the same subnet. For this experiment we first collect the traffic normally (in the absence of attacker) using wireshark. Then the well-known Spoofing software ETTERCAP-NG is installed in the attacker machine which listens to all the traffic between the victim machine and the gateway. Ettercap works by putting the network interface into promiscuous mode and by ARP poisoning the target machines. Thereby it can act as a "man in the middle" and unleash various attacks on the victims. For our experiment we have visited few websites like Facebook, Gmail etc. when the attacker is not present and again revisited the same websites in the presence of attacker. After collecting the traffic in both the attack and normal scenarios we convert it into user readable format (.arff) using tshark and then select the feature which best differentiates the normal and attack traffic. We have sorted the following feature from the list of features available "tcp. analysis.ack_rtt". This feature represents the round trip time. Figure 7 shows the difference between attack & normal traces using the above feature.

Port Scanning in EC2

Port scanning is a technique where the open ports of a server or website are probed. It is used by attackers as a means to compromise the services running on a system. We use Nmap which helps us in providing the open ports and the services running on the server. For our experiment we use Nmap to detect open ports and also any other operating system vulnerabilities by launching stealth attack as shown in Figure 8.

Table 5: Description of rented EC2 instances for ARP spoof attack

Operating System	IP Address	Type
Windows Server 2008	IP:107.23.207.107	Victim
Windows Server 2008	IP:107.23.207.115	Attacker

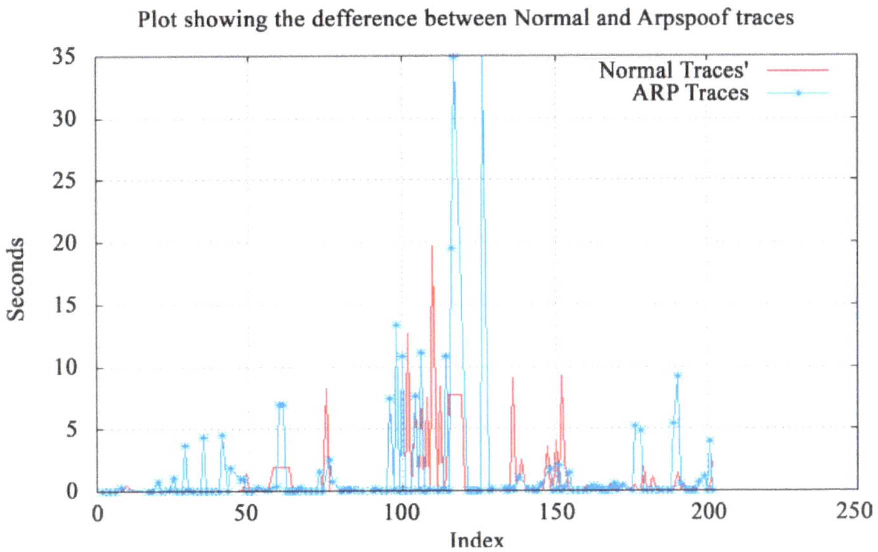

Figure 7: Difference between normal and ARP spoof traffic from same PlanetLab nodes.

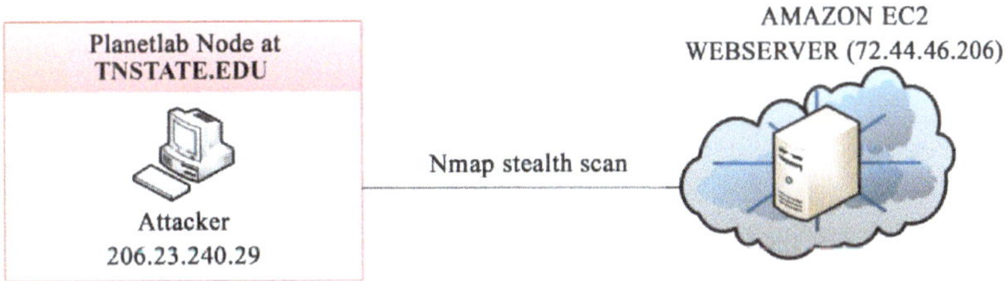

Figure 8: Portscanning using Nmap.

root@saikiran:~#sudo nmap -v -O --osscan-guess 72.44.46.206

Starting Nmap 4.52 (http://insecure.org) at 2014-11-01 18:10 UTC

Initiating Ping Scan at 18:10

Scanning 72.44.46.206 [2 ports]

Completed Ping Scan at 18:10, 0.07 s elapsed (1 total hosts)

Initiating Parallel DNS resolution of 1 host. at 18:10

Completed Parallel DNS resolution of 1 host. at 18:10, 0.08 s elapsed

Initiating SYN Stealth Scan at 18:10

Scanning ec2-72-44-46-206.compute-1.amazonaws.com (72.44.46.206) [1714 ports]

Discovered open port 3389/tcp on 72.44.46.206

Discovered open port 80/tcp on 72.44.46.206

Completed SYN Stealth Scan at 18:10, 34.46 s elapsed (1714 total ports)

Initiating OS detection (try #1) against ec2-72-44-46-206.compute-1.amazonaws.com (72.44.46.206)

Retrying OS detection (try #2) against ec2-72-44-46-206.compute-1.amazonaws.com (72.44.46.206)

Host ec2-72-44-46-206.compute-1.amazonaws.com (72.44.46.206) appears to be up ... good.

Interesting ports on ec2-72-44-46-206.compute-1.amazonaws.com (72.44.46.206):

Not shown: 1700 filtered ports

PORT STATE SERVICE

80/tcp open http

3389/tcp open ms-term-serv

6000/tcp closed X11

6001/tcp closed X11:1

6002/tcp closed X11:2

6003/tcp closed X11:3

6004/tcp closed X11:4

6005/tcp closed X11:5

6006/tcp closed X11:6

6007/tcp closed X11:7

6008/tcp closed X11:8

6009/tcp closed X11:9

6017/tcp closed xmail-ctrl

6050/tcp closed arcserve

Device type: general purpose

Running (JUST GUESSING): Microsoft Windows Vista|2008 (98%)

Aggressive OS guesses: Microsoft Windows Vista (98%), Microsoft Windows Server 2008 Beta 3 (96%), Microsoft Windows Vista Home Basic (91%)

No exact OS matches for host (test conditions non-ideal).

Uptime: 61.417 days (since Mon Sep 1 08:10:23 2014)

TCP Sequence Prediction: Difficulty = 262 (Good luck!)

IP ID Sequence Generation: Incremental

OS detection performed.

Nmap done: 1 IP address (1 host up) scanned in 38.886 seconds

Raw packets sent: 5194 (232.752 KB) | Rcvd: 36 (2092 B)

For the purposes of proper scanning and pinging we had to allow ICMP traffic through EC2. We had allowed this rule in the EC2 security groups. The first session is initiated from the PlanetLab node. Nmap is launched at the "tsuniv.edu" (206.23.240.29) PlanetLab node. It launches a stealth scan on the EC2 server which gives an approximation of the operating system and the number of open ports as shown above. The traffic is captured using the wireshark software [30] .

ETHICAL CONSIDERATION

Our experiments to implement the framework for generation and collection of network traces involve real world instances and systems. This usually raises an ethical debate as scanning remote network devices can sometimes lead to adverse attacks. At the same time, developing a robust framework for network traces without collecting data from the real world is very difficult. Simulation tools and performing experiments with a controlled lab environment cannot replicate the randomness of the real world network traffic. A recent journal article that discusses the ethics of security vulnerability research [31] , states that this type of zealous vulnerability research serves important social functions. Amazon EC2 provides students and researchers instances (Penetration Testing) that can be used for performing the experiments which involve attacks. For this the user has to get the permission from AWS before conducting any tests [32] . This approach is neither illegal nor unethical under the US laws. While accessing the instances to collect the vulnerability information we have taken utmost care not to disturb the host functions. We used minimum external resources to accurately collect the traces. The target networks in/24 blocks were scanned in a non-sequential order so that no organization is overwhelmed with our attacks. Also we did not scan any router or instance unnecessarily.

CONCLUSION & FUTURE WORK

Cloud computing offers many services to their clients including software, infrastructure etc., but they pose significant security risks to customer applications and data beyond what is expected using traditional on-premises architecture. These security risks can be well understood if we have access to the network traces in the cloud. Most of the network trace datasets are proprietary and cannot be shared due to privacy reasons; others are heavily anonymized and do not reflect current trends and lack certain statistical properties. Also, publicly available datasets are either outdated or generated in a controlled environment [1] . To the best of our knowledge; there is no publicly available dataset which captures the normal and anomalous network traces in the interactions between cloud users and cloud data centers.

Due to the ubiquity of cloud computing environments in commercial and government internet services, there is a need to assess the impacts of network attacks in cloud data centers. We present a systematic approach to design and develop an experimental platform designed to represent a practical interaction between cloud users and cloud services and collect network traffic traces resulting from this interaction to conduct anomaly detection. Our results show statistical differences between normal and anomalous network traffic traces which can be exploited by anomaly detection systems to detect and isolate adversaries in the cloud data centers. In future, we plan to implement the captured traffic on the IDS (Intrusion Detection Systems) for better understanding of anomalies and also to reduce the false positives.

ACKNOWLEDGEMENTS

This work was partially supported by Department of Homeland Security (DHS) SLA grant 2014-ST-062- 000059 and Office of the Assistant Secretary of Defense for Research and Engineering (OASD(R&E)) under agreement number FAB750-15-2-0120.

REFERENCES

1. Shiravi, A., Shiravi, H., Tavallaee, M. and Ghorbani, A.A. (2012) Toward Developing a Systematic Approach to Generate Benchmark Datasets for Intrusion Detection. Computers & Security, 31.3, 357-374. http://dx.doi.org/10.1016/j.cose.2011.12.012
2. Mukkavilli, S.K., Shetty, S. and Hong, L. (2012) Mining Concept Drifting Network Traffic in Cloud Computing

Environments. IEEE/ACM CCGRID, Ottawa, 13-16 May 2012, 721-722.

3. Shetty, S., Mukkavilli, S.K. and Keel, L.H. (2011) An Integrated Machine Learning and Control Theoretic Model for Mining Concept Drifting Data Streams. IEEE HST, Waltham, 15-17 November 2011, 75-80. http://dx.doi.org/10.1109/ths.2011.6107850
4. University of California-KDD Cup 1999 Data. http://kdd.ics.uci.edu/databases/kddcup99/kddcup99.html;2011
5. Tavallaee, M., Bagheri, E., Lu, W. and Ghorbani, A.A. (2009) A Detailed Analysis of the KDD CUP 99 Data Set. IEEE CISDA, Ottawa, 8-10 July 2009, 1-6.
6. MIT Lincoln Lab DARPA Data. http://www.ll.mit.edu/mission/communications/ist/corpora/ideval/index.html;2011
7. Sommer, R. and Paxson, V. (2010) Outside the Closed World: On Using Machine Learning for Network Intrusion Detection. IEEE Symposium on Security & Privacy, Oakland, 16-19 May 2010, 305-316.
8. McHugh, J. (2000) Testing Intrusion Detection Systems: A Critique of the 1998 and 1999 DARPA Intrusion Detection System Evaluations as Performed by Lincoln Laboratory. ACM Trans on Information System Security, 3, 264-294. http://dx.doi.org/10.1145/382912.382923
9. Brown, C., Cowperthwaite, A., Hijazi, A. and Somayaji, A. (2009) Analysis of the 1999 DARPA/Lincoln Laboratory IDS Evaluation Data with Netadhict. IEEE International Conference on Computational Intelligence for Security and Defense Applications, Ottawa, 8-10 July 2009, 1-7.
10. ISCX Datasets. http://www.unb.ca/research/iscx/dataset/iscx-IDS-dataset.html
11. Cloud vs. Traditional Data Center. http://www.businessnewsdaily.com/4982-cloud-vs-data-center.html
12. Classification of Data Center. http://www.datacenterknowledge.com/archives/2013/11/01/a-public-private-or-hybrid-cloud-debate-not-really/
13. Data Center Types. http://research.gigaom.com/2012/10/4-types-of-data-centers/
14. CAIDA Data Centers. http://www.caida.org/
15. Cloud Platform. http://mindstormtools.com/2014/02/16/amazon-web-services-aws-and-the-new-google-cloud-platform/
16. Cloud Intrusion. http://www.di.unipi.it/~hkholidy/projects/cidd/
17. AWS Data Centers. http://www.turnkeylinux.org/blog/aws-datacenters
18. Amazon AWS Instances. https://aws.amazon.com/ec2/instance-types/
19. Reddy, S., Shetty, S. and Xiong, K. (2013) Security Risk Assessment of Cloud Carrier. 2013 13th IEEE/ACM International Symposium on Cluster, Cloud and Grid Computing (CCGrid), Delft, 13-16 May 2013, 442-449.
20. PlanetLab Nodes. http://www.planet-lab.org/status
21. LBNL-The Internet Traffic Archive. http://www.icir.org/enterprise-tracing/download.html
22. Specht, S.M. and Lee, R.B. (2004) Distributed Denial of Service: Taxonomies of Attacks, Tools and Countermeasures. Proceedings of 17th International Conference on Parallel and Distributed Computing Systems, San Francisco, 15-17 September 2004, 543-550.
23. Distributed Attack. http://searchsecurity.techtarget.com/definition/distributed-denial-of-service-attack
24. DDOS Attack. http://www.crn.com/news/security/240158492/ddos-attack-behind-latest-network-solutions-outage.htm
25. EC2 Instances. http://aws.amazon.com/ec2/
26. EC2 Security Groups. http://blog.learningtree.com/understanding-amazon-ec2-security-groups-and-firewalls/
27. Load Balancing. http://www.webopedia.com/TERM/L/load_balancing.html
28. Load Balancing Tool. https://packetstormsecurity.com/files/46871/lbd-0.1.sh.txt.html
29. Slowloris Tool. https://github.com/gkbrk/slowloris
30. Wireshark Tool. https://www.wireshark.org/
31. Benson, T., Akella, A. and Maltz, D.A. (2010) Network Traffic Characteristics of Data Centers in the Wild. Proceedings of the 10th ACM SIGCOMM Conference on Internet Measurement, Melbourne, 1-3 November 2010, 267-280. http://dx.doi.org/10.1145/1879141.1879175
32. Penetration Testing Security. http://aws.amazon.com/security/penetration-testing/

CHAPTER 12

SAFAX – AN EXTENSIBLE AUTHORIZATION SERVICE FOR CLOUD ENVIRONMENTS

Samuel Paul Kaluvuri, Alexandru Ionut Egner, Jerry den Hartog and Nicola Zannone

Keywords: Access control, cloud, security-as-a-service, XACML, architectural framework

INTRODUCTION

Recent years have seen an increased adoption of cloud services, mainly driven by the explosive growth of mobile devices that often rely on cloud services (Gartner Inc, 2014). In particular, the need to have data accessible and synchronized across multiple devices (e.g., smartphones, tablets, PCs) has led to an increased pace of adoption of cloud storage services. In fact, many popular mobile and desktop operating systems already have a tight integration with cloud storage services to allow users to remotely store photos, music, movies, notes, etc. For example, Apple's iPhone is tightly integrated with its cloud storage service iCloud, Android phones with Google Drive, and Windows phones with OneDrive. There are also several other very popular storage services such as Dropbox, SugarSync, and SpiderOak. Given the number and variety of cloud services, end-users are often subscribed to multiple cloud storage services according to their needs.

Besides securely storing their data, users want to be able to share their data with others without compromising on its security. Yet, the use of different cloud providers results in users having several *islands of data*, one for each cloud provider. Thus, the user is faced with the challenging task of managing access rights across several providers.

Current authorization mechanisms implemented by cloud providers are quite primitive, in that users do not have a means of specifying fine-grained access control policies over their data. Furthermore, each cloud provider uses a custom, often *ad hoc*, solution for access control. This requires end-users to redefine their policies for each cloud storage service, which causes difficulty in synchronizing them across multiple cloud providers. The situation becomes even more challenging when users share their data with other users who are not registered to the same cloud service, as cloud providers do not have any means of verifying authorizations for unknown users.

The successful application of federated identity services in cloud environments (Hühnlein et al., 2010), where services allow their users to log-in based on credentials provided by third-party identity providers such as Google and Facebook, indicates that similar approaches in the context of authorization may be able to resolve the issue of data sharing in a multiple clouds setting. Existing access control standards such as XACML (OASIS, 2013) already provide a baseline for the development of authorization services for cloud environments (Takabi et al., 2010). However, current authorization solutions, even those based on XACML, suffer from severe limitations that hamper their adoption in these cloud environments.

In this paper, we analyze the challenges of sharing data securely in cloud environments and propose SAFAX, a novel XACML-based architectural framework tailored to the development of extensible authorization services for clouds. The key design principle underlying SAFAX is that all components are loosely coupled services, thus providing the flexibility, extensibility, and scalability needed to manage authorizations in cloud environments. SAFAX offers several advantages to both cloud providers and users. It relieves users from the complexity of specifying and maintaining access control policies for each cloud and in different formats. Moreover, users can constrain access to their data on the basis of information that can be retrieved from arbitrary external sources during policy evaluation; SAFAX invokes these services at runtime without any additional configuration by users. From a cloud provider perspective, it helps them to

Citation: Kaluvuri SP, Egner AI, den Hartog J and Zannone N (2015) SAFAX – an extensible authorization service for cloud environments. Front. ICT 2:9. doi: 10.3389/fict.2015.00009.

reduce costs associated with implementing custom solutions by outsourcing authorization decision making to an external service.

To demonstrate the feasibility of the proposed framework, we have implemented an authorization service as a web service based on the architectural principles underlying the SAFAX framework. Since the SAFAX authorization service can be used by multiple users (e.g., students, project partners, guest users), we have used the SAFAX authorization service itself as the access control mechanism in order to regulate the actions that users can perform within the SAFAX authorization service. Moreover, we have developed a Graphical User Interface to facilitate DOs in the management of policies and in the configuration of the authorization service. We have reported our experience in deploying, using, and securing SAFAX.

The remainder of the paper is structured as follows. The next section introduces a cloud scenario to illustrate the challenges of cross-domain data sharing in cloud environments. Section 3 presents the SAFAX architecture along with its main components, and Section 4 presents a prototype of an authorization service based on SAFAX. Its use in practice is then discussed in Section 5. Finally, Section 6 reviews related work, and Section 7 concludes the paper providing directions for future work.

MOTIVATION

In this section, we present a simple scenario that illustrates the challenges of enforcing access control on data stored at different cloud storage services. The scenario focuses on the mechanisms currently used to control the access to data in cloud environments. We first introduce a few terms that are used in the scenario and throughout the paper.

A Domain specifies a data set managed by a user, e.g., files stored at a specific cloud storage service.

A Domain Owner (DO) is the user to whom the domain belongs.

A Domains Controller (DC) is a host of multiple domains, possibly belonging to different DOs. A cloud storage service provider is a typical example of DC. The DC is responsible for guaranteeing the confidentiality, integrity, and availability of the data stored within the domains it hosts.

A Data Consumer is a user requesting access to some data.

Alice uses two cloud storage services offered by two independent DCs to store her data: *Domains Controller I* (DC_I) and *Domains Controller II* (DC_{II}). She stores personal files, such as music and photos, in her domain AD_1 at DC_I and documents containing sensitive information, such as a business plan, finances, and health records, in her domain AD_2 at DC_{II}. This is illustrated in Figure1.

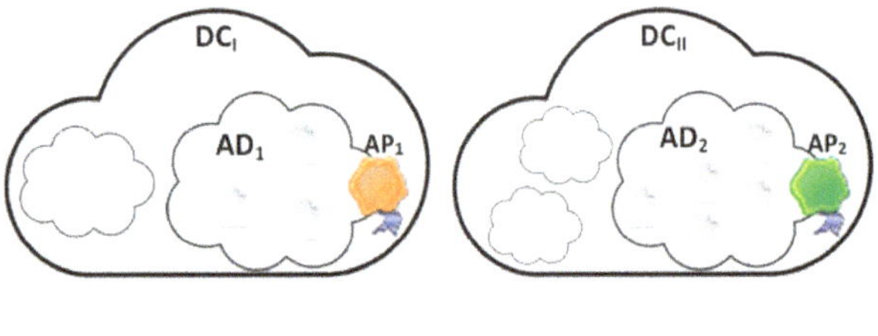

Figure 1: Alice shares resources from multiple cloud providers.

Alice wants to share her resources stored at domains AD_1 and AD_2 with other users. In particular, she has the following access requirements:

- AR_1: Bob is allowed to *view* all photos from AD_1;
- AR_2: Bob is allowed to *view* the business plan from AD_2;
- AR_3: Any neurologist from Mayo Clinic is allowed to *view* the health records from AD_2 during working hours (09:00 to 18:00);
- AR_4: Any other action (besides the ones in AR_1, AR_2, and AR_3) for any resource in AD_1 andAD_2 is denied.
- At a later point, Alice may need to update these access rights and allow Bob to *modify* the resources as well:
- $\overline{AR1}$: Bob is allowed to *view* and *modify* all photos from AD_1;
- $\overline{AR2}$: Bob is allowed to *view* and *modify* the business plan from AD_2.

Both DCs provide Alice (DOs, in general) a means of defining access control policies for sharing data with other users. In particular, DC_I enables DOs to share resources with other users in three ways: sharing with specific users (usually registered users), sharing through a link, or making the resource publicly available. This practice is adopted, for instance, by cloud storage services such as Microsoft OneDrive and Google Drive. On the other hand, DC_{II} allows DOs to define access rights on buckets and objects using Access Control Lists (ACLs). Through an ACL, DOs can define the actions (e.g., read, write) other users (or groups of users) can perform on a certain object. ACLs are currently used by a number of cloud storage services, like Google Cloud Storage and Rackspace Cloud Files, to enable DOs to control which data consumer is allowed to access their resources. Figure 2 shows the policies AP_1 and AP_2 that Alice defines to regulate the access to her data stored in AD_1 and AD_2, respectively. To make the discussion more concrete, we represent these policies using the mechanisms currently offered by existing cloud storage providers. In particular, AP_1 is expressed using the mechanism provided by Google Drive and AP_2 using the mechanism provided by Google Cloud Storage.

Figure 2: Representation of Alice's access requirements at different cloud providers. (A) Policy AP_1. (B) Policy AP_2.

One can observe that both AP_1 and AP_2 do not completely reflect Alice's intentions due to the limitations of the authorization mechanisms currently adopted by the cloud providers. Now, we discuss the challenges users have to face when specifying and maintaining policies in a multi-cloud environment.

C1: Identity-Based Policies. The access control mechanisms adopted by most cloud providers require DOs to specify, for each object, the actions that each user can perform on the object, making policy specification costly and error-prone. In addition, DOs do not always know the identity of the users, as shown with *AR3*. It is well established that introducing abstract concepts like *role* facilitates the specification and management of policies (Sandhu et al., 1996). Some cloud providers offer some flexibility in this respect by allowing the specification of policies in terms of user groups and folders (next to individual users and objects). However, the properties of users and objects that DOs can currently use in the specification of their policies are rather limited. The second rule in Figure 2B highlights this problem. Alice can define a group consisting of the neurologists at Mayo Clinic ("*neuro_group_mayo_clinic*") and specify a rule allowing the members of this group to access her health record. However, to define such a group, Alice needs to know all the neurologists at Mayo Clinic and assign them to the group.

C2: Limited Expressiveness of Policies. Cloud storage providers typically provide DOs with a very constrained language for the specification of their policies. For instance, cloud providers using ACLs (such as DC_{II}) only allow the specification of authorizations in terms of user, action, and object. DOs are not free to use other context information, such as time and location, to restrict the access to their data. The second rule in Figure 2B illustrates that Alice does not have the means to define a specific time interval in which access to her health records is allowed. As a consequence,DOs cannot specify fine-grained policies, which are often required to securely share data in dynamic and open systems. Coarse authorization control is recognized by Grobauer et al. (2011) as a main vulnerability of authorization systems currently used by clouds.

C3: Heterogeneity of Policy Specification. Cloud providers often provide DOs with *ad hoc*languages for the specification of their policies. These languages may require the specification of different policy elements to define authorizations. For instance, ACLs are defined in terms of user, action, and object. Other cloud providers do not allow DOs to specify the action that users can perform on an object; rather they only consider a general access right that allows users to perform any action on objects. This discrepancy results in DOs having to define a different policy to regulate the access to their data for each cloud service provider. For instance, Alice needs to define two different policies, AP_1 and AP_2 for the resources in AD_1 and AD_2, respectively, even if her intention is to assign Bob the same access rights (as exemplified in *AR1* and *AR2*). Moreover, the two providers force Alice to define AP_1 and AP_2 in different formats. DC_I provides Alice a visual interface for specifying AP_1 (see Figure 2A), while DC_{II} constrains the specification of AP_2 to a specific language (see Figure 2B). This introduces additional burden to DOs who have to adapt to a different language and tool for each cloud provider. Therefore, policy specification becomes increasingly complex with the growth of the number of domains, as there is no method for synchronizing policies between different domains (hosted by the same DC or by different DCs).

C4: No Support for Cross-Domain Policy Update. The lack of methods for synchronizing policies at different cloud providers can lead to additional issues in policy management. If Alice wants to change the permissions given to Bob (as shown with the updated rights $\overline{AR1}$ and $\overline{AR2}$), she has to change her policies at each cloud service provider to reflect her new access requirements. This situation could still be acceptable if DOs only have to upload the new policy to the different cloud providers. However, as discussed above (challenge C3), policies at different cloud providers may have different formats and use different information to make access decisions. This syntactical difference hinders the definition of policies portable between domains.

C5: Lack of Cross-Domain Semantic Interoperability. A DO specifying a policy to regulate access to its data at different cloud providers expects that every provider interprets and evaluates the policy based on the DOs intention. This, however, is difficult to achieve due to syntax differences between the policy languages employed by different cloud providers (challenge C3). Standards are often used to smooth these differences and, thus, to enable interoperability in distributed systems. The use of standards, however, does not solve the problem of semantic misalignment of providers' vocabularies (Trivellato et al., 2013). For instance, Google Cloud Storage uses element "role" to indicate the action that a data consumer is allowed to perform (see Figure 2A). Other providers may use the element "role" with a different meaning and/or use an element "action" to indicate the action that a certain user can perform. We cannot expect that every provider will employ common data, organizational models, and vocabularies for the specification of security policies.

C6: No Empowerment of Domain Owners. Cloud providers usually evaluate DOs' policies relying on information that is locally available (e.g., ACLs). However, this, in combination with the limited expressiveness of the employed policy language (challenge C2), provides DOs little control over their data. DOs should be able to influence the decision of granting or denying the access to their data (this is especially true when dealing with personal information). In particular, DOs should be able to define from which source the information used to evaluate their policies is fetched. In *AR3*, Alice wants to constrain the access to her health records to data consumers that are neurologists at Mayo Clinic. Those users, however, may not even be registered with the cloud provider, in which case the properties of the data consumer should be validated by an appropriate trust authority. For instance, in our scenario, the cloud provider should rely on Mayo Clinic to determine whether the data consumer is a neurologist and, thus, authorized to access Alice's health records.

We highlight two additional challenges derived from challenge C6, which reflects the perspectives of the data consumer and domains controller.

C7: Required Registration of Data Consumers. Cloud providers usually evaluate and enforceDOs' policies based on the data consumer's identity (challenge C1). Cloud providers adopt different approaches for handling data sharing with unregistered users. Depending on the provider, DOs have the option of sending an invitation to unregistered users, share their data through a link, or even make the data publicly available. The invitation often implies the alteration of the intended policy with additional constraints imposed by the provider. Cloud providers often make the resource *read-only* to an unregistered user, even if the user was given the rights to *modify* the resource. The data consumer, therefore, has to register to the provider to benefit from the intended access rights. Sharing the link has its own drawbacks. Users do not have control over their data as anyone knowing the link can access them. These issues are usually addressed by trust management (Li et al., 2003; Trivellato et al., 2014). However, trust management solutions are typically not integrated in the authorization mechanisms employed by cloud providers. Therefore, the data consumer has to be registered with each cloud provider in order to be granted access to the shared data. In the scenario, Bob is given the right to access specific data from AD_1 and AD_2 (access rights*AR1* and *AR2*), but he needs to have an account at each **DC** in order to access the data.

C8: Limited Support for Establishing and Maintaining a Web of Trust. From the DCs perspective, the problem of unregistered users could be addressed through a *web of trust*, where service providers establish a Federated Identity Management System (Buyya et al., 2010; Chadwick et al., 2011). Within a web of trust, a service provider can trust another provider to issue the credentials proving that an unregistered user satisfies the properties needed to access the data (being a neurologist at Mayo Clinic in our scenario). A risk with this solution, however, is that the web of trust becomes a closed group consisting of only few providers. This risk is aggravated by the burden that maintaining the web of trust with current solutions places on all its members. For instance, each member needs to monitor the trust relationships in the web. For a new service provider to enter a web of trust all existing service providers have to update their components in order to incorporate the new service provider. Moreover, any change in the interfaces of one of the service providers within the web of trust will impact the other service providers.

SAFAX – AN AUTHORIZATION SOLUTION FOR CLOUD SERVICES

In this section, we present SAFAX, an extensible XACML-based framework suitable for the development of authorization services for cloud. First, we provide a brief overview of XACML and its underlying reference architecture. Then, we present the SAFAX architecture along its main components. We also discuss how SAFAX meets the challenges presented in the previous section.

XACML Reference Architecture

As a baseline for the development of an authorization framework that meets the challenges discussed in the previous section, we rely on *Extensible Access Control Markup Language*(XACML) (OASIS, 2013). XACML has become the *de facto* standard for the specification and enforcement of access control policies (Liu et al., 2008); thus, its adoption would facilitate policy interoperability across domains controllers. XACML defines an attribute-based access control policy language implemented in XML as well as a reference architecture for policy evaluation and enforcement. Here, we present an overview of the XACML reference architecture. The XACML policy language is not the focus of this paper, we refer to the XACML Core specification (OASIS, 2013) for its complete description.

The XACML reference architecture is shown in Figure 3. An access request from an application is sent to the *Policy Enforcement Point* (PEP). The *PEP* forwards the request to the *Context Handler*(CH). If the request is specified in the application's native format, the *CH* constructs a XACML request and sends it to the *Policy Decision Point* (PDP) for evaluation. The *PDP* retrieves the policies from the *Policy Administration Point* (PAP). If additional attributes are required for the evaluation of the access request, the *PDP* queries the *CH* for such attributes. The *CH* retrieves these attributes from the *Policy Information Point* (PIP) and sends them to the *PDP*. The *PDP* evaluates the request against the policies and returns a response specifying the access decision (and possibly a set of obligations to be fulfilled) to the *CH*. The *CH* sends the response to the *PEP*, which is responsible for the enforcement of the decision.

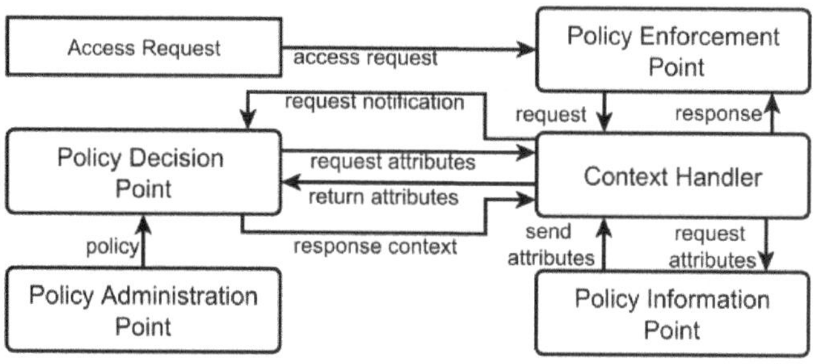

Figure 3: XACML architecture overview.

XACML provides a number of extensibility points to customize policy evaluation with respect to the needs of the application domain. The most noteworthy extensibility point is the possibility to augment the PDP with *User Defined Functions* (UDFs) for the specification of custom constraints in the policies. In the next sections, we show how UDFs can be exploited to address (some of) the challenges to be faced by authorization services for multi-cloud environments.

SAFAX – Overview

SAFAX is an XACML-based architectural framework tailored to the development of authorization services that address the challenges faced by users (DOs) while regulating access to their data on cloud storage services. In this section, we present a high level overview of SAFAX and discuss how it overcomes the challenges that were highlighted in Section 2, while the next section provides a detailed view of the main components within the tSAFAX framework.

An overview of the SAFAX framework is shown in Figure 4A. The SAFAX framework consists of three main blocks: domain-specific components (i.e., PEP, CH, and PIP); the SAFAX-CORE, which represents the baseline of the authorization service; and trust services, which can be used to evaluate custom constraints in DOs' policies. All components forming these blocks are designed as loosely coupled services. SAFAX does not prescribe who should provide these services. In Section 5, we discuss a number of deployment configurations. Here, for description purposes, we assume a configuration in which domain-specific components are under the control of DCs, SAFAX-COREunder the control of an authorization service provider and trust services under the control of some providers independent from the authorization service provider. Domain-specific components depend on the application environment. For instance, they should handle the conversion between the attribute representation in the application environment and the attribute representation in the XACML format. The only requirements for domain-specific components within SAFAX are that they adhere to the XACML specification and are offered as services and thus we do not discuss them further.

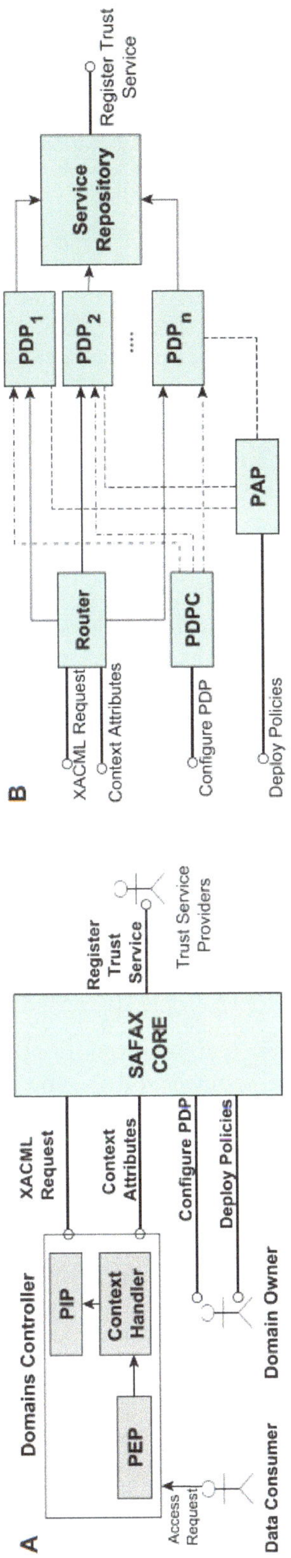

Figure 4: Overview of SAFAX. (A) SAFAX framework. (B) SAFAX-CORE architecture.

Two major problems DOs have to face when defining their policies are the limited expressiveness of the policy languages currently offered by cloud providers and the heterogeneity of policy specification. SAFAX adopts XACML for policy specification. This standard defines a canonical representation for the inputs and outputs of the PDP (which is the main component of SAFAX-CORE), thus addressing challenge C3. In particular, XACML provides an attribute-based policy language in which subjects, actions, and resources are characterized through attributes, thus addressing the inherent limitation of traditional access control models like ACL (C1). In addition, the XACML specification provides policy authors a rich set of predefined attributes as well as the possibility to use custom attributes, allowing for the definition of fine-grained policies (C2).

The use of XACML addresses some of the challenges for cloud environments and, in particular, the ones concerning policy specification. However, a key aspect is to determine whether a data consumer has the required attributes during policy evaluation. In other words, the relevant attributes of the data consumer requesting the data should be made available to the PDP during policy evaluation. SAFAX anticipates this need and allows DOs to constrain the access to their data on the basis of additional trust information that is fetched from external trust services during policy evaluation, for instance, attributes certified by a trusted authority. Intuitively, DOs can delegate part of the authorization decision making to trust service providers external to the authorization service provider. The task of connecting external trust sources with SAFAX is hidden from the DOs, thus empowering DOs with the capability of defining fine-grained access policies and at the same time relieving them from the complexity of maintaining trust sources manually, addressing challenges C1 and C6. In order to achieve this flexibility, we extend the PDP of XACML through UDFs. However, in a major departure from current XACML implementations (Dolski et al., 2007;Liu et al., 2011), we design UDFs as self-configuring clients that consume external trust services. These clients are responsible for generating valid requests for the external trust services and handling the data parsing between the external services and the XACML PDP.

We stress that the authorization service can be outside the control of DCs and can be operated instead by an independent provider trusted by DOs. Intuitively, the SAFAX framework allows eachDO to choose an authorization service and to require the DCs controlling its domains to consume this service for authorization decision making. This is similar to the authentication mechanism offered by many websites, which allows users to authenticate using the credentials provided by an external identity provider. Thus, SAFAX mitigates the need for DOs to define access control policies for each cloud service to which they are subscribed by providing a single point for deploying and maintaining their policies (i.e., a single PAP) and thus addressing challenge C4. SAFAX-COREassigns a dedicated PDP to every DO, which is identified with a unique URL (hereafter, we refer to such a URL as PDP-URL). When a DC receives an access request for a piece of data, it forwards the request to the authorization service along with the DOs PDP-URL. The authorization service uses the PDP-URL to identify the pertinent PDP for evaluation. This implies that the DCs should provide a way for the DO to specify this PDP-URL as part of their domain configuration settings.

Trust services can be used for a range of purposes such as retrieving trust information from external sources, relocating the computation of complex functions relieving the burden on the PDP and providing additional functionalities. An important example of functionality is enabling policy interoperability in distributed systems. Every DC and trust service provider may use a different vocabulary for attribute representation. While XACML unifies policy specification syntactically, it does not solve differences in semantic such as different naming or interpretation of attributes between the entities involved in policy evaluation (C5). While existing PDP implementations have no features built in to resolve this issue the extensibility of the SAFAX framework using UDFs allows resolving such issues. By connecting to external services that provides semantic alignment for the relevant attributes without the need of any human intervention (at evaluation time) SAFAXcan address challenge C5.

The DCs, who provide the cloud storage services, can greatly benefit from using SAFAX as a trusted third-party authorization service. In fact, SAFAX reduces DCs efforts of creating, maintaining, and monitoring their custom authorization solutions and, thus, they can focus on their core business.DCs simply need to consume the SAFAX service. In order to share data with consumers who are not registered with their service, the DCs do not have to establish a web of trust with other service providers. Using SAFAX, the DCs are completely relieved from this burden and can share data with any data consumer, as long as the properties of the data consumers are captured by the services used for policy evaluation, thus addressing the challenge C7. The data consumers also benefit from this approach as they do not have to register to multiple cloud storage providers in order to be able to access data (C8).

SAFAX Architecture

In this section, we focus on the SAFAX-CORE component. SAFAX-CORE exposes several interfaces that can be invoked by different entities interacting with the policy engine. The main interfaces provided by SAFAX-CORE are

- Policy Deployment: allows DOs to deploy their access control policies.
- Configure PDP: allows DOs to configure their PDPs.
- Register Service: allows the authorization service provider, DCs and external trust service providers to register their services with SAFAX.
- XACML Request: handles valid XACML requests from DCs.
- Context Attributes: allows DCs to augment access requests with additional application-specific attributes.

The components of SAFAX-CORE, as shown in Figure 4B, are designed as loosely coupled services thus breaking away from the monolithic component structure often adopted by existing XACML implementations (Dolski et al., 2007; Liu et al., 2011). We provide a brief explanation of the different services that are part of SAFAX-CORE.

Router: This service is responsible for forwarding access requests from DCs to the proper PDP based on the DOs unique PDP-URL.

Service Repository: This service allows any service registered within SAFAX to discover, bind, and consume other services in a dynamic manner. In addition, this service allows external service providers to register their services with SAFAX. Service registration requires the following details: (a) Service Identifier; (b) Service Provider's Identity; (c) Service Description; (d) Service endpoint (URI); (e) HTTP Method to invoke the service; (f) Request parameters data type; (g) Response parameters data type; (h) Request and Response Messaging format; and (i) Service Type, which indicates whether the service being offered is a PDP service, PAP service, an External Trust Service registered as a UDF, and so on. These details are necessary for services to discover other registered services, configure clients to generate valid requests and parse the responses.

Policy Administration Point (PAP): This service facilitates DOs to store and manage their access control policies regardless of the location in which the data to be protected are stored. This service also enables the PDP service to fetch the policies of a specific DO. In addition, whenever a policy associated to a DO is updated or a new policy is added, the PAP service forces the PDP service to reinitialize the DOs PDP in order to reflect the updated policies.

PDP Configuration (PDPC): SAFAX-CORE can support several PDP services; intuitively, every XACML implementation can be seen as a different PDP service in SAFAX. The PDPC service allowsDOs to select the PDP service to be used for policy evaluation. Moreover, the PDPC allows DOs to configure the selected PDP service by setting a number of parameters including the root combining algorithms[1]. These configuration settings can be changed at any time and pushed to the PDP service, which in turn initializes (or reinitializes) the DOs PDP to reflect the changes.

Policy Decision Point (PDP): SAFAX assigns a dedicated PDP to each DO. Every PDP is identified by a unique URL (PDP-URL). The PDP assigned to a DO handles all the access requests for its data regardless of the DC which sends them. The PDP fetches the policies associated to theDO from the PAP service. In addition, this service allows the PDPC service to push the PDP configuration settings specified by the DO. In SAFAX, we decouple UDFs from the XACML PDP component to allow the framework to be extensible without disrupting existing components. As shown in Figure 5A, the PDP consists of a XACML PDP and the *External Service Extensions*component that handles the invocations to external trust service. The *External Service Extensions*component contains, for each UDF, a self-configuring client that consumes the external trust service corresponding to the UDF. These clients are generic and self-configure them selves based on the information related to a given UDF that has been registered by a trust service provider with the SAFAX-CORE service. They read the external trust service description from the Service Repository and, accordingly, build a valid request and communicate with the service using the specified protocol. Moreover, they parse the response from external trust services to retrieve the trust information requested for policy evaluation.

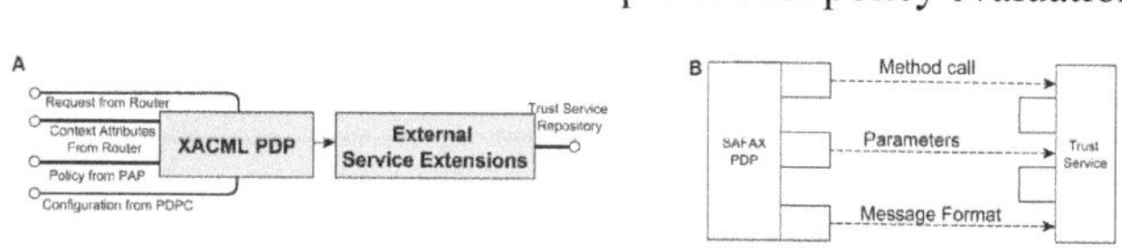

Figure 5: SAFAX PDP and its extensibility with external trust services. (A) SAFAXPDP architecture. (B) SAFAX plugins.

External Trust Services: We decouple UDFs from the PDP and implement them as external, but pluggable services, as shown in Figure 5B. This pluggable architecture allows SAFAX to be*extensible* in order to serve access requests that require complex processing in a *scalable* manner as well as consuming information from external sources. This way, the processing of trust information can be outsourced to external services while SAFAX acts as an orchestrator for these service calls based on the DOs policies. External service providers that want to plug-in their services withSAFAX need to comply with two main constraints: (i) register their service through the Service Repository of SAFAX along with a UDF Identifier which will be used by the DOs in their access control policies; and (ii) external service APIs must conform to implementation dependent specifications of SAFAX. As shown in Figure 5B, each provider that registers their service as an external trust service in the SAFAX framework must specify: (a) the *Method call* through which the service can be invoked; (b) the parameters that must be supplied to the service; and (c) the message format that indicates how the parameters will be packaged.

Message Flow within SAFAX

The services presented in the previous section give an indication of the functionality and capabilities of each component. In this section, we present the overall integrated view of the SAFAXarchitecture and its usage.

DOs specify access control policies for their data, which can be stored across multiple cloud providers (DCs). For instance, in the scenario given in Section 2, Alice wants to restrict the access to her health records to neurologists at Mayo Clinic. This access requirement can be represented using the XACML rule in Figure 6. Lines 35–42 show an example of UDF: functionurn:nl:tue:sec:pdp:1.0:udf:credentia l:user: has:credential. This UDF takes as input a user name, a credential, and an issuer, and returns a Boolean value indicating whether the user has the specified credential from the specified issuer. It is evaluated using an external credential-based trust service (see Section 4) during policy evaluation.

```
<Rule Effect="Permit" RuleId="urn:nl:tue:sec:example:sample:alice">
  <Target>
    <Resources>
      <Resource>
        <ResourceMatch MatchId="urn:oasis:names:tc:xacml:1.0:function:string-equal">
          <AttributeValue DataType="http://www.w3.org/2001/XMLSchema#string">
            healthRecord
          </AttributeValue>
          <ResourceAttributeDesignator
            AttributeId="urn:oasis:names:tc:xacml:1.0:resource:resource-id"
            DataType="http://www.w3.org/2001/XMLSchema#string"/>
        </ResourceMatch>
      </Resource>
    </Resources>
    <Actions>
      <Action>
        <ActionMatch MatchId="urn:oasis:names:tc:xacml:1.0:function:string-equal">
          <AttributeValue DataType="http://www.w3.org/2001/XMLSchema#string">
            read
          </AttributeValue>
          <ActionAttributeDesignator
            AttributeId="urn:oasis:names:tc:xacml:1.0:action:action-id"
            DataType="http://www.w3.org/2001/XMLSchema#string"/>
        </ActionMatch>
      </Action>
    </Actions>
  </Target>
  <Condition>
    <Apply FunctionId="urn:nl:tue:sec:pdp:1.0:udf:credential:user:has:credential">
      <SubjectAttributeDesignator
        AttributeId="urn:oasis:names:tc:xacml:1.0:subject:subject-id"
        DataType="http://www.w3.org/2001/XMLSchema#string"/>
      <AttributeValue DataType="http://www.w3.org/2001/XMLSchema#string">
        neurologist
      </AttributeValue>
      <AttributeValue DataType="http://www.w3.org/2001/XMLSchema#string">
        MayoClinic
      </AttributeValue>
    </Apply>
  </Condition>
</Rule>
```

Figure 6: XACML rule encoding Alice's authorization requirement *AR*3.

DOs use the PAP to deploy the specified policies and the PDPC to configure their PDP by selecting a default root combining algorithm, the PDP service to be used for policy evaluation, etc. SAFAXprovides the DO a unique PDP-URL to invoke the assigned PDP. All access requests for data belonging to the DO are forwarded to the assigned PDP through the unique PDP-URL. As a consequence, DOs should be able to configure the PDP-URL at every DC they are subscribed to.

Moreover, each DC should implement the domain-specific components (i.e., PEP, CH, and PIP) and register the Context Handler service with the SAFAX framework. This is necessary since during policy evaluation the PDP might need additional attributes from the CH of the DC such as the IP addresses of the data consumer, system time, and other attributes that can be required for policy evaluation. In particular, the CH interface to fetch the attributes should be registered with the service registry of the SAFAX framework.

Figure 7 shows the interaction of services within SAFAX. We describe the message flow by following a concrete scenario that takes place in the context presented in Section 2: Charlie (a neurologist from Mayo Clinic) wants to *view* the health records that Alice stored on a specific domain (AD_2) of the domains controller DC_{II}.

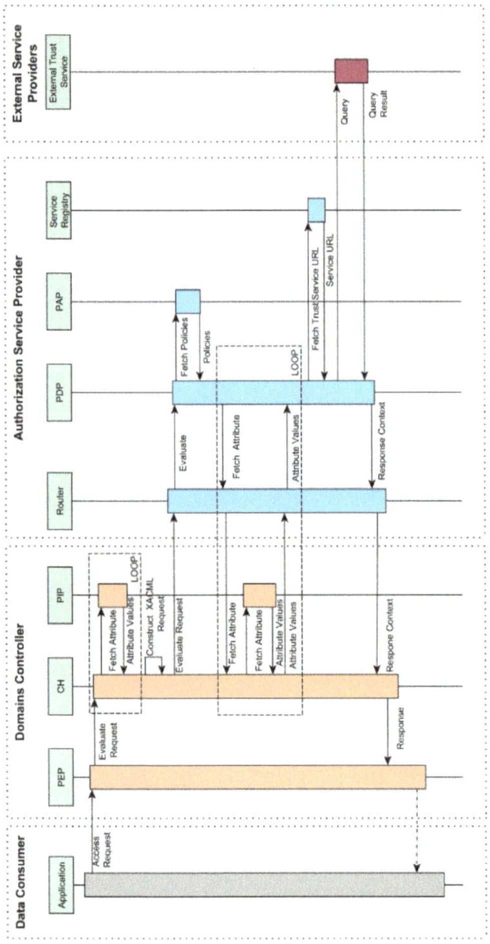

Figure 7: Message flow for policy evaluation using SAFAX.

Whenever a data consumer (Charlie) sends a request to access data belonging to a DO (Alice) to aDC (in our scenario to DC_{II}), the access request is intercepted by the PEP of the DC. The PEP forwards the request to the CH service, which first fetches additional information from its PIP, enriching the original request, and then constructs a valid XACML request. The CH service forwards the XACML request to the PDP assigned to the DO by invoking the SAFAX service. The Router intercepts the access request coming from the CH and forwards it to the proper PDP based on the PDP-URL. During policy evaluation, if the PDP needs additional attributes (e.g., timestamp), it contacts the DC's Context Handler service. When the DO specifies policies that require additional (external) trust information to make a decision, the PDP service contacts the external trust services. In our scenario, the PDP contacts Mayo Clinic, which can been seen as the trust service provider for the trust information specified by Alice in her policy (i.e., the issuer of the credential), to determine whether Charlie is a neurologist at the Clinic. After receiving the required information, the PDP computes the decision and informs the DCs Context Handler. The CH parses the XACML response and sends the decision to the PEP. The PEP enforces the decision by allowing or denying access to the DOs data to the consumer based on the given decision.

IMPLEMENTATION

We have realized the SAFAX architecture by implementing an authorization service as a web service following the architectural principles and guidelines given in Section 3[2]. The SAFAX authorization service is implemented in Java running on an Apache Tomcat server and using Jersey as the service framework. MySQL is used as a back-end persistent data storage.

The authorization service exposes interfaces that can be invoked by the PEP implemented by DCs. Moreover, for the sake of completeness and alignment with the XACML reference architecture, we have implemented examples of PEP, PIP, and CH services.

In order to ease the management of policies and configuration of PDPs by DOs, we have developed a User Interface (referred as SAFAX GUI) that communicates with the SAFAX services. SAFAX GUI is developed using HTML, CSS, and AJAX to consume SAFAX services. The SAFAX GUI enables aDO to create a *project*, which can contain multiple *demos*. Intuitively, a demo corresponds to the management point for regulating access to the data in a Domain. Each demo is associated to a single PDP, and DOs can upload their access control policies to the PAP service and configure the PDP through *Demo Management* interface as shown in Figure 8. Figure 8A shows the part of theSAFAX GUI that allows DOs to deploy their access control policies. For demonstration purposes, we facilitate DOs to upload sample access requests to test their policies. Figure 8B shows how xtbfDOs can configure their PDPs as well as providing them the URL through which their PDP can be invoked. Figure 8C shows how the sample PIP can be configured by uploading attributes that can be retrieved during policy evaluation.

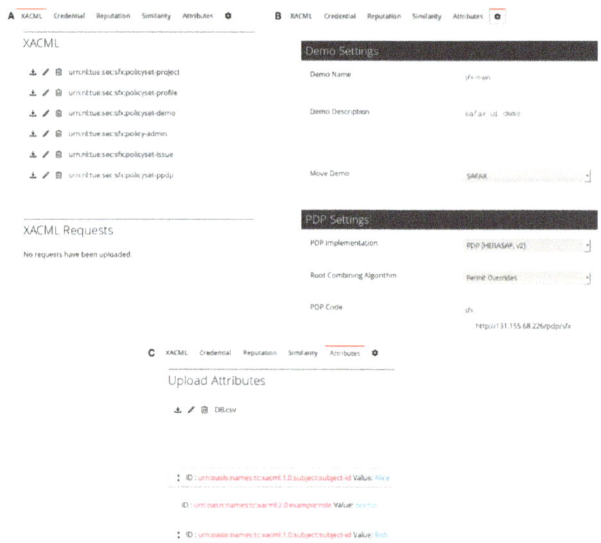

Figure 8: SAFAX GUI: management. (A) Policy administration. (B) PDP configuration.(C) Policy information point.

We have also built a service that simulates multiple DCs by allowing the DCs to evaluate their policies against different request. This service is accessible through the SAFAX GUI, which makes it possible to test the SAFAX authorization service in various scenarios. A screenshot of the GUI for policy evaluation is shown in Figure 9A. In addition to that, we provide an additional feature through which DOs can analyze the log generated during the evaluation of access requests to their PDP (Figure 9B). This is useful for DOs to gain feedback regarding their policies and correct them if necessary.

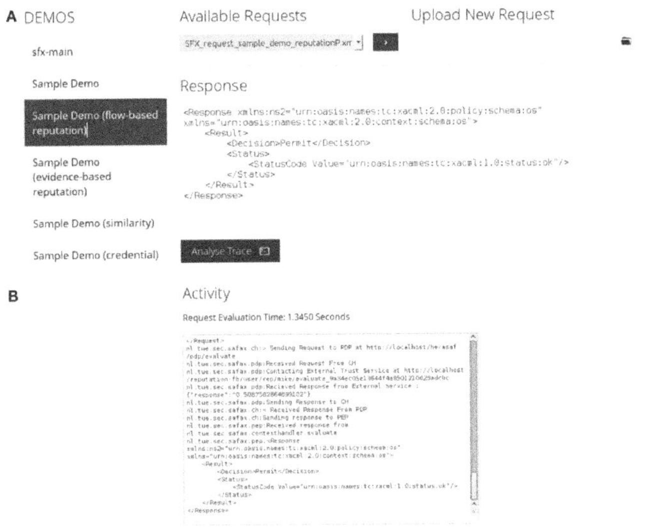

Figure 9: SAFAX GUI: evaluation. (A) Policy evaluation. (B) Evaluation log.

We have chosen to implement SAFAX services as RESTful services that strictly conform to the following constraints:

- Services are purely stateless and all information related to the state is contained either with the request or stored in a persistent database.
- Services communicate with each other either in JSON or XML.

The *Service Repository* component uses a MySQL back-end database to store the information regarding a service. Every PDP that is assigned to a DO is treated as an independent service and is registered with the service repository.

The *Router* parses the PDP-URL, which is used by the DCs to invoke the PDP assigned to a DO, extracts the code used to identify the PDP object within the SAFAX framework, and forwards the access request to that particular PDP object. For each access request, the Router generates a unique *Transaction ID*, internal to the SAFAX framework and forwards it to the PDP along with the access request. This is used for correlating the request-responses with the PDPs, and identifying the log messages generated by the PDP during the evaluation of a particular access request (Figure 9B).

Our implementation of the PAP uses a MySQL database to store the uploaded policies and make them available to the PDP. In addition to XACML policies, for demonstration purposes, we allowDOs to upload policies for external services that will be deployed on the respective external trust services. DOs can use the SAFAX GUI to upload their policies and deploy them on their assigned PDPs and trust services.

In our prototype, we used HERAS-AF (Dolski et al., 2007) as the default XACML PDP implementation. HERAS-AF was chosen since it is an open-source project, actively developed and well supported. HERAS-AF PDP component is provided as a JAR file, which we wrap as a service by exposing the interfaces for policy deployment and access requests as web interfaces. HERAS-AF supports UDFs, but they have to be bound to the PDP implementation. To circumvent this limitation, we have extended the core HERAS-AF with several classes that: (a) read the DOs configurations from the PDPC and initialize the PDP accordingly; (b) communicate with the Service Repository to fetch the configurations of external trust services based on the policies deployed by the DO; and (c) invoke external trust services and parse the response (represented in JSON) to retrieve the values from those services.

Although HERAS-AF has been used in the current implementation of SAFAX, this is not a constraint for the SAFAX architecture. In fact, the extensions to HERAS-AF are made in a manner that replacing HERAS-AF with any other XACML implementation would require changing a few lines of code in our implementation.

Our prototype implementation of SAFAX currently supports four external trust services: a credential-based trust management service, two reputation services and a policy alignment service. The credential-based trust management service is based on GEM (Trivellato et al., 2014), a distributed goal evaluation algorithm for trust management systems. One reputation service uses a flow-based reputation metric (Simone et al., 2012), which extends EigenTrust (Kamvar et al., 2003) by providing absolute reputations values. The other reputation service uses a subjective logic system centered on evidence (Skoric et al., 2014), thus providing reputation values along with uncertainty. Finally, the policy alignment service is an ontology-based service that uses semantic alignment techniques to map concepts from different ontologies (Trivellato et al., 2009), allowing domain owners to use different vocabularies and models for the specification of their policies. These services communicate with the SAFAX PDP using the RESTful protocol. This variety of trust services allows DOs to use different types of trust information within the evaluation of their policies, illustrating the flexibility of SAFAX. Note that the aforementioned trust services are simply provided as an example of how SAFAX can be extended to outsource the processing of trust information to external services. A full description of these services is out of the scope of this paper.

DISCUSSION

In this section, we present various trust models that are typically employed in cloud environments and discuss their impact on deployment configurations of SAFAX. We also discuss our experience of deploying, using, and securing SAFAX.

Trust Models in Cloud Environments

Trust models in cloud environments have a direct impact on the deployment configurations of authorization solutions based on the trust relationships and the control that entities have on the various services. We can broadly classify the trust models into three categories: (a) Centralized Trust; (b) Distributed Trust; and (c) Distributed and Delegated Trust. A representation of these trust models is provided in Figure 10.

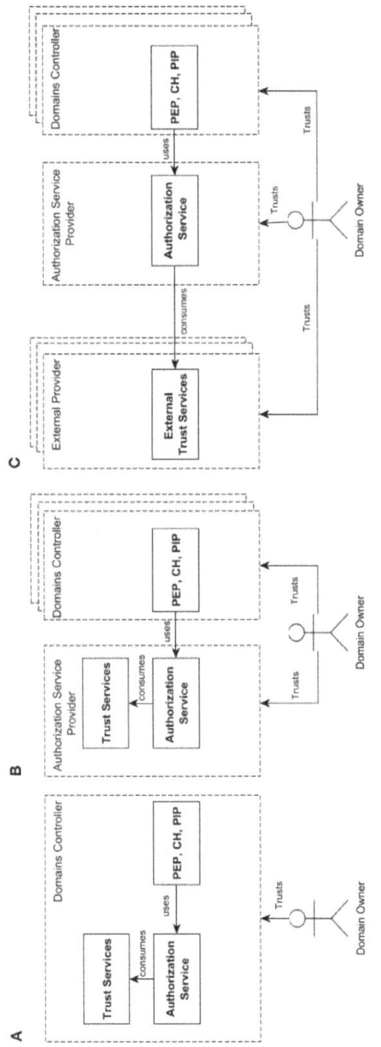

Figure 10: Trust models and their impact on SAFAX deployment. (A) Centralized trust model. (B) Distributed trust model. (C) Distributed and delegated trust model.

Centralized Trust Model

The DC has control over all the services forming the authorization service including the trust services (Figure 10A). In particular, the DC deploys the domain-specific components (PEP, CH, and PIP) as well as the SAFAX-CORE components and trust services within its organizational perimeter. However, trust services can only consume information that is internal to the DC or can be used to extend the functionality of the XACML PDP. The DO trusts the DC for the secure storage of their access control policies, for the correct evaluation of access requests from data consumers and ultimately for the enforcement of their policies. This trust model is suitable for very sensitive domains such as military clouds where the storage and evaluation of access control policies cannot be outsourced to an external entity. From the DOs perspective, this model has, however, most of the limitations discussed in Section 2 as the DO does not have the capability to freely specify its policies nor to decide which trust services should be used for policy evaluation. These aspects remain under the control of the DC.

Distributed Trust Model

In this model, the DC is not responsible for the evaluation of DOs' policies (Figure 10B). This task is outsourced to a dedicated authorization service, possibly selected by DOs. In particular, the authorization service provider deploys the SAFAX-CORE components within its organizational perimeter. Trust services that complement the authorization service are also provided by the same authorization provider and thus they are in the same domain. In this trust model, trust services are mainly used to extend the functionality of the PDP; for example, a trust service can process an IP address to determine the country to which the IP address belongs or provide support for spatial data types and spatial authorization decision functions (Matheus, 2012). In essence, trust services cannot be used as external sources of information. The DC only deploys the domain-specific components of SAFAX (PEP, CH, and PIP) for the management and enforcement of authorization decisions within its organizational perimeter and consumes the authorization service through the CH component. As shown in Figure 10B, the DO trusts the authorization service for the secure storage and evaluation of its access policies and trusts the DC to consume the authorization service for the evaluation of access requests and to enforce the authorization decision. This trust model is suited when the DO is subscribed to multiple cloud services and needs a unified means to specify and maintain its access control policies. This model is ideal for DCs that want to externalize the policy evaluation.

Distributed and Delegated Trust Model

As in the distributed trust model, the DC consumes the authorization service while implementing the domain-specific components that enforce the authorization decision (Figure 10C). However, in the distributed and delegated trust model, trust services are not only external to the authorization service but they can also be outside the control of the authorization service provider. As shown in Figure 10C, the DO trusts the authorization service to securely store its access control policies, configuration settings regarding the PDP and for proper evaluation of its access control policies. The DO trusts the DC to enforce the authorization decision determined by the authorization service. Moreover, the DO trusts the external trust services to provide accurate and complete information to the authorization service during policy evaluation. It is worth noting that the authorization service delegates part of policy evaluation to the external services even when there is no explicit trust relation existing between the authorization service and the external services. Indeed, this trust model empowers DOs with full control over policy evaluation in the sense that aDO can select the services that are used to evaluate its policies.

SAFAX supports all these three trust models, since at an architectural level we do not prescribe or constrain the deployment of the various SAFAX services. SAFAX facilitates such a variety of deployment configurations given that the individual services within the SAFAX framework are designed as loosely coupled services. The deployment of our prototype is based on the *Distributed and Delegated Trust Model* since it is the most open and extensible among the trust models. It allows our prototype to consume information from external trust sources as well as extend the functionality of the PDP.

However, given that the various components are SAFAX are essentially web services, we can easily support the other two trust models by deploying the various services in different organizational perimeters. The deployment of a service does not have any impact on theSAFAX framework, because all the services are registered to the *Service Repository* service, which in turn provides different services the information needed to consume other services. In this manner, SAFAX framework can serve different organizations with specific trust models without any changes to the framework.

Lessons Learned from Deploying, Using, and Securing SAFAX

Since SAFAX can be used by multiple DOs and DCs, a basic authentication mechanism is provided by our prototype implementation in order to identity various entities. SAFAX processes and stores data from various entities: DOs, DCs, External Service Providers, and SAFAX Administrators. This information ranges from access control policies of DOs, configuration settings of a DOs PDP, access request logs from DCs, to global settings of the SAFAX framework. In addition, our implementation supports a *Guest* mode, through which unregistered users can configure a *Test PDP*, deploy access control policies and test access requests against their policies. Finally, SAFAXsupports multiple users to act as a DO and configure access control policies in a collaborative manner and deploy them on a PDP that is shared between those users.

In order to regulate the actions that users can perform within SAFAX, we use SAFAX as the access control mechanism. In other words, SAFAX inherently plays the role of DC to control data stored within its Domain. We have developed the PEP, CH, and PIP specific for SAFAX (referred as SFX-*). Every action that a user wants to perform within SAFAX triggers an access request that is intercepted by the SFX-PEP. The request is enriched with attributes retrieved from SFX-PIP and then sent to the SAFAX-CORE service for evaluation. We specified a set of XACML policies that define the actions (e.g., create, view, edit, delete) users can perform on various SAFAX resources, essentially also playing the role of a DO. For instance, these policies are used to restrict the number of projects and demos users can create based on the groups they belong to and to limit the actions that guest users can perform.

Through this experience of securing SAFAX using SAFAX, we have gained an understanding of usingSAFAX from the perspectives of both DCs and DOs. We have observed that the SFX-PIP plays a key role in the correct evaluation of policies since the native requests coming to the SFX-PEP from the various components of SAFAX do not contain all the information necessary to evaluate the policies. The PIP needs to be aware of the various resources in its domain, the contextual information regarding those resources such as resource owners, resource types, project membership among others. In our prototype implementation, we support the two approaches described in Section 4 for attribute retrieval. In particular, attributes that are often used in policies, like resource owner and resource type, are fetched from the SFX-PIP when the XACML request is constructed. On the other hand, attributes that are checked in few specific conditions in the defined policies (e.g., number of projects and demos already created by a user) are fetched during policy evaluation.

We have observed that the DOs must be aware of the attributes that are supported by the DCs, in order to refer to them in their access control policies. Since in our case, the DO and the DC are a single entity, it is straightforward to align the various attributes. However, when a DO is subscribed to multiple DCs, it cannot be expected that they are aware of the syntax and semantics of various attributes in different DCs. For example, a DO may want to specify that a policy based on the resource's attribute such as *File Extension* for resources stored in two different clouds; however, the two cloud providers may use different attribute identifiers for the same attribute, which makes it infeasible for the PDP to match these different attributes (with different identifiers) to the attribute specified by the DO. This dependency can be avoided if the various cloud providers use a common syntax for the specification of various attributes. Another approach, which is currently used in SAFAX to remove this dependency between DOs and DCs, is by using a *policy alignment*service that is provided as part of the SAFAX framework. This service enables a semantic alignment between the concepts that can be used by different DCs based on the concept of similarity. More details regarding the policy alignment service can be found in Trivellato et al. (2009).

Overall, we have seen the advantages that SAFAX offers to both DOs and DCs in terms of ease of specification, maintenance, and evaluation of policies. Finally, the extensibility of SAFAX opens up the scope of access control to incorporate external trust sources in policy specification and evaluation.

RELATED WORK

Two main streams of research can be identified in the literature, which aim to enable secure data sharing in cloud environments. The first stream stems from the fact that outsourcing data outside the trust domain reduces the control users have on their data. Solutions in this stream often rely on cryptographic schemes, which allow users to encrypt sensitive data and distribute keys to authorized users (Blundo et al., 2010; Wang et al., 2010; Yu et al., 2010; Ruj et al., 2011). A scheme often used by these solutions is hierarchical identity-based encryption (Boneh et al., 2005), which is a generalization of the identity-based encryption scheme (Shamir, 1985) that reflects the organizational hierarchy. However, these solutions have the intrinsic problems of identity-based policies and, thus, they are not able to address the challenges for cloud. Attribute-based encryption (ABE) (Sahai and Waters, 2005) has been proposed to enable encryption of sensitive information according to an attribute-based policy in such a way that only users with certain attributes (e.g., roles) can access the information. A number of variants of the ABE scheme have been proposed since its introduction. They range from extending its functionality (Wang et al., 2010; Li et al., 2011; Asim et al., 2012) to proposing schemes with stronger security proofs (Ibraimi et al., 2010). When applied to multi-cloud environments, the main limitation of most ABE-based schemes is that they require binding the attributes to a specific domain controller or a domain owner at encryption time. Therefore, data need to be re-encrypted every time a new domain owner joins the cloud. Moreover, ABE-based schemes implicitly assume the existence of a mechanism for determining the attribute keys that their users are entitled to receive. However, the attributes of a user may depend on other attributes or conditions determined by third parties. As a result, these schemes do not address the dynamics characterizing clouds and thus fail to meet challenge **C8**. Asim et al. (2012)present a dynamic ABE scheme that does not require the encryptor to bind the attributes to a specific domain controller or a domain owner at encryption time, enabling new users to decrypt the data without the need of re-encrypting it. Yet, cryptographic schemes require a key management mechanism that determines which user is entitled to receive the key to decrypt the data. As shown in Asim et al. (2012), authorization mechanisms (i.e., solutions in the second stream) are a viable solution for key management.

The second stream of solutions to regulate the sharing of sensitive information in cloud encompasses the use of authorization mechanisms. Several proposals (Hu et al., 2009; Alcaraz Calero et al., 2010; Almutairi et al., 2012; Wu et al., 2013) adopt Role Based Access Control (RBAC) to meet the dynamic, extensible, and highly configurable security requirements of clouds. Younis et al. (2014) propose AC3, an access control model for cloud environments that combines Task-Role Based Access Control (Oh and Park, 2003) with multilevel security. One major drawback of these approaches is the limited expressiveness of the policies that can be specified (challenge C2). In this work, we used XACML (OASIS, 2013) as policy language. This choice is twofold. First, XACML has become the *de facto* standard for access control (Liu et al., 2008), encouraging its adoption by a larger number of cloud providers. Moreover, it has been shown that attribute-based access control and, in particular, XACML (OASIS, 2013) provide a baseline for the development of authorization services for cloud environments (Takabi et al., 2010). The XACML reference architecture provides a blueprint, which needs to be followed by any implementation to be compliant with the standard. Several open-source XACML implementations including SUN-XACML[3], HERAS-AF (Dolski et al., 2007), XEngine (Liu et al., 2011), enterprise-java-xacml[4], and WSO2 Balana[5] are currently available. These implementations support different versions (and in some cases, multiple versions) of XACML. Some of these implementations, such as HERAS-AF and WSO2 Balana, are actively developed compared to other implementations. In addition, some implementations have been used as a backbone for XACML-based frameworks. For instance, Lazouski et al. (2014) extend WOS2 Balana for the enforcement of usage control policies in distributed systems, while TAS3 Trust PDP (Böhm et al., 2010) extends SUN-XACML for the evaluation of trust policies. The XACML reference architecture, however, is underspecified, and existing XACML implementations of XACML may have slight variations based on implementation choices. Nonetheless, a common characteristic of existing XACML implementations is that they are implemented as a monolithic component. Although the choice of implementing the XACML reference architecture as a monolithic component may be suitable for enterprise environment, it cannot fully address the key challenges for cloud environments. This problem is acknowledged and partially addressed by Laborde et al. (2009), who extend a core XACML PDP with loosely coupled domain-dependent modules that provide non-standard security information (such as new data types). However, the approach does not discuss the decoupling of the other components of the XACML reference architecture, and does not address the fact that UDFs are typically implemented within the PDP, thus limiting the extensibility of existing implementations. By contrast, SAFAX decouples the definition and implementation of UDFs from the PDP, thus allowing domain owners to determine from which source the information used for policy evaluation is fetched. Another approach for providing authorization as a service using XACML is proposed by Lorch et al. (2003). This solution addresses challenges C2 and C3 by providing a single point for deploying and updating policies, but does not address the other challenges to be faced in cloud, especially the ones related to policy evaluation.

CONCLUSION

In this paper, we have investigated the challenges of secure data sharing in multi-cloud environments. The XACML reference architecture provides the principles to address the identified challenges. However, existing XACML implementations are monolithic, thus resulting unsuitable for handling authorizations in multi-cloud environments. To address this limitation we have proposed SAFAX, an extensible XACML-based authorization framework tailored to the development of authorization services that are suitable for (multi) cloud environments. The main characteristic of SAFAX is that all its components are designed as loosely coupled services. This design choice makes SAFAX a viable solution as it provides the necessary flexibility, extensibility and scalability to meet the dynamic, extensible, and highly configurable security requirements of clouds. To demonstrate SAFAX, we have realized a prototype by implementing the SAFAXarchitecture as a web service. The trust model underlying an application domain has a significant impact on the deployment of an authorization service. We have reviewed a number of trust models typically being used in cloud environments and we showed that SAFAX can support them. Moreover, we discussed the lessons learned from deploying, using, and securing SAFAX.

Our current implementation of SAFAX uses the XACML PDP provided by HERAS-AF. This PDP supports the evaluation of policies specified in XACML v2.0. We plan to extend the evaluation capabilities with an additional PDP service to support XACML v3.0. Our implementation allows users to verify certain types of trust information in their policies, but other types of trust (e.g., KPI, risk) and context (e.g., location) information may be needed for making access decisions. In this direction, our implementation can be easily extended with additional trust services.

ACKNOWLEDGMENTS

This work has been partially funded by the EDA project IN4STARS2.0, the ITEA2 projects FedSS (No. 11009) and M2MGrid (No. 13011), the EU FP7 project AU2EU, and the Dutch national program COMMIT under the THeCS project.

FOOTNOTES

1. ^A root combining algorithm is needed to resolve policy conflicts that can arise when more than one policy is deployed in the PDP (OASIS, 2013).

2. ^The authorization service is available at http://security1.win.tue.nl/safax/
3. ^http://sunxacml.sourceforge.net
4. ^http://code.google.com/p/enterprise-java-xacml
5. ^http://xacmlinfo.org/category/balana

REFERENCES

1. Alcaraz Calero, J., Edwards, N., Kirschnick, J., Wilcock, L., and Wray, M. (2010). Toward a multi-tenancy authorization system for cloud services. *IEEE Secur. Priv.* 8, 48–55. doi: 10.1109/MSP.2010.194
2. Almutairi, A., Sarfraz, M., Basalamah, S., Aref, W., and Ghafoor, A. (2012). A distributed access control architecture for cloud computing. *IEEE Software* 29, 36–44. doi:10.3389/fpsyg.2013.00200
3. Asim, M., Ignatenko, T., Petkovic, M., Trivellato, D., and Zannone, N. (2012). "Enforcing access control in virtual organizations using hierarchical attribute-based encryption," in *Proceedings of International Conference on Availability, Reliability and Security* (Prague: IEEE), 212–217.
4. Blundo, C., Cimato, S., De Capitani Di Vimercati, S., De Santis, A., Foresti, S., Paraboschi, S., et al. (2010). Managing key hierarchies for access control enforcement: heuristic approaches. *J. Comput. Secur.* 29, 533–547. doi:10.1016/j.cose.2009.12.006
5. Böhm, K., Etalle, S., den Hartog, J., Hütter, C., Trabelsi, S., Trivellato, D., et al. (2010). A flexible architecture for privacy-aware trust management. *J. Theor. Appl. Electron. Commer. Res.* 5, 77–96. doi:10.4067/S0718-18762010000200006
6. Boneh, D., Boyen, X., and Goh, E.-J. (2005). "Hierarchical identity based encryption with constant size ciphertext," in*Proceedings of Annual International Conference on the Theory and Applications of Cryptographic Techniques, LNCS 3494*(Aarhus: Springer), 440–456.
7. Buyya, R., Ranjan, R., and Calheiros, R. N. (2010). "Intercloud: utility-oriented federation of cloud computing environments for scaling of application services," in *Algorithms and Architectures for Parallel Processing* (Busan: Springer), 13–31.
8. Chadwick, D., Lievens, S., den Hartog, J., Pashalidis, A., and Alhadeff, J. (2011). "My private cloud overview: a trust, privacy and security infrastructure for the cloud," in *Proceedings of International Conference on Cloud Computing* (Washington, DC: IEEE), 752–753.
9. Dolski, S., Huonder, F., and Oberholzer, S. (2007). *HERAS-AF: XACML 2.0 Implementation.* Technical Report, University of Applied Sciences Rapperswil.
10. Gartner Inc. (2014). *Gartner Says Worldwide Traditional PC, Tablet, Ultramobile and Mobile Phone Shipments to Grow 4.2 Percent in 2014.* Available at: http://www.gartner.com/newsroom/id/2791017
11. Grobauer, B., Walloschek, T., and Stocker, E. (2011). Understanding cloud computing vulnerabilities. *IEEE Secur. Priv.* 9, 50–57. doi:10.1109/MSP.2010.115
12. Hu, L., Ying, S., Jia, X., and Zhao, K. (2009). "Towards an approach of semantic access control for cloud computing," in *Cloud Computing, LNCS 5931* (Beijing: Springer), 145–156.
13. Hühnlein, D., Roßnagel, H., and Zibuschka, J. (2010). "Diffusion of federated identity management," in *Sicherheit*, P-170, 25–36.
14. Ibraimi, L., Asim, M., and Petkovic, M. (2010). "An encryption scheme for a secure policy updating," in *Proceedings of International Conference on Security and Cryptography* (Athens: SciTePress), 399–408.
15. Kamvar, S. D., Schlosser, M. T., and Garcia-Molina, H. (2003). "The eigentrust algorithm for reputation management in P2P networks," in *Proceedings of the 12th International Conference on World Wide Web* (Budapest: ACM), 640–651.
16. Laborde, R., Cheaito, M., Barrere, F., and Benzekri, A. (2009). "An extensible XACML authorization web service: application to dynamic web sites access control," in *Proceedings of International Conference on Signal-Image Technology and Internet-Based Systems* (Marrakesh: IEEE), 499–505.
17. Lazouski, A., Mancini, G., Martinelli, F., and Mori, P. (2014). "Architecture, workflows, and prototype for stateful data usage control in cloud," in *Proceedings of International Workshop on Data Usage Management* (San Jose, CA: IEEE), 23–30.
18. Li, J., Wang, Q., Wang, C., and Ren, K. (2011). Enhancing attribute-based encryption with attribute hierarchy. *Mobile Net. Appl. Arch.* 16, 553–561. doi:10.1007/s11036-010-0233-y
19. Li, N., Winsborough, W. H., and Mitchell, J. C. (2003). Distributed credential chain discovery in trust management. *J. Comput. Secur.* 11, 35–86.
20. Liu, A. X., Chen, F., Hwang, J., and Xie, T. (2008). "XEngine: a fast and scalable XACML policy evaluation engine," in*Proceedings of International Conference on Measurement and Modeling of Computer Systems* (Annapolis, MD: ACM), 265–276.
21. Liu, A. X., Chen, F., Hwang, J., and Xie, T. (2011). Designing fast and scalable XACML policy evaluation engines. *IEEE Trans. Comput.* 60, 1802–1817. doi:10.1109/TC.2010.274
22. Lorch, M., Kafura, D., and Shah, S. (2003). "An XACML-based policy management and authorization service for globus resources," in *Proceedings of International Workshop on Grid Computing* (Phoenix: IEEE), 208.
23. Matheus, A., and Herrmann, J. (2012). Geospatial eXtensible Access Control Markup Language (GeoXACML) Version 1 Corrigendum. OGC Implementation Standard OGC 11-017, Open Geospatial Consortium.
24. OASIS. (2013). eXtensible Access Control Markup Language (XACML) Version 3.0. OASIS Standard.
25. Oh, S., and Park, S. (2003). Task-role-based access control model. *Inf. Syst.* 28, 533–562. doi:10.1016/

S0306-4379(02)00029-7

26. Ruj, S., Nayak, A., and Stojmenovic, I. (2011). "Dacc: distributed access control in clouds," in *Proceedings of International Conference on Trust, Security and Privacy in Computing and Communications* (Changsha: IEEE), 91–98.

27. Sahai, A., and Waters, B. (2005). "Fuzzy identity-based encryption," in *Proceedings of Annual International Conference on the Theory and Applications of Cryptographic Techniques, LNCS 3494* (Aarhus: Springer), 457–473.

28. Sandhu, R. S., Coyne, E. J., Feinstein, H. L., and Youman, C. E. (1996). Role-based access control models. *Computer* 29, 38–47. doi:10.1109/2.485845

29. Shamir, A. (1985). "Identity-based cryptosystems and signature schemes," in *Proceedings of International Cryptology Conference* (Santa Barbara, CA: Springer), 47–53.

30. Simone, A., Skoric, B., and Zannone, N. (2012). Flow-based reputation: more than just ranking. *Int. J. Inf. Technol. Decis. Mak.*11, 551–578. doi:10.1142/S0219622012500113

31. Skoric, B., de Hoogh, S., and Zannone, N. (2014). Flow-based reputation with uncertainty: evidence-based subjective logic.*CoRR*abs/1402.3319.

32. Takabi, H., Joshi, J., and Ahn, G.-J. (2010). Security and privacy challenges in cloud computing environments. *IEEE Secur. Priv.*8, 24–31. doi:10.1109/MSP.2010.186

33. Trivellato, D., Spiessens, F., Zannone, N., and Etalle, S. (2009). "Reputation-based ontology alignment for autonomy and interoperability in distributed access control," in *Proceedings of International Conference on Computational Science and Engineering* (Vancouver, BC: IEEE), 252–258.

34. Trivellato, D., Zannone, N., and Etalle, S. (2014). GEM: a distributed goal evaluation algorithm for trust management. *Theory Pract. Logic Program.* 14, 293–337. doi:10.1017/S1471068412000397

35. Trivellato, D., Zannone, N., Glaundrup, M., Skowronek, J., and Etalle, S. (2013). A semantic security framework for systems of systems. *Int. J. Coop. Inf. Syst.* 22, doi:10.1142/S0218843013500044

36. Wang, G., Liu, Q., and Wu, J. (2010). "Hierarchical attribute-based encryption for fine-grained access control in cloud storage services," in *Proceedings of Conference on Computer and Communications Security* (Chicago: ACM), 735–737.

37. Wu, R., Zhang, X., Ahn, G.-J., Sharifi, H., and Xie, H. (2013). "ACaaS: access control as a service for IaaS cloud," in *Proceedings of International Conference on Social Computing* (Alexandria, VA: IEEE), 423–428.

38. Younis, Y. A., Kifayat, K., and Merabti, M. (2014). An access control model for cloud computing. *J. Inf. Secur. Appl.* 19, 45–60. doi:10.1016/j.jisa.2014.04.003

39. Yu, S., Wang, C., Ren, K., and Lou, W. (2010). "Achieving secure, scalable, and fine-grained data access control in cloud computing," in *Proceedings of Conference on Computer Communications* (San Diego, CA: IEEE), 1–9.

CHAPTER 13

ENSURING SECURITY, CONFIDENTIALITY AND FINE-GRAINED DATA ACCESS CONTROL OF CLOUD DATA STORAGE IMPLEMENTATION ENVIRONMENT

Amir Mohamed Talib

Keywords: Cloud Computing, Cloud Data Storage, Cloud Service Provider, Formula-Based Cloud Data Access Control, Multi-Agent System and Secure Java Agent Development Framework

INTRODUCTION

Cloud computing describes applications that are extended to be accessible through the Internet. These cloud applications use large data centers or cloud data storage CDS and powerful servers that host Web applications and Web services. Anyone with a suitable Internet connection and a standard browser can access a cloud application. Cloud computing consists of multiple cloud computing service providers (CSPs). In terms of software and hardware, a cloud system is composed of many types of computers, storage devices, communications equipment, and software systems running on such devices [1] .

Heterogeneity and diversity of cloud services, and the domains' diverse access requirements in cloud computing environments would require fine-grained access control policies. In particular, access control services should be flexible enough to capture dynamic, context or attribute/credential based access requirements, and facilitate enforcement of the principle of least privilege. Such access control services may need to integrate privacy protection requirements derived from complex rules. It is important that the access control system employed in clouds is easily managed and its privilege distribution is administered efficiently. It is also important to ensure that the cloud delivery models provide generic access control interfaces for proper interoperability, which demands for a policy neutral access control specification and enforcement framework that can be used to address cross-domain access control issues [2] . Also, the access control models should be able to capture relevant aspects of service level agreements (SLAs).

Cloud Data Storage (CDS) is composed of thousands of cloud storage devices clustered by network, distributed file systems and other storage middleware to provide cloud storage service for users. The typical structure of CDS includes storage resource pool, distributed file system, service level agreements (SLAs), and service interfaces, etc. Globally, they can be divided by physical and logical functions boundaries and relationships to provide more compatibilities and interactions. CDS is tending to combine with CDS security, which will provide more robust security [1] .

Also, CDS refers to any type of data storage that resides in the cloud, including: services that provide database-like functionality, unstructured data services (file storage of digital media, for example), data synchronization services, or Network Attached Storage (NAS) services. Data services are often consumed in a pay-as-you- go model or, in this case, a pay-per-GB model (including both stored and transferred data). CDS offers a number of benefits, such as the ability to store and retrieve large amounts of data in any location at any time. CDS services are fast, inexpensive, and almost infinitely scalable; however, reliability can be an issue, as even the best services do sometimes fail. Transaction support is also an issue with cloud-based storage systems, a significant problem that needs to be addressed for storage services to be widely used in the enterprise [2] .

Confidentiality defined as ensuring that user data which resides in the cloud cannot be accessed by unauthorized party. This can be achieved through proper encryption techniques taking into consideration the type of encryption: symmetric or asymmetric encryption algorithms, also key length and key management in case of the symmetric cipher. Actually, it is all based on the CSP. For instance in [3] , Mozy Enterprise uses encryption techniques to protect customer data whereas

Citation: Talib, A. (2015) Ensuring Security, Confidentiality and Fine-Grained Data Access Control of Cloud Data Storage Implementation Environment. Journal of Information Security, 6, 118-130. doi: 10.4236/jis.2015.62013.

Amazon S3 does not. It also depends on the customer awareness where they can encrypt their information prior to uploading it. Also, The CSP should ensure proper deployment of encryption standards using NIST standards in [4] .

Access control regulates accesses to resources by principals. It is one of the most important aspects of the security of a system. A protection state or policy contains all information needed by a reference monitor to enforce access control. The syntax used to represent a policy is called an access control model. In FCDAC, principals are called cloud users. Cloud users get permissions to access resources via membership in roles. We present a new way to realize FCDAC in JADE-S. Our approach focuses not only on providing a cloud user by a user name and password but defining and enforcing expressive and flexible access structure for each cloud user as a logic formula over cloud data file attributes. Each data file is stored on the cloud in the format as is shown in Figure 1.

A multi-agent system (MAS) consists of a number of agents interacting with each other, usually through exchanging messages across a network. The agents in such a system must be able to interact in order to achieve their design objectives, through cooperating, negotiating and coordinating with other agents. The agents may exhibit selfish or benevolent behavior. Selfish agents ask for help from other agents if they are overloaded and never offer help. For example, agents serving VIP (Very Important Person) cloud users for CSP service never help other agents for the same service. Benevolent agents always provide help to other agents because they consider system benefit is the priority. For example, agents serving normal cloud users for CSP service are always ready to help other agents to complete their tasks.

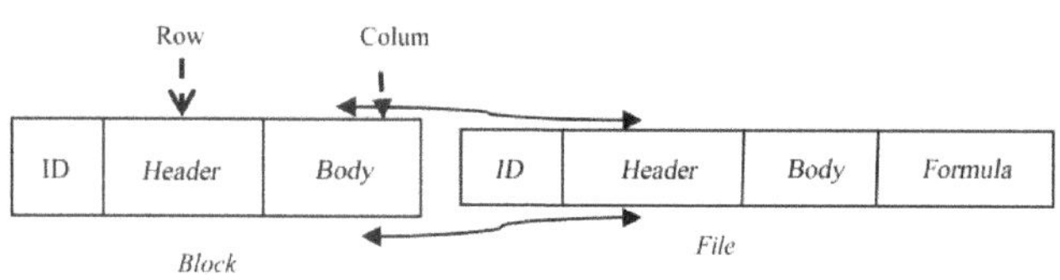

Figure 1: Format of cloud data file stored in the CDS.

Our contributions: Theoretically, this paper contributes the description of the first provably-secure and practical FCDAC which provide access structure of each cloud user by defining it as a logic formula over cloud data file attribute.

In our FCDAC scheme, we assume that the system is composed of the following parties: the CSP, many cloud users and many cloud servers or CDSs. To access cloud data files shared by the CSP or cloud users, download cloud data files of their interest from cloud servers and then decrypt. Neither the CSPs nor cloud users should be always online and they might only get online just on necessity basis. Cloud servers are always online and operated by the CSP. For simplicity, we assume that the only access privilege for cloud users is cloud data file reading. Extending our proposed FCDAC scheme to support cloud data file writing is trivial by asking the cloud user to sign the new cloud data file. Cloud servers will follow our proposed FCDAC scheme in general, but try to find out as much secret information as possible based on their inputs. More specifically, we assume cloud servers are more interested in cloud file contents and cloud user access privilege information than other secret information. Cloud servers might collude with a small number of malicious users for the purpose of harvesting file contents when it is highly beneficial. Communication channel between the CSP/cloud users and cloud servers are assumed to be secured under existing security protocols. Cloud users would try to access files either within or outside the scope of their access privileges. To achieve this goal, unauthorized users may work independently or cooperatively.

The CSP stores a large amount of information on the cloud server. Since the cloud computing environment is untrusted environment, the CSP will encrypt the cloud data before putting them on the cloud server. Here we assume that the smallest information access unit is called a "cloud file" stored in the cloud server. This is an abstract concept and it may have different meanings in different systems. To provide FCDAC, the encryption will be conducted at the file level based on our proposed MAS techniques which provide access structure of each cloud user by defining it as a logic formula over cloud data file attribute. Only the CSP can make updates to the cloud data. We also assume that there exist pre-distributed secrets between CSP and cloud server, and between CSP and cloud users. The illustration of FCDAC application scenario described as: 1) cloud user will send a data access request to the CSP; 2) CSP will provide the MAS architecture by service level agreement (SLA); 3) CSP certified the access control; 4) cloud user insert its encryption key; and 5) then only authorized cloud user can access the cloud data file, as illustrated in Figure 2.

In this paper, in Section 2 we present a discussion of the related work. Section 3 provides a brief introduction of JADE security model (JADE-S) platform. Section 4 describes our proposed FCDAC based MAS architecture. Section 5 highlights the design goals of our proposed FCDAC scheme. The implementation steps have been discussed in Section 6. Results and discussions have been described in detail in Section 7. In, Section 8 presents some concluding remarks and future work.

RELATED WORK

Many existing works close to our work can be found in the areas of "access control of outsourced data" Kallahalla et al. proposed Plutus as a cryptographic file system to secure file storage on untrusted servers [5] , Goh et al. proposed SiRiUS which is layered over existing file systems such as NFS but provides end-to-end security [6] , Ateniese et al. [7] proposed a secure distributed storage scheme based on proxy re-encryption. Specifically, the data owner encrypts blocks of content with symmetric content keys. In [8] , Vimercati et al. proposed a solution for securing data storage on untrusted servers based on key derivation methods [9] . In this proposed scheme, each file is encrypted with a symmetric key and each user is assigned a secret key. KAoS uses DARPA Agent Markup Language (DAML) as the basis for representing and reasoning about policies within Web Services, Grid Computing, and multi-agent system platforms [10] . KAoS also exploits ontology for representing and reasoning about domains describing organizations of human, agent, and other computational actors [11] . Rei is a deontic logic based policy language that is grounded in a semantic representation of policies in RDF-S [12] . However, developers of KAoS augured that the pure Web Ontology Language (OWL) based method has difficulty in definition of some types of policy [11] .

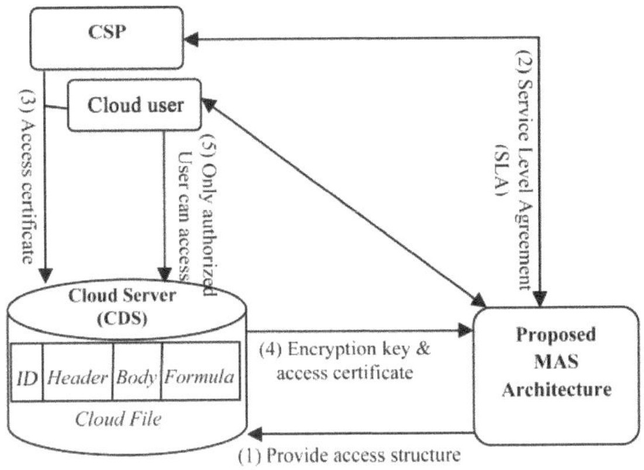

Figure 2: Illustration of the FCDAC application scenario.

An access control system is typically described in three ways: access control policies, access control models and access control mechanisms [13] . Policy defines the high level rules according to which access control must be regulated. Model provides a formal representation of the Algebra of Communicating Processes (ACPs). Mechanism defines the low level functions that implement the controls imposed by the policy and formally stated in the model.

Access Control Policies can be generally divided into three main policy categories: Discretionary Access Control (DAC), Mandatory Access Control (MAC), and Role-Based Access Control (RBAC). Early DAC models, such as the access control matrix model [14] and the HRU (Harrison-Ruzzo-Ullman) model [15] , provide a basic framework for describing DAC policy. In these models, it is the users' discretion to pass their privileges on to other users, leaving DAC policies vulnerable to Trojan Horse attacks [13] . The lattice-based multilevel security policy [16] , policies represented by the Bell-LaPadula model [17] .

JADE SECURITY MODEL (JADE-S) PLATFORM

In order to understand the role of security in the transmission of private and critical information (e.g. cloud data file) through an open environment (e.g. cloud computing and CDS), it is necessary to define the concepts that determine the diverse security levels:

ü Confidentiality: is the property that ensures that only those that are properly authorized (users) may access the information.

In the case of MAS these properties are especially important, due to the autonomy and mobility of agents. MAS without security support could not be used in an open environment such as CDS if it deals with critical cloud data, because communications could be spied or the identities of the agents could be easily faked.

JADE-S [18] is a plug-in of JADE that allows adding some security characteristics in the development of MAS, so that they can start to be used in real environments. It is based on the Java security model [19] and it provides the advantages of the following technologies:

- JAAS (Java Authentication and Authorization Service) [20] : it allows establishing access permissions to perform certain operations on a set of predetermined classes, libraries or objects.
- JCE (Java Cryptography Extension) [19] : it implements a set of cryptographic functions that allow the developer to deal with the creation and management of keys and to use encryption algorithms.
- JSSE (Java Secure Socket Extension) [21] : it allows exchanging critical information through a network using a secure data transmission (SSL).

Basic Concept

JADE platform may be located in different hosts and have different containers. In order to introduce security in cloud computing, JADE-S structures the agent platform as a multi-user environment in which all components (agents, containers, etc.) belong to authenticated (through a login and a password) users, who are authorized by the administrator of the system to perform certain privileged critical actions.

Thus, in each platform there is a permissions file that contains the set of actions that each user is authorized to perform [22] . Internally, an agent proves its identity by showing an Identity Certificate signed by the Certification Authority (provided in a transparent way to the agent when it registers in the system and provides the login and the password of its owner). Using these digitally signed certificates the platform may allow or deny certain actions to each agent.

Secure Communication

In order to provide a secure communication between agents located in different hosts or containers, JADE-S uses the SSL protocol (Secure Socket Layer) [23] that provides privacy and integrity for all the connections established in the platform. This is a way of being protected against network sniffers.

Permissions and Access Restrictions

In JADE-S platform the permissions to access resources are given to the different entities by following the mechanism defined by the new system provided by Java (JAAS [20]) for user-based authentication. Thus, it is possible to assign permissions to parts of the code and to its executers, restricting the access to certain methods, classes or libraries depending on who wants to use them. An entity can only perform an action (send a message, move to another container) if the Java security manager allows it. The set of permissions associated to each identity is stored in the access rights file of the platform (which is also unique and is loaded when the platform is booted).

Java provides a set of permissions (apart from those that may be defined by the user) on the basic elements of the language: AWT Permission, File Permission, Socket Permission, etc. Moreover, JADE-S provides other permissions related to the behavior of the agents: Agent Permission, Container Permission, etc. Any and each permission has a list of related actions that may be allowed or denied.

Authentication

As explained above, each component of the platform belongs to an authenticated user. The user that boots the platform also owns the AMS1 and DF2 agents and the main container. When a user wants to join the platform (through one of his/her agents), it has to provide his/her login and password.

These data are checked with the passwords file contained in the platform, which is stored in a ciphered way, like UNIX passwords. The passwords file is unique and is loaded with the main container. Each agent owned by this user will have an Identity Certificate that contains its name, its owner and the signature of the Certification Authority.

Certification Authority and Certificates

The Certification Authority is the entity that signs the certificates of all the elements of the platform. To do that, it owns a couple of public/private keys so that, for each certificate, it creates an associated signature by ciphering it with its private key (which is secret). Then, when the identity of an entity has to be checked, the signature may be unencrypted with the public key of the Authority (which is publicly known) and we can check that the identity of an entity wanted to prove matches the one provided by the Authority. The secure platform JADE-S provides a Certification Authority within the main container. Each signed certificate is only valid within the platform in which it has been signed.

OUR PROPOSED FCDAC BASED ON MAS ARCHITECTURE

The MAS architecture consists of two agents: Cloud Service Provider Agent (CSPA) and Cloud Data Confidentiality Agent (CDConA). CSPA interact with the cloud users to fulfill their interests. CDConA provides a CSP by definition and enforcement expressive and flexible access structure for each cloud user, in which each agent is autonomous and able to cooperate, coordinate and communicate with other agents intelligently to satisfy the cloud users' needs. CDConA has two types of sub-agents of Cloud Data Flexible Confidentiality Agent (CDFConA) and Cloud Data Expressive Confidentiality Agent (CDEConA).

Our proposed FCDAC based on MAS architecture consists of four layers: interface layer, existing access control layer, proposed FCDAC layer and CDS layer, as shown in Figure 3. At the interface layer, the CSPA receive the security report from CDConA and handle the interaction with the cloud users in terms of graphical user interface. Existing access control layer is to differentiate between our proposed FCDAC access control and other existing access control lists of identification, authorization and authentication (Access Control Polices (ACPs), Role-Based Access Control (RBAC), Access Control List (ACL), Discretionary Access Control (DAC), Mandatory Access Control (MAC)… etc.), details of these existing access control techniques highlighted in Section 2 (Related Work). At the proposed FCDAC layer, the agents are responsible for giving permissions to both VIP and NOT-VIP cloud users' requests. CDS layer is considered as the environment layer in which our proposed FCDAC scheme provided an access control.

Also, there are four types of entities: CSPs, cloud user, knowledge base and confidentiality policy rules in which our proposed FCDAC scheme obtained and utilized the information from these entities.

Description of a single agent as follow:

Cloud Service Provider Agent (CSPA)

Is the users' intelligent interface to the system and allow the cloud users to interact with the security service environment. The CSPA provides graphical interfaces to the cloud user for interactions between the system and the cloud user. CSPA act in the system under the behaviour of CSP. It is the only agent that can execute outside the main container of the platform and make remote requests through cloud server. CSPA has the following responsibilities as stated in Table 1.

Cloud Data Confidentiality Agent (CDConA)

This agent facilitates the security policy of confidentiality for CDS. Main responsibility of this agent is to provide a CDS by new access control rather than the existing access control lists of identification, authorization and authentication. This agent provides a CSP to define and enforce expressive and flexible access structure for each cloud user. Specifically, the access structure of each cloud user is defined as a logic formula over cloud data file attributes, and is able to represent any desired cloud data file set. This agent is also notifies CSPA in case of any fail caused of the techniques above by sending security reports and/or alarms.

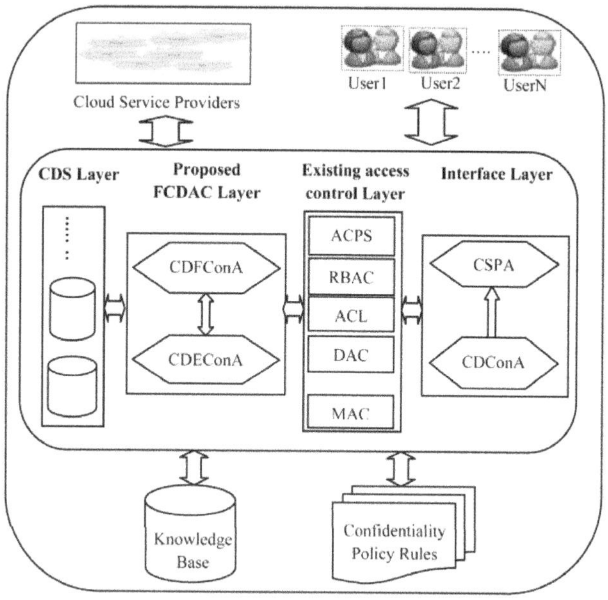

Figure 3: Proposed FCDAC based on MAS architecture.

Expressive Confidentiality Agent (CDEConA). CDFConA acts as a dispatching center, with the following advantages. Firstly, the CDFConA is the unique access point where authorization agents can contact the CDConA. Secondly, CDFConA acts as the exclusive resource access entry. This makes the cloud users are only able to access the cloud data file via CDFConA.

CDFConA is divided into two types of agent based on the exhibited behavior. The first is CDFConA-VIP, which has selfish behavior and only serves for VIP (Very Important Person) cloud users. The second is NOT- VIP CDFConA, which has cooperative behavior and serves for both VIP cloud users and NOT-VIP (normal cloud users). For example, if CDFConA-VIP is overloaded, it sends help request to the first available NOT-VIP CDFConA. If this NOT-VIP CDFConA is unable to provide the help to CDFConA-VIP, the CDFConA-

VIP sends the same help request to the next available NOT-VIP CDFConA. CDFConA-VIP keep sending the same request for help until one of the NOT-VIP CDFConA accepts or it is not overloaded. NOT-VIP CDFConA also takes the same action as CDFConA-VIP when they are overloaded. However, NOT-VIP CDFConA only has knowledge about other NOT-VIP CDFConA, but not CDFConA-VIP.

Table 1: Responsibilities of CSPA

Agent Name	Responsibilities
Cloud Service Provider Agent (CSPA)	Provide the security service task according to the authorized service level agreements (SLAs) and the original message content sent by the CDConA. Display the security policies specified by the CSP and the rest of the agents. Designing user interfaces that prevent the input of invalid cloud data. Receive the security reports and/or alarms from the rest of other agents to respect. Translate the attack in terms of goals. Monitor specific activities concerning a part of the CDS or a particular cloud user. Creating security reports/alarm systems.

There are two different types of CDConA, namely: Cloud Data Flexible Confidentiality Agent (CDFConA) and Cloud Data

Cloud Data Flexible Confidentiality Agent (CDFConA)

The architecture of CDFConA consists of five modules, as shown in Figure 4. Cloud Communication Module provides the agent with the capability to exchange information with other agents, including the CDEConA and CSPA. Cloud Register Module facilitates the registration function for CDConA. Cloud Request Management Module allows the agent to act as the request-dispatching center. Cloud Resource Management Module manages the usage of the cloud resources. Cloud Reasoning Module is the brain of the CDConA. When the request management module and resource management module receive requests, they pass those requests to reasoning module by utilizing the information obtained from the knowledge base and the confidentiality policy rule.

Cloud Data Expressive Confidentiality Agent (CDEConA)

The architecture of the CDEConA consists of two modules, as shown in Figure 5. Cloud Communication Module provides the agent with the capability to exchange information with CSPA and CDFConA. Cloud Cooperation Module provides the agent with the following mechanisms. If the CDEConA is registered as CDFConA- VIP it asks for help when it is overloaded. If the CDEConA is registered as NOT-VIP CDFConA, it always offers help to other CDEConAs when it is not overloaded.

DESIGN GOALS

To ensure the security for CDS under the aforementioned secure MAS architecture, we aim to design efficient mechanisms for confidentiality of cloud user's data and achieve the following goal: to define and enforce expressive and flexible access structure for each cloud user by defines a logic formula over cloud data file attributes, this logic formula named as FCDAC.

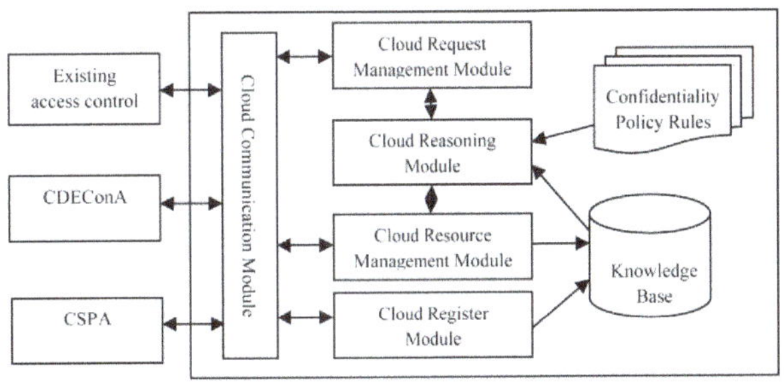

Figure 4: CDFConA architecture.

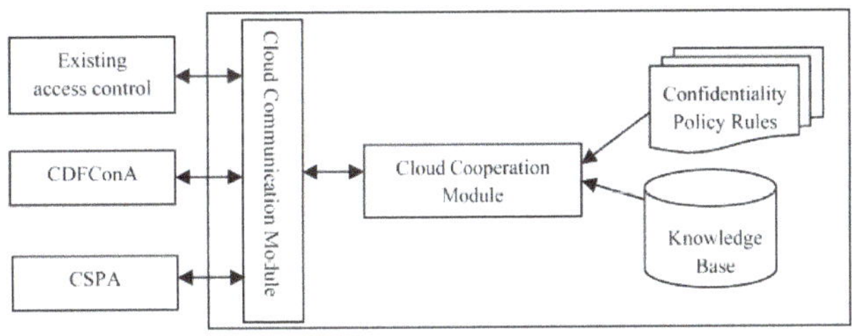

Figure 5: CDEConA architecture.

IMPLEMENTATION

Before using any security mechanism provided by JADE-S on an agent platform, first it is necessary to define a set of default Java permissions that allow executing the basic code of JADE (including network access, graphical interface, etc.). Recall that the only allowed actions are those explicitly included in the permissions file. These permissions have to appear in the "basic.policy" file, which is read by default when the platform is booted.

Formula-Based Cloud Data Access Control (FCDAC) it's an access policy determined by our MAS architecture, not by the CSPs. It's also define as access is granted not based on the rights of the subject associated with a cloud user after authentication, but based on attributes of the cloud user. In our system, CDConA provide access structure of each cloud user by defining it as a logic formula over cloud data file attribute.

Having done that, we have built, on top of the security services provided by JADE-S and data access control that is based on two levels of permissions:

- Root: the cloud user has access to all the cloud data files that may be performed on the CDS (indicated explicitly one by one in the permissions cloud data file).
- Guest: the permissions of this cloud user are quite limited. CDConA can only perform the basic actions to request services from the system (send and receive messages).

The content of the passwords cloud data file containing these two users has the same format that the UNIX passwords cloud data file. This file can be created directly with the UNIX cloud user management capabilities or through the options provided by JADE. The set of permissions of each cloud user is stored in the access policy cloud data file associated to the platform. Thus, we associate one of these cloud users to each of the types of agents:

ü Internal agents: the CDConA agent that executed within the main container of the platform (cloud servers, cloud data files and cloud users and Broker). They belong to the root cloud user; thus, they do not have any constraint on the actions they can perform. We have taken this decision to facilitate the interaction among them (they can send and receive messages from any agent, or register in the DF or the AMS. As they are internal to the platform (they execute in the main container) and they have been programmed by us, they will not perform any malicious action (kill other agents, deregister other agents, fake the identity of another agent, etc.).

ü External agents: the Personal agents that execute in an external container in another host belong to this category. They have been associated to the guest cloud user, so that they can neither access the main container (to join the other agents) nor access the DF (to modify the information of other agents). They can only communicate with the internal agents CDConA through the Broker; therefore, they cannot pretend to have the identity of other agents or kill other agents. All these constraints are necessary because we do not have any control over these agents, and they may have been programmed to perform dangerous actions.

Figure 6 and Figure 7 illustrated and show diverse windows of the interface, used to insert the parameter and start execution of our agents.

Determining Enforcement Expressive and Flexible Keys for Cloud Data File Encryption

To provide fine-grained access control, we propose to encrypt every data file with a different secret. Here we do not assume the adoption of any specific symmetric encryption algorithm and leave the choice to our proposed MAS architecture when it is deployed. However, an efficient mechanism must be designed to allow MAS, CSPs and cloud users to manage the encryption keys. In the worst case, if the CDS contain n files f1, f2,…,fn and each file is encrypted with a randomly generated secret key, the CDS overhead on the cloud user will be linear to n. At the same time, when a cloud user needs to access its data files, the communication overhead between the agents and the cloud user for key distribution will also be linear. This overhead can be overwhelming for many cloud users when we consider that the CDS can easily contain millions of files. Therefore, a more encryption key scheme must be designed.

To solve this problem, we propose the basic idea of FCDAC scheme to generate the data file encryption keys through the two types of cloud users (VIP and NOT-VIP). Every key can be derived by combining its parent key that provided by CDConA agent and some public information from confidentiality policy roles and knowledge base entities. Since the derivation procedure uses a two-way function, we can calculate the secret keys of the parent key. In this way, the CSP will need to maintain only the root keys (full information described in the first four paragraphs in the implementation section). During the key distribution procedure, the CSP receive the secret key from CSPA and send the secret key to cloud users based on their access rights. The cloud user will derive the secret key to decrypt the data files.

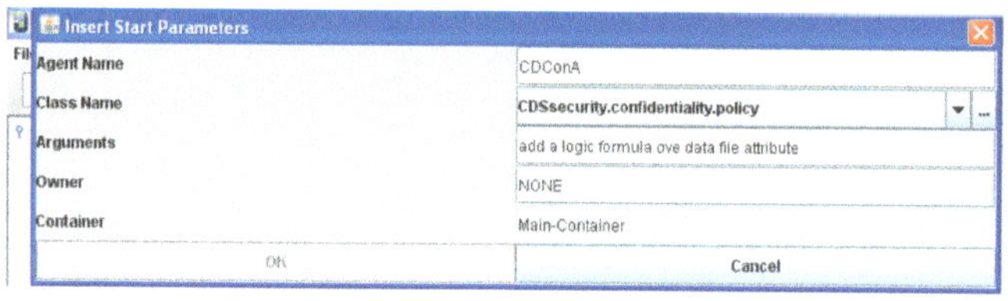

Figure 6: Define the arguments of our CDConA.

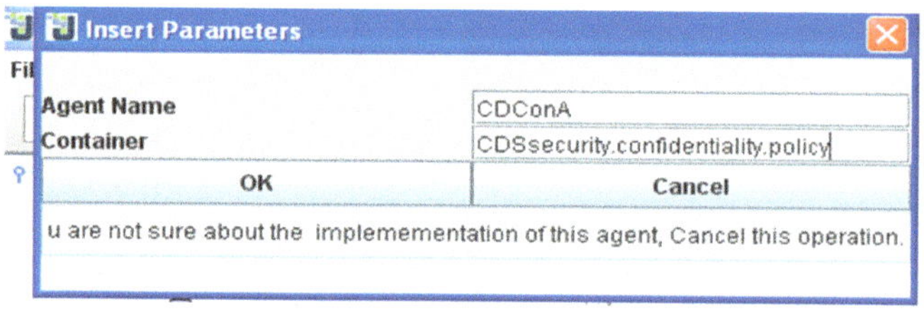

Figure 7: Insert the parameter and press ok to start execution.

The communication workflow between agents as shown in Figure 8 decreases the level of complexity in agents' platform communication. Classically, MAS architecture needs to deal with middle server such as a message brokers. By decreasing such complexity of workflow, it will increase the autonomous level that doesn't need any responds from cloud user. In agent-based communication workflow, all components will be two ways interaction and the massaging platform will use the standard messaging proposed by FIPA which is ACL (Agent Communication Language), each agent will analyze each message priorities and in which action should be taken. For example, CDConA need to receive some service from CDFConA where the receiver agent will analyze the message that received by agent-receiver. Then, it will translate it to ACL. The sender agent also will identify which platform offer, which type of service and which message type they are using. The output of these messages will be registered in cloud register module and will be stored in cloud communication module.

VIP cloud user scenario:

- 1A. VIP cloud user will request the allowance from CSP for access the cloud application.
- 2A. CSP will ask CDEConA to provide the VIP cloud user by new access control.
- 3A. CDEConA will inform CDFConA to register the

VIP cloud user request as communication ACL in cloud register module.

- 4A. CDFConA will response to CDConA that the request have been registered. Then CDConA will provide VIP cloud user by the encryption key.
- 5A. CDConA will inform CSP that the request of VIP cloud user has been provided.

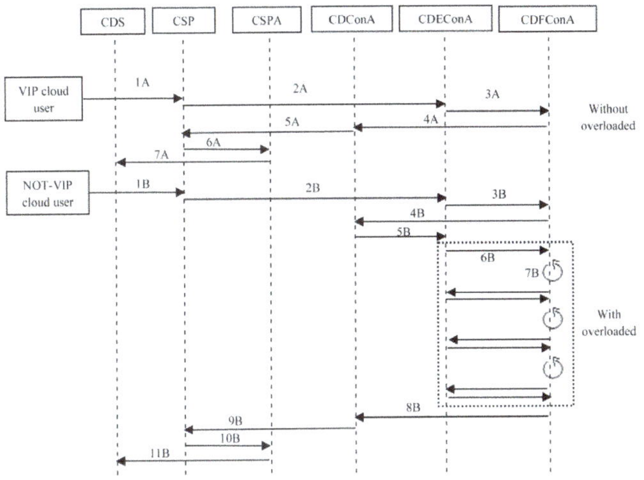

Figure 8: Agent-based communication workflow.

- 6A. CSP will provide CSPA by the SLA.
- 7A. VIP cloud user will be able to login in the CDS and access the cloud application.
- NOT-VIP cloud user scenario:
- 1A. NOT-VIP cloud user will request the allowance from CSP for access the cloud application.
- 2A. CSP will ask CDEConA to provide NOT-VIP cloud user by new access control.
- 3A. CDEConA will inform CDFConA to register NOT-VIP cloud user request as communication ACL in cloud register module.
- 4A. CDFConA will response to CDConA that the request have been registered. Then CDConA will provide the NOT-VIP cloud user by the encryption key.
- 5B CDConA will ask CDEConA to register the ACL message of NOT-VIP cloud user in cloud cooperation module.
- 6B Due to, CDFConA has a selfish behavior with a NOT-VIP cloud user then, there is no message will be registered by CDEConA. So CDEConA will send the request back to CDFConA.
- 7B CDFConA will keep sending the same request for help until one of the CDFConA accepts. This step will repeat many times unless one of CDFConA accept and serve NOT-VIP cloud user.
- 8B CDFConA will response to CDConA that the request have been registered. Then CDConA will provide NOT-VIP cloud user by the encryption key.
- 9B. CDConA will inform CSP that the request of NOT-VIP cloud user has been provided.
- 10B. CSP will provide CSPA by the SLA.
- 11B. NOT-VIP cloud user will be able to login in the CDS and access the cloud application.

EVALUATION OF RESULT ANALYSIS

To evaluate the performance of our system against the scale of the system, we measure the times required for an agent to travel around different number of cloud users before and after implementing FCDAC. The results are presented in Table 2 and are plotted Figure 9. The data show that the Round Trip Time (RTT) for an agent to travel in our system changes more or less linearly over the number of cloud users in the system, both the cases. This is due to the additional time to travel an additional cloud user. The overhead for each additional cloud user is more or less the same. The overhead introduced is due to the extensive use of the MAS architecture to encrypt and decrypt each file attribute of cloud user, which is time consuming especially when the FCDAC's key is long. But a longer FCDAC's key gives a stronger protection to the system. Hence, a trade-off between performance and security for our MAS architecture is identified.

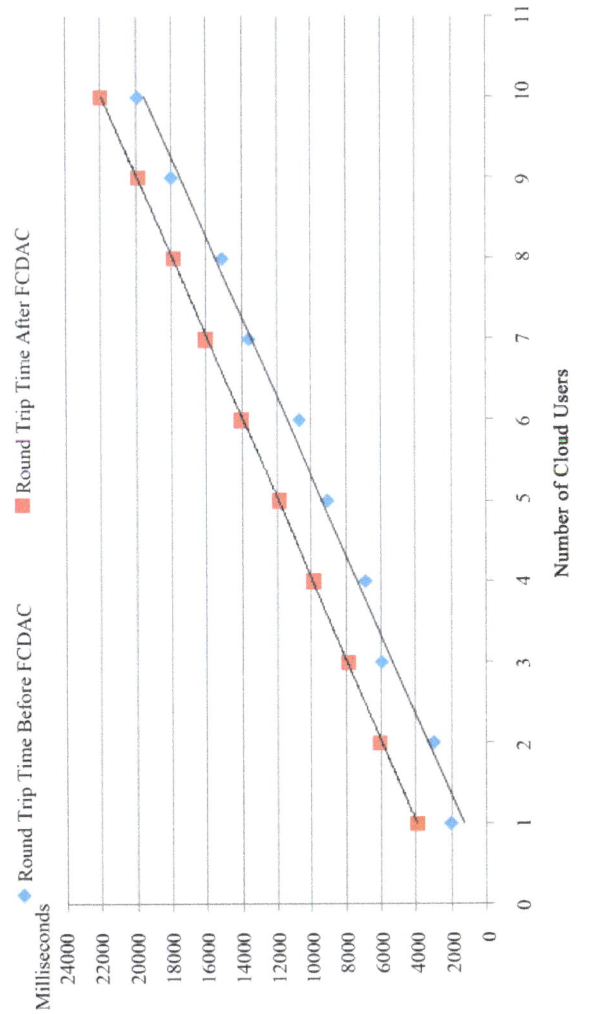

Figure 9: Average of round trip time before and after FCDAC.

Table 2: Average of RTT of our MAS in CDS

Number of Cloud Users	RTT Before FCDAC	RTT After FCDAC
1	2043.7	3988.74
2	3013.46	6098.19
3	5945.7	7908.77
4	6880.197	9921.02
5	9040.71	11900.18
6	10713.9	14066.79
7	13605.4	16080.5
8	15076.7	17913.16
9	18002.43	19893.63
10	19901.623	22000

CONCLUSIONS AND FUTURE WORK

This paper aims at formula-based cloud data access control (FCDAC) in cloud computing. One challenge in this context is to achieve fine-grained and data confidentiality, which is not provided by current work. FCDAC, it's an access policy determined by our MAS architecture, not by the CSPs. It's also defined as access is granted not based on the rights of the subject associated with a cloud user after authentication, but based on attributes of the cloud user. In this paper we propose secure MAS architecture to achieve this goal. We want to argue in this paper that secure MAS architecture is good alternative to fully implement complex programs in distributed environments such as cloud computing. Our proposed FCDAC based on MAS architecture consists of four layers: interface layer, existing access control layer, proposed FCDAC layer and CDS layer as well as four types of entities of Cloud Service Provider (CSP), cloud users, knowledge base and confidentiality policy roles. In fact, a complete prototype of the application is permanently running on a server provided by AgentCities in a worldwide agent-based network of services. Even though there is still a lot of work to be done in the security field in MAS, this paper tries to show that it is feasible to apply concepts of information security in these systems. Our results in the practical scenario defined formally in this paper, show the Round Trip Time (RTT) for an agent to travel in our system changes more or less linearly over the number of cloud users in the system measured by the times required for an agent to travel around different number of cloud users before and after implementing FCDAC.

In future work, we would focus on how we can utilize our agents system to encrypt the CDS and deploy it to real use, and we will compare the algorithm with some existing algorithms related to our work.

ACKNOWLEDGEMENTS

Amir Mohamed Talib The author would like to thank the anonymous reviewers for their valuable comments and suggestions to improve the quality of the paper.

REFERENCES

1. Talib, A.M., Atan, R., Abdullah, R. and Murad, M.A.A. (2010) Security Framework of Cloud Data Storage Based on Multi Agent System Architecture: Semantic Literature Review. Computer and Information Science, 3, 175. http://dx.doi.org/10.5539/cis.v3n4p175
2. Talib, A.M., Atan, R., Abdullah, R. and Murad, M.A.A. (2012) Towards a Comprehensive Security Framework of Cloud Data Storage Based on Multi Agent System Architecture. Journal of Information Security, 3, 295-306. http://dx.doi.org/10.4236/jis.2012.34036
3. Joshi, J.B.D. (2004) Access-Control Language for Multi-Domain Environments. IEEE Internet Computing, 8, 40-50. http://dx.doi.org/10.1109/MIC.2004.53
4. Mather, T., Kumaraswamy, S. and Latif, S. (2009) Cloud Security and Privacy: An Enterprise Perspective on Risks and Compliance. O'Reilly Media, Inc.
5. Lori, M. (2009) Data Security in the World of Cloud Computing. Co-Published by the IEEE Computer and Reliability Societies, 61-64.
6. Kallahalla, M., Riedel, E., Swaminathan, R., Wang, Q. and Fu, K. (2003) Plutus: Scalable Secure File Sharing on Untrusted Storage. in Fast, 29-42.
7. Goh, E.-J., Shacham, H., Modadugu, N. and Boneh, D. (2003) SiRiUS: Securing Remote Untrusted Storage. in NDSS, 131-145.
8. Ateniese, G., Fu, K., Green, M. and Hohenberger, S. (2006) Improved Proxy Re-Encryption Schemes with Applications to Secure Distributed Storage. ACM Transactions on Information and System Security (TISSEC), 9, 1-30.http://dx.doi.org/10.1145/1127345.1127346
9. Di Vimercati, S.D.C., Foresti, S., Jajodia, S., Paraboschi, S. and Samarati, P. (2007) Over-Encryption: Management of Access Control Evolution on Outsourced Data. Proceedings of the 33rd International Conference on Very Large Data Bases, 123-134.
10. Atallah, M.J., Blanton, M., Fazio, N. and Frikken, K.B. (2009) Dynamic and Efficient Key Management for Access Hierarchies. ACM Transactions on Information and System Security (TISSEC), 12, 18. http://dx.doi.org/10.1145/1455526.1455531
11. Johnson, M., Chang, P., Jeffers, R., Bradshaw, J.M., Soo, V.W., Breedy, M.R., Bunch, L., Kulkarni, S., Lott, J. and Suri, N. (2003) KAoS Semantic Policy and Domain Services: An Application of DAML to Web Services-Based Grid Architectures. Proceedings of the AAMAS, Melbourne, 14-18 July 2003.
12. Tonti, G., Bradshaw, J.M., Jeffers, R., Montanari, R., Suri, N. and Uszok, A. (2003) Semantic Web Languages for Policy Representation and Reasoning: A Comparison of KAoS, Rei, and Ponder. In: Fensel, D., Sycara, K. and Mylopoulos, J., Eds., The Semantic Web-

ISWC 2003, Springer, Berlin, 419-437. http://dx.doi.org/10.1007/978-3-540-39718-2_27

13. Kagal, L. (2002) Rei: A Policy Language for the Me-Centric Project.

14. Samarati, P. and de Vimercati, S.C. (2001) Access Control: Policies, Models, and Mechanisms. In: Focardi, R. and Gorrieri, R., Eds., Foundations of Security Analysis and Design, Springer, Berlin, 137-196. http://dx.doi.org/10.1007/3-540-45608-2_3

15. Lampson, B.W. (1974) Protection. ACM SIGOPS Operating Systems Review, 8, 18-24.http://dx.doi.org/10.1145/775265.775268

16. Harrison, M.A., Ruzzo, W.L. and Ullman, J.D. (1976) Protection in Operating Systems. Communications of the ACM, 19, 461-471. http://dx.doi.org/10.1145/360303.360333

17. Denning, D.E. (1976) A Lattice Model of Secure Information Flow. Communications of the ACM, 19, 236-243. http://dx.doi.org/10.1145/360051.360056

18. Bell, D.E. and LaPadula, L.J. (1973) Secure Computer Systems: Mathematical Foundations. DTIC Document.

19. Fabio, B., Giovanni, C., Tiziana, T., Giovanni, R. and Roland, M. (2007) JADE Administrator's Guide. Last Update, 2007.

20. Sun Microsystems (2010) Java Security. http://java.sun.com/security

21. Sun Microsystems (2014) Authentication and Authorization Service (JAAS).http://java.sun.com/products/archive/jaas/

22. Sun Microsystems (2014) Java Secure Socket Extension (JSSE) Reference Guide.http://download.oracle.com/javase/6/d ocs/technot es/gui-des/security/jsse/JSSERefGuide.html

23. Sun Microsystems (2014) Java Default Policy Implementation and Policy File Syntax.http://java.sun.com/j2se/1.4/docs/gui de/security/Poli cyFile s.html

24. Netscape Communication Corporation (2014) Introduction to SSL.http://developer.netscape.com/docs/manuals/security/ss-lin/contents.htm

SECTION IV:
CRYPTOGRAPHIC METHODS

CHAPTER 14 SECURING A TELECOM SERVICES USING QUANTUM CRYPTOGRAPHIC MECHANISMS

Abdallah Handoura

INTRODUCTION

The architectural model of Internet telephony is rather different than that of the traditional telephone network. The base assumption is that all signaling and media flow over an IP-based network, either the public Internet or various intranets. IP-based networks, present the appearance at the network level that any machine can communicate directly with any other, unless the network specifically restricts them from doing so, through such means as firewalls. This architectural change necessitates a dramatic transformation in the architectural assumptions of traditional telephone networks. In particular, whereas in a traditional network a large amount of administrative control, such as call-volume limitation, implicitly resides at every switch, and thus additional controls can easily be added there without much architectural change, in an Internet environment an administrative point of control must be explicitly engineered into a network, as in a firewall; otherwise end systems can simply bypass any device which attempts to restrict their behavior. In addition, the Internet model transforms the locations at which many services are performed. In general, end systems are assumed to be much more intelligent than in the traditional telephone model; thus, many services which traditionally had to reside within the network can be moved out to the edges, without requiring any explicit support for them within the networks. Other services can be performed by widely separated specialized servers which result in call setup information traversing paths which might be extremely indirect when compared with the physical network's actual topology. Most of the services and service features of ITU-T Q.1211 can be provided by the IETF's draft signaling standards for Internet Telephony, SIP (the Session Initiation Protocol) (Schulzrinne, 2001) and, for some more specialized features, its Call Control extensions (Johnston, 2002). However, The growing globalization and the liberalization of the market telecommunications, necessitates a more global infrastructure of IN that satisfies the needs of different subscribed legal implied, especially for multinational services subscribed. A lot of these services are offered on a current system, but are often realized with specialists of the system. The concepts of IN for giving such service is a coherent and stable basis (Schulzrinne, 2001). Some security functions have been introduced already in current systems, but they define constraints to user groups with the private line means, the proprietor equipment and proprietor algorithms or secrets.

There is a major difference between the realization of today service (limited) and the goals of the introduction of IN, however, the IN offer its services to a public world, open, and especially to offer the services that allow user groups to communicate by the public transmission and to change the equipment without unloading their intimacy and affluence of employment. Therefore, the services of security provides for the current network will not be sufficient for IN, the goal is more long. The defying of the aspect of the new security functions has to make then be publicly usable, economically feasible and insured all its at the same time.

INTERCONNECTING SIP AND TELECOM SERVICE APPLICATION

The IN (Intelligent Network) functional architecture identifies several entities such as the service switching function (SSF), the service control functions (SCF), and the call control function (CCF) that model the behavior of the IN network. The CCF represents the normal activities of call and the connection

Citation: Abdallah Handoura (2012). Securing a Telecom Services Using Quantum Cryptographic Mechanisms, Applied Cryptography and Network Security, Dr. Jaydip Sen (Ed.), InTech, DOI: 10.5772/33977.

processing in traditional switch, for two clients. The SSF model's additional functionality required for interacting with a service logic program executed by the SCF. The CCF and the SSF are generally co-located in specific switching centers, known as SSP, while the SCFs are hosted on dedicated computers known as SCP. The communication between the different nodes uses the INAP protocol.

Accessing IN services from the IMS network requires that one or more entities in these networks can play the role of an SSP and communicate with existing SCPs via the INAP protocol. To realize services with SIP it is important that the SIP entity be able to provide features normally provided by the traditional switch, including operating as a SSP for IN features.

The SIP entity should also maintain call state and trigger queries to IN-based services, just as traditional switches do. The most expeditious manner for providing existing IN services in the IP domain is to use the deployed IN infrastructure as much as possible. The creation of a service by SIP is possible by the three methods INVITE, Bye and options and fields of header SIP Contact, Also, Call-Disposition Replace and Requested-by that are extensions of SIP specified by IETF (Fing, 2001).

Some services are already specified by IETF (Gisin, Ribordy, 2001) by using methods and fields of already quoted header: Call, Hold, Transfer of call, Return of call, Third party control. The key to programming telecom services with SIP is to add logic that guides behavior at each of the elements in the system (Johnston, 2002). In a SIP proxy server, this logic would dictate where the requests are proxies to, how the results are processed, and how the packet should be formatted.

The basic model for providing logic for SIP services is shown in Figure 1. The figure shows a SIP server that has been augmented with service logic, which is a program that is responsible for creating the services. When requests and responses arrive, the server passes information up to the service logic. The service logic makes some decisions based on this information, and other information it gathers from different resources, and passes instructions back to the server. The server then executes these instructions (Johnston, 2002).

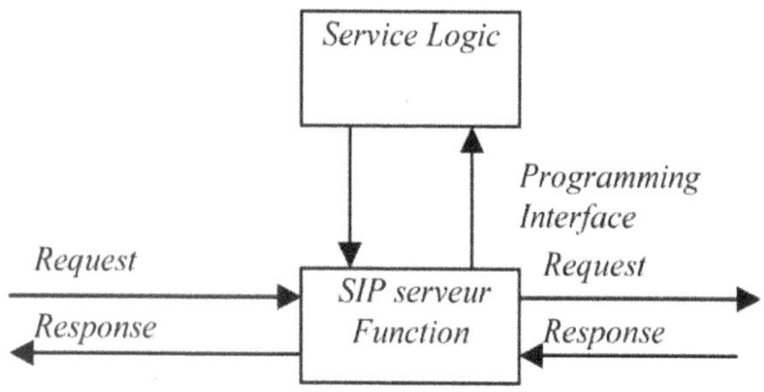

Figure 1: Model for Programming SIP Services.

The separation of the service logic from the server is certainly not new. This idea is inspired by the Intelligent Network (IN) concept (Chapron, 2001). This separation enables rapid development of new services; the idea also exists on the web.

The mechanisms used in these environments can provide valuable insight on how a solution for SIP, IN integration. SIP does not operate the model of call IN directly to access to services IN, the trick is then to bypass the machine of states of the entity SIP with the layer IN such that the acceptance of the call and the routing is executed by the native states and service machine are accessed to layers IN with the model of call IN (El Ouahidi, 2000). The model of service programming with SIP consists therefore in add on SIP server an IN layer, that manages the interconnection with the IN called SIN (SIP Intelligent Network) (Gurbani, 2002). This operation necessitates the definition of a correspondence between the model of call IN and the model of call SIP, it is to tell a correspondence between the state machine of the SIP protocol (SIP defines the header Record_Route that allows to order SIP server to function in mode with the states until the liberation of the call) and the state machine of IN. A call will be processed by the two machines, the state machine SIP processes the initiation of a call and the final reply deliverance, and the IN layer communicate with the intelligent point SCP to provide services during processing of the call (Gurbani, 2002). The figure 2 illustrates the integration SIP-IN.

Similarly to the machine of states IN, one defines the quoted calling and called the entity (OSIP) and (T-SIP) which are entities corresponding, respectively, to the O-BCSM and T-BCSM of the model IN. In the basic system of SIP, the SIP proxy with this control of call " intelligent " is defined to interconnect with intelligent network, this intelligence is realized by the use of control calls, that can synchronize with the model of call IN (BCSM). According to RFC 2543 (SIP) one can define calls of the state machine of the SIP client and SIP server [7,8]. The 11 PICs of O_BCSM come into play when a call request (SIP INVITE message) arrives from an upstream SIP client to an originating SIN-enabled SIP entity running the IN call model. This entity will create an O_BCSM object and initialize it in the O_NULL PIC. The next seven IN PICs -- O_NULL, AUTH_ORIG_ATT, COLLECT_INFO, ANALYZE_INFO, SELECT_ROUTE, AUTH_ CALL_ SETUP, CALL_SENT, O_Alerting and O_Active, can all be mapped to the SIP "Calling" state. Figure 3 below provides a visual mapping from the SIP protocol state machine to the originating half of the IN call model. Note that control of the call shuttles between the SIP protocol machine and the IN O_ BCSM call model while it is being serviced.

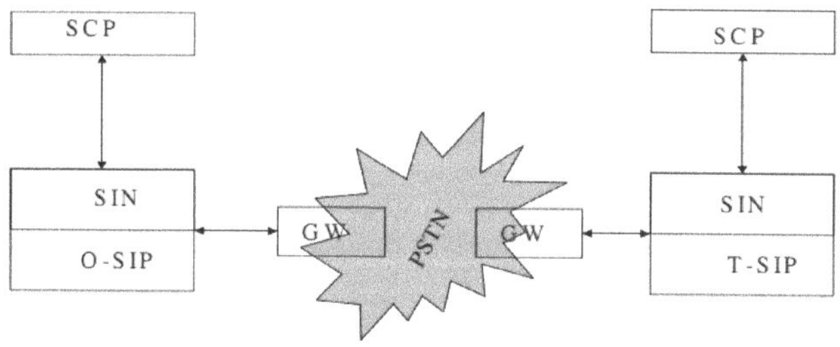

Figure 2: Interconnection SIP-IN.

The SIP "Calling" protocol state has enough functionality to absorb the seven PICs. From server of SIP proxy point of view, its initial state could be corresponded to the O_NULL PIC of the O_BCSM. Its processing state could be corresponded to the Auth_Ori_att, Collect_Info, Analyse_info, Select_ Route, Auth_Call_Setup, Senf_Call and O_Alerting PICs. Its success, confirmed and complete states could be corresponded to the O_Active PIC. Figure 4 below provides a visual mapping from the SIP protocol state machine to the terminating half of the IN Call model.

When the SIP server of termination receives the message INVITE, it creates the T_ BCSM object and initials it to the PIC T_Null, this operation is realized by the state " Proceeding " that orders the five PICs : T_Null, Auth_Ter_Att, Select_Facility, PICs of the T_BCSM. Its calling state could be corresponded to the prrsent_Call PIC. Its call processing state could be corresponded to the T_Alerting. Its complete state could be corresponded to the T_Active PIC.

The service-level call flows for Voice over IP communication where interconnecting between the PSTN and IP-based networks are necessary to complete a call.

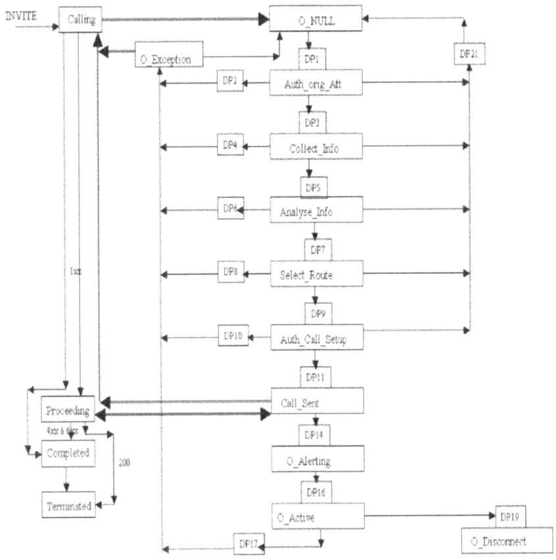

Figure 3: Mapping from SIP to O_BCSM.

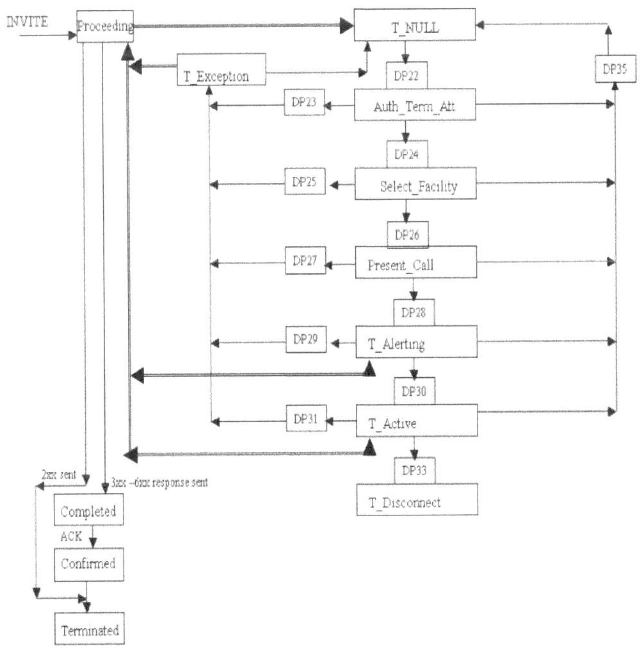

Figure 4: Mapping from SIP to T_BCSM.

THREATS IN THE INTELLIGENT NETWORK (TELECOM SERVICE)

As all elements of a network can be distributed geographically and that element of system IP is totally opened, several threats of security can rise and attack these different elements. The interconnection IN, is the process to execute a demand of service IN on the part of the user of service through at least two different autonomous areas. Typically, each area represents a system IN separated with different legal entities and entities of resource IN. The limp of the IN service is only to be executed, if the two different areas cooperates by exchanging management, control, and services of data on the basis of a legal contract (cocontract of operation). In this competition, each area applies these clean mechanisms to provide the integrity, the availability, and the intimacy of service users. If the two operators that distribute cooperate, they have to apply the same totality of mechanisms to exchange data between their SCPs and SDPs.

The main problems of security that pose in the multimedia communication area and the telephony over IP as well in a system IN under IP are following:

- Imitation of attack: users not authorized can try to access to services of IN. For example, in the case of service IMR a user not recorded can try to see video services.
- Simulating attack: A recorded user can try to avoid the policy of security and obtains illegitimately access to sensitive services. For example, a user with common access privileges can try to act as an administrator of service IN.
- Denial of Service attack: an adversary can try to block users to access to the services of IN. For example to send a great number of requests to the system simultaneously
- Communication to spy and alter: an adversary can try to spy and/or to modify the communication between a legitimate user and elements of service IN.
- Lack of responsibility: if IN is not capable to verify the communication between users and its elements of service, then it will not be possible to make these users responsible for their actions.

The list is not complete. In practice, nevertheless, one can be found confronted with others problems of security, considered as not belonging of the area of application (for example, problems linked, the policy of security, the security of the management system, to security of the implementation, the operational security or to the processing of security incidents). As well as the technological evolution on the soft, does not cease to increase in a manner not estimable, similarly, the technological connection tools to the system and the attack passive and active become impressive things?

If the system and its components are not sufficiently secured, a lot threats can occur. However, it is necessary always to consider:

- What is the probability of a threat (occurrence; likelihood)?
- What are the potential damages (impact)?
- What are the costs to prevent a threat?

Depending on these suppositions, the cost and the efficiency of security mechanisms has to be implemented. The potential of the threat depends on the implementation of IN, the specific service IN. They depend also on the implementation of security mechanisms (ex. PIN, strong authentication, placement of authentication, management of key, etc.).

Manufacturers as well as the groups of standardization make the work of the analysis of risks in the order to improve the security of systems IN. Although a many improvements have already been realized, concerning the security of access to SCP and SMP. New services and new architectural concepts necessitate supplementary improvements.

The next figure, figure 5, presents places of the different threats. Intelligent networks are distributed by nature. This distribution is realized not only to the superior level where the services are described as a collection of service feature (SF), but to too low levels, where the functional entities (FE) can be propagated on different physical entities (PE). Like the communications of various elements of the network are realized on the open and uncertain environment, the security mechanisms have to be applied.

A responsible of the system can prevent these threats of security by using the various mechanisms. The authentication has to be applied in the order to prevent users not authorized to earn the access to the distribution of services.

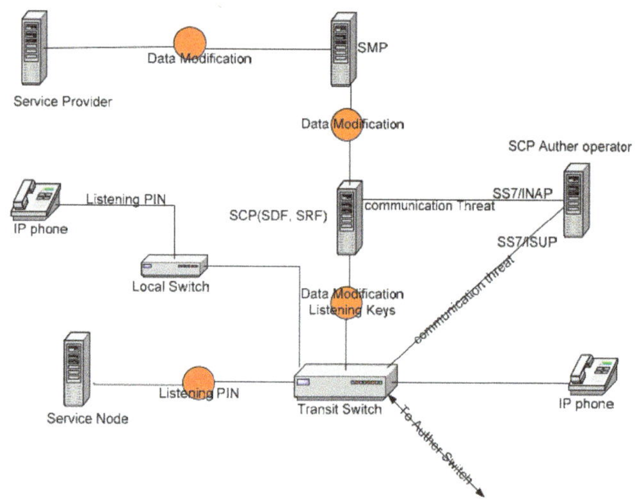

Figure 5: Places of the different threats.

SECURE THE TELECOM SERVICE WITH SIP

SIP Communication is susceptible to confront several types of attack. The simplest attacks in the SIP permit to a hacker of earning the information on users' identities, services, media and topology of the distribution. This information can be employed to excute others types of attacks. The modification of attack occurs when an assailant intercept the effort and covers the signal and modify the SIP message in the order to change a certain characteristic of a service. For example, this sort of attack can be employed for diverting the flow of signaling by forcing a particular itinerary or for changing a recording of the user or modifying a profile of service (Profos, 2002). The sort of attack depends on the type of security (or insecurity) employed (the type of authentication, etc.). These attacks can also be employed for the denial of service.

The main two mechanisms of security employed with SIP: authentication and the encryption data. The authentication of data is employed to authenticate the sender message and insure that certain sensitive information of the message was not modified in the transit. It has to prevent an assailant to modify and/or listen in SIP requests and reply. SIP employs Proxy -Authentication, Proxy -Authorization, authorization, and WWW - Authentication of areas of the letterhead, similar to these of HTTP, for the authentication of the terminal system by the means of a numerical signature. Rather, proxy-by-proxy authentication can be executed by using the authentication protocols over Internet such that, the transport layer TLS or SSL and the network layer IPSEC.

The cryptography of data is employed to, ensure the confidentiality in SIP communication, allowing only the legal receiver client to decrypt and read data. It is usual of using algorithms of cryptography such that the DES (DES: Data Encryption Standard) and Advanced AES (AES: Advanced Encryption Standard). SIP endorses two forms of cryptography: end-to-end and hop-by-hop. The end-to-end encryption provides confidentiality for all information (some letterhead and the body of SIP message) that needs to be read by intermediate servers or proxy. The end-to-end encryption is executed by the mechanism S/MIME. On the contrary, the hop-by-hop encryption of whole SIP message can be employed in the order to protect the information that would have to be accessed by intermediate entities, such that letterhead From, To and Via. The security of such information prevents malevolent users to determine that calls, or to access to the information of the itinerary. The hop-by-hop encryption can be executed by external security mechanisms to SIP (IPSEC or TLS).

Before closing this poll of security mechanisms in SIP, it is necessary to consider the efforts of standardization processing to improve the security mechanisms for SIP. The most important matter here is the problem of the agreement on the chosen security mechanism between two SIP entities (user agents and/or proxy) that want to communicate by applying a level of «sufficient» security. For this reason, it is very important to define how a SIP entity can select an appropriate mechanism for communicating with a next proxy entity. One of the proposals for an agreement security mechanism that allows two agents of exchanging their clean security aptitudes of preferences in the order to select and apply a common mechanism is, when a client initiated the procedure, the SIP agent include in the first request sent to the neighbor proxy entity the list of its mechanisms of security sustained. The other element replies with a list of its clean security mechanisms and its parameters. The client selects then the common security mechanism preferred and use this chosen mechanism (ex, TLS), and contact the proxy by using the new mechanism of security (Jennings, 2002).

With this technique, another problem should be handled. It is the problem with the assertion and the validation of the identity of the user by SIP server. The SIP protocol allows a user to assert its identity by several manners (ex, in the letterhead); but the information of identity requested by the user is not verified in the fundamental SIP operation. On the other hand, an IP client of telephony could have required and insure the identity of a user in order to provide a specific service and/or to condition the type of service to the identity of the user himself. The model of SIP authentication could be a way of obtaining such identity; however, the user agents have not always the necessary information on key to authenticate with all the other agents. A model is proposed in (Profods, 2002) for «confirmed identity» which is based on the concept of a «confirmed area». The idea is, that when a user authenticates its clean identity with a proxy, the proxy can share this authenticated identity (the confirmed identity) with all the other proxies in the «confirmed area». A confirmed area is a totality of proxies that have a mutual configuration of a security association. Such association of security represents a confidence between proxies. When a proxy in a «confirmed area» authenticates the identity of the author of a message, it adds a new letterhead to the message containing the confirmed identity of the user. Such identity can be employed by all other proxies belonging to the «confirmed area».

Using this mechanism the client UAC, is capable to identify himself to a proxy UAS, to an intermediate proxy or to a registration proxy. Therefore, the SIP authentication is applied only to the communications end-to-end or end-to-proxy; the authentication proxy-by-proxy would have to count on others mechanisms as IPsec or TLS.

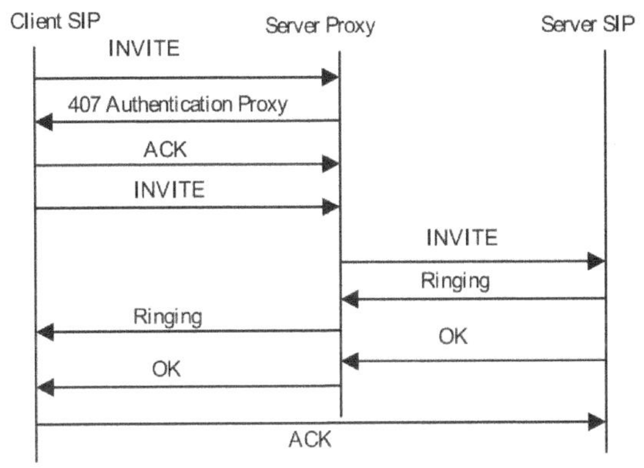

Figure 6: Authentication SIP.

The procedure of authentication is executed when the UAS, the proxy intermediate, or the necessary recording proxy for the call of the UAC has to be authenticated before accepting the call, or the recording. In the beginning the UAS sends a request of SIP message «text» (ex, INVITE). In the reception of this message, the UAS, proxy, or recording proxy decides that the authentication is necessary and sent to the client a specific SIP error message of the request of authentication. This error message represents a challenge. In the particular case, where the message of error is 401 (Unauthorized) is sent by UAS and recording, while when the message of error is 407 (Proxy Authentication Required) is sent by proxy server. The UAC receives the message of error, calculates the reply, and includes it in a new message of the SIP request. The next figure 6 shows the sequence of message for the case of request of authentication by the proxy server.

The UAC sends a message ACK immediately after that the message of error is received. This message closes the first transaction; then the second message INVITE opens a new transaction.

But this technique is a classic and it's based on a standard and classical mechanism. It will thus be preferable to propose a new technique based on sure cryptographic algorithms such as the quantum cryptography.

```
INVITE sip:xy@domain SIP/2.0
Via: SIP/2.0/UDP
To: xy <sip:xy@domain>
From: yx <sip:yx@domain>
Call-ID:
CSeq: 1 INVITE
Contact: <sip:yx@domain>
Content-Type: multipart/signed;boundary=...;
micalg=sha1;protocol=application/pkcs7-signature
Content-Length:
Content-Type: application/pkcs7-mime;
smime-type=envelopeddata; name=smime.p7m
Content-Disposition: attachment;handling=required;filename=smime.p7m
Content-Transfer-Encoding: binary
<envelopedData object encapsulating encrypted SDP attachment not shown>
Content-Type: application/pkcs7-signature;name=smime.p7s
Content-Disposition: attachment;handling=required;filename=smime.p7s
Content-Transfer-Encoding: binary
<signedData object containing signature not shown>
```

Figure 7: S/MIME encryption in SDP.

ELEMENTS NECESSITATES SECURITY IN TELECOM SERVICE

Manufacturers as well as the groups of standardization make the work of the analysis of risks in the order to improve the security of systems IN. Although a lot of improvements have already been realized, concerning the security of access to SCP and SMP. New services and new architectural concepts necessitate supplementary improvements.

The next figure, figure 7, presents places of the different threats. Intelligent networks are distributed by nature. This distribution is realized not only to the superior level where the services are described as a collection of service feature (SF), but to too low levels, where the functional entities (FE) can be propagated on different physical entities (PE). Like the communications of various elements of the network are realized on the open and uncertain environment, the security mechanisms have to be applied.

A responsible of the system can prevent these threats of security by using the various mechanisms. The authentication has to be applied in the order to prevent users not authorized to earn the access to the distribution of services.

The cryptography technique that allows detecting a spy and realized the security is the technique of quantum cryptography

QUANTUM CRYPTOGRAPHY

Quantum cryptography does not base security on unproven mathematical problems. Instead, the foundation of security lies in the properties of quantum mechanics (Gisin, Ribordy, 2001). Three such properties essential for quantum cryptography are:

1. We cannot make a measurement on an unknown quantum system without perturbing unless the measurement is an eigen operator to the quantum state being measured. This implies that an eavesdropper (conventionally called Eve) cannot make a measurement of an unknown quantum state in order to obtain some information about the key without introducing disturbances that can in turn be discovered by Alice and Bob.

2. We cannot make a copy of an unknown quantum state. This property is usually referred to as the no

cloning theorem. It prevents an eavesdropper from simply intercepting the transmission and making copies of the transmitted quantum states in order to keep copies to make measurements on, while passing on an unperturbed quantum state to Bob.

3. We cannot measure the simultaneous values of non commuting observables on a single copy of a quantum state.

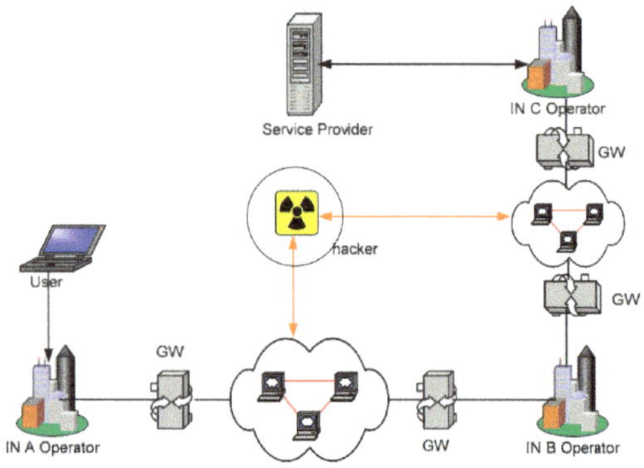

Figure 8: Place of the hacker.

It ensures that the eavesdropper cannot construct a measurement that is an eigen operator to all quantum states used for the key distribution, i.e., it guarantees that it is impossible for the eavesdropper to only perform measurements that leave the quantum states unperturbed (Hoi, 2008).

Quantum cryptography cannot securely transmit predetermined information; it can only securely generate a random key. Once generated, this random key can be subsequently used in a symmetric cipher, such as the one-time pad or one of the modern symmetric ciphers, to securely transmit data over a classical communication channel. A running quantum cryptography channel will steadily generate new secret key material. Thus, quantum cryptography is solving the most difficult problem in modern cryptography, that of key distribution.

There are mainly two types of quantum key distribution (QKD) schemes. One is the prepareandmea sure scheme, such as BB84, in which Alice sends each qubit in one of four states of two complementary bases; B92, in which Alice sends each qubit in one of two non-orthogonal states; six-state, in which Alice sends each qubit in one of six states of three complementary bases. The other is the entanglement based QKD, such as E91, in which entangled pairs of qubits are distributed to Alice and Bob, who then extract key bits by measuring their qubits; BBM92, where each party measures half of the EPR pair in one of two complementary bases.

BB84 Algorithm

BB84 is a quantum key distribution scheme developed by C. Bennett and G. Brassard in 1984. It is the first quantum cryptography protocol. The protocol is provably secure, relying on the quantum property that information gain is only possible at the expense of disturbing the signal if the two states we are trying to distinguish are not orthogonal. It is usually explained as a method of securely communicating a private key from one party to another for use in one-time pad encryption. It has the following the phases.

Step 1: Alice sends a random stream of bits consisting of 1's and 0's using a random selection of rectilinear and diagonal scheme over the quantum channel. On the other side Bob has to measure these photons. He randomly uses one of the two schemes (+ or X) to read the qubits. If he has used the right scheme he notes down the correct bits or he ends up noting down the wrong bits. This is because one cannot measure the polarization of a photon in 2 different 'basis' (rectilinear and diagonal in our case) simultaneously. For example, suppose Alice sends | using '+' scheme to represent 1 and Bob uses '+' scheme and notes down the bit as 1. For the second bit Alice sends \ using the 'X' scheme to represent 1 but Bob uses an incorrect scheme + and miss interprets it as either | or - noting it down correctly as 1 or 0 incorrectly.

Step 2: Alice talks to Bob over a regular phone line and tells the polarization schemes (and not the actual polarization) she had used for each qubit. Bob then tells Alice which of the schemes he had guessed it right. This gives the correct bits noted down by Bob. Based on this they discard all the bits Bob had noted down guessing the wrong scheme.

Step 3: The only way for Alice and Bob to check errors would be to read out the whole sequence of bits on an ordinary telephone line. This wouldn't be a wise idea. So Alice randomly picks some (say 100) binary digits out of the total number of bits that were measured using the correct scheme and checks just these. The probability of Eve being online and not affecting Bob's measurements of 100 bits is infinitesimally small. So if they find any discrepancy among the 100 digits they will detect Eve's presence and will discard the whole sequence and start over again. If not then they will just discard only those 100 digits discussed over phone and use the remaining 1000 digits to be used as one time pad (Johnston, 2002)

One advantage of quantum cryptography is the ability to detect an eavesdropper since Eve can never read the values with out altering them. For example, if Eve reads \ polarization using + scheme then he will be altering the polarization of the photon to either – or ↕, resulting in binary values 0 or 1 respectively. Eve might be able to get the actual (binary) value of 1 but ends up altering the polarization for Bob. If Bob uses X scheme to measure the values he might get either \, which is what Alice sent or /, which is an incorrect measurement.

Bit Number	1	2	3	4	5	6	7	8
Alice : Bits	1	1	0	1	0	0	1	1
Alice : Scheme	+	+	+	+	X	X	X	+
Alice : Qubit	↕	↕	↔	↕	/	/	\	↕
Eve: Scheme	X	+	X	+	+	X	+	X
Eve: Qubit	/	↕	↕	↕	↔	/	↕	/
Bob: Scheme	+	X	X	+	+	X	X	+
Bob: Qubit	↕	\	\	↕	↔	/	/	↔
Bob: Bits	1	1	1	1	0	0	0	0
Selection	√			√		√	√	√

Figure 8: Key Selection and detecting Eve's presence.

Here the bits 1, 4, 6, 7, 8 are selected by Alice and Bob since both of them use the same detection scheme. But when they randomly check bits 1, 7 and 8 they find that the values are different. Through this they can detect the presence of the eavesdropper.

BB92 Algorithm

In 1992, Charles Bennett proposed what is essentially a simplified version of BB84 in his paper, "Quantum cryptography using any two non-orthogonal states". The key difference in B92 is that only two states are necessary rather than the possible 4 polarization states in BB84. As 0 can be encoded as 0 degrees in the rectilinear basis and 1 can be encoded by 45 degrees in the diagonal basis. Like the BB84, Alice transmits to Bob a string of photons encoded with randomly chosen bits but this time the bits Alice chooses dictates which bases she must use. Bob still randomly chooses a basis by which to measure but if he chooses the wrong basis, he will not measure anything; a condition in quantum mechanics which is known as an erasure. Bob can simply tell Alice after each bit she sends whether or not he measured it correctly.

This security feature results from the use of a single or two photons. We know from quantum properties of photons that the measurement of spin of one gives the spin of the other. So if a given pulse sent from Alice is formed by entangled photons then Eve can split these photons using a beam splitter in such a way that he can direct one photon to his polarization detector and another to Bob's. But if only single photons are generated then in presence of a beam splitter the photons have to choose between Eve's and Bob's polarization detectors. This increases the error rate which the BB84 protocol will detect.

Thus, it is the singleness of the photon that guarantees security (Mohamed, 2007). The figure 9 represents a probability to spy detected vs photon number:

Pdet(n) = Pr{MBB84 |= Φdet} with Φdet = a PCTL equation, is True if spy is detected.

PCTL : probabilistic temporal logic (Xu, 2009)

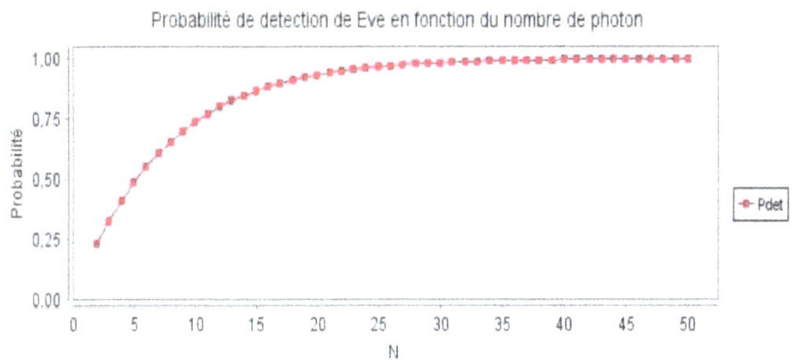

Figure 9: Probability to spy detected.

Quantum Key Distribution QKD

The BB84 protocol and its variants are the only known provably secure QKD protocols. Other QKD protocols (BB92), although promising, have yet to be proven secure. The benefits of QKD are that it can generate and distribute provably secure keys over unsecured channels and that potential eavesdropping can be detected (Mohamed, 2007). QKD can defeat the current computationally complex key exchange methods. Because QKD generates random strings for shared secrets, attaining a QKD system and reverse engineering its theory of operation would yield no mechanism to defeat QKD.

IMPLEMENTATION A QUANTUM CRYPTOGRAPHY IN SIP PROTOCOL OVER IMS NETWORK

The IMS has been originally conceived for mobile systems, but with the addition of TISPAN works in the 7 version 7, the PSTN are equally supported. The IMS is a structured of the architecture of Next Generation Network (NGN) that allows the progressive introduction of voice application and multimedia in mobile and permanent network.

The IMS is used with all types of systems (permanent, mobile or wireless), including a switching functions, as GPRS, UMTS, CDMA 2000, WLAN, WiMAX, DSL. An open interface between control and service layers allows mixing calls/session in a different access networks. The IMS used a cellular technology to provide an access in every position, and Internet technology to provide services.

The principle of the IMS consists on the one hand in clearly separate the transport layer of the service layer and on the other hand to use the transport layer for control and signaling functions so as to insure the quality of service wished for the desired application. IMS aims, to make the network a sort of middleware layer between applications and the access.

Applications are been SIP, or not SIP, they pass by a Gateway before the connection to the controller of sessions.

Despite considerable advantages of the IMS, several limit render the IMS all alone is incapable to be beneficial for the creation and the exploitation of services by operators to the near users, it is in order that, one uses IN service into SIP protocol. In my Application, I'm proposing a several IMS networks nodes for mobile application (figure10). The signaling into the different elements is assured with SIP over MAP (Mobile Application Protocol).

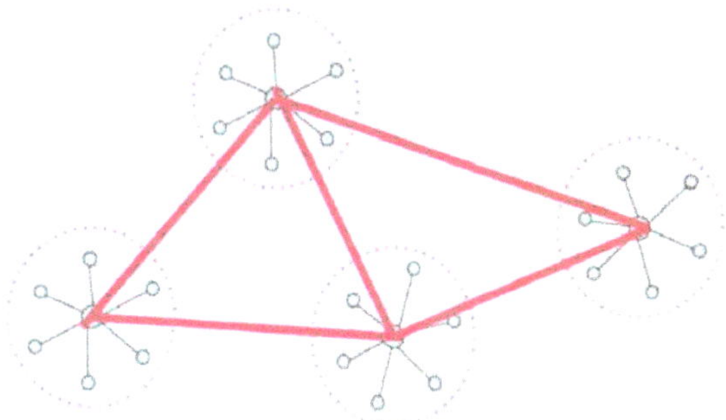

Figure 10: IMS Network node.

After this I'm developing a quantum cryptographic key distribution in SIP Body based on the BB84 algorithm (Bernhard, 2003), named qc:

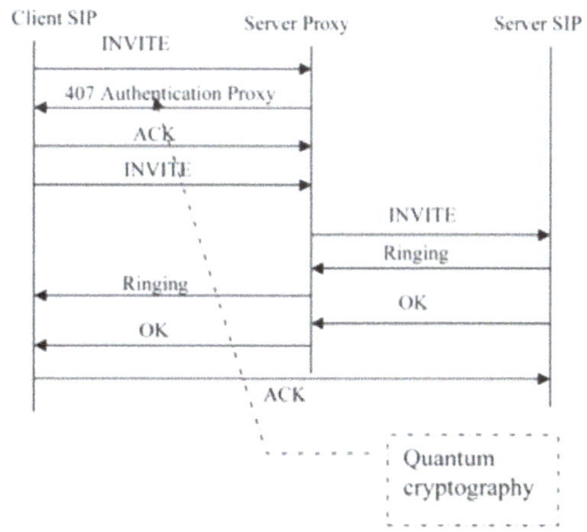

```
INVITE sip:xy@domain SIP/2.0
Via: SIP/2.0/UDP
To: xy <sip:xy@domain>
From: yx <sip:yx@domain>
Call-ID:
CSeq: 1 INVITE
Contact: <sip:yx@domain>
Content-Type:
multipart/signed;boundary=…;
micalg=sha1;protocol=application/quantum
cryptography
Content-Length:
Content-Type: application/quantum
cryptography;
smime-type=envelopeddata; name=qc
Content-Disposition:
attachment;handling=required;filename=qc
Content-Transfer-Encoding: binary
<envelopedData object encapsulating
encrypted SDP attachment not shown>
Content-Type: application/quantum
cryptography;name=qc
Content-Disposition:
attachment;handling=required;filename=qc
Content-Transfer-Encoding: binary
<signedData object containing signature
not shown>
```

Figure 11: QC into SIP request.

The different ID of IMS clients is registered in a database developed with sql in QC server. I am proposing one QC server for one IMS server (see figure) and the transaction into these IMS servers is authenticate with BB84 protocol like a Kerberos protocol (Butler, 2006), figure 12. After this, I am implementing my application over an IMS core (http://www. openimscore. org) open source IMS network and IMS client is UCT client IMS (http://uctimsclient. berlios.de). The figure 13 show a SIP client Request and figure 14 show an IMS network with QKD server.

CONCLUSION

Mobile networks has adopted the IN technology to provide to users of the new services that can be only obtained in the permanent system and improved management of mobility. With the SIP protocol under IP an attempt of the Mobile connection has IP and IN to define the new services as well as to exploit advanced techniques in the security developed for IP network becomes possible especially for IMS network. The SIP authentication is the alone technique proposed by SIP for the security for the terminal and subscribed. With quantum cryptography mechanism into SIP Authentication, the security between IMS client and PCSCF or I-CSCF is assured and sure.

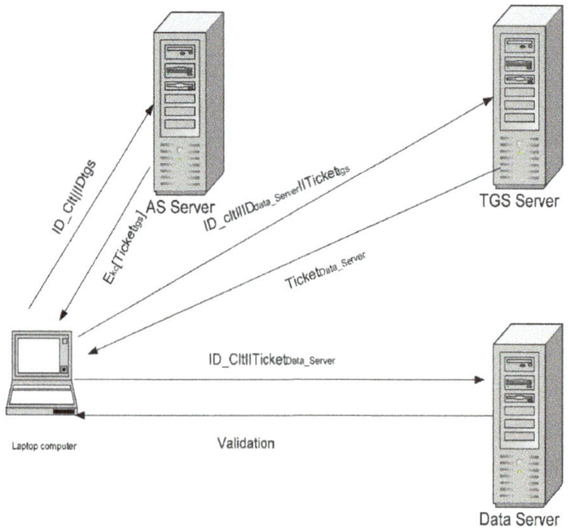

Figure 12: Kerberos mechanism.

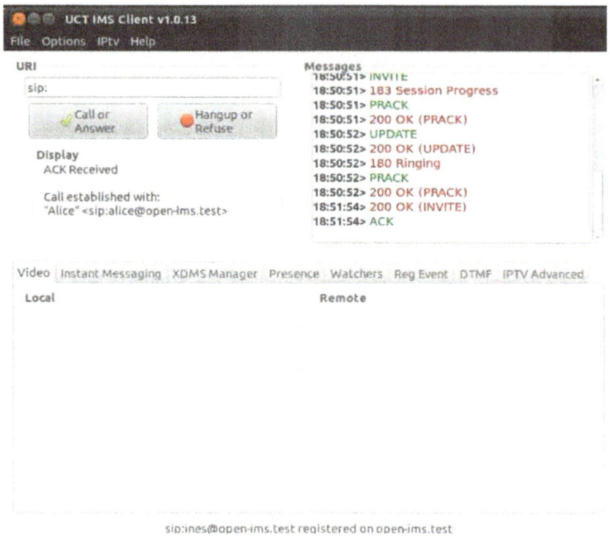

Figure 13: SIP client request.

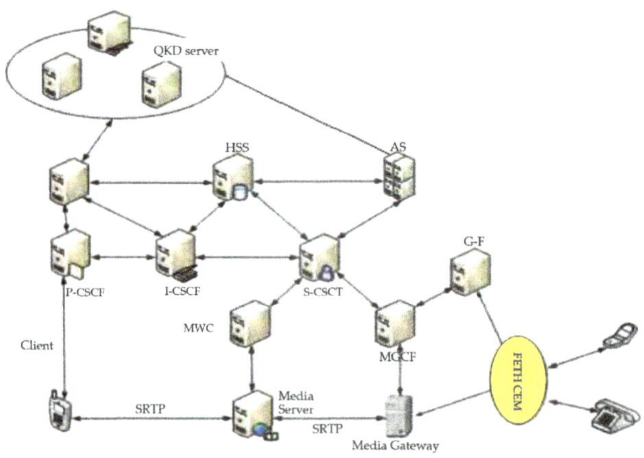

Figure 14: IMS network with QKD server.

REFERENCES

1. Bulter, F. I, Cervesato, A. D. Jaggard, A. Scedrov,C. Walstad, Formal analysis for Kerberos 5, Theoretical Computer Science 367 (2006) 57 – 87.

2. Schulzrinne, H. The Session Initiation Protocol (SIP); hgs/SIP Tutorial may 2001. Johnston, A & al, SIP service examples; draft-ietf-sip-service-examples-03.txt, June 2002.
3. Chapron, J. B, Chatras, An analysis of the IN call model suitability in the context of VoIP; Compter Networks 35 (2001) 521-535.
4. Hoi-Kwong Lo and Yi Zhao, Quantum cryptography. arXiv:0803.2507v4,1 Apr 2008.
5. El ouahidi, B & al, Internet/Telecommunication integration : Towards IN-capable SIP network; Revue internationale: Calculateurs parallèles réseaux et systèmes repartis, Hermès-Editions, Edition spéciale ingénierie des services de télécoms, 12(2) :259- 280, December 2000.
6. Internet Draft , VK. Gurbani, Interworking SIP and Intelligent Network (IN) Applications; draft-gurbani-sin-02.txt, June 2002
7. EEEurescom Project P916 Supporting of H323 by IN, Providing IN functionality for H323 telephony calls, October 2000.
8. Gisin, N. G.Ribordy, W.Tittel and H.Zbinden, Quantum cryptography. arXiv:quantph/0101098v2 18 Sep 2001.
9. Fing, Principes et conditions de mise en oeuvre du standard ENUM en France; http://www.art-telecom.fr/publications/index-cp-enum.htm. 18 juin 2001.
10. Bernhard Omer, Classical Concepts in Quantum Programming. arXiv:quant-ph/0211100v2 29 Apr 2003.
11. Mohamed Saleh Mourad Debbabi, Verifying Security Properties of Cryptoprotocols: A Novel Approach. Fifth IEEE International Conference on Software Engineering and Formal Methods, IEEE 2007.
12. Xu Wei, Ma Yan, Liu Nan, Wu Dong-ying, A Formal Method for Analyzing Fair Exchange Protocols. 2009 WASE International Conference on Information Engineering.
13. Schweizer.L, Scripts et APIs pour la gestion de serveurs SIP ; www.tcom.ch; 23/12/2001. http://www.openimscore.org.
14. Profos.D “Security requirements and concepts for Intelligents networks” , Ascom Tech AG Bielstrasse 122, 4502 Solthurn.
15. Jennings, C. Peterson, J and M. Watson,“Private Extensions to the Session Initiation Protocol (SIP) for Asserted Identity within Trusted Networks”, <draft-ietf-sip-assertedidentity-01>, June 2002.

CHAPTER 15

EVOLUTION OF AN EMERGING SYMMETRIC QUANTUM CRYPTOGRAPHIC ALGORITHM

Omer K. Jasim, Safia Abbas, El-Sayed M. Horbaty, Abdel-Badeeh M. Salem

Keywords: AES, Encryption/Decryption, Quantum Computations, QKD, Symmetric Algorithm

INTRODUCTION

Recently, two distinct ciphers for cryptography processes are defined, symmetric and asymmetric cipher [1] . Symmetric is a form of cryptosystem in which encryption and decryption processes are preformed based on the same key. While, asymmetric encryption and decryption processes are depending mainly on performance using the keys mechanism (public and private) [2] . A Key is a numeric or may be a special symbol which is used through the time of encryption and decryption. The selection of key in cryptography is very important since the security of encryption algorithm depends directly on it. The strength of the encryption algorithm relies on the secrecy of the key, length of the key, the initialization vector, and how they all work together [3] .

Asymmetric encryption techniques are about 1000 times slower than symmetric encryption which makes it impractical when trying to encrypt large amounts of data [4] . Also to get the same security strength as symmetric, asymmetric must use a stronger key than symmetric encryption technique [5] . Therefore, in this paper we focus on the symmetric cipher technique.

Generally, symmetric technique divided into two broad categories: stream cipher and block cipher [2] [3] . In a stream cipher, an encryption/decryption process embraces on a symbol by symbol at a time. While, a block cipher divides a plaintext into a number of equal blocks (b > 1), these blocks are encrypted together to produce a cipher text [4] [5] .

Citation: Jasim, O. , Abbas, S. , Horbaty, E. and Salem, A. (2015) Evolution of an Emerging Symmetric Quantum Cryptographic Algorithm. Journal of Information Security, 6, 82-91. doi: 10.4236/jis.2015.62009.

Moreover, a block cipher transforms 64; 128; 192 or 256-bit to string of the same length under the control of secret key [6] . All block cipher systems rely on substitution-permutation boxes, which are fixed and do not have any relation with a secret key. It is adding more complexity to the cipher text by changing the location of the plain text character into a new position [7] .

This paper discusses the AES block cipher symmetric algorithm. Scalability, easy to implement and resistance against attacks are well-known features for such algorithm [6] [8] [9] . AES algorithm utilizes the same key for encryption/decryption process with length 128; 192; 256-bits. This key is grouped (XOR-gate) with separate equal blocks of a plain text [10] . Additionally, the length of secret key determines the number of rounds in such algorithm (Nr). Thus, AES-128 bits needs 10 rounds, 12 rounds for AES-192 bits and 14 rounds for AES-256 bits; for more details see [6] .Table 1 shows the relation among key length (Nk), input block (Nb) and number of rounds (Nr) in the AES algorithm.

Unfortunately, most of modern encryption algorithms rely entirely on a complex mathematics computation in the key generation and distribution and management. So, it is vulnerable to quantum attack and the man-in- the-middle attack. Quantum computation especially QKD is the first solution to these problems.

QKD is an important practical application of quantum computation. It is based on laws of physics rather than computation complexity of mathematical problems. It can generate security keys between two communications and guarantee security of sensitive data (for more details see [11] [12]).

This paper discusses and analyzes the structure of Substitutions boxes (S-boxes) in the traditional AES. Moreover, based on a quantum cipher key, a dynamic quantum S-Boxes

(DQS-Boxes) is generated. Finally, a new version of AES by integration between the enhanced version of AES and QKD in two implemented modes (on-line and off-line) is presented.

The rest of the paper is organized as follows: Section 2 surveys the existing study for AES optimization and cryptanalysis. The developed architecture for QAES and integration modes are given in Section 3. Section 4 explains the inferences obtained from the results and discussion. Section 5 presents the conclusion and future works.

EXISTING METHODS

Recently, there are few authors are focused on the enhancing and cryptanalysis of the AES algorithm, because most of AES attacks appeared lately.

For example, Sekar et al. [2] propose a new innovative method to enhance the AES algorithm by increasing the key length to 512 bits and thereby the number of rounds is increased in order to provide a stronger encryption method for secure communication. This method doesn't modify the structure of AES, but only increase the number of rounds. Therefore, this algorithm increases the processing time which will limit the use of AES in real applications.

Kazys et al. [13] present a new version of AES by generating random S-Boxes coinciding with every secret key generation. The authors described in details how to generate random S-Box, key-independent, and ratio of independence for the S-Box elements is computed. The breach of this study was not debating any type of cryptanalysis attacks.

Table 1: AES key, input block, and rounds

Cipher	Nk-words	Nb-words	Nr
AES-128	4	4	10
AES-192	6	4	12
AES-256	8	4	14

Shaaban et al. [14] develop a powerful algorithm for cryptography, it's based on AES to generate different sub keys from the original key and using each of one to encrypt a single AES round. It becomes resistant against the analysis attacks such as a brute force attack and others. Moreover, the authors classified secret keys as real key and PRNG, each one used in special cryptographic mode. However, this algorithm is slower than classical AES, therefore, it is apt to the timing attack.

However, contrast to above studies, the first cryptanalysis deployed by Alex B. et al. [7] [15] when they evaluate the cost of cryptanalytic attacks on the full AES by using a special-purpose hardware in the form of multi- core AES processors. Also, they analyze different time-cost trade-offs and evaluate the implications of progress in VLSI technology under the assumption that Moore's law will continue to hold for the next ten years. These calculations raise some concerns about the long-term security of the AES.

S. Hadi et al. [9] propose a new related-key impossible differential attack on 7-round AES-128, which is the first attempt using this technique. They attacked 7-round AES-128 with the time complexity of $(105)^2$, the fastest attack of all the previous ones from time and pre-computation complexities points of views. This attack is the first related key impossible differential attack which is applied to 7-round AES-128. A fundamental point to construct such attack is using a special property of Mix Column operation of AES.

Other studies [12] [16] -[19] discuss the weakness of key schedules (key expansion [6]) which may be used in attacking the block cipher system, until now not have any key schedule attack have been fully broken the AES algorithm.

Finally, we can conclude that many studies have attempted to enhance the strength and efficiency of AES algorithm without changed in a core of AES structure. In other hand, not fully rounds hacked by the attackers, the best states reached to seven rounds (out of ten) for AES-128, and ten (out of 12 or 14) rounds for AES-192 and AES-256.

QAES ARCHITECTURE

This section illustrates the QAES development steps based on two different modes (on-line and off-line modes). The main machine utilizes the Core i5 (4.8 GHz) with 8 GB of RAM with 500 GB-HDD, while, the simulator is programmed using Visual Studio Ultimate 2012 (VC#).

QAES Development

The QAES developed system incorporates both the QKD and an enhanced version of the AES in order to provide an unconditional security level [20] [21] for any cipher system built on symmetric encryption algorithms. As shown in Figure 1, the AES enhanced version utilizes the dynamic quantum S-Box (DQS-Boxes) that is generated from the QKD and exploits the generated key in the encryption/decryption process.

The DQS-boxes enjoy the dynamic mechanism, in which the contents of each S-Box changes consequently in each round with the change of the key generation. Such dynamic mechanism aids in solving the mechanism problems associated with the traditional S-Boxes. Avoiding the off-line analysis attack, overcoming the DS-Box [14] , and resistance to the quantum attack are examples of the associated problems.

Since the unconditional security depends on the Heisenberg uncertainty principle (core feature in quantum theory) [20] [21] , instead of the complex mathematical model in key generation, more attack resistance is assured and the cipher system is hard to be attacked.

Integration Modes

The integration between the enhanced AES and the QKD uses two different modes the online and the off-line is explained in this section.

Online Mode

During the negotiation between the two parties (master, slave), as shown in Figure 2, the encryption/decryption process is achieved coinciding with quantum key generation.

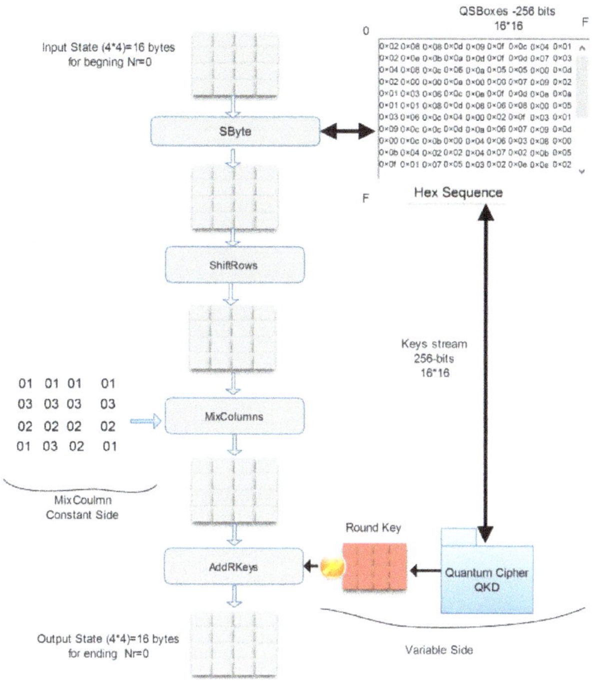

Figure 1. QAES architecture for single cycle.

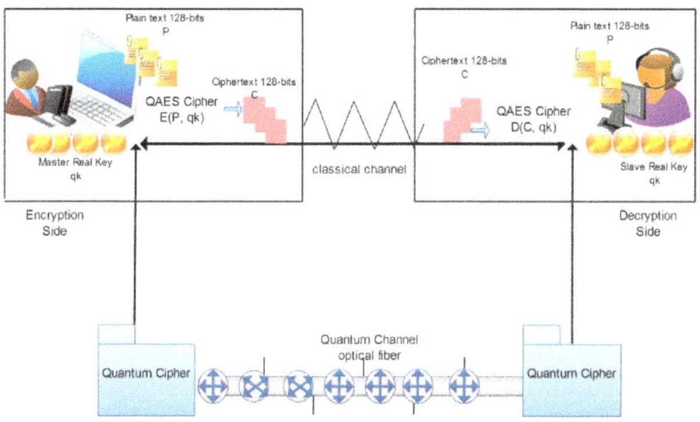

Figure 2: On-line mode architecture.

The on-line mode follows the following steps:

- The quantum secret key is generated over the quantum channel using BB84 protocol.
- The master and slave parties check the online compatibility for the generated secret key.
- The master and the slave choose the appropriate key length (128; 192; 256 bits) through the classical channels in order to perform the encryption/decryption process.
- The two parts deploy the selected final quantum secret key (q_k) to the symmetric encryption algorithm (AES).
- The system automatically creates the DQS-Box based on the secret key generation with length 256-bits.
- Encrypt the first block input file (P1-128 bits) by the AES stages—using qk_1 which generate by QKD round1.
- $E(P_1 \oplus qk_1) = C_1$
- Finally, Encrypt final block input file by the AES stages—using qk_n which generate by QKD $round_n$, where $n = Nr = 10$; 12; 14.
- $E(P_n \oplus qk_1) = C_n$
- The decryption process start with the end of the encryption process (inverse methodology).
- $D(C_n \oplus qk_n) = P_n$

Due to the key availability (KA) associated with QKDs [21] [22] , the online mode is provided by a sequence of unrelated keys $(qk_1, qk_2, \cdots, qk_n)$ in each round, illustrated in Figure 3, these unrelated keys prevent the attackers from detecting the next key generation. Then, each QAES round, will consider the generated sequence of keys $(qk_1, qk_2, \cdots, qk_n)$ as a sequence of sub keys, which in turn are used in the encryption/decryption process.

Finally, this mode can be used with any type of encryption modes such as cipher feedback (CFB) mode, output feedback (OFB) mode, and the counter (CTR) mode.

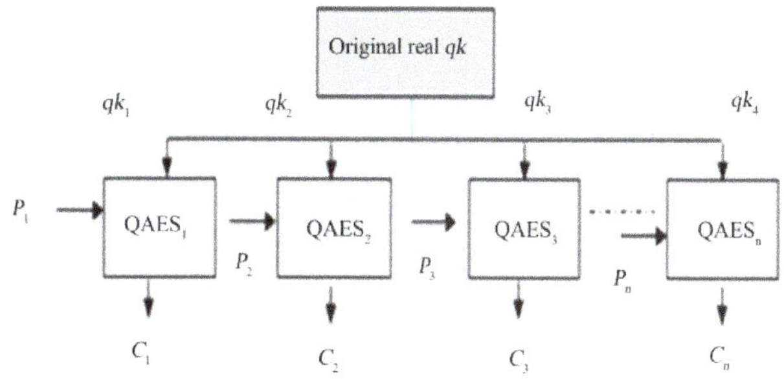

Figure 3. On-line encryption mode.

Offline Mode

Despite of many positive criteria for QKD such as KA, key distribution and management, they depend on exchanging photons between parties over limited distances (314 km) [23] [24] . Various randomness tests for qubits generation from QKD based on NIST, DIEHARD, and others were implemented previously [21] and reveals an astonishing fact, that all tests generate truly random bits, that used a key for the encryption/decryption process, in both suggested modes.

As shown in Figure 4, the architecture of this mode consists of quantum device, key controller and two communication parties (master-slave). The quantum cipher (QC) used to generate sequence qubits between parties. The QC responsible of exchanging and replacement of keys in both parties (master-slave) and system (user- system).

The off-line mode follows the following steps:

- Generate the random qubits from QKD, these qubits act as secret key (k).
- Based on this K, the system creates DQS-Box.
- Using classical AES-key scheduler, the sub-keys for each AES-round are generated.
- Finally, steps (4, 5, 6, 7 and 8) in the on-line mode are typically performed.

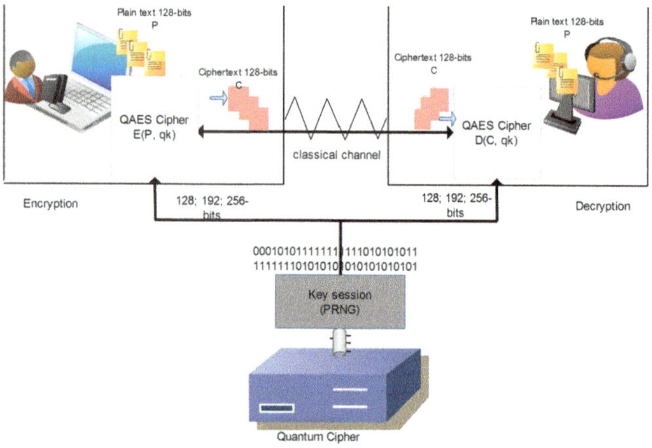

Figure 4: Off-line mode.

Due to the results of the random tests implementation mention in [21] , the unrelated key generation offers a highly secured cipher system. The differences between the QAES and the classical AES are the DQS-Boxes and the generation method of the sub key. As shown in Figure 5, this mode can be used with any type of encryption such as CFB, OFB, and CTR.

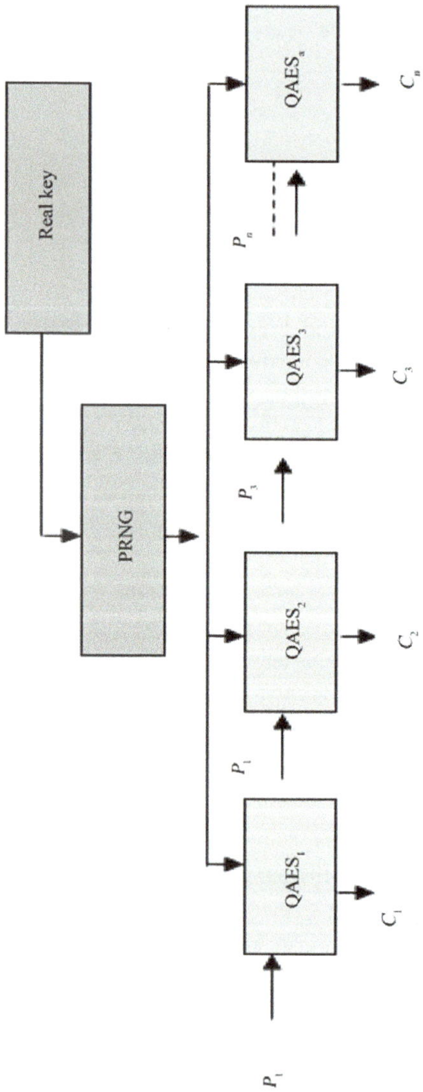

Figure 5: Off-line encryption mode.

RESULTS AND DISCUSSIONS

In this section the ratio of independency for DQS-Box and the time of encryption process have been implemented, measured and analyzed based QAES. After then, the results are compared when the same processes are implemented based classical AES.

DQS-Box Analysis

The ratio of independent mainly depends on Equations (1)-(4), these equations are used for the classical S-boxes correlation and independency computations [2] [9] . Accordingly, the ratio of independence based the DQS-Box are calculated. The results show that using the DQS-Box produces higher ratio and lower correlation coefficient between different rounds. This guarantees a better security and more resistance against the almost of cryptanalysis attacks and build a stronger encryption algorithm.

$$y = \frac{x - \text{mean}(x)}{std(x)} \tag{1}$$

$$\text{mean}(x) = \frac{\max(x) - \min(x)}{2} \tag{2}$$

$$std(x) = \sqrt{\max(x) - \min(x)^2 / 16} \tag{3}$$

$$\text{ratio} = \frac{std(CORR)}{\max(x)} \tag{4}$$

where CORR is a ratio of correlations.

For example, regarding to the simulation environment for QKD, two DQS-Boxes are generated with 256 bits (matrix 16 × 16). According to Equations (1)-(4), the ratio of correlation functions and independence between DQS-Box1 and DQS-Box2 are shown in Figure 6, Figure 7.

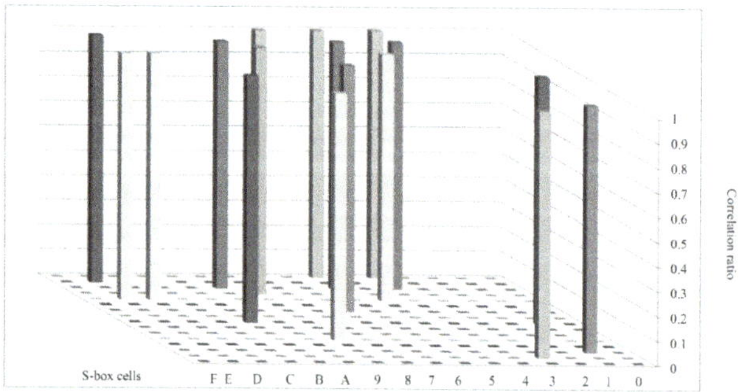

Figure 6: Correlation between QS-Box1 and QS-Box2.

As shown in the above figures, the ratio of correlation (CORR) coefficient is 6.606%, while the ratio of independence is 93.359%. Exactly, the ratio of independent ranging between (72.78% - 100%) for each corresponding row between two DQS-Boxes, [for more details see Appendix], which indicates that the QAES provides a highly unrelated Box that led to a more secured connection. Moreover, the DQS-Box generation process enjoys the advantage that the intermediate generation done during the encryption/decryption process which avoids the offline analysis attack associated with the S-Box.

Efficiency of QAES

In the following analysis, both the AES and QAES algorithms have been implemented using several input files sizes: 500 kb, 1000 kb, 1500 kb, 2000 kb, and 3500 kb.

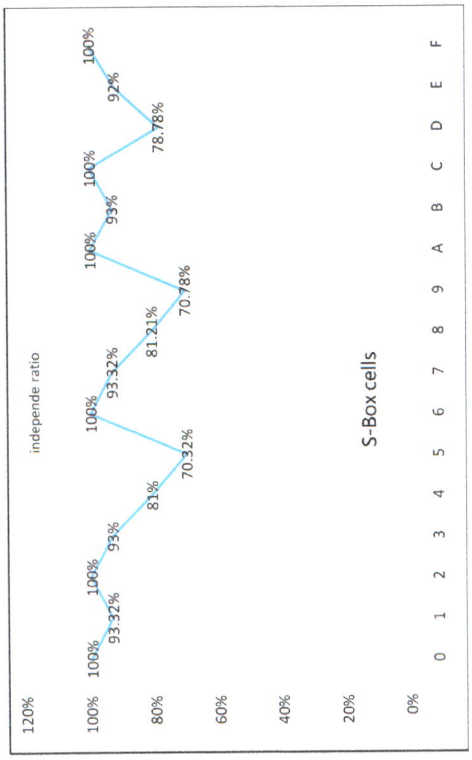

Figure 7: Ratio of independence.

Figure 8 and Figure 9 represent the running time of the implemented algorithms using the local machines described above, the running time is calculated in milliseconds (ms) and the input size is taken in kilobytes.

Comparing the QAES with traditional AES encryption algorithms reflects a higher security level. However, as shown in Equation (5), and Figure 10, this algorithm takes time more than others due to the time required for quantum key generation (time for key negotiation (T_{QKG}) and time required for the encryption/decryption process T(Enc(P)).

$$T_{qencryption} = T_{QKG} + T\left(E\left(P_n\right)\right) \quad (5)$$

where T_{qenc} = Total encryption based QAES and P_n = plain file.

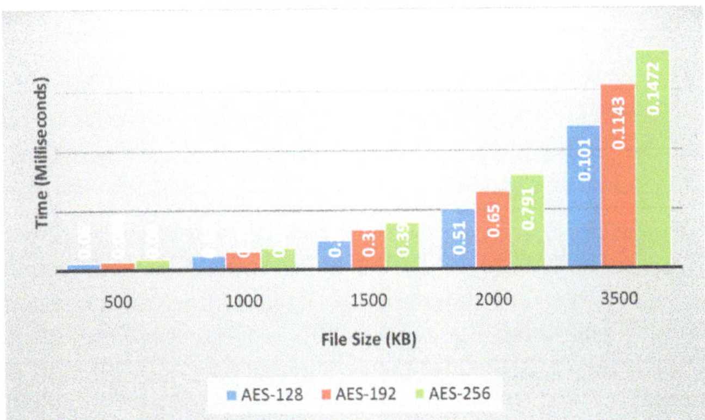

Figure 8: AES efficiency.

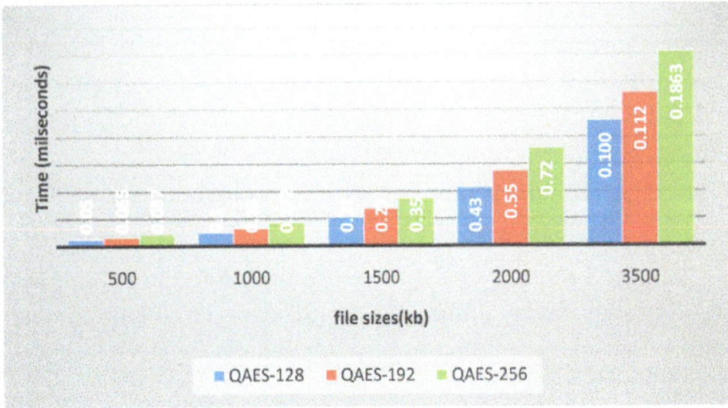

Figure 9: QAES efficiency without key generation time.

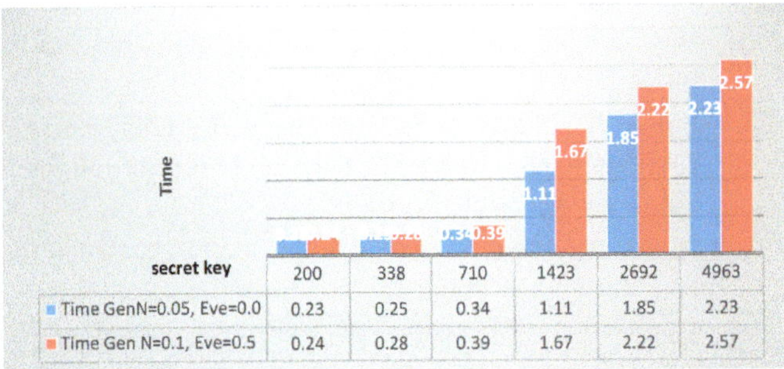

Figure 10: Secret key generation with viarouse configurations.

As showed in Figure 10, any change in the eavesdropper activity or noise level directly impact on the length of the secret key and the time of generation it. For example, in order to get 200 from 500 qubits are pumped under the influence of noise 0.05 GHz and there is no Eve influence, we need 0.23 milliseconds to generate it. Usually, this time simultaneously grows with the increasing of the noise or Eve influence. However, the practical environment is faster than the simulator environment, due to the light nature [8] [24] .

Generally, we can conclude that the QAES is a little bit slower than the AES. For example, according to Figures 8-10, and Equation (5), the encryption time of AES-128 bits is 0.101 ms for file size 3500 kb. While, QAES-128 bits takes 0.23 ms for key generation has length 200-qubits and 0.100 ms for file encryption. So, the total time for QAES-128 is 0.123 ms and 0.135 ms for QAES-192.

Finally, since the QAES follows the same architecture of the AES, the input file size has always changed during encryption process and the details of the processed file remain unchangeable.

CONCLUSIONS AND FUTURE WORKS

In this paper a developed version of AES algorithm, annotated as QAES, based on quantum encryption mechanism and dynamically S-Boxes have been introduced, implemented and discussed. The paper shows that the QAES development and design do not contradict the security of the AES algorithm, since all the mathematical criteria remain unchanged. The QAES symmetric encryption algorithm has been revealed depending on the integration between the AES and the QKD using two different modes, the On-line and the Off-line. The experimental results and the analysis show that the QAES produces more complicated un-breakable keys, hard to be predicted by attackers than the keys generated by the AES. However, the speed of encryption of the QAES is tiny higher (0.409 seconds) than that using the AES. The strength of the QAES lies in its ability of generating a high ratio of independence between DQS-Boxes, see Appendix; this ratio aids in achieving a more secured environment against most types of cryptanalysis attacks.

In the future, in order to assure the strength of the QAES, the algebraic and quantum attacks are going to be implemented, and the results are going to be analyzed.

REFERENCES

1. Rose, H. and Hag, J. (2012) Using a Cipher Key to Generate Dynamic S-Box in AES Cipher System. International Journal of Computer Science and Security, 6, 19-28.
2. Sekar, A., Radhika, S. and Anand, K. (2012) Secure Communication Using 512 Bit Key. European Journal of Scientific Research, 52, 61-65.
3. Kinga, R., Aline, A. and Christian, E. (2012) Generation and Testing of Random Numbers for Cryptographic Application. Proceeding of Romanian Academy, 13, 368-377.
4. Daemen, J. and Rijmen, V. (2002) The Design of Rijndael: AES—The Advanced Encryption Standard of Information Security and Cryptography. Vol. 22, Springer Verlag, Berlin, 231-240.
5. Warren, D. and Smith, W. (2014) AES Seems Weak, Linear Time Secure Cryptography. International Association for Cryptologic Research, 1-24.
6. Stallings, W. (2012) Cryptography and Network Security Principles and Practice. 5th Edition, Prentice Hall, Upper Saddle River, 330-337.
7. Alex, B. and Johann, G. (2012) Cryptanalysis of the Full AES Using GPU-Like Special-Purpose Hardware, Journal Fundamental Informatics—Cryptology in Progress. 10th Central European Conference on Cryptology, 10-12 June 2010, Vol. 114, 221-237.
8. Matthew, G. (2013) Statistical Tests of Randomness on QKD through a Free-Space Channel Coupled to Daylight Noise. Journal of Light Wave Technology, 3, 34-35.
9. Hadi, S., Alireza, S., Behnam, B. and Mohammadraze, A. (2013) Cryptanalysis of 7-Round AES-128. International Journal of Computer Application, 10, 21-29.
10. Biryukov, A. and Nikolic, I. (2010) Automatic Search for Related-Key Differential Characteristics in Byte-Oriented Block Ciphers: Application to AES. In: Gilbert, H., Ed., Advances in Cryptology EUROCRYPT 2010, Lecture Notes in Computer Science, Vol. 6610, Springer, Berlin, 322-344.
11. Geiselmann, W., Januszewski, F., Kopfer, H., Pelzl, J. and Steinhardt, R. (2007) A Simpler Sieving Device: Combining ECM and TWIRL. In: Rhee, M.S. and Lee, B., Eds., Information Security and Cryptology—ICISC 2006, Lecture Notes in Computer Science, Springer, Berlin, 118-135. http://dx.doi.org/10.1007/11927587_12
12. Sumalatha, M. and Malal, M. (2013) Design of High Speed 128 Bits AES Algorithm for Data Encryption. International Journal of Current Engineering and Technology (IJCET), 20, 338-343.
13. Kazys, A. and Janus, K. (2012) Key-Dependent S-Box Generation in AES Block Cipher System. Informatica, 20, 23-34.
14. Shaaban, S., Wisam, E. and Shadi, A. (2013) Enhancement the Security of AES against Modern Attacks by Using Variable Key Block Cipher. International Arab Journal of E-Technology, 3, 17-26.
15. Bernstein, D., Chen, H., Chen, M., Cheng, C., Hsiao, C. and Lange, T. (2009) The Billion-Mulmod-Per-Second PC. In SHARCS '09: Special-Purpose Hardware for Attacking Cryptographic Systems, Lausanne, 131-144.
16. Neetu, S. (2010) Cryptanalysis of Modern Cryptographic Algorithms. International Journal of Computer Science and Telecommunications, 1, 166-169.
17. Julia, J., Ramlan, M., Salasiah, S. and Jazrin, R. (2012) Enhancing AES S-Box Generation Based on a Round Key. International Journal of Cyber-Security and Digital Forensics, 1, 65-72.
18. Amit, C. and Damodar, T. (2012) Analysis of AES Algorithm Using Symmetric Cryptography. International Journal of Computing, Communications and Networking, 1, 57-62.
19. Cukier, M., Berthier, R., Panjabi, S. and Tan, S. (2006) A Statistical Analysis of Attack Data to Separate Attacks. Proceedings of the International Conference on Dependable Systems and Networks (DSN 2006), Philadelphia, 25-28 June 2006, 123-142.
20. Payal, P. and Soni, D. (2013) An Invention of Quantum Cryptography over the Classical Cryptography for Enhancing Security. International Journal of Applied or Innovation in Engineering and Management, 2, 243-246.
21. Omer, J., Safia, A., El-Sayed, M. and Abdel-Badeeh, S. (2014) Statistical Analysis for Random Bits Generation on Quantum Key Distribution. Proceedings of the 3rd IEEE International Conference on Cyber Security, Cyber Warfare, and Digital Forensic, Beirut, 29 April-1 May 2014, 45-51.
22. Christain, K. and Mario, P. (2010) Applied Quantum Cryptography (Lecture Notes in Physics, Book 797). Springer, Berlin.
23. Solange, G. and Mohammed, A. (2014) Applying QKD to Reach Unconditional Security in Communications. European Research Project SECOQC. www.secoqc.net
24. Ammar, O., Khaled, E., Muneer, A. and Eman, A. (2013) Quantum Key Distribution by Using RSA. Proceeding of the 3rd International Conference on Innovative Computing Technology (INTECH), London, 29-31 August 2013, 35-44.

CHAPTER 16

INFORMATION PROTECTION BASED ON SHIFT REGISTER WITH NON-LINEAR FEEDBACK FUNCTION

Saleh Al-Omar

Keywords: Pseudorandom Sequences, Non-Linear Feedback Function, Information Protection

INTRODUCTION

In tasks of information protection, statistical monitoring and diagnosis, modeling and designing, generators of pseudorandom sequences are widely used. The effectiveness of these generators in informational technologies is defined by specific features of using them [1] .

Pseudorandom objects are very important in modern systems of information protection [2] . Especially important role in this dynamically developing domain is played by pseudorandom binary sequences, which are used as a baseline for one of three types of information security algorithms—flow algorithms [3] . Pseudorandom sequences are widely used for generation of keys for the symmetrical data protection algorithms and pseudorandom binary strings for protocols of authentication of remote users in integrated systems [4] . In modern conditions of productivity growth of computational systems and possibilities to unite a huge number of computers in a network for solving problems of security breach, the problem of adequate increasing the reliability of information security becomes more actual, including methods of improving means of obtaining and using pseudorandom sequences.

Protective features of pseudorandom sequences and functional transformations in theoretical plan are defined by the principal impossibility of analytical solutions of the systems of non-linear Boolean equations [5] . This feature of Boolean transformations lies in the heart of using binary sequences and Boolean functions in information security systems. That is why the level of protection of data with using pseudorandom sequences is directly dependent on the nonlinearity of Boolean functions, which are used to generate pseudorandom sequences. From this, important reserve for increasing effectiveness of means of information protection, which use pseudorandom sequences, is in improving means of formation such sequences in the direction of increasing the nonlinearity of Boolean transformations, which they use.

Thus, at the current stage of development of information protection, the problem of developing methods and approaches for increasing effectiveness of hardware-software means of generation of pseudorandom binary sequences is actual.

ANALYSIS OF THE CURRENT STATE OF THE PROBLEM OF EFFECTIVE GENERATION OF PSEUDORANDOM SEQUENCES FOR INFORMATION SECURITY PROBLEMS

Modern Generators of Pseudorandom Sequences Oriented to Be Used in Systems of Information Protection Are Built on the General Principles [5]

- Divergence—the notion which came from the theory of dynamical systems and consisted in the fact that algorithm of a generator should provide diverging sequence of binary n-bit words, that is the sequence, the repetitive cycle of which tends to 2^n [5] .
- Nonlinearity of used functions of transformations, which provides complexity of recognition of generation functions of pseudorandom sequences.
- Computing complexity which means computational incompressibility of the procedures for pseudorandom sequences generation.

Mentioned principles, formulated on the theoretical level, are not strictly defined and partly overlap each other

Citation: Al-Omar, S. (2014) Information Protection Based on Shift Register with Non-Linear Feedback Function. Journal of Information Security, 5, 218-227. doi: 10.4236/jis.2014.54020.

[6] . The notion of divergence is often used if the base for the functional transformation, which lies in the base of the generator, is a special case of the theory of numbers [6] . For bit transformations the problem of divergence which means to provide the repetitive cycle of $2^n - 1$, theoretically can be solved only for linear feedback functions: they must be isomorphic irreducible polynomials in Galois fields. For nonlinear functions of the bit transformation, divergence problem has a solution only for special cases [7] .

A Criteria of Quality of the Generators of Pseudorandom Sequences Oriented to Be Used in Systems of Information Protection the Following Indicators Are Mostly Used [8]

- Statistical criteria which allows to estimate the probability characteristics of the generated sequence [6] ;
- Divergence criteria of generator work—is estimated by the minimal length of cycle appeared during the run;
- Unpredictability of the generator—is estimated by the complexity of the special algorithm-recognizer which allows to distinguish the generated sequence from random [7] ;
- Rate of sequence generation.

Really important when these criteria are considered is the principle, formulated in [8] and postulating that the criterion for determining the randomness is always determined by the class of the problems in which this randomness will be used, that is: use should determine the target probability distribution with the specified degree of approximation and the importance of each of the above criteria.

The third of mentioned earlier criteria of quality of pseudorandom sequences generators is their algorithmic unpredictability, which stipulates the complexity of the algorithm which can predict next values by using data from previous samples [9] . From the point of reliability of data protection it is the third criterion is a determining, because all breaches in security provided by using pseudorandom sequences are reduced to the extrapolation of the recent [9] . It is proved that irreversible transformations should be used to make the sequence meet the unpredictability demand. For flow algorithms widely used in data transfers across networks and telecommunication systems, high speed of generation of the sequence is very important [3] . Exclusion of the possibility of gaining access to programs which implement the generation process is also very important. Based on the last two demands, more preferable is a variant of hardware realization of the generators. In this case, significant criterion of quality of means of pseudorandom sequences generation is their complexity. In practice, the most important class of generators of pseudorandom sequences is the generators based on shift registers with linear feedback—LFSR (Linear Feedback Shift Register). The main advantage of such generators is the fact that due to the developed method of synthesis of the feedback functions their acyclic work is provided (it means the cycle is $2^n - 1$ with n-bit shift register) along with the simplicity of circuit implementation on a hardware level and high performance [8] . So far as the maximum number of different combinations of n binary digits is 2^n, period of the generated sequence cannot exceed 2^n. If LFSR gets into a state with zero values of all bits, it cannot go to another state. That is why zero state shouldn't appear if the initial state nonzero. Therefore, the maximum number of possible states is $2^n - 1$. Maximal length sequence will be provided in case when the feedback function is a simple polynomial in Galois fields [4] . Thus the number G(n) of simple polynomials in Galois fields, and therefore the quantity of sequences with length of $2^n - 1$ formulated by LSFR is determined by the formula:

$$N_L(n) = \frac{\phi(2^n - 1)}{n} \quad (1)$$

where $f(2^n - 1)$—Euler number—quantity of integer, including ones, which are less than $2^n - 1$ and those, which don't have common divisors with $2^n - 1$.

Theoretically the maximum possible number of states of n-bit shift register equals 2^n. Respectively, maximum repetition period of the binary sequence formulated by a nonlinear shift register of such length is 2^n too. Such sequences are called Bruijn sequences. Number N(n) of nonlinear feedback functions of n-bit shift register which provide the maximum repetition period is determined by the formula:

$$N(n) = 2^{2^{n-1}-n} \quad (2)$$

For example, for the 6-bit shift register (n = 6) according to (1) exist only 6 simple polynomials in Galois fields and respectively 6 linear functions which provide period of $2^6 - 1 = 63$ which is close to the maximum, though that number of nonlinear feedback functions for the register with the same bit number which provide the maximum period—2^6 according to (2) is $2^{26} = 67108864$.

Despite such a big number of nonlinear feedback functions, providing the maximum period of repetition of the sequence, finding them is a challenge, which hasn't acceptable solution to date [4] . So, for n = 6 assuming that the total number of functions is 2^{64}, the maximum period is provided, on average, only by one of $2^{64-26} = 2^{40}$ functions.

METHOD OF FINDING NONLINEAR FEEDBACK FUNCTIONS

The state of a shift register is characterized by w code which corresponds to the binary vector of X_w values of register bits:

$$X_w = \{x_0^w, x_1^w, L, x_{n-2}^w, x_{n-1}^w\}$$

During the register shift new value of v code is determined by the following method:

$$X_v = \{x_1^w, x_2^w, L, x_{n-2}^w, f(X_w)\}, \quad v = (2 \cdot w) \bmod 2^n$$

Suppose $f(x_1, x_2, \ldots, x_n)$—Boolean feedback function of n-bit shift register for which the following condition is true:

$$f(x_0, x_1, L, x_{n-1}) = 1 \oplus f(x_0 \oplus 1, x_1, L, x_{n-1}) \quad (3)$$

If the feedback function $f(x_1, x_2, L, x_n)$ satisfies the condition (3), then each v code in the register is preceded by only one w code. A set of codes which sequentially formulated in shift register with feedback feature which satisfies the condition [4] we will name the ring. Each of 2^n possible codes in n-bit register is included into one of the rings.

Suppose we have two rings—A and B. If code w is included in A and the symmetrical to it code $v=\left(w+2^{n-1}\right) \bmod 2^n$ is included in B, then inverting the value of the function in these codes will lead to unite of A and B rings.

Proof: Binary vector $X_w=\{x_0^w,x_1^w,L,x_{n-2}^w,x_{n-1}^w\}$ of state of the register corresponds to w code. Code e follows after w in the A ring: $X_e=\{x_1^w,x_2^w,L,x_{n-2}^w,f(X_w)\}$. When inverting the value of the feedback function on code w, the following after w will be code u: $X_u=\{x_1^w,x_2^w,L,x_{n-2}^w,f(X_w)\oplus 1\}$. Code v is symmetrical to w:

$X_v=\{x_0^w\oplus 1,x_1^w,L,x_{n-2}^w,x_{n-1}^w\}$. According to (3.1) $f(X_v)=1\oplus f(X_w)$, that is why code u follows after v in the B ring. When inverting functions on code v, the following code will be e: $X_e=\{x_1^w,x_2^w,L,x_{n-2}^w,f(X_w)\oplus 1\}$.

Therefore, when inverting functions on symmetrical codes which are included into different rings A and B, after w code there will be transition to code u $\in$ B. Later, serial pass of all codes of the ring B is performed, last of which is code v. From this code transition to code e $\in$ A is performed. Further all codes of the ring A are passed serially. Thus, rings A and B are combined into one ring.

Offered method of synthesis of the nonlinear feedback function which provides full period is based on basic procedure of combining rings, obtained during cyclic shift.

The function of cyclic shift of the shift register equals to senior bit of the current code K.

$$f(X_n)=\left[\frac{k}{2^{n-1}}\right]=x_0^k \quad (4)$$

Obviously, that function (4) satisfies the condition (3). Function (4) forms N_R rings, each of which includes codes with equal number of ones. Let's denote with R(k) the ring, which includes code k. Suppose L(A)—num- ber of ones in codes of the cyclic ring A. For example, when n = 4 and k = 6: R(k) = {6(0110), 12(1100), 9(1001), 3(0011)}, L(R(k)) = 2.

Each of rings has only one minimal code. It is obvious that for any cyclic ring A ≠ R(0), minimal code q = min(A) is an odd number $\left(x_{n-1}^q=1\right)$. It means that nonzero minimal code q of the cyclic ring can always be represented as q = 2·d + 1.

THE BASIC PROCEDURE FOR COMBINING CYCLIC RINGS IS IN PERFORMING THE FOLLOWING SEQUENCE

1. Initial value of the current code j is chosen randomly, 0 < j < 2^n. Counter of h codes, for which the value of the feedback function is determined, is set to one: h = 1.

2. u = (2·j) mod 2^n + 1 is calculated. If calculated code u is minimal in its ring, which means u = min(R(u)), then the value of the feedback function on code j is determined as an inversion of the cyclic shift: $f(X_j)=\left[\frac{j}{2^{n-1}}\right]\oplus 1=x_0^j\oplus 1$, otherwise $f(X_j)=\left[\frac{j}{2^{n-1}}\right]\oplus 1=x_0^j\oplus 1$, where [x]—the less of integers, which is greater than x.

3. The new value of the current code j: = (2·j) mod 2^n + f(X_j) is calculated. Increment of the counter is performed: h: = h + 1. If h ≤ 2^n, then return to item 2, otherwise-end.

The function of cyclic transfer forms N_R rings. Described procedure provides a connection of all these rings into one.

Proof: Combining of the rings is performed in pairs. Let's consider random ring B, which consist of codes which include m ones (0 < m < n), minimum of them is denoted as $\beta_{\min}=\min(B)$. Previous to his code is $\beta\geq 2^{n-1}$ what is more $\beta_{\min}=2\cdot\beta-2^{n-1}+1$. Obviously that code $\alpha=\beta-2^{n-1}$ differs from code β only with one in senior bit and therefore belongs to another ring A. Since $\beta_{\min}=2\cdot\alpha+1$, then respectively to mentioned procedure the feedback function will change its value on a X α set in a way in which code α will be followed by the code $\beta_{\min}$. Value of the function in code β will also be changed in a way when this code will be followed by the code $\alpha_{next}=2\cdot\alpha$. In this way the described procedure provides a union of the rings A and B.

Transfer to the minimal code of the B ring possible from one code of the ring A: L(B) = L(A) + 1 except the situation when L(B) = 0. In this case one code is a predecessor of minimal codes for both rings. For example, when n = 4 code 1(0001) precedes the minimal code 0 of the ring {0} and the minimal code 1(0001) of the ring {1, 2, 4, 8}.

The minimal code of each of the rings (except the ring, which consist of zero code) is preceded by the code with less number of ones from other ring. It means that described procedure provides a binding of all rings, made by cyclic shift.

When k = 1 according to (4) RN(5,1) = 1 and, respectively, exist only one partial ring G_1^1, which includes only one set X_w = {10000}. Respectively, $X'_w=\{0000\}$ and j(0000) = 1.

When k = 2 there are two partial rings: G_1^2, G_2^2. When j = 1 from G_1^2—first partial ring, set X_w = {10010}; $X'_w=\{0010\}$ and j(0010) = 1 is chosen randomly. When j = 2 from G_2^2—second partial ring, set X_w = {11000}

and, respectively, $X'_w=\{1000\}$ и j(1000) = 1 is chosen. When k = 3 there are two partial rings: G_1^3, G_2^3. When j = 1 from G_1^3—first partial ring, which contains 3 sets, set X_w = {11010} is randomly chosen. Respectively, $X'_w=\{1010\}$ and j(1010) = 1. When j = 2 from G_2^3—second partial ring, set X_w = {11100}: $X'_w=\{1100\}$ and j(1100) = 1 is also randomly chosen. When k = 4 there is only one partial ring G_1^4, which includes 4 sets. For example, second of them is randomly chosen: X_w = {11101}. Respectively, $X'_w=\{1101\}$ and j(1101) = 1. When k = 5 there is only one partial ring G_1^5, which includes only one set X_w = {11111} for which $X'_w=\{1111\}$ and j(1111) = 1.

The resulting table of the values of the Boolean function $\varphi(x_1,x_2,x_3,x_4)$ is showed in Table 1.

In algebraic normal form the synthesized function $\varphi(x_1,x_2,x_3,x_4)$ has the following form: $\varphi(x_1,x_2,x_3,x_4)=1\oplus x_1\oplus x_3\oplus x_1\cdot x_3\oplus x_3\cdot x_4\oplus x_2\cdot x_3\cdot x_4\oplus x_1\cdot x_2\cdot x_3\cdot x_4$. Therefore, the feedback function of the shift register providing repetitive cycle 2^5 will have the following form:

$$f(x_1,x_2,x_3,x_4,x_5)=x_5\oplus\varphi(x_1,x_2,x_3,x_4)=1\oplus x_1\oplus x_3\oplus x_5\oplus x_1\cdot x_3\oplus x_3\cdot x_4\oplus x_2\cdot x_3\cdot x_4\oplus x_1\cdot x_2\cdot x_3\cdot x_4$$

.

Let's demonstrate that the proposed method of synthesis of the feedback function is constructive. An operation of setting value of the function $\varphi(x_1,x_2,\ldots,x_{n-1})$ into one which is used in this method corresponds to coupling of

the ring which includes code $X_i=\{x_1,x_2,\ldots,x_{n-1},x_n=1\}$ and the ring which include code $X_j=\{x_1,x_2,\ldots,x_{n-1},x_n=0\}$, where $i\in\{1,\ldots,NR(n,k)\}$, $j\in\{1,\ldots,NR(n,k-1)\}$. As the proposed method suggests a choice of one X code from all rings then it means that each ring is connected with one of the rings, codes of which have less number of ones. Thus all rings are connected into one that provides the maximum period of 2^n repeats of the code in the shift register.

Described procedure for constructing the nonlinear feedback function opens opportunities for optimizations of parameters of generated pseudorandom binary sequences by choosing the ring from set of G. Since the procedure is consistent and includes element of choice, then choice can be done from selected criteria, for example, criterion of the maximum of nonlinearity or compliance to avalanche effect.

For comparative analysis of the effectiveness of the proposed method it is important to estimate the number of nonlinear feedback functions, which can be obtained from its use. The number NF(n) of Boolean functions which allow to synthesize the proposed method is determined by number of variants of choice of codes from partial rings. Since this choice is independent for each partial ring, then numeric value NF(n) is determined as a product of a number of variants for choice. With fixed number of k ones in the code of the ring, which contains n codes, number of variants to choose the code from partial ring is k. The total number of such rings is NF(n), numeric value of which is determined by the formula (2.12). Therefore, the total number of variants for choice of the code which contains k ones from the rings with length n is $k^{NR(n,k)}$. For rings with less length the number of variants of choice of the code is $\frac{k\cdot d}{n}$, where d—divider of n and number of such rings is $NR\left(d,\frac{k\cdot d}{n}\right)$. Thus, the total number of

Table 1: Values of $\varphi(x_1,x_2,x_3,x_4)$

X	φ(X)	X'	φ(X')
0000	1	1000	1
0001	0	1001	0
0010	1	1010	1
0011	0	1011	0
0100	0	1100	1
0101	0	1101	1
0110	0	1110	0
0111	0	1111	1

NF(n) feedback functions which allows to synthesize the proposed method is defined by the following expression:

$$NF(n)=\prod_{k=1}^{n-1}k^{NR(n,k)}\cdot\prod_{d=2}^{n/2}\psi(n,k,d),\text{где}$$

$$\psi(n,k,d)=1:\xi(n,d)\cdot\xi\left(d,\frac{k\cdot d}{n}\right)=0$$

$$\psi(n,k,d)=\left(\frac{k\cdot d}{n}\right)^{RN\left(d,\frac{k\cdot d}{n}\right)}:\xi(n,d)\cdot\xi\left(d,\frac{k\cdot d}{n}\right)=1 \quad (5)$$

Analysis shows that developed method allows synthesizing 10 times more functions comparing with knows methods.

For n = 5 the proposed method allows to obtain NF(5) = 144 feedback functions, when the existent methods propose not more than 15 functions [8] . At the same time the proposed method is quite simple and technological [4] that provides higher performance compared to known methods. The proposed method is realized in software and successfully passed all tests.

The disadvantage of the method of building LFSR based on described procedure of combining elements of closed code groups is the fact, that time and amount of memory proportional to 2^n is required for its implementation. A modification is proposed to significantly decrease computational complexity by narrowing the class of synthesized feedback functions and optimization of the procedure of building the function in disjunctive normal form.

Suppose the current vector of the values of bits of n-bit shift register is $R=\{r_0 r_1\ldots r_{n-1}\}$. As it was proved earlier feedback function f(R) provides full repetition period if on sets to which the minimal in its ring

$$w=\sum_{k=0}^{n-1}r_k\cdot 2^{n-k-1}$$

code corresponds, f(R) equals the inversion of the senior bit of the set:

$$f(R)=r_0\oplus 1$$

and $f(R)=r_0$ **on other sets**.

Feedback function will formed as:

$$f(R)=\overline{r_0}\cdot\mu(X)\vee r_0\cdot\overline{\mu(X)}$$

where $X=\{x_0,x_1,\ldots,x_{n-1}\}=\{r_1,r_2,\ldots,r_{n-1},1\}$—vector of bits obtained by shifting R to the left by one bit with filling vacated junior bit with one; m(X)—function which takes zero value if X corresponds to the minimal value of the code in the ring and one otherwise.

m(X) can be formed as disjunction of all t_{ij} terms:

$$t_{ij}=\mathop{\&}_{k=0}^{i-2}\left(x_k\oplus x_{(j+k)\bmod n}\right)\cdot x_{i-1}\cdot x_{(j+i-1)\bmod n},$$
$$i=1,\ldots,n-1,\ j=1,\ldots,n-1.$$

Set cannot be minimal if it contains at least one sequence of bits $S_j=\{x_j,x_{j+1},\ldots,x_{(j+i-1)\bmod n}\}$ with length i, with initial bit in position j, $0<j<n-1$, if numeric value of such sequence is less than value of the sequence with the same length of i senior bits of the set $S_0=\{x_0,x_1,\ldots,x_{i-1}\}$.. (If j + k > n, then senior bits of the set are used).

In particular, the set isn't minimal if i – 1 of corresponding senior bits of this sequence are equal and the junior bit of the sequence S_0 is greater than junior bit of the sequence S_j:

$$x_0=x_j,$$
$$x_1=x_{(j+1)\bmod n},$$
$$\vdots$$
$$x_{i-2}=x_{(j+i-2)\bmod n},$$
$$x_{i-1}>x_{(j+i-1)\bmod n}.$$

In each term t_{ij} check of satisfying this condition is performed. If $i-1$ of corresponding senior bits of sequences S_0 and S_j are equal, and $x_{i-1}>x_{j+i-1}$, then t_{ij} is equal to one that means that this set isn't the minimal in its ring.

Condition is checked for all length of sequences $i=1,\ldots,n-1$, and for all values distances between initial sets of sequences $j=1,\ldots,n-1$. Combining all conditions through the operation of disjunction as it is during formation of the m(X) function, provides a check if the value of the code, to which vector X corresponds, is minimal in the ring. In Table 2 there is an example of formation all terms t_{ij} for a 5-bit register.

To extend the procedure of formation of the feedback functions, which provide full period, the previously described method of pre-unification of the two rings can be used. Let's consider examples of work of the $f_1(X)$ function for n = 5 with different values of bits vector X.

Example 1. $X=\{x_0,x_1,x_2,x_3,x_4\}=\{0,0,1,0,1\}$

Let's determine terms for sequences with the length of one. The sequence of senior bits is $S_0=\{x_0\}=\{0\}$. Next, let's compare X_0 with each bit x_1, x_2, x_3, x_4:

$$t_{11}=x_0\cdot x_1=0,$$
$$t_{12}=x_0\cdot x_2=0,$$
$$t_{13}=x_0\cdot x_3=0,$$
$$t_{14}=x_0\cdot x_4=0.$$

Note that for all sets with zero senior bit, values of t_{1j} will always be zero.

Let's determine terms for sequences with length i = 2 : S_0 = {0, 0}.

$$p_{21}=(x_0\oplus x_1)=(0\oplus 0)=1,\ t_{21}=p_{21}\cdot x_1\cdot x_2=1\times 0\times 1=0;$$
$$p_{22}=(x_0\oplus x_2)=(0\oplus 1)=0,\ t_{22}=p_{22}\cdot x_1\cdot x_3=0\times 0\times 0=0;$$
$$p_{23}=(x_0\oplus x_3)=(0\oplus 0)=1,\ t_{23}=p_{23}\cdot x_1\cdot x_4=1\times 0\times 1=0;$$
$$p_{24}=(x_0\oplus x_4)=(0\oplus 1)=0,\ t_{24}=p_{24}\cdot x_1\cdot x_0=0\times 0\times 0=0.$$

It is obvious that all t_{2j} have zero value. As long as values of the following t_{ij} depend on p_{2j}, we will determine terms only for those values j, where p_{2j} has value of one, thus j = 1 and j = 3. The length of the sequence i = 3, S_0 = {0, 0, 1}. Let's find terms for j = 1 and j = 3.

$$p_{31}=p_{21}\cdot(x_1\oplus x_2)=1\times(0\oplus 1)=0,\quad t_{31}=p_{31}\cdot x_2\cdot x_3=0\times 0\times 1=0;$$
$$p_{33}=p_{23}\cdot(x_1\oplus x_4)=1\times(0\oplus 1)=0,\quad t_{33}=p_{33}\cdot x_2\cdot x_3=0\times 0\times 1=0;$$

Zero values of p_{31} and p_{33} during calculations of the following terms convert the result into zero. Therefore, all t_{ij} for this set are equal to 0. $f_1(X)$, formed as disjunction of all t_{ij} terms, also obtains zero value. It means that code w, corresponding to X = {0, 0, 1, 0, 1} set, has the minimal value in the ring. Really, w = 16 × 0 + 8 × 0 + 4 × 1 + 2 × 0 + 1 × 1 = 5 and the ring, where it is included, is {5, 10, 20, 9, 18}. We can see that 5 is the minimal value.

Table 2: Terms t_{ij} for n = 5

	j = 1	j = 2	j = 3	j = 4
i = 1	$x_0\cdot x_1$	$x_0\cdot x_2$	$x_0\cdot x_3$	$x_0\cdot x_4$
i = 2	$(x_0\oplus x_1)\cdot x_1\cdot x_2$	$(x_0\oplus x_2)\cdot x_1\cdot x_3$	$(x_0\oplus x_3)\cdot x_1\cdot x_4$	$(x_0\oplus x_4)\cdot x_1\cdot x_0$
i = 3	$(x_0\oplus x_1)\cdot(x_1\oplus x_2)\cdot x_2\cdot x_3$	$(x_0\oplus x_2)\cdot(x_1\oplus x_3)\cdot x_2\cdot x_4$	$(x_0\oplus x_3)\cdot(x_1\oplus x_4)\cdot x_2\cdot x_0$	$(x_0\oplus x_4)\cdot(x_1\oplus x_0)\cdot x_2\cdot x_1$
i = 4	$(x_0\oplus x_1)\cdot(x_1\oplus x_2)\cdot(x_2\oplus x_3)\cdot x_3\cdot x_4$	$(x_0\oplus x_2)\cdot(x_1\oplus x_3)\cdot(x_2\oplus x_4)\cdot x_3\cdot x_0$	$(x_0\oplus x_3)\cdot(x_1\oplus x_4)\cdot(x_2\oplus x_0)\cdot x_3\cdot x_1$	$(x_0\oplus x_4)\cdot(x_1\oplus x_0)\cdot(x_2\oplus x_1)\cdot x_3\cdot x_2$

Example 2. $X=\{x_0,x_1,x_2,x_3,x_4\}=\{0,1,1,0,1\}$

2.1 Since x_0 = 0, then terms $t_{11}=t_{12}=t_{13}=t_{14}=0$.

2.2 Let's determine term for sequences with length of i = 2:

$S_0 = \{0, 1\}$.

$$p_{21} = (x_0 \oplus x_1) = (0 \oplus 1) = 0, \quad t_{21} = p_{21} \cdot x_1 \cdot x_2 = 0 \times 1 \times 1 = 0;$$
$$p_{22} = (x_0 \oplus x_2) = (0 \oplus 1) = 0, \quad t_{22} = p_{22} \cdot x_1 \cdot x_3 = 0 \times 1 \times 0 = 0;$$
$$p_{23} = (x_0 \oplus x_3) = (0 \oplus 0) = 1, \quad t_{23} = p_{23} \cdot x_1 \cdot x_4 = 1 \times 1 \times 1 = 0;$$
$$p_{24} = (x_0 \oplus x_4) = (0 \oplus 1) = 0, \quad t_{24} = p_{24} \cdot x_1 \cdot x_0 = 0 \times 0 \times 0 = 0.$$

All terms for t_{2j} have zero values. Among values of p_{2j} there is only one value $p_{23} = 1$, which can be used for further calculations. The rest of these values turn terms, to which they are included, into zero. Let's consider the sequence of length i = 3. The sequence of three senior $S_0 = \{0, 0, 1\}$. For all j values except j = 3, terms t_3j will be zero. Determining p_{33} and t_{33}:

$$p_{33} = p_{23} \cdot (x_1 \oplus x_4) = 1 \times (1 \oplus 1) = 1, \quad t_{33} = p_{33} \times x_2 \times x_3 = 1 \times 1 \times 0 = 1.$$

If we have at least one term with value of 1, the value of the function $f_1(X)$ will also be one.

Therefore, for X = {0, 1, 1, 0, 1}, $f_1(X) = 1$, it means code w = 13 isn't a minimum in its ring. Let's make sure that it is true. We obtain a ring by cyclic shift: {13, 26, 21, 11, 22}. Here we can see that the minimal value in this ring is 11, not 13. Table 3 shows the result of construction of the feedback function for a 5-bit shift register with minimal repetitive cycle.

Complexity of the developed algorithm of construction of the feedback function in Zhegalkin's algebra is equivalent to the function itself.

Let's estimate the complexity of the $f_1(X)$ function. To calculate one term t_{ij} the following number operations are required:

· i – 1 operations NXOR $(\oplus)$ to compare corresponding bits of the sequences;

· 1 operation AND to check the condition $x_{i-1} > x_{(j+i-1) \bmod n}$;

· i – 1 operations AND to unite all conditions.

So, in total we have 2i – 1 operations. The total complexity of calculation the terms for all values i and j is:

$$\sum_{i=1}^{n-1}\sum_{j=1}^{n-1}(2 \cdot i - 1) = 2 \cdot (n-1) \cdot \sum_{i=1}^{n-1}(2 \cdot i - 1) = 2 \cdot (n-1)^3 \quad (5)$$

Another $(n - 2)^2$ operations OR are required to unite all terms, that is to calculate the function m(X) $2(n - 1)^3 + (n - 2)^2$ operations are required, therefore, the complexity is proportional to n^3.

As we can see, the function is redundant. In each term t_{ij} calculations, which are made for t_{i-1j}, are performed. During paired comparison of the elements of the sequences S_0 and S_j with length of i > 2 the results of the first i – 2 elements are known form the previous step. That is why the formula to determine t_{ij} can be written as:

$$t_{ij} = p_{i,j} \cdot x_{i-1} \cdot x_{(j+i-1) \bmod n},$$

where $p_{i,j}$-term, which compares for equality senior i – 1 bits of the sequences.

p_{ij} can be determined as:

$$p_{ij} = 1, \text{if } i < 2, \qquad p_{ij} = \left(x_{i-2} \oplus x_{(j+i-2) \bmod n}\right) \cdot p_{i-1j}, \text{if } 2 < j < n-1.$$

Since for calculations of each t_{ij} constant number of operations is performed (1 operation when i = 1 and 4 otherwise), the complexity of the function m(X) will be proportional to n^2: $4n(n-1) + 2n = 2n(2n-1)$.

The amount of memory required to perform the algorithm is determined by necessity to save all terms t_{ij}, $i = 1, \ldots, n-1$, $j = 1, \ldots, n-1$. Therefore, memory expenses are proportional to n^2.

CONCLUSIONS

An approach is proposed for the construction of the important element of the contemporary systems for the protection of information-generators of pseudorandom binary sequences with the repetition period 2^non the basis of n-bit shift register with the nonlinear feedback function. Such generators are considerably simpler and more efficient compared with the generators constructed in the form of LFSR system and nonlinear inverter.

Table 3: Construction of the feedback function

No.	R	X	μ	f
0	00000	00001	0	1
1	00001	00011	0	1
2	00010	00101	0	1
3	00011	00111	0	1
4	00100	01001	1	0
5	00101	01011	0	1
6	00110	01101	1	0
7	00111	01111	0	1
8	01000	10001	1	0
9	01001	10011	1	0
10	01010	10101	1	0
11	01011	10111	1	0
12	01100	11001	1	0
13	01101	11011	1	0
14	01110	11101	1	0
15	01111	11111	0	1
16	10000	00001	0	0
17	10001	00011	0	0
18	10010	00101	0	0
19	10011	00111	0	0
20	10100	01001	1	1
21	10101	01011	0	0
22	10110	01101	1	1
23	10111	01111	0	0
24	11000	10001	1	1
25	11001	10011	1	1
26	11010	10101	1	1
27	11011	10111	1	1
28	11100	11001	1	1
29	11101	11011	1	1
30	11110	11101	1	1
31	11111	11111	0	0

Saleh Al-Omar Within the common approach, based on the technology of the association "rings", realization of which requires memory with size 2^n, is developed with high-tech modification, which makes it possible to build the generators of pseudorandom sequences on the basis of the shift register with the nonlinear feedback function of with the use of memory, proportional to n^2. The use of the method proposed makes it possible to build a suitable for the practical use in the telecommunication technologies. An experimental study made it possible with the use of the method proposed to build generators of word length up to 128 bit.

REFERENCES

1. Obeidat, A. (2012) Burst Error Correction Method Based on Arithmetic Weighted Checksums. Engineering, 4, 768- 773. http://dx.doi.org/10.4236/eng.2012.411098
2. Luby, M. (1996) Pseudorandomness and Cryptographic Applications. Princeton University Press, Princeton, 273 p.
3. Golomb, S.W. (1982) Shift Register Sequences. Aegean Park Press, Laguna Hill, 324 p.
4. Menezer, A.J., Van Oorschot, P.C. and Vanstone, S.A. (1997) Handbook of Applied Cryptography. CRC Press, Boca Raton, 780 p.
5. Sarkar, P. and Maitra, S. (2001) Efficient Implementation of "Large" Stream Cipher Systems. Proceeding of 3th International Workshop "Cryptographic Hardware and Embedded Systems" (CHES-2001), Springer-Verlag, 319-332.
6. Key, E.L. (1976) An Analysis of the Structures and Complexity of Nonlinear Binary Sequence Generators. IEEE Transaction on Information Theory, 22, 732-736. http://dx.doi.org/10.1109/TIT.1976.1055626
7. Sidorenko, V., Richter, G. and Bossert, M. (2011) Linearized Shift-Register Synthesis. IEEE Transaction on Information Theory, 57, 6025-6032.
8. (2000) NIST Special Publicaion 800-22: A Statistical Test Suite for Random and Pseudorandom Number. 348 p.
9. Gutierrez, J., Shparlinski, I.A. and Winterhof, A. (2003) On the Linear and Nonlinear Complexity Profile on Nonlinear Pseudorandom Number Generators. IEEE Transaction on Information Theory, 49, 60-64.

CHAPTER 17

C3SM: INFORMATION ASSURANCE BASED ON CRYPTOGRAPHIC CHECKSUM WITH CLUSTERING SECURITY MANAGEMENT PROTOCOL

Moad Mowafi, Lo'ai Tawalbeh, Walid Aljoby, Mohammad Al-Rousan

Keywords: Wireless Sensor Networks, Security, Message Authentication Code, Cryptographic, Node Capture Attack

INTRODUCTION

Wireless Sensor Networks (WSNs) are highly distributed and self-organized system that is based on collaborative effort of a large number of nodes, where each node has the ability of sensing, computation, and communication. WSNs suffer from various malicious attacks because the environment is open to the public. Thus, an enemy can easily listen to the wireless communication and intercept the traffic. To prevent such malicious attacks, secret keys should be used to encrypt wireless communication and establish data confidentiality, integrity and authentication among sensor nodes. An enemy can also capture a sensor node and access its data and communication keys. This type of attacks is called node capture attack, and forms a main challenge to develop a security mechanism for WSNs.

In wired and wireless networks, information assurance is attained by data encryption and authentication. Many complex security algorithms are developed such as public-key cryptography (e.g., RSA [1] and Diffie-Hellman [2]), digital signature and trusted third-party authentication schemes [3]. In WSNs, the sensor node does not have sufficient memory to store a lot of keys or support a complex public key algorithm. Moreover, the computation overhead and energy consumption make traditional security mechanisms not suitable for WSNs. Therefore, it is necessary to develop an appropriate security mechanism for WSNs to distribute secret keys among the nodes, encrypt communication and form authentication. However, the challenge does not lie in the development of a secure mechanism merely, but on how to efficiently create, distribute and manage the secret keys among the nodes.

In this paper, we introduce a new security protocol called Cryptographic Checksum Clustering Security Management (C3SM) that operates under clustered hierarchical network architecture. The proposed scheme provides sufficient security regardless of how many nodes are compromised and achieves efficient energy consumption with low key storage overhead. In C3SM, every cluster selects dynamically and alternately a node called Cluster Security Manager (CSM) which distributes a periodic shared secrete key for all nodes in the cluster. Then, the cluster head (CH) authenticates the identity of the cluster nodes, and establishes a unique pairwise key for each node in the cluster. The authentication is achieved by cryptographic checksum or Message Authentication Code (MAC). To enhance confidentiality between the cluster nodes and the CH, we design a local, random, dynamic, periodic and unique pairwise key for each path between the CH and sensor node. These key properties make the security in WSNs stronger, and attain high connectivity with low memory cost and low energy consumption.

To enhance integrity and authenticity among nodes, we use cryptographic checksum (variable tiny segment of code) appended to control messages. Moreover, the proposed scheme has strong resilience against node capture because it has an alternating CSM that distributes keys at regular period of times in normal (safety) mode, monitors the cluster nodes for attack, and changes keys directly in case of an attack occurs (threat mode). The rest of this paper is organized as follows. In Section 2, we provide a review of related work in key management for WSNs. In Section 3, we describe the proposed system architecture. In Section 4, we present and analyze the system model. In Section 5, we evaluate the system performance and present simulation results. Finally, we conclude the paper in Section 6.

Citation: M. Mowafi, L. Tawalbeh, W. Aljoby and M. Al-Rousan, "C3SM: Information Assurance Based on Cryptographic Checksum with Clustering Security Management Protocol," Journal of Information Security, Vol. 3 No. 4, 2012, pp. 272-280. doi: 10.4236/jis.2012.34034.

RELATED WORK

The existing approaches for solving the key distribution problem in WSNs can be classified into four categories [4]: Network-wide keys schemes, full pairwise key schemes, matrix-based schemes, polynomial-based schemes, and probabilistic schemes. In the network-wide keys scheme, a single master key is loaded into all sensor nodes. This scheme provides perfect connectivity since all deployed nodes share the same key, and also new added nodes can be loaded with the same master key and connect simply. Several schemes have adopted this approach [5-7]. The shortcoming of the network-wide scheme is that a capturing of a single node will comprise all the nodes and their communication. Moreover, malicious nodes can be easily injected into the network. In the full pairwise key scheme, each node from n nodes stores n-1 pairwise keys in order to communicate with every other node.

This scheme provides a high level of security but its main drawback is its demand for very large memory storage. Matrix-based schemes are originally created for establishing a pairwise key by Blom [8]. In Blom's scheme, each node i has the ith row and the ith column of secret and public matrices, respectively. By exchanging their columns, any two nodes i and j can create their pairwise key $K_{ij} = K_{ji}$. In this scheme, if no more than t nodes are compromised, no more keys are compromised. Increasing t can improve the scheme resilience; however more secret information needs to be stored. Extensions of Blom's scheme have been proposed in [9,10]. The polynomial-based key management schemes are originally initiated by Blundo [11] as a special case of Blom's scheme.

In Blundo's scheme, each node i has a polynomial f (x,y) over a finite filed. By evaluating their polynomials, any two nodes i and j can create their pairwise key f (i,j) = f (j,i). Several schemes have adopted Blundo's scheme [12-14]. The main drawbacks of the polynomial-based approach are its demand for large memory to store the polynomials, and the computational power of the multiplication and exponentiation operations [4]. In the probabilistic approaches, the security services are divided into phases in order to offer high security as the pairwise key approach and lower storage as the network-wide key approach, and to find suitable tradeoff between security and overhead. In general, the probabilistic approaches pass through three phases [4]: Key predistribution, shared-key discovery, and path-key establishment. Our work belongs to such approaches and presents a security mechanism for each phase, aiming at attaining effective security, efficiency, and flexibility. Several schemes, related to our work, have been proposed [15-20]. In [15], a random key pre-distribution scheme is proposed.

It prepares a very large size key pool, chooses randomly a subset of keys, and then stores them in the node's memory before deployment. After the discovery process performed between the nodes that intend to communicate, the nodes can establish a connection if they share one or more of the common keys stored in their memories. The common key then becomes a shared key for the link between the nodes. Nodes that cannot find a shared key with each other can generate a path key through what so-called a connected secure graph. This scheme requires a large key storage in large scale networks. Moreover it does not support node authentication, and its resilience to node capture attacks is weak since any captured node can compromise other nodes keys. In [16], a scheme called efficient pairwise key establishment and management (EPKEM) is proposed.

In this scheme, each node stores randomly a row and column from a key matrix, and any two nodes create a distinct pairwise key by combining their common keys and node identities. If a node is compromised, the communication between non-compromised nodes remains secure. However, this scheme has high communication overhead in large scale networks, needs large key storage, and consumes energy when adding nodes.

A scheme for large-scale hierarchical WSNs is presented in [17]. It uses polynomial key calculations to create a distinct pairwise key between any two nodes. This approach assumes three phases for key management: key pre-distribution, inter-cluster pairwise key establishment, and intra-cluster pairwise key establishment. The scheme shows good security mechanism against node capture attacks, but the establishment of one pairwise key for each node needs the cluster head to communicate with other cluster heads to authenticate node connectivity. In [18], a rekey-boosted security protocol in hierarchical WSNs is proposed.

In this approach, clusters are formed based on LEACH, and random key pre-distribution is used to establish node-to-node security and authentication. A cluster key is used to secure the cluster head-to-node communication, and a key created by the cluster head is used to protect the cluster head-to-base station communication. In this scheme, the cluster head carries much overhead because it is used for both routing and security. In [19], the proposed scheme stores a master key and random vector in each node, and any two nodes create a pairwise key by combining their random vector with the stored master key. In addition, each node stores a cluster key to communicate with the cluster head. The cluster key is derived from the preloaded master key and identification number of the cluster head. Hence, an enemy that knows the master key and the identification number of the cluster head can extract the cluster key and easily attack the cluster.

A protocol for securing the paths among the nodes in WSNs is proposed in [20]. In this protocol, the network area is partitioned into a virtual grid with identical cells. It is assumed that each node stores four keys: individual key to communicate with the base station, cell key to communicate with nodes inside the cell, eight pairwise keys to communicate with other cells, and broadcast keys. By capturing any of the cell nodes, the adversary can extract the key and then easily attack all the nodes inside the cell.

System Architecture

The system is organized in a multi-tier architecture according to the recourses and functionality. The resources variability divides the system into two-tier architecture. One tier represents the base station (BS) and another tier represents the deployed sensor nodes. The BS is assumed to have no computational, storage and communication limitations and is located far from the sensor field. The sensor nodes are assumed to be resource-constrained in energy, processing, and storage. The sensor nodes are homogenous, have the same resources, and start with the same level of energy. The sensors nodes are capable of control their power to vary their functionality.

From the functionality viewpoint, the system is divided into four-tier architecture as shown in Figure 1. The first tier represents the BS that will be considered as a powerful data processing unit that performs heavily operations, a storage center that collects data, and a key distribution center before deployment. The BS is assumed to be trusted and temper resistant. The second tier represents the CH that will be considered as a collector for sensed data from other members in the cluster, an aggregator for the collected data, and a sender for the fused data to the BS in a single-hop path, as depicted in Figure 2. The third tier represents the sensor nodes that sense data and report the target field states to the CH as depicted in Figure 2.

The fourth tier, the lower layer of our proposed stack model, represents the contribution of what we target in this research that is the clustering security management layer. This layer appears dynamically in each cluster by targeting one of the sensor nodes other than the CHs that is the CSM as depicted in Figure 2. The CSM will manage the cluster security because it works as a key distribution center and as a guard for cluster sensor nodes against an adversary. The CSM periodically constructs a key and distributes it to its cluster members and to the CH.

SYSTEM MODEL AND ANALYSIS

The C3SM scheme consists of two parts: The first part deals with key distribution and managing methodologies while the second one deals with network monitoring and resilience against the node capture attack and its implications.

Key Distribution and Managing Model

Before deploying the nodes in the target field, each sensor node will be assigned two types of key. One key to encrypt and authenticate aggregated sensing data from a CH to the BS. And the other one used for a period of time after the deployment to encrypt and authenticate exchanged data between the CH and its sensor node members. After the deployment of sensor nodes and formation of clusters, each cluster will candidate one node to become a CSM that will protect the cluster against an adversary attacks, and distribute (re-keying) keys for the nodes in the cluster including the CHs. This procedure will constitute a distributed cluster among all clusters in the network with cluster members called CSMs. The key management scheme consists of two phases: key setup phase and path key establishment phase.

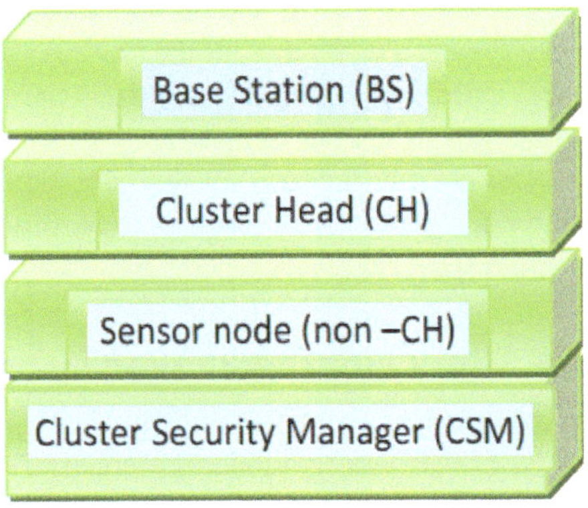

Figure 1: Four-tier clustering security model for WSNs.

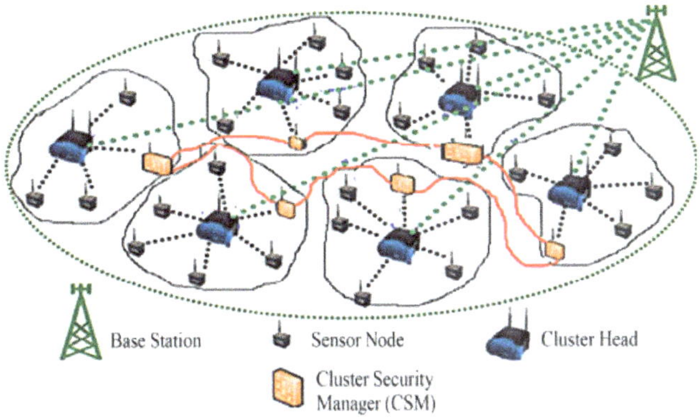

Figure 2: A clustering security architecture for WSNs.

Key Setup Phase

When the nodes are deployed, each node is preloaded with an initial shared key (K_p) which assumed to be a large number symmetric key assigned for all nodes in the network. The preloaded key can be used by any sensor node to generate its master key as a function of the node ID. An authenticator MAC function (C-function) is used to generate the keys. For example, node i uses K_p and its ID to generate its master key (K_i) as follows:

$$K_i = C\left(K_p, ID_i\right) \quad (1)$$

The symmetric key K_p is just used after the sensor nodes deployment for a short period of time between the CH and cluster members to create a master key. This key is changed periodically by the CSM, thus, any attack to any node in the cluster does not affect its security.

After formation of clusters, the CH will broadcast its ID (ID_{CH}) and an advertisement message (Adv) encrypted by the preloaded key K_p to the cluster members. It is assumed that every node can know the Adv message.

$$CH \rightarrow N: \quad ID_{CH} \| C\left(K_p, \text{Adv} \| ID_{CH}\right) \quad (2)$$

After the above formatted message is broadcasted, each authorized sensor node receives the message and performs the same function, $C\left(K_p, \text{Adv} \| ID_{CH}\right)$Figure 4. Node-to-CH message authentication. Equ , and Equation (5) ase ill be established (6) This technique can alleviate the trad pair nction a cryptographic checksum function p CH , as the CH and compares with the received MAC, as depicted in Figure 3. Then, each member of the cluster will respond with its ID (ID_N), and a message contains a join signal (Ack), the CH's Adv and the node ID (ID_N), encrypted by its preloaded key K_p, as shown in Figure 4.

$$N \rightarrow CH: \quad ID_N \| C\left(K_p, \text{Adv} \| ID_N \| \text{Ack}\right) \quad (3)$$

When the CH receives a reply from its cluster members, all of them can generate a secure master key as shown by the following equations:

$$K_{CH} = C\left(K_p, ID_{CH}\right) \quad (4)$$

$$K_N = C(K_p, ID_N) \quad (5)$$

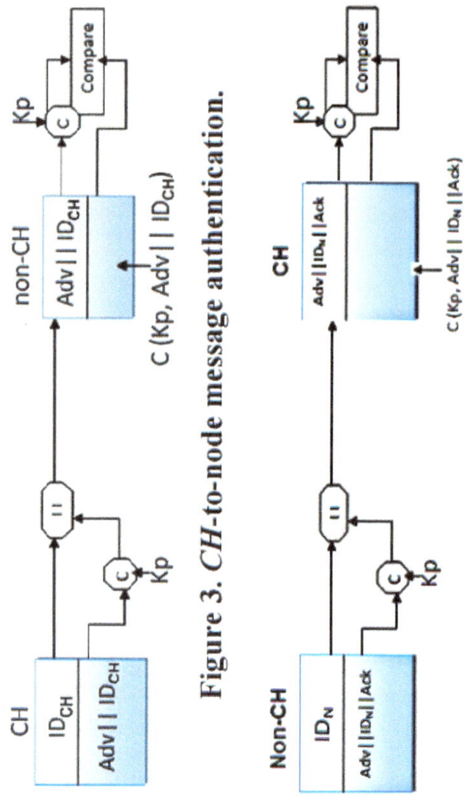

Figure 3. *CH*-to-node message authentication.

Figure 4: Node-to-CH message authentication.

Equation (4) represents the master key of the CH and Equation (5) represents the aster key of any member node N. After each node in the cluster generates its master key, the cluster will translate into next phase, which is called the path key establishment.

Path Key Establishment Phase

In this phase the pairwise key K_{CH-N} will between the CH and each cluster member node N. The pairwise key maintains a unique key for a path between the CH and each node in the cluster. Hence, it provides a sufficient security against node capture attacks since any compromised node will not affect the secure communication among non-compromised nodes. Moreover, this approach does not require a large storage for each node to store the whole pairwise keys in the network because the CH node just stores the pairwise keys of its cluster members. The pairwise key is derived as follows:

$$K_{CH-N} = C(K_N, ID_{CH}) \quad (6)$$

This technique can alleviate the tradeoff between the pairwise key supported security and the key storage overhead.

C-Function

The C-function is a cryptographic checksum function that is usually called message authentication code or MAC. However, the domain of C-function consists of a message of some arbitrary length, whereas the range consists of all possible MACs and all possible keys [21]. There are three types of MACs in our proposed system, as shown in Equations (4)-(6). The left hand side of each equation represents the generated fixed length authenticator that can be exploited to perform the following functionalities: authentication to assure that received messages are from alleged nodes, confidentiality to protect the traffic as long as the generated authenticator used as a unique pairwise key between the CH and its cluster members, and resiliency against node capturing because the key for each path is unique and is managed periodically by the CSM. On the other hand, the right hand side of the equation represents the variable length message which is the ID of the node and either the secret shared key between all nodes in the cluster such as K_p or the unique key between the CH and its cluster members such as K_N.

Clustering Security Management

After completing the formation phase for each cluster in the network, the role of security is triggered in order to protect the network against malicious attacks. The security of the network is managed by distributed nodes throughout the network, forming a security cluster.

The security cluster is a distributed cluster through all the data clusters in the network, as shown in Figure 2. In the safe mode, the construction of the cluster is assumed to take place at the beginning of the second half of the current data cluster cycle and remain to the ending of the first half of the next data cluster cycle.

The CH in each data cluster can candidate one of its cluster members to be a CSM which carries out three tasks. First, the first CSM creates a schedule in which order the cluster member nodes are elected as CSM and repeats the same process after the member nodes in the cluster are already pass the turn. The CSM checks its energy and if it is less than a threshold, the CSM will broadcast a release message to its cluster nodes. The node in schedule will take the turn and become a CSM. By this property the CSM guarantees the fairness in energy consumption among the cluster nodes. Second, the CSM can work as a key distribution center to construct and distribute periodically a shared master key for each node inside the cluster and also to the CH in order to re-keying them. By the master key, all the nodes in the cluster can use this key as a secrete key for establishing a new pairwise key (re-keying) between the CH and each sensor node in the cluster. Third, the CSM carries out monitoring and controlling the cluster member nodes against any attack. The CSM will exchange periodic messages with the cluster member nodes, and if one of the nodes does not reply, the CSM assumes an adversary captures the node, and then it will change all the keys in the cluster. In case that any CSM are captured, the nodes can tell through the disappearance of the control message sent by the captured CSM, and consequently the turn for the next appointed CSM arises to work for a period of time equals to the time of the data cluster. Figure 5 summarizes the C3SM algorithm.

Malicious Attack and Threat Model

The malicious attacks can be divided into passive and active modes. In the passive mode, the enemy listens to the communication among the nodes to seize private data, while in the active mode it captures nodes in the network. When a node is compromised, the stored secret keys or information are revealed and, hence, false messages can be injected or the transmitted messages can be modified or dropped.

Next, we analyze the system security under node capture attacks, considering three types of sensor nodes: a cluster member, the CH, and the CSM.

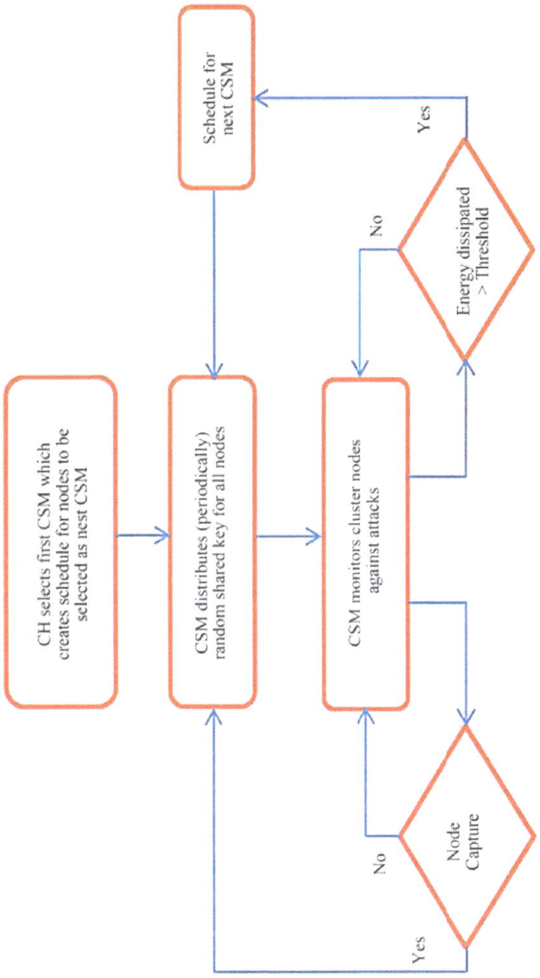

Figure 5: C3SM algorithm.

Sensor Node Capture Attack

In our scheme, after nodes deployment and cluster formations, in a short period of time, each CH will establish a unique pairwise key (K_{CH-N}) for each link with a cluster member node. In addition, after the CSM distributes a shared secrete key for the nodes in each cluster, the CH can also establish a unique pairwise key (K_{CH-N}) for each link with a cluster member node, and so forth. Thus, if adversaries deploy their own malicious nodes, these malicious nodes cannot be connected to the cluster because the communication with the CH requests from the node to know its master key (K_N) which is a cryptographic checksum or MAC from the node ID and the shared key K_p as shown in Equation (5). In case that a sensor node is physically captured, the adversary can read the contents of the node memory and discover its pairwise key with the CH, however it cannot compromise other non-captured nodes because the pairwise key is unique for each pair of two communicating parties. On the other hand, the CSM will lose the communication with the captured node, and distributes a new master key for the attacked cluster.

Cluster Head Capture Attack

In our scheme, the CH stores all the pairwise keys of the member nodes in the cluster. The CSM monitors the nodes in the cluster and exchanges periodic control messages with them. So, if the CH is captured, the CSM will detect the capture and broadcast messages to all the nodes in the cluster to set up a new round, and candidate a new CH. The CSM also distributes a new shared key for all the nodes in the cluster. Then, the new CH will use the shared key to establish a unique pairwise key with each node in the cluster. So, the adversary cannot compromise any node in the cluster because all the cluster node keys are changed and the communication is also changed to a new CH.

CSM Capture Attack

In our scheme, each elected CSM in a cluster can create a schedule to determine when each node in the cluster is elected as a CSM. In case that the CSM is captured, all nodes in the cluster lose communication with the CSM. After a short period of time the node in responsible in the schedule will take the turn to become a CSM.

PERFORMANCE EVALUATION

Security algorithms for WSNs include a tradeoff between the security level and resources consumption. In this section, we evaluate by simulation the performance of our proposed scheme, and compare it with current schemes in [15,16]. The simulation was performed by a self developed simulator using the simulation settings as follows. A deployment region of 100 ´ 100 m^2 is considered. The frequency of key refreshment is 5 time units, and the frequency of control messages is 1 time unit. The control message size is 50 bytes.

Communication and Computation Overhead

The communication per bit in WSNs is more costly than computation [22]. In C3SM, communication is performed inside a cluster, which means there is no longer transmission. In addition, the computational operations of key management are simple and performed locally (inside the cluster). A network of 10 clusters with 12 nodes per cluster was used. The Friis free-space model was used to estimate the communication energy consumption [23]. Figures 6 and 7 show the energy consumed by the CSM, CH, and data sensor node (non-CH) of a randomly chosen cluster, for performing key management operations: key setup, re-keying and nodes monitoring. Figure 6 shows the accumulated dissipated energy after completing 100 rounds, while Figure 7 shows the dissipated energy d ring one round. As shown in both figures, the CSM consumes more energy compared to CH and non-CH nodes because it performs monitoring and re-keying tasks frequently while the CH only performs key setup and authentication with its cluster nodes.

Figures 8 and 9 show the consumed energy for each phase of key management: Setup, re-keying, and monitoring which are performed at randomly chosen cluster. Figure 8 shows the accumulated dissipated energy during each phase at a random cluster after completing 100 rounds, while Figure 9 shows the energy dissipated for each phase during one round. As shown in both figures, the monitoring task consumes approximately four times energy compared to re-keying task because in the monitoring task the CSM exchanges periodic messages with the cluster nodes in order to protect the network against node capture attack. On the other hand, the re-keying task consumes energy only when the CSM discovers an attack or its dissipated energy reaches a threshold. The energy consumed by the setup phase is mostly done when the CH performs authentication with its cluster nodes.

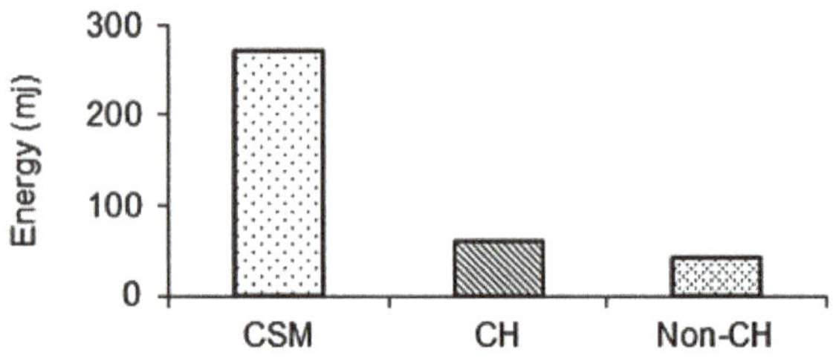

Figure 6: Consumed energy by cluster nodes of a randomly chosen cluster.

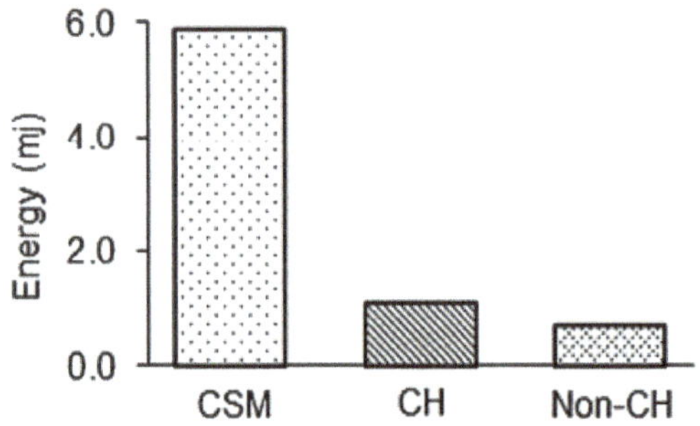

Figure 7: Consumed energy by cluster nodes of a random cluster during one round.

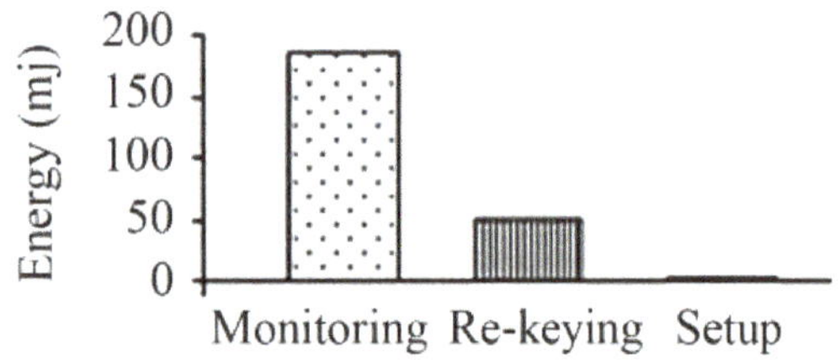

Figure 8: Consumed energy for key management phases at a randomly chosen cluster.

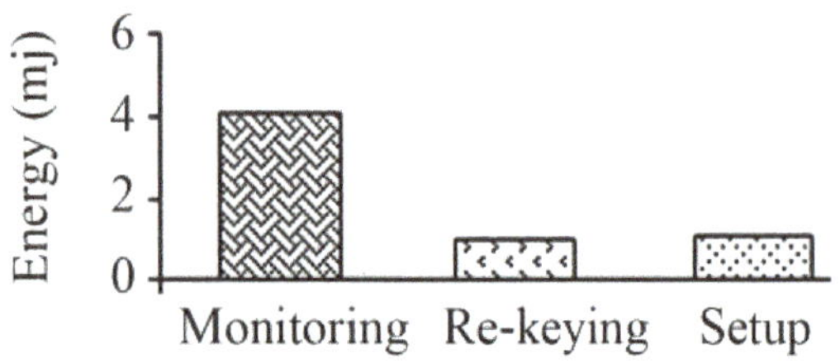

Figure 9: Consumed energy for key management phases at a random cluster during one round.

Resiliency to Node Capture

Because the resources of a sensor node are very limited, complexity of computations or long term transmission affects the lifetime of the network. Many approaches try to solve the problem of node capture attack. However, most of them still suffer from overhead or compromising nodes attack. In the random pre-distribution scheme in [15], the same keys are used by different nodes and, hence, if a node is captured, the secure communication among other nodes is compromised. In EPKEM [16] and our proposed C3SM, pairwise keys are stored in every node and, hence, the resilience against node capture is improved. C3SM prevents key compromise for noncompromised nodes, even if many of the sensor nodes are captured. Figure 10 shows the network resilience against node capture attacks for our C3SM scheme in addition to the random key pre-distribution scheme in [15] and the EPKEM scheme in [16]. It is shown that in the random key pre-distribution scheme, the fraction of compromised keys in non-captured nodes increases as the number of captured nodes increases, while in EPKEM and C3SM it remains at low fraction regardless how many nodes are captured. In C3SM, each sensor node receives periodically a shared key from the CSM, and then the CH uses this key to establish a pairwise key with each node in the cluster. Pairwise keys are different for each path and cannot easily be derived because the MAC used is many-to-one function. Namely, there are many keys to produce the correct MAC; consequently the opponent has no way to know the correct key. Furthermore, keys are refreshed periodically.

Key Storage Overhead

In random key distribution, to achieve the required network connectivity, each sens r node is required to store a certain number of keys in its memory. Figure 11 shows the number of keys stored in each node versus the network size for the three schemes: C3SM, EPKEM, and the random key pre-distribution scheme. It is shown that the number of keys per node increases linearly in the random key pre-distribution scheme, and increases sub-linearly in

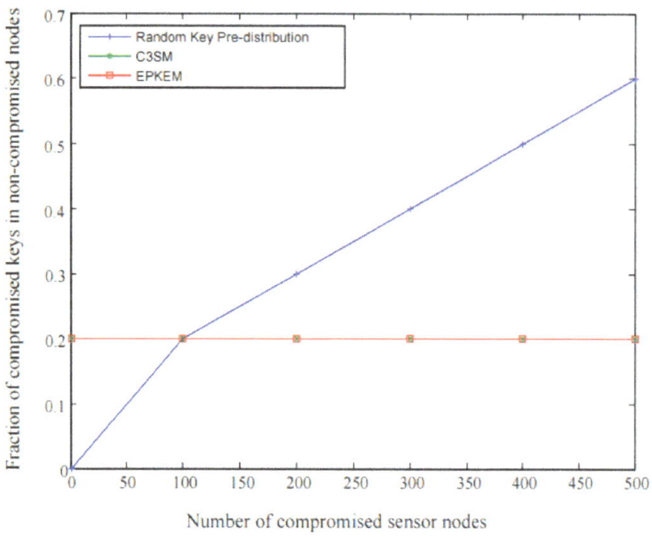

Figure 10: Network resilience against node capture attacks.

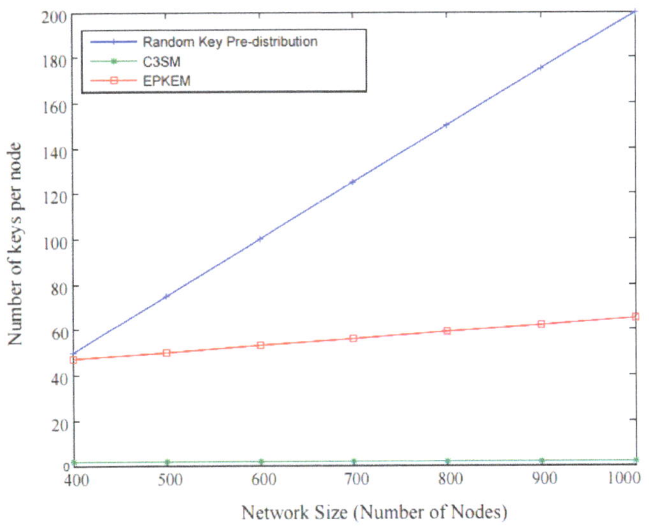

Figure 11: Key storage overhead versus network size.

EPKEM. On the other hand, C3SM has the lowest key storage overhead. In C3SM, each node only needs to store a pairwise key with the CH and a key with the BS in its memory no matter how many nodes are in the network.

CONCLUSIONS

In this work, we propose a cluster-based security protocol for WSNs, called cryptographic Checksum Clustering Security Management (C3SM). Our protocol uses cryptographic checksum to authenticate communication among nodes. In C3SM, each node only stores two keys despite the network size, which reduces the key storage overhead especially in large scale networks.

To enhance confidentiality between the cluster nodes and the cluster head, we use a local, random, periodic and unique pairwise key for each path between the cluster head and the sensor node. These key properties make the network security stronge while achieving high connectivity with low memory cost and low energy consumption. Compared to existing schemes, C3SM achieves better network resilience against node capture attacks with lower key storage overhead.

ACKNOWLEDGEMENTS

The authors would like to thank Jordan University of Science and Technology, and the Scientific Research Support Fund at the Ministry of High Education in Jordan for supporting this research.

REFERENCES

1. R. L. Rivest, A. Shamir and L. M. Adleman, "A Method for Obtaining Digital Signatures and Public-Key Cryptosystems," Communications of the ACM, Vol. 21, No. 2 col for WSNs, called Cryptogra ing Security Management (C3S cryptographic checksum to authenticate communication among nodes. In C3SM, each node only stores two keys despite the network size, which reduces the key storage overhead especially in large scale networks. To enhance confidentiality between the cluster nodes and the cluster head, we use a local, random, periodic and unique pairwise key for each path between the cluster head and the sensor node. These key properties make the network security stronge while achieving high con- r , 1978, pp. 120-126. doi:10.1145/359340.359342
2. W. Diffie and M. E. Hell an, "New Directions in Cr tography," IEEE Transactions on Information Theory Vol. 22, No. 6, 1976, pp. 644-654. doi:10.1109/ TIT.1976.1055638 m yp- ,
3. Y. Jararweh, L. Tawalbeh, H. Tawalbeh and A. Moh'd, "Hardware Performance Evaluation of SHA-3 Candidate Algorithms," Journal of Information Security, Vol. 3, No. 2, 2012, pp. 69-76. doi:10.4236/jis.2012.32008
4. M. A. Simplício Jr., P. S. Barreto, C. B. Margi and Carvalho, "A Survey on Key Management Mechanisms for Distributed Wireless Sensor Networks," Computer Networks, Vol. 54, No. 15, 2010, pp. 2591-2612. doi:10.1016/j.comnet.2010.04.010 T. C.
5. B. Lai, S. Kim and I. Verbauwhede, "Scalable S Key Construction Protocol for Wireless Sensor Networks," IEEE Workshop on Large Scale Real-Time and Embedded Systems (LARTES), Austin, December 2002, p. 6.
6. ession Y. Zeng, B. Zhao, J. Su, X. Yan and Z. Shao, "A Loop-Based Key Management Scheme for Wireless Sensor Networks," Proceedings of the 2007 Conference on Emerging Direction in Embedded and Ubiquitous Computing (EUC'07), Taipei, 17-20 December 2007, pp. 103- 114. doi:10.1007/978-3-540-77090-9_10
7. B. Dutertre, S. Cheung and J. Levy, "Lightweight Key Wireless Sensor Networks by Leveraging echnical Report, System Design LaboraManagement in Initial Trust," T tory, Menlo Park, 2004.
8. R. Blom, "An Optimal Class of Symmetric Key Generation Systems," Proceedings of the Eurocrypt 84 Workshop on Advances in Cryptology, Paris, 9-11 April 1984, pp. 335-338.
9. H. Chien, R.-C. Chen and A. Shen, "Efficient Key Pre-Distribution for Sensor Nodes with Strong Connectivity and Low Storage Space," Proceedings of the 22nd International Conference on Advanced Information Networking and Applications (AINA'08), Okinawa, 25-28 March 2008, pp. 327-333.
10. W. Du, J. Deng, Y. Han, P. Varshney, J. Katz and A. Khalili, "A Pairwise Key Pre-Distribution Scheme for Wireless Sensor Networks," ACM Transactions on Information and System Security, Vol. 8, No. 2, 2005, pp. 228-258. doi:10.1145/1065545.1065548
11. C. Blundo, A. Santis, A. Herzberg, S. Kutten, U. Vaccaro and M. Yung, "Perfectly-Secure Key Distribution for roceedings of the 12th Annual onference on Advances in Crypce of the IEEE Computer and Communications Societies (INFOCOM'05), Miami, 13-17 March 2
12. D. Liu and P. rwise Keys in Dis- . 8, No. 1, 2005, pp. 3287 Dynamic Conferences," P International Cryptology C tology (CRYPTO'92), Santa Barbara, 16-20 August 1992, pp. 471-486.
13. H. Chan and A. Perrig, "PIKE: Peer Intermediaries for Key Establishment in Sensor Networks," Proceedings of the 24th Annual Joint Conferen 005, pp. 524-535.

Ning, "Establishing Pai tributed Sensor Networks," Proceedings of the 10th ACM Conference on Computer and Communications Security (CCS'03), Washington DC, 27-31 October 2003, pp. 52-61.

14. D. Liu, P. Ning and R. Li, "Establishing Pairwise Keys in Distributed Sensor Networks," ACM Transactions on Information and System Security, Vol 41-77. doi:10.1145/1053283.105 ber 2002,

15. L. Eschenauer and V. D. Gligor, "A Key-Management Scheme for Distributed Sensor Networks," Proceedings of the 9th ACM Conference on Computer and Communications Security, Washington DC, 17-21 Novem pp. 41-47. doi:10.1145/586110.586117

16. Y. Cheng and D. P. Agrawal, "Efficient Pairwise Key Establishment and Management in Static Wireless Sensor Networks," Proceedings of the 2nd IEEE Intern Conference on Mobile Ad Hoc ational and Sensor Systems, Washington DC, 7-10 November 2005, p. 7. doi:10.1109/MAHSS.2005.1542842

17. Y. Cheng and D. Agrawal, "An Improved Key Distribution Mechanism for Large-Scale Hierarchical Wireless Sensor Networks," Ad Hoc Networks, Vol. 5, No. 1, 2007, pp. 35-48. doi:10.1016/j.adhoc.2006.05.011

18. Y.-Y. Zhang, W.-C. Yang, K.-B. Kim, M.-Y. Cui and M.-S. Park, "A Rekey-Boosted Security Protocol in Hierarchical Wireless Sensor Network," Proceedings of the 2nd International Conference on Multimedia and Ubiquitous Engineering, Seoul, 24-26 April 2 .

19. D. P. S. E. Christina and R. J. Chitra, "Energy Efficient Secure Routing in Wireless Sensor Networks," Proceedings of 2011 International Conference on Emerging Trends in Electrical and Com Tamil Nadu, 23-24 March 2011, pp. 982-986.

20. S. G. Yoo, S. Kang and J. Kim, "SERA: A Secure Energy and Reliability Aware Data Gathering for Sensor Networks," Proceedings of 2010 International Conference on Information Science and Applications (ICISA), Seoul, 21- 23 April 2010, pp. 1-11. doi:10.1109/ICISA.2010.5480347

21. W. Stallings, "Cryptography and Network Security: Prin ciples and Practice," 5th Edition, Pearson-Prentice Hall, Upper Saddle River, 2011.

22. J. Hill, R. Szewczyk, A. Woo, S. Hollar, D. E. Culler and and H. Balakrishnan, K. S. J. Pister, "System Architecture Directions for Networked Sensors," Proceedings of the 9th International Conference on Architectural Support for Programming Languages and Operating Systems, Cambridge, 12-15 November 2000, pp. 93-104.

23. W. R. Heinzelman, A. Chandrakasan "An Application-Specific Protocol Architecture for Wireless Microsensor Networks," IEEE Transactions on Wireless Communications, Vol. 1, No. 4, 2002, pp. 660-670. doi:10.1109/TWC.2002.804190

CHAPTER 18

A VISUAL CRYPTOGRAPHY BASED DIGITAL IMAGE COPYRIGHT PROTECTION

Adel Hammad Abusitta

Keywords: Image Watermark, Pattern, Visual Cryptography, Digital Image, Copyright

INTRODUCTION

The proliferation of digitized images has made the digital images to be modified, distributed, duplicated and accessed easily. It is creating a pressing need to develop copyright protection methods. A watermarking technology is now providing highly attention as a desired method and technology for protecting copyrights for digital data [1-7]. A watermarking has been defined as the practice of embedding identification information in an image, audio, video or other digital media element to provide privacy protecttion from attackers [8-9]. The identification information is called "watermark pattern" and the original digital image that contains watermark pattern is named "marked image". The embedding takes place by manipulating the contents of the digital image [10]. Also, a secret key is given to embed "watermark pattern" and to retrieve it as well. Figure 1gives summarize of standard watermarking embedding scheme.

Basically, if the owner wants to protect his/her image, the owner of an image has to register the image with the copyright office by sending a copy to them. The copyright office archives the image, together with information about the rightful owner. When dispute occurs, the real owner contacts the copyright office to obtain proof that he is the rightful owner. If he did not register the image, then he should at least be able to show the film negative. However, with the rapid acceptance of digital photography, there might never have been a negative. Theoretically, it is possible for the owner to use a watermark embedded in the image to prove that he/she owns it [11].

A typical image watermark algorithm must satisfy the following two properties: transparency and robustness. Transparency means that the embedded watermark pattern does not visually spoil the original image fidelity and should be invisible. Robustness means the watermark pattern is not easy to detect and remove illegally. Moreover, any modifications of the image values have to be invisible, and the watermark method has to be robust or fragile in order to provide protection against attackers.

In 1994, Noor-Shamir proposed the concept of visual cryptography [12]. The concept nowadays is being developed and/or improved several times for different purposes of applications by authors [13-24]. A good survey on visual cryptography can be found in [25]. Actually, Visual cryptography is describing as a secret sharing scheme extended of digital images, this will be discussed in the next section. Hwang [26] is the first author proposed a method of how to take a benefit of visual cryptography to create digital image copyright protection. According to Hwang method, the watermark pattern does not have to be embedded into the original image directly, which makes it harder to detect or recover from the marked image in an illegal way. [27-30] improved different methods to overcome Hwang method's shortcomings. We will come to these shortcomings in Section 3.

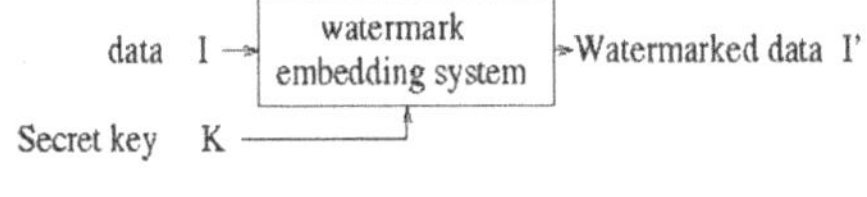

Figure 1: Watermarking embedding scheme.

This paper proposes new digital images copyright protection based on Hwang method. The proposed method

Citation: A. Hammad Abusitta, "A Visual Cryptography Based Digital Image Copyright Protection," Journal of Information Security, Vol. 3 No. 2, 2012, pp. 96-104. doi: 10.4236/jis.2012.32012.

is based on visual cryptography defined by Noor-Shamir and Hwang method. Marking images will be conducted without embedding patterns into images. This leaves marked images unchanged with sizes exactly equal to the original ones. This paper is organized as follows. Section 2 reviews the concept of visual cryptography and digital image copyright protection. Section 3 presents our proposed digital image copyright protection method. Section 4 reports some experimental results and makes some discussions concerning our method. Finally, conclusions appear in Section 5.

VISUAL CRYPTOGRAPHY AND RELATED DIGITAL IMAGE COPYRIGHT PROTECTION

Naor and Shamir in 1994 proposed the concept of visual cryptography during EUROCRYPT 94.Figure 2 from [31] demonstrates a simple version of visual cryptography. In their method, they introduced encoding scheme to share a binary image into two shares Share 1 and Share 2. A pixel P is divided into two subpixels in each of the two shares. If P is white one of two rows above in Figure 2 is selected to create Share 1 and Share 2. But, if P is black one of two rows below in Figure 2 is selected to create Share 1 and Share 2. A binary image at the end becomes secret image or invisible unless both shares are superposition.

Hwang created the first and typical idea for a digital image copyright protection based on the visual cryptography. The method use a simple (2, 2) visual threshold scheme defined by Naor-Shamir. Referring to Hwang's algorithm, the owner must select h × n black/white image as his/her watermark pattern P and a key S which must be kept securely. Then, verification information V is generated from the original k × 1 image M and the watermark pattern P using the key S; as follows:

1) Use S (the secret key) as the seed to generate h x n different random numbers over the interval [0, k × 1]. (Ri represents the i-th random number).

2) Assign the i-th pair (Vi1, Vi2) of the verificatin on information V based on the following Table 1:

Collect all the (Vi1, Vi2) pairs to construct the verification information V. This verification information must be kept by neutral organization. When the owner of an image M wants to claim the ownership of an image M' as

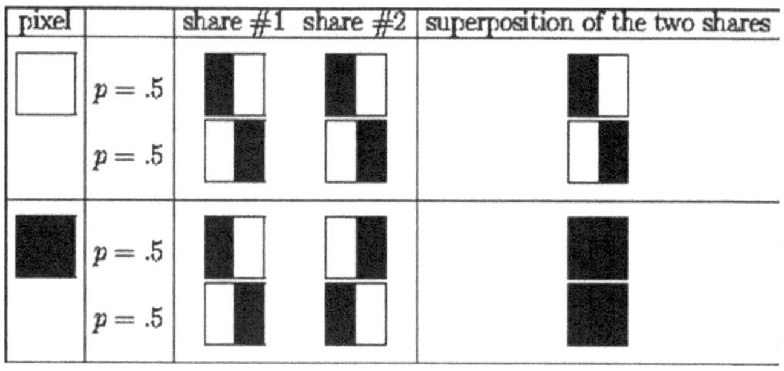

Figure 2: Naor and Shamir's scheme.

Table 1: The rules to assign the value of verification information

The color of the i-th pixel in watermark pattern is	The left most bit of the Ri-th pixel of Image M is	Assign the i-th pair, (vi1, vi2), of *verification information V* to be
Black	"1"	(0,1)
Black	"0"	(1,0)
White	"1"	(1,0)
White	"0"	(0,1)

a copy of the original image M, the owner has to provide the secret key S, and the watermark pattern P is restored using the image M' and verification information V as follows:

- Use S as a seed to generate h × n different random numbers over the interval [0, k × 1]. (Ri represents the i-th random number).
- Assign the color of the i-th pixel of the watermark pattern P' based on the image M' as follows:
- Get the left-most bit, b, of the Ri-th pixel of image M', and if b is 1 then, assign fi = (1, 0); otherwise assign fi = (0, 1).
- If fi is equal to i-th pair of V then assigns the color of the i-th pixel of P' to be white; otherwise, assign it to be black.
- If P' can be recognized as P through the human, the neutral organization shall adjudge that the image M' is a copy of M.

According to the previous method and also the related methods, these methods are strongly related to the values of the most significant bits of pixels selected randomly from the original digital image; therefore, if the most significant bit to some pixels selected randomly has been changed, the modified image M' will fail to retrieve the watermark pattern P successfully. Also, since the method does not consider the relationship between pixels and its neighbors, the watermark pattern would not be retrieved, if part of image has been cropped. Moreover, if we have an image X with some similarities with the original image M. The watermark pattern P might be restored successfully, despite the image X is not the same as the image M.

THE PROPOSED DIGITAL IMAGE COPYRIGHT PROTECTION

In this section, we present the proposed watermark method. The method acctually use the relationship between 8- neighbours pixels of pixel P(x, y) as a base of embedding algorithm as you will see later. Figure 3 shows the 8- neighbours of pixel P(x, y).

We assume that the owner wants to embed the h × n watermark pattern into the image M that is a k × 1 256 grayleveled image. The owner embeds the watermark pattern P into the image M by generating the secret key, S, and the verification information, V, as the following steps.

Step Embedding-1. Select number S randomly as the secret key of the image M.

Step Embedding-2. Use S as the seed to generate h × n different random numbers over the interval [0, k × 1]. Where Ri is the i-th random number.)

Step Embedding-3. Calculate the number of Ri-th pixel's

neighbours pixels from its 8-nieghbours pixels that are less than or equal to the Ri-th pixel, this number named, Number_of_neighbors_less_or_equal_Ri-th_pixel. Also, calculte the number of Ri-th pixel's nieghbour pixels from its 8-nieghbour pixels that are greater than Ri-th pixel, this number named Number_of_ neighbor_greater_ Ri-th_pixel.

For example, as in Figure 4, the Number_of_neighbors_less_or_equal_Ri-th_pixel = 3, because we have three pixels {97, 98, 100} less or equal the Ri-th pixel, which equals 100. Also, Number_of_neighbors_greater_Ri-th_ pixel = 5, because we have 5 pixels in the following set {101, 103, 101,105,111} greater than Ri-th pixel.

It is obvious, in case the Ri-th pixel is a border pixel, this pixel do not have a full 8-nighbours. In this case, the available nighbours should be considerd and calculate Number_of_neighbors_less_or_equal_Ri-th_pixel and Number_of_neighbors_greater_Ri-th_pixel same as in step Embedding-3.

Step Embedding-4. Find the i-th pair (vi1, vi2) of the verification information V based on Table 2.

Step Embedding-5. Assemble all the (vi1, vi2) pairs to create the verification information V.

Note that Step Embedding-5 constructs the verification Information V based on the watermark pattern P and the relationship result between Number_of_neighbors_ less_or_equal_Ri-th_pixel and Number_of_neighbors_ greater_Ri-th_pixel as shown in Table 2, and moreover the proposed method does not make any change into image M or alter any pixel of image M.

The verification information V genrated from Step Embedding-5 must be given to the notarial organization. If an image M is appropriated by somebody as the image M', The owner of an image has to provide the secret key S to the notarial organization. The notarial organization retrives the verification information V and the watermark pattern P, which the owner has registered, and verifies the ownership of the image M' as follows:

X − 1, y − 1	X − 1, y	X − 1, y + 1
x, y − 1	x, y	x, y + 1
X + 1, y − 1	X + 1, y	X + 1, y + 1

Figure 3: 8 Neighbours pixels of pixel P(x, y).

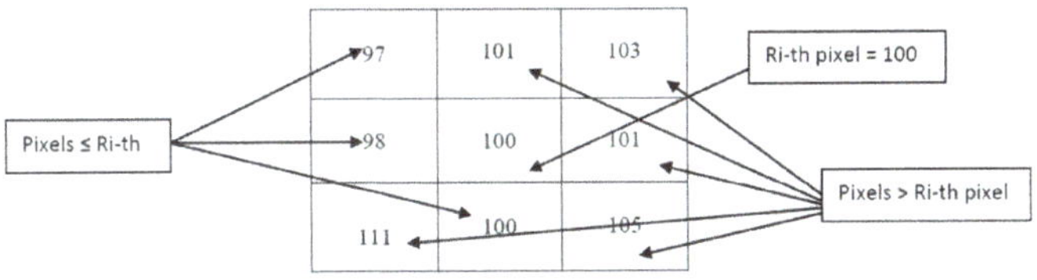

Figure 4: Example of Ri-th pixel's neighbors.

Step Verification-1. Use S as the seed to generate h × n different random numbers over the interval [0, k × 1]. Where Ri is the i-th random number.)

Step Verification-2. Assign the color of the i-th pixel of the watermark pattern based on image M' as follows:

If (Number_of_neighbors_less_or_equal_Ri-th_pixel ≤ Number_of_neighbors_greater_Ri-th_pixel) AND (the i-th pair, (vi1, vi2), of verification information V = (0,1)) then Assign the color of the i-th pixel of P' to be white Else If (Number_of_neighbors_less_or_equal_Ri-th_ pixel ≤ Number_of_neighbors_greater_Ri-th_pixel) AND (the i-th pair, (vi1, vi2), of verification information V = (1,0)) then Assign the color of the i-th pixel of P' to be black Else If (Number_of_neighbors_less_or_equal_Ri-th_ pixel>Number_of_neighbors_greater_Ri-th_pixel) AND (the i-th pair, (vi1, vi2), of verification information V = (1,0)) then Assign the color of the i-th pixel of P' to be white Else If (Number_of_neighbors_less_or_equal_Ri-th_ pixel > Number_of_neighbors_greater_Ri-th_pixel) AND (the i-th pair, (vi1, vi2), of verification information V = (0,1)) then Assign the color of the i-th pixel of P' to be black.

Table 2: The proposed method's rules to assign the value of verification

The Color of the i-th pixel in watermark pattern is	The relationship between *Number_of_neighbors_less_or_equal_Ri-th_pixel* and *Number_of_ neighbors _greater_Ri-th_pixel*	Assign the i-th pair, (vi1, vi2), of *verification information V* to be
Black	*Number_of_neighbors_less_or_equal_Ri-th_pixel* ≤ *Number_of_neighbors_greater_Ri-th_pixel*	(0,1)
Black	*Number_of_neighbors_less_or_equal_Ri-th_pixel* > *Number_of_neighbors_greater_Ri-th_pixel*	(1,0)
White	*Number_of_neighbors_less_or_equal_Ri-th_pixel* ≤ *Number_of_neighbor_greater_Ri-th_pixel*	(1,0)
White	*Number_of_ neighbors_less_or_equal_Ri-th_pixel* > *Number_of_neighbors_greater_Ri-th_pixel*	(0,1)

Step Verification-3. If P' equals the original watermark pattern P or can be recognized as it, then the notarial organization can conclude that image M' is a copy of M.

Note that the code written in Step Verification-2 can be concluded directly from Table 2 which displays the proposed method's rules to assign the value of verification information.

The security of the proposed method is based on the relationship of pixels selected randomly and their 8- neighbor's pixels. This happened because whenever a change is applied into original digital image pixels, the result of the relationship mostly becomes the same. In other words, the relationships between Number_of_ neighbors_less_or_equal_Ri-th_pixel and Number_of_neighbors_greater_Ri-th_pixel will not be affected by some majer changes in image pixels' bits. Experimental results in the next section will reflect that fact.

EXPERIMENTAL RESULTS

The proposed algorithms are studied using Matlab 7. Images used are 256 × 256 pixels images Lina, Baboon and F-16 (shown in Figure 6). In Matlab 7, we made some changes in the three images before applying the proposed method. The changes are applied in the most significant bits of randomly selected pixels. Also, we did make changes in images quality using Adobe Photoshop CS 5 by applying diverse compressions in the three images. The watermark pattern used in the experiment is "cheng" in Figure 5. From the results shown in Table 3, we find that the watermark pattern "cheng" get some noise but still can be recognized even if the three images have been compressed and the size of those files is changed.

CONCLUSION

This paper presents a digital image copyright protection method using watermarking technology. The method proposed in this paper does not require that the watermark pattern to be embedded in to the original digital image. Instead, Verification information is generated which will be used to verify the ownership of the image. This leaves the marked image equal to the original image. The proposed method is tested and shows that a watermark pattern can be retrieved easily from marked image even the image is attacked by major changes in pixels bits.

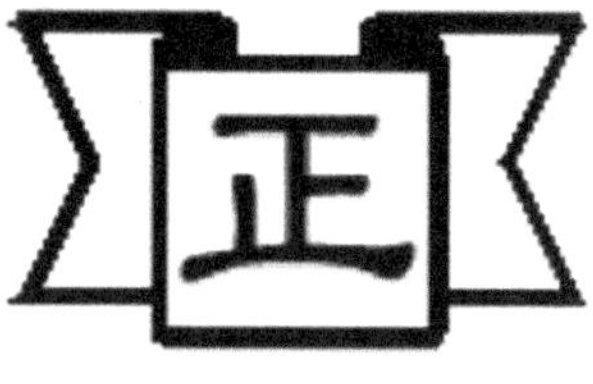

Figure 5: The watermark pattern "cheng".

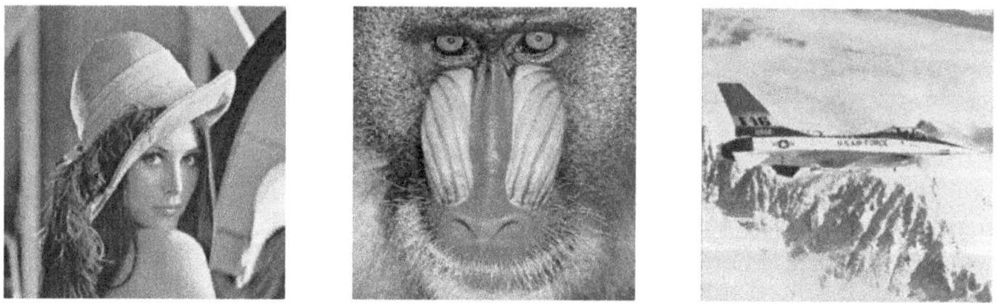

(a) Lena (b) Baboon (c) F-16

Figure 6: Three images of our Experiments.

Table 3: Experimental results

(a) Use the proposed method to embed "Cheng" into "Lena"

The Marked Image	The Digital Image Quality with Adobe Photoshop CS 5	The Recovered Watermark Pattern "Cheng"
	0/low (the size of compressed file is 10.463 Bytes)	
	1/low (the size of compressed file is 12.501 Bytes)	
	2/low (the size of compressed file is 13.830 Bytes)	
	3/middle (the size of compressed file is 15.643 Bytes)	
	4/middle (the size of compressed file is 17.344 Bytes)	
Marked Image = Original Image	5/middle (the size of compressed file is 17.139 Bytes)	

	6/high (the size of compressed file is 19,113 Bytes)	
	7/high (the size of compressed file is 24,385 Bytes)	
	8/maximal (the size of compressed file is 30,930 Bytes)	
	9/maximal (the size of compressed file is 39,177 Bytes)	
	10/maximal (the size of compressed file is 48,199 Bytes)	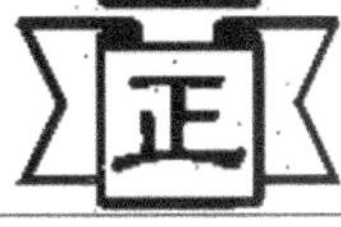

(b) Use the proposed method to embed "Cheng" into "Baboon"

The Marked Image	The Digital Image Quality with Adobe Photoshop CS 5	The Recovered Watermark Pattern "Cheng"
	0/low (the size of compressed file is 17,930 Bytes)	
	1/low (the size of compressed file is 22,112 Bytes)	
	2/low (the size of compressed file is 23,856 Bytes)	
	3/middle (the size of compressed file is 27,115 Bytes)	
	4/middle (the size of compressed file is 30,103 Bytes)	
Marked Image = Original Image	5/middle (the size of compressed file is 27,992 Bytes)	
	6/high (the size of compressed file is 33,120 Bytes)	
	7/high (the size of compressed file is 38,004 Bytes)	
	8/maximal (the size of compressed file is 44,759 Bytes)	
	9/maximal (the size of compressed file is 53,992 Bytes)	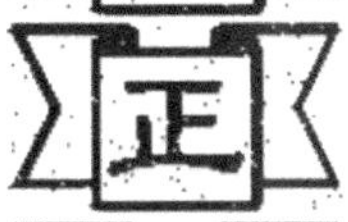
	10/maximal (the size of compressed file is 62,951 Bytes)	

(c) Use the proposed method to embed "Cheng" into "F-16"

The Marked Image	The Digital Image Quality with Adobe Photoshop CS 5	The Recovered Watermark Pattern "Cheng"
	0/low (the size of compressed file is 9850 Bytes)	
	1/low (the size of compressed file is 11,451 Bytes)	
	2/low (the size of compressed file is 12,344 Bytes)	
	3/middle (the size of compressed file is 13,949 Bytes)	
	4/middle (the size of compressed file is 16,278 Bytes)	
Marked Image = Original Image	5/middle (the size of compressed file is 14,929 Bytes)	
	6/high (the size of compressed file is 17,930 Bytes)	
	7/high (the size of compressed file is 21,125 Bytes)	
	8/maximal (the size of compressed file is 25,920 Bytes)	
	9/maximal (the size of compressed file is 32,852 Bytes)	
	10/maximal (the size of compressed file is 40,877 Bytes)	

The watermark pattern cannot be retrieved from the marked image unless the key is given, and the key is only known by the owner. Also, the watermark pattern cannot be retrieved from the marked image unless the secret key and the verification information are given.

REFERENCES

1. B. Surekha and G. N. Swamy, "A Spatial Domain Public Image Watermarking," International Journal of Security and Its Applications, Vol. 5, No. 1, 2011, 12 p.

2. R. J. Anderson, "Information Hiding," First International Workshop, Vol. 1174, 1996, pp. 1-7.

3. I. J. Cox, M. L. Miller and J. A. Bloom, "Digital Watermarking," Morgan Kaufmann Publishers Inc., San Fransisco, 2002.

4. M. Kutter and F. A. P. Petitcolas, "Fair Benchmark for Image Watermarking Systems," Proceedings of the Conference on Security and Watermarking of Multimedia Contents, San Jose, 25 January 1999, pp. 226-239. doi:10.1117/12.344672

5. G. C. Langelaar, J. C. A. van der Lubbe and J. Biemond, "Copy Protection for Multimedia Data Based on Labelling Techniques," Proceedings of the 17th Symposium on Information Theory in the Benelux, Enschede, May 1996, pp. 33-39.

6. M. S. Fu and O. C. Au, "Joint Visual Cryptography and Watermarking," Proceedings of the IEEE International Conference on Multimedia and Expo, Taipei, 30 June 2004, pp. 975-978. doi:10.1109/ICME.2004.1394365

7. R.-H. Hwang, "A Digital Image Copyright Protection Scheme Based on Visual Cryptography," Tamkang Journal of science and Engineering, Vol. 3, No. 2, 2002, pp. 97-106.

8. H. Inoue, A. Miyazaki, A. Yamamoto and T. Katsura, "A Digital Watermark Technique Based on the Wavelet Transform and Its Robustness on Image Compression and Transformation," IEICE Transactions on Fundamentals of Electronics, Communications and Computer Sciences, Vol. 82, No. 1, 1999, pp. 2-10.

9. G. W. Braudaway, K. A. Magerlein and F. C. Mintzer, "Protecting Publicly Available Images with a Visible Image Watermark," Proceedings of the SPIE, San Jose, 1 February 1996, pp. 126-133. doi:10.1117/12.235469

10. L. Hawkes, A. Yasinsac and C. Cline, "An Application of Visual Cryptography to Financial Documents," Technical Report TR001001, Florida State University, Tallahassee, 2000.

11. C.-N. Yang, "A Note on Efficient Color Visual Encryption," Journal of Information Science and Engineering, Vol. 18, 2002, pp. 367-372.

12. M. Noar and A. Shamir, "Visual Cryptography," Advances in Cryptography Eurocrypt'94, Vol. 950, 1995, pp. 1-12.

13. W.-P. Fang, "Non-Expansion Visual Secret Sharing in Reversible Style," International Journal of Computer Science and Network Security, Vol. 9, No. 2, 2009, pp. 204- 208.

14. J. Weir and W.-Q. Yan, "Sharing Multiple Secrets Using Visual Cryptography," Proceedings of the IEEE International Symposium on Circuits and Systems, Taipei, 24-27 May 2009, pp. 509-512. doi:10.1109/ISCAS.2009.5117797

15. Z. X. Fu and B. Yu, "Research on Rotation Visual Cryptography Scheme," Proceedings of the International Symposium on Information Engineering and Electronic Commerce, Ternopil, 16-17 May 2009, pp. 533-536. doi:10.1109/IEEC.2009.118

16. X.-Q. Tan, "Two Kinds of Ideal Contrast Visual Cryptography Schemes," Proceedings of the 2009 International Conference on Signal Processing Systems, Singapore, 15- 17 May 2009, pp. 450-453. doi:10.1109/ICSPS.2009.119

17. H. B. Zhang, X. F. Wang, W. H. Cao and Y. P. Huang, "Visual Cryptography for General Access Structure by Multi-Pixel Encoding with Variable Block Size," Proceedings of the International Symposium on Knowledge Acquisition and Modeling, Wuhan, 21-22 December 2008, pp. 340-344. doi:10.1109/KAM.2008.91

18. M. Heidarinejad, A. A. Yazdi and K. N. Plataniotis, "Algebraic Visual Cryptography Scheme for Color Images," Proceedings of the IEEE International Conference on Acoustics, Speech and Signal Processing, Las Vegas, 31 March-4 April 2008, pp. 1761-1764. doi:10.1109/ICASSP.2008.4517971

19. F. Liu1, C. K. Wu and X. J. Lin, "Colour Visual Cryptography Schemes," IET Information Security, Vol. 2, No. 4, 2008, pp. 151-165. doi:10.1049/iet-ifs:20080066

20. W. Qiao, H. D. Yin and H. Q. Liang, "A Kind of Visual Cryptography Scheme for Color Images Based on Halftone Technique," Proceedings of the International Conference on Measuring Technology and Mechatronics Automation, Zhangjiajie, 11-12 April 2009, pp. 393-395. doi:10.1109/ICMTMA.2009.294

21. L. M. E. Bakrawy, N. I. Ghali, A. E. Hassanien and A. Abraham, "An Associative Watermarking Based Image Authentication Scheme," Proceedings of the 10th International Conference on Intelligent Systems Design and Applications (ISDA 2010), Cairo, 29 November-1 December 2010, pp. 823-828. doi:10.1109/ISDA.2010.5687160

22. V. V. R. Prasad and R. Kurupati, "Secure Image Watermarking in Frequency Domain Using Arnold Scrambling and Filtering," Advances in Computational Sciences and Technology, Vol. 3, No. 2, 2010, pp. 236-244.

23. P. Fakhari, E. Vahedi and C. Lucas, "Protecting Patient Privacy from Unauthorized Release of Medical Images Using a Bio-Inspired Wavelet-Based Watermarking Approach," Digital Signal Processing, Vol. 21, No. 3, 2011, pp. 433-446. doi:10.1016/j.dsp.2011.01.014

24. A. De Bonnis and A. De Santis, "Randomness in Secret Sharing and Visual Cryptography Schemes," Theoretical Computer Science, Vol. 314, No. 3, 2004, pp. 351-374.doi:10.1016/j.tcs.2003.12.018

25. P. S. Revenkar, A. Anium and Z. Gandhare, "Survey of Visual Cryptography Schemes," International Journal of Security and Its Applications, Vol. 4, No. 2, 2010, pp. 49- 56.

26. R. Hwang, "A Digital Image Copyright Protection Scheme Based on Visual Cryptography," Tamkang Journal of science and Engineering, Vol. 3, No. 2, 2002, pp. 97- 106.

27. M. A. Hassan and M. A. Khalili, "Self Watermarking Based on Visual Cryptography," Proceedings of the World Academy of Science, Engineering and Technology, October 2005, pp. 159-162.

28. A. Sleit and A. Abusitta, "A Visual Cryptography Based Watermark Technology for Individual and Group Images," Journal of Systemics, Cybernetics and Informatics, Vol. 5, No. 2, 2008, pp. 24-32.

29. A. Sleit and A. Abusitta, "A Watermark Technology Based on Visual Cryptography," Proceeding of the 10th World Multi Conference on Systemic, Cybernetics and Informatics, 2006, pp. 227-238.

30. A. Sleit and A. Abusitta, "Advancedd Digital Image Copyright Protection Based on Visual Cryptography," Proceeding of the 4th International Multi Conference on Computer Science & Information Technology, Amman, 5-7 April 2006, pp. 365-375.

31. D. Stinson, "Doug Stinson's Visual Cryptography Page," 2003. http://www.cacr.math.uwaterloo.ca/~dstinson/visual.html

INDEX